...In a Van Down by the Ocean

A Homeless Memoir Part 1

By
David Walter Smith

PublishAmerica
Baltimore

© 2011 by David Walter Smith
All rights reserved. No part of this book may be reproduced, stored in a retrieval system or transmitted in any form or by any means without the prior written permission of the publishers, except by a reviewer who may quote brief passages in a review to be printed in a newspaper, magazine or journal.

First printing

PublishAmerica has allowed this work to remain exactly as the author intended, verbatim, without editorial input.

Hardcover 978-1-4560-2328-7
Softcover 978-1-4560-2327-0
PUBLISHED BY PUBLISHAMERICA, LLLP
www.publishamerica.com
Baltimore

Printed in the United States of America

For the kind people of Santa Monica and Venice; all the broken folks that they allow to dwell there; and the public libraries there within—Universities of the Poor

For the Raven: *"For as long as she is listening..."*

And as always, for Aubrey, the breeze-child; she, more than anyone, paid the price for who I am

CHAPTER ONE

I was not without hope but I was not hope-full. I had tried; I would continue to try. As the ensuing years unfolded I would come to envy those who knew how to quit. I could see the "whens" and "whys" all around me, but "how" remained elusive to my soul. All my life I never understood suicide. I couldn't fathom the concept of letting go of existing. The thought of nothingness scared the bejesus out of me to be sure but it went beyond that in my mind. Maybe it comes from all those years of playing team sports or from the blue collar my Dad wore regardless of his attire. After all this time, as the last four years lay dormant waiting to be relived, relayed and reframed, I still could never kill myself. Although for the first time in my life I do understand.

In late August of the year two thousand my brother Chris and I left the home we grew up in on the northwest side of Chicago. We had left before, together and apart, only to return to the gracious, loving support to which we had been privileged our whole lives. The last time was in the spring of ninety-three. Chris and I had gone to Nashville to sell our songs. The years previous to this saw us in various bands seeking the redemption of the masses. The masses never grew beyond a handful of drunks, a couple of friends and family members. We were good, we were flawed, we were busy seeking out us assuming others would follow. We still are.

When we first headed to Nashville I had a wife and daughter. By '96 my marriage ended and the next year saw my ex-wife, Donna taking our daughter Aubrey back to Chicago. Within six months Chris and I followed.

It was not our talent that failed in Nashville. You will be hearing that kind of statement throughout this book. Understand now: When it comes to writing and performing a song, Chris and I are the shit! Rock-folk-blues is our mainstay but we can write pretty much anything from jazz standards to a country song that would make Hank Sr. cry. I say this now because it is our talent, combined with an undying dedication to said talent, in the face of a world that doesn't have the interest, energy or wherewithal to see our beauty and worth, that holds the heart of my story.

On our return from Nashville Chris and I knew we would leave again. My parents wouldn't have had it any other way. They love us, enjoy our company and want to be of help but they had raised their six children, of which I am the youngest, and held dearly to the hope of one day being somewhat free of them; those poor sonsabithches. Even before we left Nashville Chris and I talked about going to California.

The brightest side of going to Nashville was that we met talented people who were after what we were after. One such person was Steve Goodie. He did comedy, musical and otherwise, as well as running his own recording studio. Through Ty Hager, another great, ignored songwriter, we started recording with Steve and became friends. Actually it was Eric Teplitz who ended up being the glue that brought us all together. Eric was around twenty then while the rest of us were in or near our thirties. He had the highest hopes and therefore took the hardest fall I think. Great talent though—The world will never know. Yeah, there's a lot of that going round. Together we formed the core of what we called "The Nashville Underground," the most talented, ambitious (artistically anyway) writers who, because of the aforementioned artistic ambition, had the least chance of making any money. Meeting the three of them became a watershed moment for Chris and I. We never felt the slightest encouragement from our chosen industry but Eric, Ty, and Steve saw in us what we saw in them; the next Dylan, Jackson Browne, Beatles or whatever name you want to add. Steve applied to this on a lesser extent for he was and will always be more for the comedy. Hell of a funny guy and for all my love of myself, for I do think more of mine and Chris' writing than anyone else's, Steve is and always will be a better musician; Eric too. But Chris and I are the ones I'd pay to see play. Call it ego or accurate classification, I don't care anymore.

Most important is that I love them. They are not of my blood but they are in it.

Steve, the only business man among us decided to sell his house and move to California. He had come to Nashville years before us and felt that the time had come for a new scene. He left a month before Aubrey and her mother. Once he had settled into his new studio he announced that we all should follow.

By that time Eric was a mess over all his efforts in getting his CD heard by anyone from Tennessee to New Mexico to the tune of a biblical "whatever," while Ty continued to be the one forever on the cusp breaking through. Steve made a decent living at his trade but Ty generated interest from the other side of the wall; where Steve stood grass-roots and self-sufficient, Ty laid in the penniless shade of whispers toward greatness. He actually had meetings with "SUITS", but they all came to the same end. "We love your stuff, but we don't know what to do with it." MORONS! How do these people get their power and money? No vision, no guts, no soul.

So Eric crawled into a bed at his parents' house back in Philadelphia; Ty went on making sandwiches for the "Subways" of the world waiting for the "SUITS" to get their heads out of their asses; and the brothers Smith started talking about California as we planned our trek back to Chicago.

Did I mention that Chris and I are alcoholics? Never lost a job over it and we've had plenty of jobs. See, that is where all of this is leading. From the time we quit high school to be this thing we've become we worked day jobs—meaningless, time-consuming, soul-draining day jobs. I didn't want to be a truck driver who attended his dreams between a punched clock and an early morning alarm. I moved furniture, delivered lumber; Chris drove from Nashville to Memphis and back as a courier; and we both knew first hand the horrors of telemarketing. "Enough," we cried. "Enough!" The compromise had run its never ending circle enough times for us to see that it led nowhere beyond a paycheck that covered nothing more than living expenses and the bottom of a bottle that could only numb the frustration until the next bottle.

The plan was clear: Work for a year or so to save enough money for a large, trustworthy, cargo van and a cushion in a bank account.

In order for us to save any kind of money we thought it best to go back to Chicago. My parent's still lived on the second floor of the two-flat that my grandma owned. She lived on the first floor, which left the basement apartment where the four Smith boys spent the larger part of their misspent youth. In the years of our absence, our perpetually temporary flights of quasi-independence, the basement served as my Dad's office.

My oldest brother Joel, who taught Chris and I along with our other brother Art, how to love then play guitar, still resided there but not in the basement apartment. Back when rock-n-roll first infested his pubescent soul, Dad had built a jam room for Joel and his future loud sounds. It held the corner of the basement opposite the apartment with a laundry area offering them both space to be separate. Joel lived there then as he lives there now: A brilliant musical mind hounded by voices born of a genetic chemical imbalance. At the tender age of seventeen Joel suffered a nervous breakdown brought on by schizophrenia. From the time it all happened to the day Chris and I came back from Nashville, Joel had endured a journey I could never possibly understand let alone relate to others. I have seen him tortured by his own mind, isolated by paranoia and amused to no end by the visions and commentary of an entity that is as real to him as anything you or I have ever gripped in our hands or owned with our eyes. He has had days, bad and worse—days, good and better. In his early twenties Joel left for a year once and hitchhiked as far west as Washington state, as north as Minnesota and as south as Texas. At the time we didn't know where he went or if he was alive. One night he showed up looking more skeleton than flesh and quoting the bible. The only other time he left home was when the folks enrolled him in an institutional program on Chicago's near south side. He had to be almost thirty then and I'm pretty sure it lasted less than a year.

Through it all the man has been student of music and a soul in search of beauty

The next oldest brother would be Art. On our return he was busy raising his three kids Tim, Shaun and Erin—in a house being paid for by fixing trucks for the city—fighting with his wife, and being mad at the world. Never has such a sweet man been so at odds with himself. Art wanted to be a big shot, a man of material substance. The thing about Smith men is that their souls tend to search for something money can't buy and power won't explain.

Eileen, the oldest, was just finishing up getting her teaching certificate. She had a house in the neighborhood with her husband Scott and two kids, Keeley and Jake. The folks had been helping her out because of the manic depression that left Scott bedridden for months at a time. I've seen marriages fall apart over untied shoes laces but the vows were not wasted on my sister. She kept her family together and forged ahead. Eileen is one hell of a broad, in the best and truest sense of the word. As time went by she would start teaching, get Scott help, and secure her own financial ship.

Josefa was the closest sibling to me in age, one year older with Chris one year older then her. (Mom had six kids in six years; talk about tough broads.) Josefa lived in Ann Arbor, Michigan with her Husband Ross and their two boys Guthrie and William. They have added a third boy, Rory, since I have been in California. She loves her family and would love them even more if she could live next door. She has never moved back home nor needed to hit the folks up for money. She and Art had that in common until Art's marriage fell apart and he moved into the basement apartment vacated by Chris and myself.

I tell their brief incomplete stories to paint a picture. To illustrate all the emotional and financial balls juggled by two, sweet fools that decided to raise six wonderful, sick, intelligent, artistic and angry children. Children who would grow to take all the wisdom given by the aforementioned sweet fools and make it their own to varying degrees of success and failure and in some cases throw it back in their sweet foolish faces. Bless them—bless us. I love us all.

It took me close to three years to buy the van get it road worthy and pad my checking account. I say I because Chris didn't get a job this time. He had already reached the breaking point. That was fine with me after some initial whining. Chris spent his time writing, sleeping and attempting to get us gigs; we did a handful of gigs locally just to keep our chops up. As our departure approached Chris started to plan some road dates between Nashville and California. All the phone calls, all the mailed packages only garnered six paying gigs. A few in and around Little Rock, Arkansas, a couple in Oklahoma and one in New Mexico. He tried so hard; I tell you I hate this fucking business.

The rest of our time, when I wasn't working or spending time with Aubrey, Chris and I were drinking booze, smoking pot, snorting coke and tripping on acid or mushrooms; the weekends mostly. I only missed one day of work because of the binges.

The coke and hallucinogenics didn't get as frequent until Aubrey and Donna moved back to Nashville. I had been back in Chicago for about a year and a half when they left. Before she left, I once more tried to convince Aubrey to stay with me. I told her I would forget about California and keep my truck-driving job in Chicago. I had made a similar offer when her mother and I first split up back when she was six. She said the same thing both times, "I want to be with my mother." It was hard for me to take because for all my flighty dreaming I was the one who spent the most time with her. For more than a few years I was a stay-at-home dad. I taught her how to ride a bike, how to swim and, for the most part, how to read. We were great together. When I look back on it now I think maybe she knew that I had somewhere I was supposed to be. Mom once said that Aubrey feared, given too much space, that Donna would be gone from her life. In some ways, even though they always lived in the same house, her mother was already gone. I think I could have made it work and that we would have built a good life and been relatively happy. That being said I was glad to be set free.

I started seeing a girl from work about six months before we were to leave. I told her from the beginning that it had to be a fling. After the end of my marriage I had no interest in falling in love. I had enough commitment on my plate: Aubrey and music. Her name was Angel and we had a good time, it turned out to be just what I needed. Her being twenty-three while I had just turned thirty-five posed no real problems for me over the short term. It would have never worked beyond that and not just because of the age difference. She loved music but never saw my greatness; she thought me talented and cute, but not great. She may even have thought me great. But whenever I heard her raving about other musicians that couldn't lick my boots with a two-story latter, I could hear in her voice and see in her eyes an excitement that she lacked for my work. Say what you want about me for it, I had to be seen as great. I've worked my whole life toward it and she couldn't see......I'm sorry. I am an egomaniac but I make up for it by being every bit as good as I say I am.

On our last night in Chicago one of Chris' oldest and dearest friends gave us a small care package for the road along with a hundred dollars each. There could only be one course of action: Get an eight ball. But then we thought better of it and only got a sixteenth. So Chris, Steve Paulson and I snorted blow, drank some of Steve's prized imported beers, and talked the night away. After managing a few hours of sleep Chris and I loaded up the van.

The loading consisted of a full sized futon mattress, which we laid down first starting from the back double doors and ending where the sliding side door began. Behind the driver's seat sat two milk crates stacked and stuffed with radiator fluid, water, chains, motor oil and some ratchet straps. Crammed in the same area stood a floor jack, an ax and a sledgehammer. Moving toward the back we laid our two three-by-two PA speakers, the long ways parallel to the van's dashboard, tucked toward the driver's side. Three three-by-two Tupperware storage containers; one of which held our archaic computer; the second housed tools, surplus hoses and belts for the van, a couple of plastic tarps and jumper cables; the third for cookware and food were placed evenly behind the speakers bringing us to the back door. By the side door went our Marshall amp and speaker, our bags and four guitars. In the crevices, corners and thrown over top of other things were boxes filled with Chris' many novels and screenplays, and our collective countless song lyrics; seven small boxes holding fifty each of the CD we recorded in Nashville; a four-man tent you could set up in five minutes; a thin, puny, twin mattress with miscellaneous pillows, blankets and a sleeping bag; and more boxes with more tapes of our recording history, video and audio. Outside the back door we attached a rack for the bike I chained to it and on the roof we rigged a platform for the spare tire.

We left the basement apartment in a shambles; tornados and hurricanes showed more respect. Shame on us is all I can say about it, shame on us.

Sorry, Mom.

Sorry, Dad.

A few nights before we left there was a party thrown in our honor. Family and friends gathered to wish us well, a typical affair at the Smith household; good food, warm smiles, hearty laughs born of great conversation, and a song or ten. It always amazes me to think of how profoundly I love to be with these people who have made up so much of who I've become and how necessary it is that I leave them.

On the day we left only mom, grandma, Angel and a sunny, warm August early, afternoon bore witness. Eileen, I think, showed up with her two kids, Jake and Keeley, but just for a moment, on their way to where they had to be. Dad had a sales meeting out of town, and just as all the others who were not us, led their lives according to their needs, immediate and long term. Mothers, grandmothers and girlfriends alone set the day aside to stand curbside and wave goodbye. Before that there were hugs and kisses, a few large bills slipped from palm to palm, and a silent gaze between loved ones that knew how silly and useless words could be. Chris drove first and as we pulled away we gathered up mom in our respective side-mirrors stepping out into the street, and we knew she was cheering us on.

Tears filled our eyes but soon laughed at their own folly. Yes, a long unknown road lay out before us but everything and everyone important was behind us and always would be. The truth of our tears lied in a debt we both feared would never be paid. At least that is how I felt. All my folks wanted of me was not to need anything from them. As much as I wanted to succeed for myself, I wanted for them to be right for believing in us.

CHAPTER TWO

The trip to California would start from Nashville. I had see to Aubrey once more before I left. We arrived mid-evening and I can't remember how long we stayed. I'd ask her but Aubrey's memory is not any better than mine—probably a couple of nights. The night before we did leave, Aubrey and I went for a walk alone. She took me to see her school and we sat by some steps. The sun left the sky slowly as if needing to hear what we would say. A blue hue clung to the light asking the dark to wait like an old lady hushing an intruder upon her stories.

"I'm sorry, kid."
"It's okay, dad."
"I need to do this."
"I know."
"I talk too much, uh."
"Yeah ya do."

Sitting there I looked at this kid on the verge of being twelve who had lived in the three different states, two of them twice; I lived in one house from the time I was ten months old until I moved into my first apartment at the age of twenty. Off the tip of my head I count seven times she had been moved between the ages of three and twelve. In less than a year of her mother and I splitting, Donna took a lover into their home. Larry was only seventeen or eighteen when he moved in with them, just ten years older than Aubrey. All the yelling she had to endure between Donna and myself. When I told Aubrey that her mother and I were breaking up, this sweet, tough six-year-old girl looked up at me and said with a simple, direct understanding, "It's about time; you guys fight too much."

"How are you and Larry getting along?"

"He's okay, when he doesn't try to act like my dad. I just hate the way mom always takes his side."

"Try and cut her some slack, Breeze-child. You're gonna grow up and leave and she doesn't wanna be alone. This may be her last chance."

"But I'm just a kid."

"In some ways so is she. But she is a good provider. Ya got a roof, clothes, food, and she don't beat ya. What can I tell ya, kid; you've got legitimate complaints against us both; hell, I couldn't live with her; look, none of this is fair, but you chose her." I rambled on.

"I was six years old and I wanted to be with my mother!"

"I understand."

"I just-"

I put my arm around Aubrey's shoulders, tucked her in against my chest and kissed her forehead.

"All I'm saying is that if you were with me you'd have to live with my shit; we're your parents so whatta ya gonna do? I am sorry though and whenever you wanna yell at me for all I've put you through I'll take it."

"I don't want to yell," she whined. "Can we just sit here and not talk."

"Shutting up is not what we do best, but let us give it a try."

"You're such a dope, dad." Aubrey laughed through a sniffle.

We sat for a little longer then walked through the playground and talked of lighter things, the things that life fills its days with without concern or drama.

The other priority I had in Nashville was to see Madison, my niece. She was the daughter of Donna's identical twin sister Alice. I had enough of a hand in raising Madison to consider her a second daughter—considerations only go so far. She had a father, albeit not much of one, who lived in Wisconsin. Madison and I shared streets and homes on and off through eight years. When I had Aubrey on the weekends in Nashville I took Madison as well. I taught her how to ride a bike and attempted to teach her how to swim; if she were mine she would have learned sooner than later. Our time together was sporadic and my power limited.

I remember trying to get her to eat some green peas once. Her parents fed her a strict vegetarian diet from the beginning and she took to it, I believe, of her own accord. The problem was that she didn't eat enough vegetables. During one stint of Madison and her mother living with us I had the kids to myself as I often did. For lunch I gave Madison some ramen noodles and a bowl of peas. I had been worried about all the cheese, pasta and junk food she ate. She did eat some beans but lacked dearly in vegetables. When she went to leave the table without eating the peas I said flatly, "You're not going any where until you eat some of those peas." She made a fuss at first, pouted and squirted a few tears, then proceeded to plant her fists in her chin and elbows on the table; the kid settled in for the long haul. I made her sit there for almost three hours and she probably had three maybe four spoonfuls.

Now all of that speaks more to her strong will then any dynamic in our relationship. Although if it had been her mom, a good woman doing the best she could, the battle of wills—if there had been one at all—would have lasted ten or fifteen minutes and no peas would have gone down; she wasn't my kid. We did have that battle and we did have other times; she knows what I'm about and I know her. For all the guilt I had in leaving Aubrey there would be plenty left for Madison.

When I said goodbye to Madison at her house it was a short affair. I'd add sweet but she kept any real emotion at a safe distance—not at all cold. I'm not in any place of superiority to be bashing people, parents or otherwise, but Madison had kind of always been on her own. Her mother showed Madison genuine love and affection, as did her father; they are decent folk. She did not have the free exchange and anchor of accountability with her parents that Aubrey and I shared. Whatever shortcomings I have or scars I've laid upon her psyche, Aubrey knows where to hang her hat and trust its fate. I have tried to give Madison the same sense of emotional security; the words have been said and I hope the actions have met them in her heart.

On the morning we left, Chris and I woke under the heavy burden of the coming goodbye. The van was loaded and Aubrey waited in her living room wiping the nights sleep from her eye. I let Chris go in first as I stood outside the screen door with my eyes on the ground in front of me. I could see their knees huddled together and heard Chris singing an old familiar song softly through the tatteredness of a voice that encouraged sweet humor as opposed to gut-wrenching, emotional pain.

"I'm so glad we had this time together. Just have a laugh and sing a song. It seems we-."

I imagine the ringing accuracy of the next line, *"It seems we just get started and before you know it, comes the time we have to say, 'So long,'* proved too much for Chris and he broke away.

My knees buckled as he walked past me toward the driver's side of the van. I paused with screen door resting slightly ajar against my palm. Aubrey's shoulders shook, as the blinded eyes in her drooped head didn't have the strength to try and find me. I wrapped her up in my arms and tried to squeeze the life out of us both. My hands took in the back of her head as I kissed her forehead.

"I love you so much, kid."

"I love you too, daddy."

"We're gonna be okay."

"I know."

"I'll call when I can and I'll write."

It all lasted probably less than twenty seconds or it could have been longer; time had never been so insignificant. I only know that at that moment I needed her to know how much she meant to me and that words weren't going to do it; I held her harder. Aubrey squeezed back like she had never done before or since.

I pulled back to see if our eyes could meet through all the salty water. I blurted out a short, harsh laugh and kissed some of tears off her cheek.

"I am so proud to be your dad." I measured each word carefully.

"Thank you." She barely managed.

"I have to go." I stepped back.

Her tears slowed for a moment before she crumbled beneath them again.

"Be good, Breeze-child."

And I left.

In the van I fell apart all over again and just gave Chris a wave to get us the hell out of the there. Aubrey did not come out to see us off.

She told me later that she crawled into bed with her mom and cried most of the day away. Donna had taken the day off to be with her as Aubrey had stayed home from school to say goodbye.

Once we were a few blocks away and about to get on the highway I started to gain a modicum of composure.

"God, I am one selfish asshole!" I laughed through the remaining tears.

"You're a good dad." Chris answered plainly. "Shall we goo."

"Onward goo."

It might surprise you to hear that Nashville has the best Chinese buffet in the world, but indeed it does. We had discovered the "Golden House" when we moved there years before and became regulars. All the food there was amazing, well the egg rolls were only so so, but they had one dish that topped anything we had ever experienced. The moo goo giapan was physically addictive. It consisted of the choicest strips of chicken breast with mushrooms, broccoli and snow peas in a white sauce that defies explanation. Chris and I had been there once already while we were in town, with Aubrey and Madison. The night before Chris suggested that we stop in once more on our way out of town. Who was to say that it would still be in business the next time we made it back to Nashville.

Not so surprisingly, by the time we settled into our table at the restaurant we had a healthy appetite. The draining, emotional, roller coaster ride of abandoning ones daughter for a life of music on the road left one quite peckish.

The goo was good.

The goodbyes were over and we headed down forty-west with an eye on stopping off to check out Memphis' famous Beale St. Chris had heard a lot about it from other musicians and from his many visits as a courier. Little did Chris and I know that we'd be getting a glimpse of our future.

Memphis was the last stop before entering Arkansas, and Beale St. sat at the edge of town not far from the bridge that would carry us over the Mississippi river. After parking the van we walked around to get the feel of the place. In and around Beale St. you could feel the tourist vibe but it lay in the shadow of industry. For all I know it could have been the history of a river town that hung in the air with no current function; the structures that looked like factories could now be trendy lofts. Cobblestones poked at the soles of my shoe altering my steps to their texture. Every few corners held street musicians or clowns making balloons look like animals, all for the benefit of atmosphere in the hope of a buck.

Before the sun faded altogether Chris and I decided to go back to the van and grab a couple of acoustic guitars and join the carnival. We didn't expect much—we were not disappointed. People walked by our chosen post sometimes taking note with a smile while others saw us as part of the furniture, which is to say not at all. Chris and I tried a couple of different spots with the same results. It felt good to play; the music kept us in quite good company. By the time the sun had fallen we acquired a buck or two and a few "sounds good guys" but more importantly we had a good practice in the warm evening air. There was a band playing on a makeshift stage behind a restaurant so Chris and I took in a few songs then talked about their shortcomings as we moved on down the line.

Chris recognized the name of a bar someone had told him about so we went in to see about a booking or maybe an open-mic. The manager said if we hung around that between sets of the band booked for the night we could get up and play a few. It was all on a lark, we had no idea when we would be back this way but in the name of "what the fuck" we hung around. The band on stage looked like college kids but the kids could play. They were a horn based jazz band. I don't remember a guitar player but the sax and trumpet player traded licks while the bass and drums laid down the groove as the keyboards padded the sound. The manager wasn't to be found between sets and he didn't leave word with anyone about us getting up there so as the band began their next set Chris and I headed back to the van.

The Mississippi conversed with itself beneath us as Tennessee fell behind and with every rotation of the tires we were traveling further south then we had ever been in our lives. Once across the bridge Arkansas sat in the dark on either side of the road, unknown and silent.

It had been almost midnight when we left Memphis so after a couple of hours on the road we pulled into a rest stop just outside of Little Rock to get some sleep. Up until then all we knew of where we were was colored by the wind of a van moving at seventy miles an hour. The second I turned off the ignition I felt the thick, hot, night air drape itself on my skin with suffocating wings that left no pore unclogged—with the windows rolled down no less. It took a minute or so for the mosquitoes to join the heat on their attack of my skin. I tried to let my heavy eyes fall away from their pestilence as Chris had already done. The day began so long ago and had been piled upon with emotional stress, a king-sized meal, a four-hour drive to Memphis where more energy got spent, and then two more hours on the road. I was fucking exhausted! Surely the heated mosquitoes were no match for such a day. I looked at Chris in a fury of envy that would soon turn to admiration. Here was a man whom from sleep could not be deprived. I rolled the window up to feel the heat grip me internally, rolled the window down to feel my breath mugged by the Arkansas air and pushed back down my throat, while mosquitoes swam in my sweat. I at last settled on the window being bit more than a quarter opened. Oddly enough it slowed the flow of the minutely winged vampires enough to make more of a difference than the way the night air chose to strangle me with my own salty discharge. I leaned my head against the window moving only to slap my wrist, elbow, cheek, neck, thigh, when I felt that a given bloodsucker had reached his legal limit.

I felt Chris stir enough to know that though he might be asleep he was not sleeping well. As petty a man I am, from this I drew no comfort. At one point I declared the nightmare winner and stepped out of the van to stretch my legs, give the annoying little beasts a moving target, and maybe create a small, merciful breeze of my very own. I achieved momentary relief, at least in my imagination, or simply from the dynamic of a different kind of torture; my joints ached, my head bobbed and my eyes burned until I had to sit again.

Time in the moment of time passing is its own little mystery but the memory of time passing, is aforementioned mystery squared. I'm sure T.S. Eliot would chuckle at the time wasted considering time at all.

Anyway, the clocked ticked at the night in drops of sweat, eating away at the misery that I fed on becoming less and less nourished with every bite. I remembered camping with Dad as a kid, or just being home on a humid, Chicago, summer night; nights when you could feel the sun beating on you through the dark. Being young I fought physically as if I could out maneuver the heat by angling myself in positions it would never presume me to be. Dad suggested playing opossum, arguing that my useless movements only made it hotter. In other words, accept the present fate instead of making it worse. It took a discipline that over the years I came to master. The Arkansas heat laughed, "Be still, do the hokey-pokey: Your ass is mine." Chicago could never claim this kind of heat. In Arkansas the sun did not simply beat through the night, it wore the night and stole its way down from the heavens to sit among us, to get close enough to be intimate with our breath, determine our breakfast consumption.

In sleepless fever my eyes spied, in the side mirror, a creature waddling across the grassy medium. The moon shone a soft light, which I never once accused of giving heat. My tired eyes were spooked by the unfamiliar movements made under the innocent moon's glow. The creature shuffled to the left and muddled about before shuffling back from whence it came. If it sought out food it either had a bad case of O.C.D. or was just too dumb to realize where it had been moments previously. Back and forth it went while my eyes reflectively followed and time dripped off the night. I didn't realize then how grateful I was having something to look at and how the distraction eased my suffering. Oh, the suffering continued, but it seemed less important. I leaned this way and that as not to let my sight be lost to its movement. The question then started to play in my mind. What is it? Being a city kid my first thought was a big southern rat. The next obvious guess came in the form of an opossum. That thought made me think that my heated brain was physicalizing my Dad's advice. Maybe I fell asleep and this was a dream. I indulged that fantasy for a moment and smiled. I would take on any ghoulish being, my squirmy sub-conscious could conjure, over the reality of being awake. As I pondered its species, the plump little bugger wandered out of my mirror's realm.

Exhausted beyond the limits of my wits, feeling as far as I've ever been from home, and being a born coward, I decided to let the night's entertainment drift. The heat welcomed back my full attention and the mosquitoes said, hey. I rolled down the window gingerly looking about for the mystery beast. Disappointed, I turned to face the windshield and took note of all the bugs that had found their final resting place there. "So," I said, to the swarm out for my blood, "it's a vendetta is it?" More time passed, T. S. Eliot laughed and awareness conversed with suffering exclusively. I left the window down in defiance of the night as if to say, "Come and get me." My head lay on my palm, erected by the elbow as I stared into the beastless side mirror. Suddenly the little bastard waddled furiously across my field of vision; I saw a tail, short, thin and wiry. In that brief appearance it revealed more of itself than when it languished seductively taunting my curiosity. In that flash of movement I detected something reptilian. Now I had to know. I grabbed a baseball bat that we had brought along for just such occasions and eased myself on to the pavement keeping my eyes on the last known whereabouts of the critter in question. Not willing to stray too far from the van I stretched my neck into the darkness while reaching my hand towards the van door. Of course the little guy would probably not come back with me hovering about. Or so I thought until I saw a lumpy ball of shadow within the distant dark slowly move my way unassumingly. It paused to investigate here and there but moved steadily. Apparently it had missed out on or got away from whatever inspired its rabbit's pace, because presently it seemed to be out for a Sunday stroll. I took the van's door handle in hand but bravely held the rest of my ground. Not so suddenly the beast was upon me with nothing but ten yards of asphalt and four feet of grass between us . Out of the shadows and into the moonlight, aided only by the faint bulb affixed to the restrooms some twenty yards over my shoulder, the beast made itself known to me. It did not so much as ignore or not notice me as it didn't think to consider either concept. I don't know if this is a common behavior amongst the armadillos of Arkansas, or if that particular one had some brash sense of ownership. One thing remained clear: I stood on his turf and he didn't care one way or another.

You might think it anti-climatic or at least disappointing but I smiled until I laughed. Not because of how silly I had been, although yes color me silly personified, no, I laughed because I had never seen a real live armadillo before. I mean maybe in a zoo but let's face it, armadillos are not really what one goes to zoos for to see. Still here I was on the adventure of my life, almost a thirty-six year old man, gambling all respectability and even the love of his daughter on the egocentric belief that he was too good to be denied, and on my first night out on the road to unseen fortune or failure, I met my first armadillo in person. The armadillo could not see the significance of it all but I did not expect that of him. After all he was from Arkansas. (I realize the sexist implications of my assuming that it had been a male and I own that.) He meandered about as I marveled and moved closer, but not too close. I followed him until he slipped into the woods.

Time had passed—fuck Eliot—time had passed and the sun bled from the east into the dark blue sky. I walked back to the van and leaned on the hood to think more about the armadillo and all that he represented. Playing on the streets of Memphis was the perfect way to start our trip; it announced us and our music to the road. The horror of that muggy, mundane, sleepless night in Arkansas introduced the road to me while giving notice to an armadillo whose apathy echoed that of the Memphis streets.

CHAPTER THREE

    Chris and I pulled into a gravel parking lot of a campsite with the sun only threatening the day and set up camp. Visions of glorious state parks bursting with nature's wonders, asking only a meager seven to sixteen dollars a night were, at least temporarily, blinded by this twenty-three dollar cemetery plot of the road. Our folks were veterans of travel and filled our heads with tales of the country's plentiful and affordable state parks. Of course we had to be in specific proximity with the gigs we had in and around Little Rock so this would have to do for now. I set up my modern wonder of an accessoriless tent while Chris set up the back of the van for his bed. My tent had more than enough room but Chris preferred the solitude, which would be defeated soon enough.

    Through my exhaustion I still managed to giggle with affection for the tent I held so dear, and planned to live in for the coming year. When we were kids setting up the tent was a family project. Dad, the chief engineer, Art, his right-hand man because of his knack for the tearing apart and putting things together, and because Joel had a talent for disappearing or not being there at all—then the rest of us kids serving as nameless, faceless builders of the pyramid: Spreading out the massive, mildew ridden canvas, driving the stakes to anchor the soon to be rising monstrosity, sorting through all the poles needing to be inserted and snapped to other poles then slid through loops to come out on the other end to be inserted and snapped again. Once all was inserted, snapped and looped, inserted, snapped and looped, the structure would rise in increments according to poles being steadied and properly angled; it took a family to raise a tent. I dreaded the moment of every camping trip when Dad turned off the engine and I knew that big lump of an erector set from hell on the roof or atop the trailer waited to be assembled. That being said, we joked, argued, laughed and had the best time every time. When the tent stood I felt like I had been apart of something worthy and good, not at all being able to imagine that on the next trip I would dread it all over again.

The tent of my present had nothing in common with that of my youth. It unfolded like an umbrella with all its parts self-contained. You did have to insert a handful of times but it snapped all by itself, and stakes were involved though not always necessary. Being an idiot it took me longer than most to master it but the whole thing, at its worst, was up in less than ten minutes. When I camped with Aubrey and Madison I didn't really need their help but in honor of tradition we made a project of it anyway.

I got the tent up, laid out my bedding and went to sleep before the sun noticed me and got angry. I slept victoriously in defiance of all elements and despite waking drenched with sweat I felt great. The afternoon heat ruled the day but I had already won.

Chris and I showered then went in search of our first gig. Showtime was hours away, but being in a strange town we wanted to get the lay of the land. The area we were in could have been any where in the country; malls spewing strip malls with business parks added for the community's architectural enhancement. Our gig was beside a strip mall adjacent to a business park. Appropriately we were playing at a nationwide chain called the Coffee bean. After going inside and talking to the manager to see where we would set up, we decided to stay close by for fear of getting turned around. In finding the place we had to ask a few people for directions. The directions we received were poor and inconsistent, except for the resentment and hostility, which were rich with consistency. Our northern accents had marked us as unwanted invaders. The people of Little Rock, Arkansas went so far as to sneered at our money—even the French love our money.

The afternoon encounters with the locals left us concerned as to what kind of reception we would get when we played. That fear was alleviated as soon as we started playing. I wouldn't say we killed, but the small crowd of twenty to thirty patrons were at the very least warm.

There was one table of slightly above middle-aged women that made us feel quite welcomed and another table offered a young couple that appreciated our being there. We were paid seventy-five dollars and given free food, made twenty plus in tips and sold three CDs. In my frail book of failure that was a booming success. Chris and I knew we weren't going to make enough off the road to pay for our trip. Well, maybe somewhere we allowed the irrational hope that we'd sell CDs by the box full, get tips hand over fist and be taken home by young beautiful women every night, but they were just dreams whispered between breaths on our pillows.

For one night we felt the possibilities encouraged by a specific reality. Back at the campsite we went over the mistakes, squabbled over details remembered differently and called it a night before harmless disagreements led to destructive accusation. Chris and I have a long history of arguing. I don't think there is anyone we need, respect or count on as much as each other so it stands to reason that there is no one who can annoy, hurt or enrage the other more. The funny thing about any given moment is that it can be perceived differently by two people as it's happening, leaving the coming memory of said moment open to even more disparity. Throw in a shared history, which breeds' familiarity, that while sometimes giving one a clearer understanding of the other, it also convolutes with running unresolved issues and assumed agendas. In end you can know someone too well but not as well as you think to the point where taking what he or she says at face value becomes impossible. This eventuality is made more frequent by all the times you're right in your assumptions of their agendas. It gets to the point where you read more into the expressions and tones than the actual words, which can reveal more truth but also can be over interpreted. Add to all of this that no one wants to be caught being an asshole and that we all, sooner or later and often, are guilty of being assholes. There would be dramatic scenes depicting all of these factors but that night we let it brew to be consumed another time.

Being on the wagon didn't help anything. Chris and I were both obese. I stood at five-ten and weighed three hundred pounds and Chris was six-two at three-fifty to four. I had dark, wavy, long hair that curled and mustache with a goatee covering my chin while Chris had long, straight—what I'd call strawberry-blonde—hair. (I think he would say dishwater blonde and I'm sure under the right circumstances we could argue about it to the point of bringing the fiber of our respective characters into question.) Chris had a Grizzly Adams motif going on around his face. Every time he shaved his beard a baby's face would squirt out from within his huge melon. We weren't just fat, but big-boned, former jocks, with an appetite as big as the great outdoors—ya know, gluttons. Chris and I had the hunger for every thing from knowledge and wisdom to booze and drugs, from sex and art to pizza and ice cream; hardcore extremist hell bent on self-destruction through self-gratification with a course set for self-discovery. One can, and would be better off to discover the self void of all the destruction and indulgence, it's just who Chris and I happened to be and, although it would have been nice to be different, I have had a good time with no regrets. What can I say—born in the sixties, raised in the seventies and made to endure the eighties.

So.

Out on the road we had hoped to strip things to the bone. I had about four grand in the bank but that, we hoped, would be for the van. We would live on what money music provided and the pounds of rice and beans we had stored up in the van. Clean up, lose weight and our talent could not be over looked. Our last drink had been in Chicago but there was a half a bottle of Ten High left in the van and I didn't have the gumption to pour it out. Chris wanted none of it which was for the best since it wasn't really enough for even one of us. I drank it down that night after our first gig on the road with the belief that it didn't really count as falling off the wagon because I barely got drunk off a half of a fifth—a friendly buzz though

That morning we woke to the heat and steamed some rice on our little two-burner propane stove. Our tank was about the size of a quart and would cook three to five meals depending on the length it took to cook each meal. Cooking the rice proved a tricky thing to get right. I was always thought of as the cook between us but Chris had the better touch with rice. In the coming months getting the rice not to be crunchy and mushy at the same time became an on going battle. After breakfast we broke camp because the next gig would be twenty-five miles north in a little town called Conway. The night before we talked about how to kill the day. We had no idea what would, if anything, be in Conway. Throughout the trip we took turns worrying about money. I was the biggest pain in the ass about it; that is of course until I wanted to do something. I consistently spoke of the money as a communal thing, a joint asset, but I worked for it so I'm sure when push came to shove I acted as though my decisions carried more weight. (I admit that now but would have been indignantly offended and righteously enraged if Chris ever even remotely implied such a crude concept to me then.) In looking for the Coffee Bean the day before we came upon a movie theater and Chris suggested that today we get the fuck out of the heat for a couple of hours and go see a movie; maybe hop screening rooms and catch two. I protested long enough to appear the more steadfast one then gave in as I had wanted to, and knew I would all along.

I don't remember what we saw, I can only recall that the ticket taker, true to Arkansas form, resented us and that the theater was dark and cool. I remember getting popcorn and irking Chris because I had been such a prick about wasting money on a movie then turned around and wasted money on soda and popcorn. Chris had an old saying he used to turn to in such situations, which I relished in throwing back in his face.

"In for penny; in for a pound."

Walking out of the theater we found that the heat had gained strength while it waited. The temperature had been hovering around one hundred and ten ever since we hit town but after the air-conditioning of the movie house whatever tolerance we had built-up melted away.

Arriving in Conway we located the gig then sought out a campsite but there were none to be found and for that we were grateful. Motel room! Motel room! The gig was at a ma and pa coffee house and went off uneventfully. Chris and I played our songs to a small gathering that offered a few tips, bought no CDs, but seemed grateful for an evening's entertainment. At the end of the night we collected our thirty dollars and free sandwiches from management and went back to our cool room. The bed felt good as we lay in the dark but neither of us we're able to sleep. If we weren't in a dry county, that night, I think, we may have jumped wagon. Chris spoke with a positive verve, as was his way when he needed to reassure himself. It's not that he was being pretentious although I sometimes thought that of him, but no, simply a need to gear himself up in the face of the challenge that lay waiting. Looking back at those moments I realize now how unsupportive I could be. On that night I remember a good feeling keeping us company but only because Chris had created it.

Every moment is based on the chemistry that we bring to the experience. Depending on the amount of good will verses negative energy adding to that the varying degrees of desperation or exhaustion combined with a million other variables in two given psychological make-ups at a certain point and time wrapped in common and separate pasts, the results could differ from slightly to completely. For example if there had been even a hint of a false note in Chris' good will that night it would have pissed me off; forced positive energy in some instances can make you actually feel positive, while in others it can cause a negative explosion.

"This is going to work. I'm done wasting time on bullshit."

"There was some bullshit tonight."

"Unfucking comparable to all the other shit we've endured. Dave, you played in Little Rock last night and moved on to the next town. When have you ever done that?"

My eyes were closed as his voice softly owned the room.

"No, this is going to work. We are too fucking good and now we are putting it all out there. I'm not talking about anything grand ever again. Just work."

"We'll need more than just six gigs."

"We'll get'em."

"Final Call was good tonight."

"I'm not getting the marriage on that last chorus."

At Chris' most Pollyanna he'd never gloss over a performance and not give it his strictest eye.

"I like having it be a bit loser in the end."

"No, it was good and it'll get better."

Chris coached us some more and I surrendered to the sermon until sleep came for us both.

In the morning we lingered in our room until checkout and bummed around town because we had one more gig at another ma and pa coffeehouse in the neighborhood. We decided that after the gig we'd drive through the night into Oklahoma and find us a real state park to camp in for a couple of days. To kill time we wrote letters home and read, I had started James Joyce's FINNEGAN'S WAKE but gave it up for something less impossible to follow like Ralph Ellison's, THE INVISABLE MAN. All I could gather from the first thirty pages of the Joyce book was that somebody died. I assumed his name was Finnegan. Before the sun fell we parked by the coffeehouse on the edge of town near some tracks and took a few pictures to send home. We called ourselves R&R CROSSING so the shots by the tracks and their accompanying signs seemed like a good photo-opt.

The show was going well enough as we played to another small group—not many tips but enough applause. Toward the end of the second set the place started to fill up with a gaggle of young retro-hippies. At first Chris and I thought we should just keep playing straight into the third set, but then figured that management might prefer we take a short break to encourage the people to spend some money on their fine coffee and related food products.

"Let's keep it short and then kick their asses," I said excitedly under my breath.

"Let me check with manager and see if it's cool that we keep it to five." Chris walked off the stage.

"You dudes are excellent man," a hippie wanna-be offered as he approached the step-off-the-floor of a stage.

Chris thanked him and kept moving.

"Do you know the band?"

Having no idea what he was talking about I smiled, "All my life."

"They should be here any minute, they're driving in from Memphis."

"What band?"

"Head from the Dead; they're going on after you."

"Oh, I didn't know there was another act playing tonight."

Chris returned to tell me that we were being told to forget the last set. They had a friend in this tribute band to the Grateful Dead that had called in the afternoon asking if they could do an impromptu set that evening; telling us had slipped their minds.

"Look at all these asses we could be kicking," I shouted through a whisper to Chris as we slowly wrapped up our chords.

Chris paused to take in the burgeoning crowd. "Godammit." He returned to the task of getting our stuff packed away and off the stage.

"On the bright side, they would have ignored us anyway." I smiled and waited for Chris to join the humor.

"These are Dead Heads; we would have owned this room."

Within minutes the band and a horde of others pulled up out front. The coffeehouse was under siege by the sixties as seen from the eyes of those who wouldn't be born until the eighties. The small establishment had at least as twice as many people huddling around the front steps than they could ever fit inside. Chris and I had to squeeze through the youthful humanity hungry for music with our equipment held over our heads. On reaching the front steps we could see the band unloading enough gear to fill the Aragon ballroom stage. By the time we loaded the last piece through the Ford's sliding, side door we over heard someone saying that they'd have to set up outside.

"Chris, we could make our way back inside, set-up and get in another ten or twenty songs before they plugged in their first guitar," I said retrieving chord bag from the van.

"We'd have to ask first."

I immediately worked my way back inside and found someone behind the swamped food counter who appeared to be in charge.

"The manager's not here and I'm pretty sure the police we'll be here to shut all this down anytime now," she shouted over the counter through the increasingly obnoxious flower children, none of whom had seen a shower in days. Her voice did not plead nor demand but you could hear the beginnings of a meltdown tickling beneath the surface.

"But what if-" Her eyes cut me off at the knees.

Chris and I leaned against the three-quarter ton, white whale that had carried us so far and would carry us further still taking in the excitement at a safe distance. By the time the band was close to being ready to play the clock ticked toward midnight. There were drums, keyboards, two guitars and a bass player. This small dry town was not built for such a spectacle. It was in fact built by those who detested and feared all about to transpire. My guess is that the owner's of the coffeehouse had to fight tooth and nail just have permission to book the likes of Stopher and myself. The sound-check shook the meager porch that the band had so foolishly perched themselves upon. Chris and I shook our heads.

"We would have given them such a nice little show." Chris smiled sadly.

"This could only have happened to us, Stopher."

On the highway, miles away, we lost the sense of our humor and spewed bitterly down the road, bringing into question not only the priority of the masses, but also the merit of the masses' chosen few. Once we spit out the last of our contempt it became all too funny again. The laughter would subside and we would talk about other things or not at all until one of us cracked an unattached smile that connected us both to that sight of profound uselessness.

"Did you see the bowing of that porch?"

"What? No string sections?"

Chris drove, then I drove; the night was no match for us. The sun joined us in Oklahoma, slowly creeping up our backs try to get a glimpse of where we'd be going next. Monday morning had nothing for us to do. There were no trucks full of lumber or stacks of pipe going anywhere that I'd be taking them. We had played our first three dates in Arkansas and didn't have to be in Bixby, Oklahoma until Friday. All Monday morning told us was that we couldn't drive forever and that we might as well find a sweet piece of land that held a hole full of water and let the rest of the week fend for itself. Fountainhead State Park was all that and more; a filling station for the soul and only twelve dollars a night.

The brown state sign called us off the road and led our trusty Ford down a long isolated path leaving the humming highway to those with some place to be. There were a handful of campers left over from Labor Day weekend, most of whom would join the civilian work week soon enough. By the time we picked a sight amongst the greenery of tall trees, the outside world couldn't be heard or seen. The van sighed it's relief as the oil dripped into the pan leaving all moving, metal parts to rest in frictionless harmony. The Oklahoma heat wafted harmlessly over a dry, well-meaning breeze that never allowed the ninety-five degrees to get mean. This was not the thick, humid one hundred plus Arkansas heat that banned anything remotely resembling a breeze from its state lines, unless sent directly from the fires of hell.

On our way in we made sure to locate the way to the lake—poetry aside it was still fucking hot. Letting all chores simmer under the mid-morning sun, Chris and I slipped on some shorts and followed the winding, foot, trodden path from our site through the woods out into an opening of grass that rose up and sloped down giving way to the sand and rocks that introduced the water to our feet. At first you had to step carefully among the jagged edges but that soon gave way to rounded gravel, then squishy mud, then finally nothing but water cool as it was warm. On that first morning we were too tired to swim and had not much to say. The water took us in and cleansed our concerns as we gave ourselves completely to the expectationless beauty of the wet quiet; silence but for the movement of water against itself and our bodies.

Throughout the rest of our stay we would make our way back down the path together or alone. Three full days and nights of embryonic peace (I was in a band called "Embryonic Peace"—A tribute to "The Osmonds") whenever we sought it, waited down the path, open without arms, understanding without knowledge, and soothing without caring. The water offered nothing but the acceptance of our bodies and whatever else we wanted to leave there.

Somewhere in our travels we picked up food supplies to compliment our rice and to give us a break from it. On one night I'd chop up the chicken breast, green peppers and onions into a big pot where I'd add garlic, basil, oregano and cayenne pepper on one burner while Chris tended the rice on another. While the rice simmered I'd add a couple of large cans of whole peeled tomatoes and then some paste. When the rice was done we'd mix it all into the big pot and eat like kings. We called it cayenne chicken. On other nights we'd simply fry up some burgers or boil hot dogs. Of course when we didn't feel like cooking at all there was peanut butter and jelly.

In anticipation for life on the road I bought an ax, a sledgehammer and a wedge. I assumed that we would be chopping a lot of firewood. The propane stove was a last second gift from the folks because they had been given a new one. I took it along but never expected to get much use from it. The thought of chopping wood every night for my dinner made me feel like an old pioneer living amongst the elements as I blazed a trail out west. What I didn't know about the west was that because of the dryness and the time of year, most of the state parks banned any open fires. Even when they are allowed you have to purchase the wood they supplied.

The only use my treasured ax and sledgehammer have provided me over these last four years is the comfort of security. So like Hank Hill I am a loyal subject to the kingdom of sweet Lady propane and propane accessories.

On one of the nights spent at Fountainhead Chris and I practiced a little bit for the next gig. I don't remember if that started the huge argument we had, but working on music had always been a good way to get on each other's nerves in the past. Neither one of us likes to be told what to do or that our ideas aren't satisfactory. Sometimes a fight begins with a disagreement over who was flat or out of time. What begins a fight rarely if ever has anything to do with what makes it escalate or what really is at the heart of what's bothering or hurting the other person. Sometimes it has more to do with the way the other person is arguing and the way the other person is arguing can be related to just about anything under the sun except the specific thing that the argument at hand is supposedly about. Mostly it comes down to: How are you treating each other? Are you really listening? Is the way you remember what just happened as important as you think? Do you absolutely have to be agreed with? The last two were the fulcrum on which the first two were catapulted out the window every time.

A pattern may have already been established, or begun on the road, of me really hurting Chris to the point where he had felt dismissed. The hard part about grasping that was because, for me, our history had been based on the older brother keeping the little brother in line. Two years difference as children was colossal in the first place and in the second, Chris, had always been the teacher and when everything had been hashed out in our youth I was left feeling that two things were consistently true: Chris had been over bearing and too hard on me but that he was ultimately right. Somewhere along the way I became a leader although not in any pure form, but enough of one to set off a change in our dynamic. A change that I remained unconscious of to the point where I thought he was still being too hard on his little brother when in fact I was attacking him. This wasn't the case in every situation and I have no idea what transpired that night. I only remember him saying, "You are too quick to take away my reality." I would hear that over the next few years, as well as, "You talk to me like an idiot-child." The funny thing is that a part of me felt like I was forever on shallower ground than him but that, yeah, at times he seemed more of an idiot to me than I would have ever thought of him before. The tricky thing was that I couldn't differentiate my feelings of superiority from those of inferiority and either could he so we surrounded ourselves with these evolving roles and unanswered hurt emotions.

We drove each other nuts that night. At one point I literally tore at my hair. I just wanted out of the arguing but couldn't give him what he wanted even when I understood what that was. When I saw it and tried to give it, it was a half-hearted, short-lived, pretentious attempt that only fueled his rage. I would have reacted the same way.

"Why don't you just take your righteous rage and break something, you fucking, selfish child." Chris shouted through the dark night sitting on the bench lit only by our battery lamp.

"You are so fucking superior, none of this is your fault." I stomped around the van wishing I could get away but not at the expense of being wrong.

"It is my fault, because you never do anything wrong! It's always my fault!"

The circle ran true to form and the calm would come. Chris would apologize and take all the blame; I would apologize and feel him not wanting to share it so he could resent me on a later date. That is probably a cheap shot because Chris doesn't know how to be insincere. When he is angry with you everything is magnified until your faults envelope you into being the sum of their parts. Afterward he can only see the shame upon himself and nothing you offer can trespass.

I started writing my first song since leaving Chicago the day before we broke camp. I only had one line and three chords. Chris and I were talking about how for the last few years we had spent too much time in our heads. We were all thought and no action, stuck between all we had done and how much was left to do. Life had taken its toll leaving me uncertain as to what I had left in the tank. The line was as follows:

It seems I've been searching for a compromise
between giving up and trying again

I usually jump into a song running without stopping before I have a verse or two and a chorus. Being in the midst of such a dramatic change in my life I guess I decided to tread lightly. Adding another song to my already over stuffed catalogue had not been a pressing concern for me in quite some time. Chris and I could never write a song again and still die with a body of work to rival anyone from Dylan to Gershwin. No, songs came for their own sake now and this one felt important; I let it dangle.

The days at Fountainhead in my memory stand out as a landmark. I can see us now wallowing in our own private lake embracing everything we were and all that waited for us to accomplish. None of it seemed then, or feels now, like pie in the sky optimism or the meanderings of a couple of delusional dreamers. No we have not achieved half of what we hoped for and yes failure of both financial and personal natures continue to surround our every effort to this very day; but there in the lake, cradled in those moments, we basked in the light of the Holy Grail. The road lay out in front of us, long and impossible, and still does, but it is the right road for us. Dreaming amongst the trees that circled the water to protect it—the promises whispered and declarations shouted there—from a workday world that feared everyone might try to do the same, we confirmed our resolve, accepted the fate it implied and said, YES! I want to go back there one day to tell the trees, to show the water that Chris and I have kept our word.

CHAPTER FOUR

Bixby was only a two to three hour drive from Fountainhead so we pulled out late Thursday morning with an eye at getting to Mike and Marsha's in time to have shook the dust off our boots and restocked some supplies. Chris and I first saw the Calvert's hosting a writer's night at a roadside bar called Guitar Jacks in Nashville. Mike did the hosting and his wife Marsha along with his sister Carol joined him on stage throughout the night to bless us with some of the sweetest sounds I had ever heard in my life. Mike used to introduce them on stage by saying, "This is my wife and sister; I don't know who the chick on the end is." What followed were three part harmonies so closely knit they formed a single silky blanket that slipped round your shoulders and corralled the senses into surrendering your soul. I do go on but when they sang it was perty. On top of that, Mike's songwriting had an earthy poetry both rustic and mythical, straightforward and esoteric. They called themselves Blazon Pearl and I am even more amazed that the world doesn't already know of them than I am about my own anonymity. Mike actually may have coined the phrase, "Nashville Underground" but they were so wildly beloved in the fringe community that I just assumed they'd break through to the other side. Blazon had made a living on what Mike called meat and potato tours before settling in Nashville with the hopes of getting signed. Making a living on the road however meager was enough to make them my heroes. They started hosting writer nights in various places while building a reputation and making semi-influential friends. Once they added Terry Baye on second guitar their sound was even more complete. But like all the others that I thought the most worthy, Blazon never seemed to catch the right fish. Of course Mike had turned some offers down. I never knew the particulars but assumed that they would have been good enough for me. (If for no other reason than Chris and I being so willing to be taken advantage of by anyone in the business, we should've been picked up on a long, long time ago.) So like the rest of us, Blazon went back home. Home for Mike, Marsha and Carol was around Tulsa and Terry, knowing a good thing when he was in it, went with.

Carol lived across the street from Mike, Marsha and Terry with her two teenage boys. The three Calverts managed some properties for a local real estate firm while Terry made extra money playing in a couple of popular local bands and giving guitar lessons. Blazon had someone paying them to record a CD that seemed destined never to be finished. Mike crippled himself perpetually with never ending second-guessing and delusions of perfection. Where Chris and I stacked song on top of song Mike preciously nit-picked himself into a corner he rarely vacated long enough to finish any of the many potentially great songs he started. He had more than enough material to complete an album but unfortunately he applied the same self-imposing entanglements to recording as he did writing. All the finality and the details of mixing enabled him to tinker it to death.

We pulled up in front of the address that Carol had given us over the phone and paused a moment before getting out. It had been years since we had seen them and Chris only talked to Carol the one time for directions since Nashville. You could call us friends but we were probably closer to associates. Blazon was a friendly bunch, the kind to give you long time reunion hugs even if you all had dinner the night before. Chris and I were not what you'd call cold or uptight except maybe in comparison to them. No matter how welcomed we knew we'd be it still felt like an intrusion. Chris and I did have a special affection for Mike; he kind of made think of what Joel might have been like if he never went crazy (not that Mike didn't have a crazy all his own). Nothing so exact as you could put your finger on but something of a more kindred-spirit nature. There was always a cowboy in Joel somewhere and Mike was an Oklahoma native son of a preacher; grandson of a rancher. I liked the rest but Mike was the magnet that drew me to them. Chris always said that Mike, like Joel, moved like an artist; it was in their walk, it was in their manner. I remember the first time I saw Mike sitting on a stool with a guitar gingerly cradled inside his arms and the neck nestled warmly under his fingers. That was how the guitar looked when Joel held it; home for Christmas dinner after months out on the road. Mike played a fine guitar but no would ever confuse him with a picker of any virtuosity but the guitar smiled gentle and easy at his touch.

Sitting nervously in the van, we waited for the courage to stir us when from across the street Carol bounced out from her house and made for the van. She was as beautiful as a specimen as nature could claim; blue, sparkling, circular pools for eyes and a windswept, prairie smile. Her slender silky frame held her beauty in kind and never failed to make me weak in the knees.

"Welcome to Oklahoma, boys!"

Our feet dropped from the van as we each took her in for a gander in our arms, letting the distance and time ease our shame long enough to feel justified in holding her a little longer and harder then we otherwise would have allowed ourselves.

"You look incredible as always my, dear," Chris said respectfully.

"A sight for sore eyes," I added a mite less than awkward.

Carol had been good friends with Donna and Alice. Her kids got together with our kids so I saw her outside of the usual gatherings a few times back in Nashville. After Donna and I split we had some nice talks, although being the fat slob I was I never thought she saw me in any romantic sense. But we had some nice moments and she was so very sweet as well as beautiful that one's mind does wish to think beyond the realistic on occasion.

Carol led us into Mike and Marsha's living room before heading out to run some errands.

"Someone should show up pretty soon, make yourself to home."

The house was small and cozy with a friendly porch. The living room held a couch and a loveseat forming the corner of the room opposite a lazyboy chair, Mike's throne no doubt, surrounding the television that sat kitty-corner from the front door. The coffee table in the middle of it all sat worn and littered with remotes, ashtrays and magazines.

Mike walked in sporting a swollen belly in the center of his tall frame. He stopped to face us and raised his arms above his square shoulders in a question mark, then ran his right thumb and middle finger through his dark, graying, stringy hair to clear it from his face and send down his back as an answer.

"We got us some Chicago boys sittin' in the parlor."

"Hey, Mike," Chris and I said in unison as we took turns in the tradition of hugging then standing about trying to find a place to put our eyes.

Once back to sitting on the couch, Mike sat in his chair and Chris and I relaxed. The conversation followed the news of life from Nashville to Chicago to Oklahoma. Mike was Mike, affable to a fault without being pretentious. The three of us enjoyed tickling the edgier side of our humanity together. I think that is probably what Mike liked about us. He was a positive spiritual person, as were Marsha, Carol and the rest of crowds they ran with back in Nashville. With a lot of them lip service ruled the day and even Mike would lay it on thicker than my taste could suffer now and again. As we got to know each other though, Mike indulged his darker side in our company. A collector of jokes, he would display the meatier ones for Chris and myself. Mike has told us countless jokes and I can't remember a single one in its' entirety. There is the one about the all-star band in hell with a chick singer; the one about how God doesn't like Mexicans, and a million others I don't know enough to tell. He is not a misogynist or a racist but funny is funny.

As people started showing up, Marsha then Terry, various other friends from the neighborhood, Chris and I looked at each other in agreement: Beer, lots and lots of beer. The wagon was to be parked in Bixby and re-boarded at a time and place to be later determined. We slipped out and returned as the guitars came out and a good old fashion round commenced. Oh, to hear Blazon sing again, what a joy, what a joy. I let Terry have the first couple to himself but threw in my two-cents worth of riffs in after that. I had secretly wanted to be the second guitar player even before Terry showed up on the scene. He had a better all around knowledge of music than I, his chordings and the way he played off the chords was truly a thing of beauty. But when it came to lacing along with a melody, I was second to no man, woman, or beast. That night music flowed, voices rang and the beer bubbled our senses.

The first night winded down and people drifted on home. I let Chris take the couch and retired to my beloved tent, which I had set up in the back yard earlier. The warm evening was made hotter by being inside with the air-conditioning all night but once I settled into the Bob Smith opossum-sleeping method I passed on to a deep slumber. Oh, and being drunk helped too.

The next day everyone was out busy working and Chris and I practiced for the gig we had that night. I don't remember a thing about the show; we played, got paid, and then met up with Blazon at a late-night restaurant that they played at every Friday. They asked us to come up to sing a few but we had already suffered through enough indifference at our own gig and the group here looked more interested in buffalo wings than music. Chris and I stayed for a set then decided to meet the crew back at the house. I could already feel the itch to get back on the road but we had another gig in Tulsa on Saturday plus the idea of watching football with Mike on Sunday had an appeal because who knows when it'd be offered again. I wanted this new life I chased but old comforts died hard.

The Ribcage was a roadside bar just outside of Tulsa. That made for an hour drive from Bixby. It actually felt good to play in a bar again. Something about the well lit, clean cut atmosphere of the coffee houses made me feel out of place. The bars had obnoxious drunks, smoke soaked oxygen and there was always someone who'd rather listen to the jukebox. (I was in a band called "Smoke Soaked Oxygen"—a tribute to Rod Stewart) The coffee houses at their worst ignored you politely where as if you displeased the rabble washing another workweek down their throats it could and usually did get ugly. Now I may be a raging alcoholic but I hate bars for the most part; people are annoying enough sober. The fact is, though I am most definitely a poetic, sensitive, intellectual writer of deep, profound insights into the human heart and soul; I am also one bad motherfucker of a blue-collar rock and roll star. When you're playing the bars you have only one job: Kick ass; simplicity invites clarity, and clarity liberates the senses. To be fair, the coffee houses are fine gigs and I can see myself playing them the rest of my life if they'll have me, and furthermore if I had to play bars every night I know it would wear thin. And yes, the second Chris and I walked into the Ribcage that night a feeling of dread over came me. When you reach a certain age most folk tend to avoid fights so of course a heavy sigh accompanies that moment when you see the inevitable forming your future. But soon enough the challenge seduces you, and that part of you that never wanted to grow up in the first place grabs hold of the gut to squeeze whatever remaining juvenile glory you've got left out on to the floor.

Chris started out singing a few easygoing covers with my sweet guitar dancing along. Being in Oklahoma, we covered Hank's ON THE BAYOU—rural is rural and Hank is Hank—and that raised a smile or two. Before long there was the obligatory request for FREE BIRD, which to their surprise, we rocked out like no two other men could. Hoops and hollers greeted us at the song's end as if we had a five-piece band pulsing beneath us the whole way. The victory lived only as long as it took for someone to request a song we didn't know. Chris knew most of the covers and compared to the average working bar band that was not much. We were writers and of course that meant nothing to nobody but us. That's not to say that some of our songs didn't go over well; people can't have their preconceived notions on the defense at all times.

Here is one example that informs you that you are playing in a bar. Some drunk comes to the stage asking for Jim Croce. Lucky for him, Chris is quite versed in the work the man and proceeds to spit out a few. The drunk applauds gratefully, enthusiastically even, for each song then comes up twenty minutes later screaming, "I said I wanted to hear some Jim Croce, goddammit!"

Of course the best part about playing in a bar is the free booze. By the end of the fourth set we had a good beer buzz going as we settled on some stools by the manager. She couldn't have been happier with our work and not only gave us shots, but bumped our pay from one-fifty to one seventy-five, bought a couple of CDs and told us we were welcomed back any time we came through town. That is a successful evening.

The drive back to Bixby was all smiles and congratulations. The house was alive with music on our return so we jumped in with both feet because the water was fine. Chris had Terry pick us up some weed earlier that day so he twisted a few and smiles were passed all around. It could have been Chicago in the back alley or Nashville in our apartment; it was as if we had fit it all into a suitcase. Different faces told old stories that happened to us all and we crammed the circle of life in the bouncing bubble of clear, fragile liquid that floated us along back and forth through time threatening to end and never end alternately.

All of ourselves that we tried to leave back in that Chicago basement caught up with us at the Calvert's. Still it was good for Chris and I to reconnect with the Calverts for old times sake as well as to see them walk among their own homebred demons. Every night Marsha went through the house until the wee hours of the morning cleaning like a hired ghost-maid while Mike sat in their bedroom whittling on some piece of wood, both attempting some sort of symbolic effort to control, organize, or bury their past. I didn't see them as looking forward but that is just my perception. I love using various drugs but never understood speed. Maybe they were just afraid to sleep. Blazon had been teased with the taste of life changing success while Chris and I had been consistently ignored. They're returning home may have held a more profound significance. Mike once told me that all he really wanted was a good spit of land and a hundred head of cattle; Marsha owned the ambition beyond that. Carol had her boys to raise and anytime she got on a stage was a good thing. So there they all were, their feet seeped in soil that birthed their roots feeling a thousand miles away in either direction.

Before we left Mike told us to get off interstate forty and see his country.

"Take 412 up through the panhandle to 325 into the Black Mesa, boys," he smiled a spark that tickled his memory with fondness and marked the weariness of too many years since going there himself.

Mike had written a magical song about his grandfather and a place in the country of his youth. One line in that song is map to Mike Calvert's soul: *He knew where he was, when he was where he came from; like the back of his old grandfather's hand.*

I have not talked to any of the Calvert's since that visit but heard through Alice that Marsha still lives near Tulsa and so does Carol. Terry went to his own roots in Colorado and Mike sought out his true one. Somewhere up in the panhandle on a spit of land in the company of some cattle left to the land by his long since passed grandfather, sitting on a porch with his boots on a wooden rail—no doubt in need of mending—sits a cowboy minstrel cradling a guitar as he serenades the cottonwood trees and they him.

During our stay there another line came to me for the song I was working on. Every morning I heard dogs barking as if in response to the wind. I don't know why it struck me as such. The sun was hours away; a breeze would find me in my tent; a dog barked to another dog barking. The sun got closer; the wind picked up; the dogs would bark. In my half-sleep a rhythm both poked at my slumber and soothed it encouragingly. After two mornings of this I looked at the lyrics I had started and added:

Dogs barking at the wind; trying to finish before I begin
It all dies down, till I lose the sound, the memory forgets
But the senses hound
And I'm searching, without moving
Searching, without moving

The road felt good rumbling under the tires of my faithful Ford companion. Every mile added to my affection for this eight-cylinder monster chewing at the distance with its extended body swaying in winds that burst across open fields on to the highway offering humility to man-made machinery. Chris and I gossiped about the Calvert's to pass the time and make us feel better about ourselves; it's what we do isn't it? None of it held malice, only mindless observations and idle speculations.

As 412 took us deeper into the handle, civilization bid farewell and the land devoured our sight. Green pastures held distant mounts speckled with trees diminished by the magnitude of space; the green gained variance from rocky desert patches as the road narrowed to the greedy consumption of nature's will. Once on 325 the sun grew tired in the sky with reaching arms for earth's unseen territories, leaving only enough light behind for us to see the dark coming. Chris and I had so arrived at being nowhere that only two radio signals came in each being from Christian stations. The land spoke for God all on its own so we turned the radio off. The map told us that the state park was not only there but all around us. Never has so much space felt so claustrophobic. Fear crept through our spines on tiptoes with a devilish grin. As spooked as we were it was funnier still to the point of laughing and laughing hard. We stared out into the vast monument to our miniscule consequence in the mass configuration of existence, then looked at each other and laughed again. The laughter ended abruptly as it started then erupted again. The road got smaller and rougher as the light grew dimmer. Of the few offshoots from the so-called main road we saw they all seemed to be private drives. At the point, where the road almost completely ceased to be a road, we spied what we thought might be some RVs. Approaching with skeptical caution we prepared ourselves to be assaulted by shotgun wielding, wilderness men who hunted misguided tourist for sport. What we found were some old kindly retired folks who had gone in search of their country and found it in the middle of nowhere. They welcomed us with a sympathetic sense of our bewilderment and pointed to the camper where we could register.

We set up our tent near two black spotted boulders
By the base of rise where the bobcat receives
The key to this land that just keeps getting older

Those are some lyrics from the bridge of a song Chris wrote about our experience called, THE BLACK MESA. That is just what we did that night. Again Chris slept in the van while I took the tent. The lyric describes perfectly the little cove formed by the rising brush hovering over the massive rocks, where we sat on a picnic bench to see the resident feline peek through a tall, grassy patch, standing on rail-thin path no doubt created by himself, carefully inspecting the trespassers of this land to which he justly lay claim. Like the armadillo of Arkansas, I at first suspected some sort of attack from the beast. Unlike the hard-shelled, glorified rodent of the Deep South, the bobcat harbored a concern as to our agenda: What did we want? Did we bring any food? Did we eat bobcats? For two nights he showed up with these questions; on the third he went else where for other answers.

It was in the tranquil space of the Black Mesa that I finished the song I had started at Fountainhead. Chris and I had once again boarded the wagon after the indulgences of Bixby; sober but not yet clean. We still had a little weed left to share with the warm mesa air. The song I had begun was one of those that I had to finish before I knew why I started or more to the point what it had to say. Which is not to say that I didn't have a clue to the feeling for in fact the feeling was all I had. I felt something in Fountainhead that gave me the first line and a few chords; dogs barked at the sunless, morning wind in Bixby and that spoke to the first line; being further from home with every next step in the Black Mesa than I had ever been crystallized the feeling into a single theme. Fountainhead and the Black Mesa were bookends to Bixby, which might as well have been the basement in Chicago where my story, this journey all began—specifically the last two years leading up to our departure. In that time I went inward to the mind using drugs and alcohol, seeking stillness, hiding but exploring; escaping but discovering; stagnate but adventurous. Now the road with all its uncertainty holding new sights and challenges requiring movement, demanded the mind be brought out from the dark, meandering, intellectual, insulated world of conjecture and abstract speculation and into the physical act of sinking or swimming. So the song said write me and I did:

It seems I've been searching for a compromise
Between giving up and trying again
Dogs barking at the wind
Trying to finish before I begin

Then it all dies down 'til I lose the sound
The memory forgets but the senses hound
And I'm searching without moving
I'm searching without moving

Swirling wind returns
Them dogs are barking again
Decisions need not be made
Still I crave an action
I wanna let be
But them itches are for scratchin'

Then it all dies down 'til I lose the sound
The memory forgets but the senses hound
And I'm searching without moving
Just searching without moving

I think I just wanna be happy
I think sometimes I don't know what that is
I think I better keep looking
I think I know it isn't here

So some compromises can't be found
It's gotta be one way or the other way bound
Cracks runnin' through a foundation
Sooner or later gonna hit the ground

Rip it apart and build it up, play with the pieces
Make a new machine; junk is a junkman's dream
And I'm still searching without moving
Just searching without moving

Happiness is in a moment
And that moment is always fleeting
Lately my moments all blur into one
Not one worth repeating

Rip it apart and build it up, play with the pieces
Make a new machine; hell, junk is a junkman's dream
I think I'll get moving, leaving the searching
I said moving, fuck the searching

I know, it's too long for the radio—fuck the radio.

On our first day at the Black Mesa we walked a trail that started parallelling a creek on the side of a dirt road before spiraling upward around a rocky mount of hardened sand. Rising up we traveled from the campsite into a cowboy movie. Cactus sprouted here and there along with wild sage, patches of green in the form of a shrub imitating a tree stood sporadically in open defiance to the glaring sun and the occasional cream colored boulder offered protection from gunfire should bandits appear. After a mile or so the trail split, one way rose and fell off in the distance winding and looping until its destination remained a guessing game from the vantage point of the fork, the other continued up to what we estimated to be a two or three story peek. City boys that we were we chose the assured finite path and arrived at the top in short work. The peek lay flat in a circle the size of small parking lot. In fact on the side opposing the trail was an entrance for automobiles.
  "We needed the exercise any way," I said to Chris.
  "Whatever," Stopher huffed through a puff.
  On the trail side of the peek rolled the rocky cowboy exterior that held other peeks similar in stature. The trail's other fork could be picked up for further inspection as it went on for miles before vanishing behind another mount that probably wore it like a sash up its belly round and round all the way choking its neck until finally slapping it on the head. Further still amongst the rises and falls of the land a ribbon of

black top pavement slid into view from some unknown source of the so-called civilized world forging its smooth will, cutting in and out of the horizon leading the eye curiously, "Who and why saw the need? What is out there that requires...?" Standing on the other side of the mount, adjacent to the dirt road entrance you saw directly below, the road and creek, to the right the campsite with its handful of trees, to our left the beginning of some woods, but straight out beyond all things immediate sat an eternity of prairie. Cowboys roamed there as well, but not the movies' thrilling gunfight scenes amidst the desert boulders. Here, pensive greens mingled in greater frequency with the rock, laden coarse sand; the horizon's edges were framed by pines holding up the sky; and the deepest distance the eye could absorb perched the promise of even more green pines steadfastly steeped in a softer more forgiving soil. The ocean of land swallowed the eye and swam in your blood. Chris and I stood silently letting the warm wind die in the strands of our hair only to be reborn in places better left not understood, better served by magic than science.

Later that day we asked about the ribbon of black top and if maybe a town could be found on it in a reasonable distance. Chris wanted to mail a letter and I hoped to find a grocery store. Indeed the dirt road that led us in the night before and ran beneath the mount we stood upon, rambled on through the small wooded area out on to the black top that led to a small town only ten miles away. The town was really a street and the street only a few blocks long. We came across a post office, a museum, and what may have been a school but they were all closed. Another black top intersected with the main street of the town by the post office but only offered a chance to wind off into bigger mounts and more parts unknown. The last building before the black top turned into a reddish, clay, dirt road was a general store that appeared to be open.

The owner was a middle-aged, squat man with a friendly disposition who filled the role of welcoming committee, historian and tour guide. He even graciously accepted our mail with the promise it would be expedited in a timely manner. The man of the town went on to tell us about the dinosaur tracks that were the town's claim to fame. On a shelf he had some plaster castings of the tracks with a few toy dinosaurs placed around them for, I assumed, theatrical effect. Chris got kind of excited about the whole thing and asked where the actual tracks were. I still hadn't convinced myself that any of it were true or even possible, but no money was being asked of us so we took the map, bought a couple of ice cream bars and thanked him for his time.

Outside the store we sat on a bench and looked down the dust red road of dirt.

"That sign says 325," I noted.

I got up, went to the van to get the Atlas map book of the entire country and opened it on the hood.

"The old RV folks back at the campsite said they came from New Mexico that way," Chris said from the bench.

I stepped out on to the black top just fifteen feet from where it gave way to the dirt.

"That looks like a cool ride," I said as I turned back to the map. "I bet it's a more direct route to where we're going too. It runs right into 25, then that takes us straight down to Albuquerque."

Chris rose from the bench to eye the road.

"It's not much of a road," he said cautiously.

"Old, Betsy can handle 'er," I grinned, slapping her hood.

"It'd definitely would be something see," Chris said easing himself into the idea. "Let's ask the guy inside and see what he says about it."

I walked back into the store and the man smiled with the hope that a long conversation beckoned his lips.

"That's highway 325 out there, right?"

"Yes, sir, that'll take you down into New Mexico then on to interstate 25," he responded excitedly before realizing that he may have been too efficient in his answer there by ending the need for any other exchanges.

"That doesn't look like much of a road, how rough is it?"

"Oh, she'll give ya a ride," he chortled. "How are yer tires?"

"I just got'em before leaving Chicago. They can't have more than two thousand miles on'em, if that."

"Let me take a look." The little man shuffled off his stool and waddled his way happily around the counter. A sense of helpful importance planted itself in each step as his waddle morphed into a stride. His round, joyful face flashed a smile at me as he strolled by on his way to be of service.

"Them some good tires," he congratulated me as he circled the van. "Solid tread."

He circled a second time then stuck his stubby forefinger into the grooves of one tire in the back and then one in the front. The man tried unsuccessfully to wear his inspector's face void of glee as to give us faith in his judgment. He planted himself in the road to give it a good stare then shot his sharp eyes on the tires, then the road, then the tires.

"That is one scenic drive you'll be taking there. Be sure to take it easy on them shocks; this ain't a road built for speed."

"No, we'll take it slow," I assured him.

"You got some fine tires, you won't be having any problems there."

We thanked him for his expertise and concern and he shucked our praise off as he lapped it up. His stride settled back into a waddle as the helpful man waved over broad but lumpy shoulders to us driving off, on his way up the three steps into the store, back to his post to wait for the next person in need of service.

The next day Chris and I went in search of the dinosaur tracks. I can't say that we found them any more than I could say we did not. We did go where they were supposed to be but there were no clear markings or signs that pointed to a specific spot. A sign offered the general area but no more. Chris and I walked along a grassy ditch taking turns saying, "Is that it?"—"This looks like something?"—"Hey-oh wait, forget it." Yet we left feeling satisfied that we had been in the presence of something prehistoric. Part of it was the trust we put in the sincerity and reliability of the man at the general store, and the other less tangible part was something in the air; the fresh, tall blades of grass; or maybe just in us. All I know is that when I think back on the spot we were standing in I can feel the time before time pulling at my center. There was something about the land we stood on that made it make sense, that I should believe the tale told; I don't believe in God but I know it is nice to believe in something once in a while.

Later that day we drove the van up to the mount we had hiked up the day before and got out our guitars to play. I've always liked playing by water, in parks around campfires and in nature in general. Of course I had never played in scenery like this in my life. The space took in our music and sang it back to us, the wind wrapped up every note to carry away and drop wherever, whenever, in no particular order, carelessly without thought, and the sky stretched out above never looking down or up, only being reached for, forever beseeched. We sang with strength, we sang in gratitude, our shut eyes felt the beauty caressing, pounding; whispers shouted through the lids, indifferently calling, "You can't help but see."

During one song a hawk joined us, gliding in a circle in front of the mount, starting roughly a couple hundred feet above where we stood and gradually working his way down to our eyes' level, hovering before us and the mount's peek, then engaging his wings effortlessly, the hawk rose to where he began just so he could float, sinking through the circle again. One may have knowledge of hawks that proved otherwise but Chris and I were convinced that the bird liked what he heard. I wish I could remember what song we were playing or how long the hawk hung on the air in front of us; moments are made to flee while memories make moments stand still, favoring essence over fact. When the hawk had enough he lifted himself above the trees to our left then disappeared among them only to reappear over the prairies miles away.

"There's something you don't see everyday," said Chris.

"Indeed."

Our time in the Black Mesa went slowly and even got a little boring but in a good way. Chris would read while I went for a walk, I'd read word for word Chris' steps, music got played my song written, and we talked our dreams into reality then returned them to their proper place. On one walk I found at the creek's edge a stone that stood out from the others with its rusty orange color and ivory, marble stripes. Smoothed by time its oval shape and perfectly rounded sides, an eighth of an inch thick, had a calming effect in my hand. I had gathered up other stones in our travels, but this one was the one that the others had to be collected for to be found.

(Here is the funny thing about memory: I am almost sure that I found the stone in question at Fountainhead. Chris is the one who insists that it came from the Black Mesa. A month or two after landing in Santa Monica I decided to send Aubrey the stone as an attempt to share my journey across the country with her. Chris loved the stone too because, he said, it came from the Black Mesa. The Mesa meant a lot to me as well but I do think Stopher was even more affected by the experience. Fountainhead was our first real break from the road and taste of nature as well as having a place to swim. I can see clearly, me hunching by the shore picking at stones with the water swooshing through my fingers. I actually started looking at stones with Aubrey in mind because I knew that she liked to collect them. You see we both have a specific association that magnifies our memory to the point of claiming it as fact. In this case we are left with two opposing facts. I'm sure we argued a lot about this at the time. I know Chris and I argued a bit about me sending the rock to Aubrey because he knew she'd just lose it, but he backed off quickly because he also knew how important it was for me to reach out to her in any way I could. We argue a lot in general, but those first few months in Santa Monica, tensions ran particularly high. I think I may have backed off on the origin argument, who the fuck really knows? What I do know is that yesterday when Chris and I were talking about the respective books we were writing—Stopher is writing about the last four years as well—I told him that I was going to have the stone be found at the Black Mesa. He didn't remember that I had once contended that it had been found elsewhere and further more, although he maintained his memory of the matter, he would not be at all surprised to find that he was wrong. We have grown up in our small way, but God, it has taken a shit load of time and wasted energy spent.)

The Black Mesa served us well and like so many before we offered it nothing—to be fair it didn't ask. The white Ford rolled off the forgiving black top on to a red, cantankerous road no better suited for travel then a dying man on dialysis. I dared not push pass thirty as my faithful companion bobbed and bucked over the stilted terrain's many mini-peeks and valleys as the dust shouted after us, "What the hell are ya doing out here you masochistic, sadistic freaks." Roller coasters had a gentler disposition. I don't know how many miles of this we subjected our much-abused trooper to but we had to be on that road for hours before the reprieve of a black top stretched itself out beneath her aching joints. Chris and I too were forced to endure the rocking of the road's unsatisfied anger at being trespassed upon but at least we could reap the benefits of the surrounding vision: Red Mesas littered the horizon in every direction without even beginning to dwarf the open desert space that seethed between each bulking mass of rock, while both rock and sand baked under the sun's unflinching eye. Two hours went by before coming across another soul to comfort us with some sort of proof that maybe there was another side to this planet we found ourselves inhabiting. As the four-wheel jeep went by I caught the driver's eye and he seemed equally happy to see me.

"It's like being on the moon," said Chris aloud to himself.

"Well, it's perttier," I offered in my best Mortimer Snerd, "and whole lot redder!"

We laughed nervously as the red moon ate us whole.

Whenever we left Chicago the agenda had always been tied to forging a career in music that would finally allow us to be seen as what we already knew we were. And make money; preferably lots of money, but any modest amount would have sufficed. Out in the middle of the red moon I saw Dad smile and heard Mom saying, "Oh, David, it sounds wonderful." So much of my youth and early adult years were spent leaning on the hopes that someone would see my talent and then send me out into the world to show it off. I am basically a coward who had a nice nest that he had to be cooed from. No one cooed and the years flew away. By the end of my twenties I started to figure out that I was gonna have to show the world to myself; it's what my folks had been saying all along. Every once in a while I tell myself to forget why I'm out in the world; set aside what it is that I'm looking for, and soak in where I am; what it is that I have found; and for a moment, a single fleeting moment, I appreciate it all, even the failure, because it takes everything that happens to put you where you are. Aubrey, who is in high school now, sent me a paper she did on Voltaire's Candid, and he was saying that very thing in the sixteenth century; nothing new under the sun, people, only in our eyes.

I drove across a red moon in my trusty white Ford van with the guy I count on most and through our mutual apprehensions we agreed that it was one of the coolest things that we had ever done or ever will do.

The tires hit the black top in a hushing hum as the rattling of the previous miles ceased in an abrupt switch. The van fell deafeningly quiet, afraid to question its present fate like a soldier in a foxhole after the shelling emptied from the skies. Any attempt to look up or tempt the peace with inquiry might very well invite the wrath's return. The van simply rolled to the tune the road sang and happily hummed along.

Not long after arriving on the more civilized passage Chris and I stopped in at a gas station to fill up the tank and inspect for damage. The back doors as well as the van's whole tail end roof to tires were covered in red dust, and when we opened them more red dust revealed itself on everything in proximity with the aforementioned doors. As far as two feet inside, the red moon had smuggled aboard caking itself, upon whatever it could, clinging to the foot of futon, saturating the sheet we had hung on a wire to keep human eyes outside. If not for the sheet, who knows how far the hands of the red moon would have grasped into their dusty clutches. I grabbed a broom while Chris removed the sheet from the wire and shook it out. The cakes were reduced to stains but it would be months before the stains faded in with the accumulation of other stains. The red moon hung in the van's rear as a marker of where we had been. Chris also believed it responsible for the van suffering the loss of a timing chain three months later. The van's gas mileage steadily decreased over the next six months as well and I suspect that the red moon crept up through our exhaust and slowly choked her from the inside. If our separate suspicions were proven to be true and we could go back in time and take a different, softer route, I think we'd both choose the red moon.

Back on the road we saw a tourist sign boasting of a volcano that you could drive up to the top of and walk round its outer edge. With all the bumpy sitting we had been doing a long walk sounded refreshing. The drive up round the dormant beast of the last million years or so was steep and narrow. Chris sat in the passenger's seat trying not to look out the window. The higher we climbed the closer the road's tightrope of terror inched toward the tires. His back straightened as if a pole had been shoved so far up his ass it that it knocked out his front teeth. Chris leaned away from the door with both hands attached to fully flexed extended arms, white knuckled against the dash bracing him, while his wide eyes formed a perfect circle in their sockets not wanting to watch but unable to let the gravity he imagined pulling at our tires out of his sight. To his credit, Chris didn't say much for fear of distracting me.

"Go slow." He managed a couple of times along with a few sounds that wordlessly explained his growing concerns.

I, being on the side without all that falling-down-the-side-of-a-mountain-scenery and having the steering wheel in my confident hands, felt very much at ease. Chris took a moment to breath on the flat edgeless earth firmly attainable to his feet once we parked the van safely. I took on the whole three-mile trail around the volcano and Chris meandered about closer to the van. The hike did me good and the view was spectacular, both down in the volcano and out into the surrounding world. The inside was filled with plant life, trees and birds. It surprised me to see such vibrant living going on inside a volcano but since it has just been a big hallowed out rock oh theses many years I guess it shouldn't have. On my return to the van Chris sat on a bench that offered up the sky.

"You get to stare death in the face this time."

The trip down definitely tasted a mite more treacherous. Chris lounged casually smiling at the solid wall of rock with the visual comfort of limited possibilities. My only comfort came from feeling the tires' movement in my hands. Chris and I trust each other's driving ability, but there is something about being that close to the possibility of your demise that, while not diminishing your faith in someone, certainly informs you of the potential for helplessness.

Early Friday evening we pulled into Albuquerque with a mouthful of road in our throats. We stopped near a restaurant that was managed by one of our cousins. Growing up, the Smith kids shared a close relationship with my Mom's sister Dorothy's kids. They lived in

Providence, Rhode Island but between our family trips out east and theirs to the Midwest we managed to bond. Dorothy married her high school sweetheart Bob Jungels who happened to be a dear friend of my Dad's. Dad actually dated my aunt Dorothy once, before Mom; it was all very incestuous. So the four parents were as much friends as family with a common view on life and art, which they passed on to their respective kids. I use the word common loosely being that they all lived lives and loved the arts. Keith was one of three boys and two girls that my Dad's sister Nancy raised. Unlike the five Jungels kids, the Roesslers lived closer most of the time but we saw them much less. Dad loved his sister and during the time Dad's mom was dying of stomach cancer in the early eighties, my Mom and Nancy became very close. There are those you love and like to see and those who have attached themselves to something vital in the fabric of your soul. Barbara and Bob—Dorothy and Bob; it was that way before any of the children were born.

Keith, or it could have been Kevin (they are identical twins) heard about our stopping in Albuquerque and, through our moms, offered us a free meal. We were having a hard time finding the place so I got out of the van to ask around. On finding our way I went back to the van, jumped behind the wheel, turned the key in the ignition and the van said: "huggghhuugg, hugghhuugg, huggghuugg." I said: "Don't mouth off to me motherfucker." The van repeated its refrain and my heart slunk into that hole in your chest set aside for those moments you want to hide yourself from what you don't want to know. Chris stared at the key stunned, then at me with an open mouth empty of words; I mirrored his gaping mug.

"Fuck," I finally said.

I tried to start the van again. The van had nothing new to say. I stepped out and walked around to the hood although I did not pop it before doing so; I don't know shit about this stuff other than that it was probably the starter. The good news was that we had the money, I just had hoped to get along a little further…it wasn't this starter that spread the cool sense of doom down my spine. The starter was just the beginning. I could suddenly see all the things that would go wrong, and not just with the van—neither Chris or I were the picture of health, of the three the van had best chance of a prosperous old age. I saw the money melting away, job applications being filled out, my breath struggled, trapped deep in my lungs unable to find air; I had only begun to touch the kind of freedom imagined by poets, with the tip of my tongue stealing it off of my lips. I let my head fall giving its weight and the weight of all that it carried down against myself and I climbed into the driver's seat.

"Try it again?" Chris spoke.

I turned the key and the van spoke too. It spoke of miles to come; it spoke impatiently of waiting on us to come calling, as if we had been the ones sputtering; it spoke to the tune of sparks igniting, pistons pounding, power surging and life waiting. God bless my white whale of a Ford. Even through the joy I knew there could still be a problem, that I would have to find a mechanic and that the next time it not might start, but it DID START, BY ALL THAT IS HOLY IT STARTED!!!

Chris and I took turns slapping the dash and singing her praises as we headed for the restaurant.

Kevin (I'm just gonna say it was Kevin. Sorry Keith) walked up carrying his six-foot plus, squarely, chiseled frame with a hearty smile on his soft, tanned face under silky, thin blonde hair and gave us a firm handshake and warm hug. The extended family is a wondrous thing. I know we shared a few sleepovers but if not for his loving his mother and our love for her brother this moment of sincere affection does not exist. I would have felt it on my own at some point but Kevin carried our mutual lineage in his stride. Chris and I both thought of ourselves as imposing the will of family history on someone who could easily consider us strangers as we asked the hostess to see the manager. Kevin's warmth dismissed that the instant his eyes lit up at our standing there. I don't mean to overstate, but I have always seen myself as being privileged and more than a little lucky in the manner and amount in which I have been loved. When I say manner, I am alluding to a kind of wisdom and intelligence not often tied to love. Either way I have always felt privileged. But then to walk into a restaurant in Albuquerque, New-fucking-Mexico, and to be met with such genuine kindness and regard by virtue of being blessed a million times over already for having Bob Smith as my father, well it simply shames me for all the times I have complained about my life and all the times I will most assuredly complain again. (Note to reader: The coming pages are jammed-pack with shameless complaining.)

Not only did Kevin supply us with a first rate meal accompanied by several imported beers, but on top of that he had us booked in a four star hotel for the two nights we would be in town. Unfortunately he had to catch a plane that night to Arizona. I truly would have liked to spend some time getting to know him; he seemed like a hell of a guy.

Chris and I ended up only nibbling at our meals because the beer tasted so very good. Kevin joined us for one before he left and encouraged us to order whatever we needed. It was agreed that being greedy would be unbecoming so we had a few each, had our food wrapped up to go, then picked up a case of Heineken at a local liquor store and went in search of our hotel. Everything was in walking distance but after getting the beer we had to drive to the hotel to have the van safely kept over night. I didn't remember a thing about the van almost not starting until we were sitting up in our beautiful room. We drove two blocks from one parking lot to another without incident; she turned over like a champ as if nothing had ever happened.

The gig was on Saturday so Friday went wetly down our throats with a long day's journey. Sitting up in bed that night we concurred that this was how it was supposed to be: Every night a different town to play and hotel room waiting, paid for in advance by somebody else. If it never happened again it at least had been once—kings of the road. More dreams found starry words as the cable television glowed pleasantly through the night though nothing worth watching was on most of the time.

"Is this so much to ask?" I indicated the room.

"You deserve nothing less, Vuma." Chris confirmed my desires as reasonable.

The next morning I got up and headed out to have the van looked at while Chris slept. The mechanic said that I might need a starter or it could have just been that the van felt a bit finicky from the long drive. (Curse of the Red Moon?) He encouraged my worrisome side but only half-heartedly. When I asked how long the starter would hold out he said that from what I had told him it'd be at least a few months before it burned out completely if at all. I went back to the hotel where, with Chris, I decided to wait until I found a mechanic I could trust in California. (I still have the same starter in my van to this day.)

The rest of the day was given to recovery through bedridden television therapy interrupted only for bathroom breaks. On one such excursion I heard Chris scuffling with himself in the toilet. It sounded as if was losing. A short burst of pain shot from his mouth followed by the counter receiving a clump from the bulk of his weight. Momentary silence gapped the inching of Stopher out of the bathroom by part leaning part falling against the wall all the way back to his bed.

"What happened?" I asked, once he had completed his collapse to begin cringing under the covers.

It took a few minutes for Chris to find a position free from the pain.

"I just finished beating-off for the second time today when this massive pain seared through the right side of my back."

"Does it still hurt?" I chuckled a little.

"At the moment only if I try to move." Chris either didn't sense the humor or was simply too preoccupied.

"I'm sorry," I started laughing, "are you okay?"

"Besides the fact that I am now afraid to touch myself, EVER AGAIN! And that one of my organs may have literally ripped in half, I'm feeling better."

I howled while Stopher cracked a pencil thin smile.

I recovered enough to consider that he might need a doctor. "Are you gonna be alright? Should I make some calls?"

"I just need to lie still."

"I am sorry but Jesus," I started to laugh a bit then stopped.

Chris laughed but the pain cut him short. I began to worry and Chris caught my eye.

"I'm fine. It probably was from drinking too much after not drinking at all and then beating-off twice."

"Now that is one those sentences you just don't see coming—no pun intended. Speaking of which, how does that even enter into it?"

"I don't fucking know. All I know is I came that second time and I got this crippling pain shooting up my side."

"Has that ever happened before?"

"Thank God no."

"Least ya didn't go blind."

"It'd been less painful."

"I was just thinking of giving myself a little love but now…"

"I just hope I can play tonight."

"Is it that bad?"

"At the moment it is."

"I've heard a lot stories about sex and rock-n-roll, but this, this could only happen to us."

Chris remained still and a few hours later he felt fine and as far as I know, that particular chain of events never came to pass again. Oh sure, he would come to endure plenty of more back spasms and organs squealing out their dismay from repeated alcohol abuse but at least he was able to cum void of undue discomfort. As for me, I rose above my fears and beat-off twice that very day—what a hero.

The gig went well, we played outside on the terrace and the evening air laid lightly over our shoulders with warm, friendly breezes. The people were all receptive and kind; a few even tipped us. Between sets we got to conversing with a gentlemen who dressed like, and claimed to be, a biker. The gentleman made a special point of letting us know that he was also a lawyer; the duality that occupied his daily life bubbled from his being as a great source of pride. I almost had the feeling of being pitched an idea for a television series. There was nothing about us that could have solicited any hope on his part that we could further any aspirations he might have so Chris and I figured that every encounter he had was another episode in the life of, BIKER LAWYER GUY. He did tip us a twenty—lights, camera, action!

"People want other people to fit in their perception of whatever label they deem fitting," he waxed philosophically.

"Comfort lies in definition," Chris offered.

"Comforts a drug, man," Biker-Lawyer guy cooed under a deep, heavy breath.

"I prefer 'shrooms," I smiled.

"Break the molds and you find the truth." He deflected my attempt at humor.

The second people start talking in terms of grand truths my eyes start to glaze over. If you meet someone and the first thing out of their mouth is, "I'm up front and honest," or "I have lots of black friends," then you can rest assured that they're full of shit racists. (Oh, and people who always demand respect tend to suck at giving it.) The need to advertise on billboards means one is selling and I have no interest in being sold.

Biker-lawyer guy was all right, just another poor schmuck out on the town spreading the fascination of his existence out for him to see others see. The truth is he was an interesting, intelligent person and I enjoyed meeting him. I kid the earnest because I am one of them and as I get older it is a suit that doesn't wear very well. Earnestness is good in a mixed drink but only Wild Turkey straight goes down smooth.

The last set found Chris and I finding our groove. In the beginning of the night you try to play songs people know and that most folk can agree on. A Jim Croce song has never, as far as I know, offended anyone; do a Croce tune and most will go along for the ride. As the night moves on you slip in a few originals, some Elvis Costello, Eagles and of course Beatles, and the crowd will at least be appeased; the obligatory Buffet song, "Margarita Ville", speaks to just about any demographic. The second set we tend to jam a bit more but you still have to temper it depending on the room. We do a nice funky-bluesy version of "All along the Watchtower" that accommodates Hendrix and Dylan both. By the third set the night is what the night is gonna be, you release yourself from the pressure of pleasing others and your fingers are completely oiled. This was our final gig before hitting California so we cut loose on the last set with an added fervor. The place still held a handful of gracious observers so Chris and I let'em have it main line. We received some whoops and hollers and when the night ended we packed it up with sweaty smiles.

In our time on the road Chris and I played things close to the chest where strangers were concerned. On that night we got to talking with a forty-something Mexican who at one point transferred the topic of conversation from music to marijuana, bless his heart. I waged in against any such venture that involved us following anyone through the unknown streets of Albuquerque. The thought of getting caught buying weed and being thrown in jailed accompanied visions of getting mugged or worse. I am a coward. Chris is an even bigger coward but true addiction makes heroes of us all. Once Chris entertained the concept of having an eighth of weed for the last leg of our trip he was a hound on the scent.

"Chris, this is just plain stupid."

"Sniff, sniff, sniff."

"We don't know the town; we don't know him."

"Sniff, sniff, sniff."

He had a come back for every argument and soon all I could say was, "Sniff, sniff, sniff."

We agreed that neither of us would leave the van, the engine stayed running, and no money would be given until the merchandise was inspected. The ride didn't take long; a few traffic lights, take a right, then another right down a dark side street for a few blocks. The car we followed pulled over. Our man got out and went in the side entrance of a little brick building that should have been a small family home but was in fact partitioned into four different dwellings bursting with large families. Unseen voices filled the dark street. Shapes moved about, some cheerfully others less so but none holding much menace. Life in the barrio on a Saturday night pulsed and we sat uninvolved van-standers; hopeful ghosts. Apprehension built on the time passing; the longer we stood there the more we were observed. We couldn't see them notice us but felt the pauses in their movements, heard loud voices shrink into murmurs and laughter fade. It could have easily been the natural flow of an evening's breath but we saw ourselves as the white elephant inserted into its throat. Before it got too quiet our messenger returned and showed Chris his offering. Whatever procedure we had previously discussed went quickly from our minds, the exchange was made void of formality and as the money left Stopher's palm for the other's I had the van rolling away.

The liquor stores had already closed so there was nothing left for us to do but return to our room at the Sheraton, twist one up and let the night sink until the sun rose.

CHAPTER FIVE

There were no more gigs to play and no one left to visit. A strange sensation surrounded me as the road opened up once again. Soon enough we'd find out what exactly in the hell we were going to do with the rest of our lives. Of course that is one of the many jokes people are always playing on themselves. Just because you worked in a factory from eighteen to sixty it doesn't mean that at anytime in your life you couldn't have done something else; maybe you couldn't have, but not by virtue of that being what you did. Crossing the state line into Arizona I saw California as a destination of a definitive kind. My wildest dreams coming true aside, it was still the end of something beside the road or country. All that water said stop! No record contracts were waiting, I knew that. I allowed a corner of my mind to roll film on a few cinematic scenarios where we somehow get plugged into the machinery of the industry making money ever after doing what the brothers Smith were born to do: Write, play music, create and inform the world of its humanity or lack thereof. So if I knew that that wasn't, more than likely, going to happen, then what did I see? Nothing, because I couldn't, I wouldn't see day jobs. Maybe I saw the years revert to the days of Steinbeck and Guthrie, where a man got by on his wits and skill; where, in this fantasy, Chris and I would roll into some camp of workers and take the day off their backs and turn aching sweat into soft warm smiles; take their stories—give them songs, unleash their sorrow—birth their strength, reveal them in us—find us in them.

Chris and I both read THE GRAPES OF WRAITH before we left Chicago.

I had long since gave up on trying to change the world like Martin, Malcolm or Lennon, or saving the sick and hungry like Teresa and Chapin, but I had still hoped to be of use in the way that I felt most useful. My worth as a writer and musician along with the love of my family are the only things of which I am certain.

Chris had talked about seeing the Grand Canyon so when the sign stuck out from off the road we decided to pull over, look at the map and do the math. I wanted to keep moving but Chris had us going whether I conceded or not. (We have, over the years, taken turns being the one to lead the other where they needed to go and I owe Chris on this one.) I worried about time; California was not expecting me—I worried about the money; it would be pissed away one way or another. Chris knew the detour was not a detour but a direct path to a moment. The Grand Canyon previously sat in my thoughts as a place that the unimaginative masses assembled at because the guidebook said so; The Brady Bunch shot an episode there for God's sake; bourgeois, passé', cliché', take your pick.

Go. Just go.

The road from the interstate ran through pleasant enough scenery, rolling greens and the like. I almost didn't notice us rising upward at first. At one point it leveled off into a flat desert and I thought we missed a turn somewhere. The sign said press on so we did. Trees returned as the road winded up then up some more. I believe we entered from the south, I've been told that the north is ever so much more breathtaking. (Yes, I'm well aware that your mountain is better than my mountain—people will argue over anything, especially the right to feel superior.) As the van rose toward the top we began to see cars parked on the side of the road and when we reached the peak the parking lot squirmed like big city traffic. I turned around and found a patch of dirt off to the road's side. The sun was not long for the sky as we hustled behind some others through the trees and brush. When we stepped out into the opening all chatter that buzzed about from all parties trekking through the woods crumbled into a symphony of oohhs and ahhhs. They were the only words that could be formed and, in the end, the only words appropriate. If God existed and was a sculptor this would have been the piece he taunted Michelangelo with, "Fuck David, Mikey; check this out." Every nook and cranny cut out its own significance among the vast configuration of rock to stand apart as one; each jagged edge colored the flats as they defined the rise and fall of every edge; my eyes floated above the entirety, descended through the details, bounced from scopes narrow to broad and varieties in between; staring down at the depths of the canyon I think even the sky hesitated with the thought of giving into gravity. Chris called me from the ledge as a personal favor.

The western horizon held the sun on its shoulders, but like a head sliding down the spine, the sun showed signs of surrender to a gravity of its own. Chris and I hurried back to the van to roll a quick one. We smoked making our way back through the woods and returned just in time to witness day's release. The beheaded horizon glowed in burnt orange remains that bled across the sky tainting the clouds, white and puffy, gray and drawn. People dispersed evenly as burnt oranges turned to purple pinks. Chris had not planned it but we had come at a popular and prized time. The tourists had dinner plans to keep and motel rooms or campsites to settle their evenings in but Chris and I were not tourists; we were explorers with the night beckoning our expertise. The colors of the sky followed the crowds out, leaving gradually but steadily. A few hangers on saw the night wrap itself up in billions upon billions of stars—there could have been more starlight than night; the dust of the stars alone was almost enough to read by.

With a couple more rolled, we made ourselves at home on a fenced lookout post with guitars in tow. Our voices echoed then disappeared into the vacuum but every note told me how lucky I was to be there. I couldn't stop smiling at my fortune; Fountainhead, the Black Mesa, the Grand Canyon; the vacation that was a life. I knew it wasn't always going to feel this way; anything becomes commonplace if you do it everyday. I still envisioned finding a state park close enough to L.A. to basically live there so the stars would bid me goodnight ritually. I kept telling myself, remember this, collect the moment and store it safely in a special place; don't let it fade. I do remember, it glows inside me but has faded. I could conjure up words as I have throughout these pages to varying degrees of success, but I can no more put a finger on an emotion so precise than a photo can deliver the scent of pines on a breeze. The one thing consistent in all of my adventures up to that point and beyond was the voice that surged deep from my belly saying, this is right; you are supposed to be here. It is easy to believe the voice when nature unfolds itself holding nothing back, arching its splendor unashamed of seduction. The time would come when the voice spoke in the face of unrelenting disappointment and the downright browbeating of even the smallest of my faintest dreams, within a breath of submission. The voice would come then too, every bit as clear, confident and unforced. My response to the voice would surely suffer from weary doubt, fevered rage and humble requests for strength to give up. This voice of which I speak gathered its resolve from Fountainhead to the Canyon so it could show it to me when I needed it most; it is all one journey. So as my story is told look for the Canyon so grand in my despair and you will understand its worth.

While taking a break in between songs a young couple from St. Louis joined us out on the post. They were in their twenties and on vacation. When Chris told the brief tale of our adventure, what we had hoped to achieve, excitement bubbled in their young eyes. They begged to hear some music, which we provided gladly. After a few songs I asked if they smoked weed and they smiled. The smoke induced a welcomed quiet as attention gave itself to the chore and the magnificence of our darkened muscular host, dissolving while the respectful silence lingered as our collective buzz subjectively fed upon the spectacle. (Marijuana is the subjective drug; whatever you are experiencing, it insists that you do it to the fullest.) Deep breaths seemed to be the choice of communication as we all tried to stow away the moment into our lungs. A song was once again requested and we complied; it's our fucking job. The time for traveling approached and as I saw it coming I excused myself to retrieve our CD from the van. On my return I offered it to the young couple as a reminder of the shared moment and as proof that they had met the great Smith brothers on the cusp of their triumphant debut in the west. Chris insisted that they take down our home address in Chicago and write us their thoughts on the CD. They graciously accepted, agreed and we never heard from them again. I like to believe that they on occasion listen to it and wonder whatever became of us. That is if they are together or even alive.

The debate of catching a couple of hours of sleep before hitting the road was dismissed by Stopher's being wired from the majestic caffeine that was the Grand Canyon. I stayed awake to help Stopher navigate his way back to the interstate then let the road's hypnotizing hum have its way with my heavy eyes.

I intermittently awoke to check on Chris to find his eyes fixed ahead as if he had just seen a flying saucer and expected it back any second.

"You okay," I inquired sleepily.

"I got it."

I don't know any one person who worries more than Chris or who harbors more determination to a given effort; I took him at his word and drifted off. This is not say that Chris and failure don't hold hands at the movies. His talents are very specific. He is either the dumbest genius, or the most brilliant moron, but when he does say he has got it, it is gotten. One example is that he is the best, drunk driver that ever lived. In fact I would rather have him driving drunk than a lot of sober folk I know. I can hear the offended gasps from here and you are right, but go fuck yourself, he is a greatest drunk driver and I'm the second greatest.

I came to for good the last hour before the California state line. I asked Chris if he wanted to switch but he had entered one of his O.C.D. (Obsessive Compulsive Disorder) states; he had to get us to California. By the time we pulled up to the inspection booth at the state line, Stopher feared he appeared drunk, dangerous, or at the very least suspicious. His eyes burned with water and his ears stung from the drop in elevation. Luckily the trooper on the passenger side decided to ask the questions so I did all the talking. The trooper was pleasant, I was pleasant, and Chris held on to the steering wheel. He had spent all of his faculties on keeping the road in line and now his brain had only that ability. We passed through void of incident and Chris turned off at the first exit and into a motel parking lot.

"Let's keep going; I'll drive," I insisted.

"I need to lie still; I need a bed." Chris sounded zombified.

"We've wasted enough money." I wanted to get a room as much as he did.

Chris turned toward me with ignited eyes that suggested the zombie was hungry. "I need to get off the road. This van has been through enough for the night."

"The van is fine!" Oh, I was being accusatory.

"Look, I'm in no shape to cross a dessert."

"Better to do it now while the sun's down."

You could feel the heat even then. You could feel the heat at sixty-five miles per hour with windows rolled down.

"I need a bed. I need some air-conditioning."

I argued some more about the money.

"Fuck the money and fuck you."

This was one of those moments that we would relive: Chris needing me to simply see him as more important than the details. As big as a baby as he could be, Stopher was the ultimate team player and usually made demands like this only when he absolutely had to have something. In reflection I see those exchanges clearly and as reasonable. Then? Then I worried about money until I was the one who simply had to have.

In the room we made a late call to Steve to let him know we were close. To our surprise he picked up. I don't know the exact time but it had to be well past midnight. Chris handed me the phone to get directions to Steve's doorstep. With that settled we took to our beds and gave the room to the dark.

"I'm sorry," Chris said with a shake in his voice.

"For what?"

"For being a baby, for needing a bed." No one ever has to tell Chris about himself once he has time to gather his thoughts.

"No, I'm an asshole." I see me too.

"Yeah, but we could've made it."

The dark, as it had done for us our entire lives growing up in a room with our brothers, settled the nerves; fostered something softer, encouraged understanding.

"No, it's better we get some rest. The van too."

Before falling asleep we put in for an early wake up call for sunrise. By getting on the road before seven, we figured to cross the dessert under the sun's lesser grip and hit Santa Monica by early afternoon.

During the early part of the drive Chris told me how he had to stand in a corner of the motel room singing softly aloud to himself to distract him from the pain in his ear. As bad as I felt for him I sensed in my voice an underlying criticism. I can't explain it, there were times when he got sick or experienced pain in these kinds of extreme and as bad as I truly felt for him, I also got angry or annoyed with him on some level: Projection? For not taking care of himself? Misplaced hero worship? Or maybe I thought he wasn't being as tough as I thought I would be in his shoes? I don't know if he ever picked up on any negative vibe or if I was able to corral these instances of unreasonable resentment. Along with my parents, Chris had done more than any other to teach me about whom I want to aspire to be, and more than anyone, what fragile athletes we all are in that endeavor.

Heat permeated from the earth, shouting it back to the sun. Chris and I were simply caught in the crossfire. Echoes of Arkansas tugged at my brow. Surely we didn't drive all this way to end up in a greenless dryer version of the Deep South. The dessert gave way to the valley, the valley spilled into L.A. and the heat stayed hot on our trail. I tried with all my might to be still of mind, restful in spirit. The country was having a heat wave; the weather had no personal agenda against me or any related dreams. September had little more than a week left and even sunny California had to acknowledge the change of season in some form. Then, on interstate 10 between Fairfax Avenue and the 405, a rush of cool magically embodied the air. The oppression lifted not gradually, but instantly like walking into a different dimension. Chris' face wordlessly mirrored the change. He turned to me and I him smiling.

Finally I said, "Someone turned on the air-conditioning?"

"God bless the ocean."

"He sure did."

Just before pulling off the highway all the dread of the unknown, the haunting of unanswered details, and the weight of dreaming too big, risking all, whooshed away with the sea's breath, eroded in the mouth of the salt air. On the exit ramp after the first left turn, it all came back. Where would we sleep? No one wants us here, just another industry town feeding on its young and the young of others.

Knocking on Steve's door, a garage revamped into a recording studio, a whisper hovered over every other thought that I had, "Nobody wants you here."

The studio/garage sat kitty-corner from Sukey's, main house, backdoor. Steve received us almost as if he didn't really expect us. I don't mean to say unhappy or intruded upon but his warmth held distance. The fact that we had no real plan seemed to suddenly dawn on him. When he arrived Steve had a place to stay, a source of income expected from his studio and some capital left over from the sale of his house in Nashville. Chris and I had a van. On the phone over the last few years he talked excitedly about being in the same town again, here in the room with him I could see the math adding up in his head where he gets stuck babysitting us.

"I may have some work for you." Steve announced as a way of talking about something other than the math.

"Well it's about time," I ruffled.

Steve went on to describe the situation in nervous detail: Sukey had co-written a musical about the Wright brothers' first flight called KITTY HAWK. She had co-written it with the guy who wrote SUMMER OF '42. (Our first day in town and already we're rubbing shoulders with Hollywood's storied past, indirectly as it may have been.) The musical was set to open in six weeks and they needed someone to play guitar in the band for a handful of shows that Steve would be unavailable for. I could make as much as two hundred dollars and more if Steve, the drummer or bass player took sick on a given night. Steve knew the bass and drum parts as well as the guitar so he'd understudy them while I understudied him.

Steve told me up front that he had put an ad in the paper to audition other guitar players but he would be willing to tutor me as much as I needed to learn the songs. In the other words I had the job if I could learn twenty songs in four weeks. I am a terribly slow learner when it comes to music—even simple stuff. If it's something I wrote there is nothing I can't play but it is all very organic with me; it has to come from me. Chris and I were both offered the opportunity but Chris begged off after the first rehearsal. I was actually glad that he did; we had enough music and life to fight about as it was.

On that first day in California I told Steve that I was in but assumed once he saw how inept I was at that sort of thing he would politely give the job to someone more qualified. Unfortunately for him, Steve had no doubt that I could pull it off.

But the first order of the day was to find a State Park cheap enough to afford over the long term and close enough to commute back and forth from. We looked through the phone book then made some calls out of Steve's studio.

"I could ask Sukey to let you stay a night or two in one of the guest rooms but..."

Steve's voice trailed off and we knew where and why. He lived in the garage and the house belonged to his long time friend Sukey whom I had met a handful of times in Nashville. (She lived there for years and that's where she and Steve met long before I had even thought about going to Nashville. In fact Steve ran his studio out of the back of her house there until she packed up and went to California—She might have gone to New York first. They started off dating but she was at least ten to fifteen years his senior—computer dating—but they did become friends to the point of siblings even.)

In her youth she had worked in theater and had done some commercials but Sukey came from money, or her mom had married into it, so she moved about as she pleased. A short plump of a pixie, Sukey had bright eyes that bounced about her face when she talked. I can't say that I got to know her beyond the surface over the last four years and I know even less of her history, but she is one of those people whose core is very much apparent. I don't mean to imply transparent; just because you can see through the water doesn't mean that it is without depth. She would have been fine with opening her house to Chris and I then as she has done in so many other wonderful ways since that day.

If Steve had already talked to her about Chris and I staying for a night or two before hand, I still would have wanted to get started learning the ropes of what my daily life was going to look like. The closest thing we could find was Malibu State Park. The twenty-three a night, if we stayed a minimum of three, would do for a transitional stint but only until we got the lay of the land. We got directions from Steve and made plans to get together the next day.

Back in the van we drove the remaining thirteen blocks down to see the ocean. There was too much to do to find parking and walk to the shore so we just got close enough to pull to the side of a road that ran along the parking lots. At Ocean Park and Ocean Ave. we stepped out of the van to look across the green lawn lined with palm trees, over the bicycle path that ran around Perry's food and rentals, out passed the soft, lazy sand and on to the water.

"There it is." Chris announced.

"Hard to miss."

"Okay, let's go home."

The sun wouldn't be setting for a few hours so it rested firmly on our smiles. The heat burned more friendly than harsh at the ocean breeze's insistence. I felt the journey's miles at my back whoosh by me, and tug at my heels. Nothing ended here; just a moment to be savored and savor we did.

"You can smell the salt." I noted.

The breeze picked up lifting our hair filling our ears with sounds we couldn't speak. The moment passed and each of us took turns attempting to convey something but the words never formed—in our heads, from our mouths. Chris did emit a phrase that expressed our mutual separate states; a joke which eased the weight of…that eased the weight:

"There it is." Repeating his previous announcement.

"There it is," I agreed.

On the Pacific Coast Highway heading towards Malibu the ocean held our hands. Logistical questions rumbled in my brain with each one fighting to be answered first. The door to any clear thought was stopped-up like something out of a Stooge's short, "Spread out." I could tell Chris had as many mysteries to be solved but confidence painted his expression. He had that, "You are not getting that weak-ass shit by me again," look on his face that he wore when a pitcher had gotten the best of him. Forget that the guy threw as nasty a slider as the Portage Park schoolyard saw on a given summer day. The rubber ball would not be allowed in the square anymore—foul tips, squib grounders, harmless pop-ups, yes—but the ball and his bat would have words. Sooner or later all the tips, squibs and pops would translate into line drives—never home runs, but solid smashes sprayed about generously.

I tend to keep quiet when speculation, decorated with all its "ifs" and "thens," lean on one another creating castles of straw in a windstorm. I let them bubble in my head until I either attach the loose ends to something solid or I internally collapse. Chris and I both talk things to death. In fact there is probably not one thing that I could say about Chris that I could not also say about myself and vice versa. That being said, the pattern is true enough, Chris needed to get excited, determined and or angry, while I needed to let it all surround me as I philosophically and or pathetically surrendered to failure until I could boil it down to some manageable task.

We had a hell of a time finding the entrance to the state park. I expected to see a brown sign like they have all over the country but this sign was white with blue lettering—big as Mack truck, but my mind insisted on brown. After passing one way we doubled back and missed it again going the other. Finally we saw the words through the colors and turned up the drive that curved as it rose steeply. As it turns out I don't think it was a real State Park. The twenty plus fee should have been the first clue. Maybe it did have some sort of affiliation with the State but then where were the fucking brown signs! It was a nice enough place with a great view of the ocean off a bluff, but it felt corporate somehow.

"Illinois plates, where ya from?" The young man behind the office counter asked.

"Chicago."

"The windy city; that's a hell of a long drive. How long you staying in Cal? "

"I don't know, somewhere between a while and forever." In my heart I had always believed that any magnificent success I had aside, I'd end up back in Chicago sooner or later. I said what I said because I liked the way it sounded.

"That's the way to ride a wave, dude."

Yes, he was a surfer.

Back in the van I followed the road's curves as they swirled forth and back around the many roaming homes of the road. It was mainly a campsite for RVs. That was another clue—Malibu's RV State Park. That was the name of the place. All I heard over the phone was State Park. There had to be, at least in the neighborhood, a hundred campers ranging from to cute bungalows to mammoth condos on wheels; the majority filled the middle, but edging towards the bigger sizes. The village bustled as children darted across the road, older folk sat in lawn chairs under canopies atop grass colored mats, and parents shouted that dinner waited but would not wait long. All the sights and sounds varied from pleasantries to threats. Wet bodies sprinkled with sand that had spent the day across the highway with the surf, above on boards or within unaccessorized, walked along the road laughing and thinking of food. Smoke permeated from one source after another all speaking pretty much the same menu. The smell of burgers dominated the air. No wood burned so that left coals and propane, mostly propane. You could detect the lighter fluid for the coals along with the meat but not like you would have when I was a kid. The smell that would have been the wet fluid or crackling wood was replaced by the odorless hiss of tanks feeding burners. But there was enough of the past in the present to breath it in.

When the road leveled off it emptied the van into a small parking lot that held fifty cars tops. Another village emerged on the other side of the lot beyond the showers and bathrooms. Tents bubbled from the ground with similar activities of the town below being replayed for those that think life differed from one station to the next. There were less children (technically) and I didn't see any senior citizens. Demographics and economics aside, life imitated life. Usually campsites have a place for you to park next to, or in, it but here all the cars were in one place and all the sites in another. The campers were supplied with wheel barrels to haul what was needed from the car to the site. The visual of all the tents growing from their respective plots gave one the feeling of coming upon a medic camp during the civil war. There were no trees, just open land for the wounded, and a sky to offer your prayers.

Chris and I made camp before starting dinner. The sun held up long enough for us to finish most of our chores and walk to the edge of the bluff and say goodnight to the ocean. In our first year we would not catch as many sunsets by the water as the ensuing ones, when it became a ritual. The clouds that evening were more like smoke emanating from a pink-orange fire; thinly seeping almost creeping like an accomplice from the scene of the crime. The evening's true arsonist, circular and cocky, even though fading in power and scope, held to the court denying nothing. Once relinquished, the sky dimmed and the land to prepared to be dark.

Chris and I dined in the remaining light on some rice concoction quietly. After the chore of dishes we talked of the next day. I think we both knew then that we would be sleeping in the van very soon. The remaining hope was to go to the welcoming center for tourists at the Beverly Center in Beverly Hills to see if maybe my hope of a true State Park in the area could be fulfilled. Neither of us believed it, but an education is an education so that was our first stop the next day.

Usually when I think of welcoming centers it is right off the highway, an oasis just out of town. Leave it to L.A. to put one inside a mall for the rich and richer. I stayed with the van while Chris went on re-con. Finding a nearby pay phone, I put in a call to the folks, and looked around for a bathroom, but spent most of my time feeling very out of place. I had come all this way and felt imprisoned by an inability to devise a plan. Every idea concerned me because they involved expenditures and mysteries like, "Will they let us do that?" and "Will we get in trouble?" or possible threats like, "Hey, let's kick these guys out of our state!"

Chris came back with the answer we knew he would. "We're gonna have to live in the van. "

Steve took us out to lunch that afternoon and we talked more about KITTY HAWK.

"I'm definitely gonna try but…"

"You can do this."

"There's no way in hell we can do this."

"Come on, it's like driving into Wisconsin."

"I got the shit kicked out of me in Wisconsin."

"Dave, you write weirder shit than this in your sleep."

"That's the point, if I write it I can play anything; when I learn stuff it has to go through my brain."

"His brain, Steve," Chris repeated. "You know what a problem area that can be."

"Just don't worry; you'll be fine."

"Like my old man says: 'I'll show up'."

"Wanna stand in line with me on a Hollywood street corner in the blazing heat tomorrow?" Steve asked wide-eyed and bushy-tailed.

"Would we ever!" I cheered.

"That does sound sweet," Chris waxed nostalgically.

"I'm doing the open mic thingy at the Laugh Factory; wait in line for eight hours for four minutes, you know the drill. If you bring a guitar, I'll have mine and we can get started on KITTY HAWK."

"What time?"

"I'll be there at ten."

We went on to tell Steve that we would in fact be living in a van down by the ocean. He was fine about us getting our mail at his place and extremely happy to let us store our vintage one hundred watt Marshall in his studio; the bike and rack he would have to check with Sukey about but he figured there'd be plenty of room in the yard and there was. Chris asked the location of the nearest park to his house and after unloading our extras at Steve's we headed to Marine Park, on Marine avenue and Sixteenth, to turn that van into a home. It came off a lot easier than I had worried. Doing physical work in the head leads to ulcers; put the problem in my hands and solutions introduce themselves. In the side door we laid my luggage bag and the guitars stacked on top of that. My twin mattress laid behind the driver's seat next to them. On the passenger's side Chris would lay on the futon with the guitars at his head and the back door at his feet. Chris suggested staying in the van that night, hell he'd been sleeping in it all along. The campsite had already been paid for the next two nights so we would wait.

The next thing would be to decide where we'd park at night.

I found some free parking only a few blocks a way from the Laugh Factory. I am my father's son; I don't pay for parking. Steve and I got to work on a few things and for a moment I thought that maybe I could pull this off. Then the moment passed, but Steve's faith in me never wavered. Standing in a line stacked with all those hopeful young comics I was struck by two thoughts: There should be a therapist handing out cards; and I'm funnier these schmucks. Chris even had begun to write a bit that he could do that night. Something about how he was shocked at his doctor for suggesting that he had a weight problem. He should've done it but alas. Whether we could be funny in the restraints of a stand-up routine or not, hanging out with them on a street corner Chris and I were getting the most laughs. It got competitive too. I think some were trying to psyche each other out and they had no idea that we were there just to work on some songs.

At one point I took a walk to a nearby Kinko's to copy the charts Steve wanted me to work with. I remember feeling really good when I left the line. There I was hanging at the famous Laugh Factory in Hollywood making funny people laugh, working off a chart for a musical and then making copies. Somewhere between going and coming something in my gut swallowed itself leaving me with that sinking sensation you get toward late afternoon on a day when you had ditched school and would have to go back tomorrow. This life could not be sustained. I tried to shake it out of me but instead the feeling grew from inside me into a heavy winter coat that was easier to wear than carry.

The next couple of days we kept our eyes open for good places to park at night wherever we drove, in Santa Monica or Venice. We drove around quite a bit to get familiar with our new home. To relieve the pressure of what we didn't know we decided to see a movie and that is when we discovered the Third St. Promenade.

The Promenade is three blocks that run from Broadway to Wilshire. On them the only traffic allowed are the shoppers, vendors and performers. They call it an outdoor mall but it reads more like a carnival. On the sidewalks you found the usual fare: stores, restaurants, jewelers a few movie theaters and some high-falooten boutiques. On the side walks just off the street, stood old fashion carts, the kind that you would expect to see in an old time movie selling cotton candy to Shirley Temple. (They were essentially big wooden boxes on two huge wagon wheels, and two wheels the size of a large bagel.) Here they sold every thing from old fashion kettle popcorn to cellular phone accessories. In the streets the performers ranged from jugglers and animal balloon makers to first class flamenco guitar wizards and authentic, genuine, blues men. Occupying the middle are hacks of all kinds.

The first block starts, running from south to north, at Broadway and runs to Santa Monica Blvd., the second from Santa Monica to Arizona, and the third Arizona to Wilshire; these intersecting avenues allow regular traffic. The promenade streets are paved with inlayed six sided bricks to give it that old time cobblestone feel while being more appealing to the feet and easier to maintain; old school in a modern motif. In the center the cobblestones give way to a smooth cement strip about two feet wide shaped ever so subtly to curve up on either end and dip in the middle like a gutter; sleekness de-accents mundane function. Each street has a couple of creatures formed from wire owing its likeness to one breed of dinosaur or another on a large patch of elevated grass surrounded by a three foot wall of cement that has a two-tier rail running along the inner side of the cement ledge on the grass, except on either side of the structure's whole where the elevation of the grass drops to no more than a curb and is held from the public by a shin-high rail. The extinct, wired monstrosities are invested with leafy vines depicting these once lumbering giants of the pre-historic world as glorified novelty bushes. There are actually two elevated plains of grass sporting its own beast separated by a small courtyard. The two elevated specimens, the courtyard and the lower level patch of grass in front and behind, depending on which structure you refer to, of each dinosaur complete the structure. On the middle block two large herbivores (even though each wears a metal face sporting bloodthirsty fangs) face each other while the homeless lounge away the day in the square beneath their faux threatening yet empty gazes. On either end of the promenade the dinosaurs are of the smaller feistier variety and they face in opposite directions spitting water into a pool. The courtyards on these end streets are smaller than the one in the middle and although the homeless do meander about there on occasion they do not lay the consistent predatory claim demonstrated for the larger one in the very center of the promenade. Other than those differences the three structures are pretty much the same—the platforms for the dinosaurs on the northern Wilshire end are higher off the ground than the others—they all own the same over all oval shape and demand the same portion of the street, allowing passage for the crowds on either side—the center street structure seems a tad larger than the other two but maybe only because the dinosaurs are taller, fatter and more majestic there. Each courtyard has three steps leading down from the elevated grass for weary shoppers to take a load off and the day in, and as I said the center structure being for the most part been confiscated by the homeless.

It was in and around this center grouping of the obsolete, bushes and people, that Chris and I would toil away the next few years facing north with the tip of a dinosaur tail, also metal, but with no fangs, at our back.

I don't remember the movie but I remember coming out of the theater and hearing music float on the breeze. The sun glowed upon the buzz bequeathed me by a cheap bottle of vodka. I hate vodka but in the name of fiscal sense I decided to switch to Chris' poison of choice and buy one half-gallon rather than two fifths. (That and vodkas is cheaper than bourbon in the first place.) This was to be our first night sleeping in the van. At Marine parked we asked one of the maintenance guys about a public shower and he told us the drill. We had a few ideas on where to park but that would be an education in process like everything else. I can't say for sure whether this was our first night sleeping in the van.

Like so much of what I've said or am going to say, it is all coming from a memory blurred by events both similar and varied not to mention marinated in liquor spiced with weed. Our first night could have been sober and anxious in Albertsons' parking lot (A large supermarket) as Chris remembers and what I'm about to relate could have been the second night. That being said, I will plow along as best I can and relay it all however my addled brain transcribes.

Chris asked one of the performers on the street that day about the rules, if any, on getting permission to play there ourselves. Thirty-seven dollars for the calendar year for a permit was all it took. There would be plenty of guidelines we had to follow and they would be given to us once we went to city hall to get the permit. It seemed like a good way to make a few bucks while we figured something else out but I worried about the initial thirty-seven dollars. Chris scoffed, saying that we'd make it back within a day or so. I had KITTY HAWK to prepare for, and there was the open mic Steve hosted at a local coffee house on Friday night where we could start building a reputation, so I didn't think much of the street performer thing other than it might be fun, if we got around to it. Chris talked a bit more excited about the possibilities.

"We could make a killing out here."

Oh, someone would die.

We hung around for a bit and watched a couple of black guys, one sitting on milk a crate the other on their amp of similar stature, a few feet off the curb bluesing up "Proud Mary." The one singing lead vocal and sitting on the crate strummed an old beat-up box of an acoustic while the younger, that is to say maybe only in his early fifties, played lead on a slightly less tattered flying V electric. The older one had a sweet clear tone in his voice with a hint of smoked, graveled molasses and smiled warmly out from under his snow white, full mustache that matched perfectly the curly trimmed fro that squirmed out of a baseball cap. The man on the V played it like an appendage from birth, dancing around the melody with triads and voicing the chords like watercolors of waterfalls. His hair sprouted wildly from his head sporting only strands of gray within the black mop while his teeth ran crookedly about his mouth.

The men I just described were Mel and James. The older one, James was from New Orleans although he had been playing on the promenade for roughly ten years. Mel came from L.A. and had been playing lead guitar for James a handful of years; Mel had a gift for curved answers that led you back to questions empty handed. They, James particularly, would be first to welcome Chris and I to the street performer's fraternity. He took a liking to us, but as much as that he respected what we did.

We left the promenade to go check out the famous Venice beach. I had yet to dip my feet in the western sea and was anxious to do so. The drive up and down Pacific Avenue or Ocean Avenue, or Nielsen Way, depending on which stretch you drove, took a while before yielding a parking spot. In time I would come to know all the best places to look for free parking that didn't leave one with a hike to get to the ocean. (I am my father's son.) Somewhere between Venice Blvd. and Washington a space appeared after the umpteenth pass. We packed up our guitars along with a bag of water bottles and booze bottles and made for the water.

People don't exist much for me that night. If I were to remember walking down the boardwalk during that time of day, around five-thirty, last late September, I'd recall the usual rotation of beach dwellers, tourists, and shopkeepers that routinely saw their days end there. I'd see on the boardwalk, painters packing up their easels and unsold works; tables being folded by tarot card readers; boxes being stuffed with sage, beads, glass figurines; and hand made signs, each paragraph written in different color marker, that warned of governmental conspiracies and the Pope's plan to impregnate my sister or daughter, being stacked and stored for tomorrow's revelatory display of inspiring revolution. I'm sure they were all the there along with basketball players shuffling up and down the courts; old drunks waiting for the peace of a dark empty beach to be allowed to crawl into a doorway, between buildings, under the lifeguard's perch, behind the bathrooms; and the older or at least middle aged competitors playing what looked like tennis with racquet ball rackets fenced in on diminished courts that made me think of people being shrunk down to a size that enabled them to stand on a ping-pong table.

They were there, but all I can see on that day from this one was the sky wrapping itself around the water so that the sand couldn't spill and the water wouldn't seep from their proper places. The sun had waited on our goodbye, then retired leaving its usual trail of burnt orange-pinks and dusty purples. Chris and I had found a bathroom close to the shore that had a cement walk circling the building. From there we saw the clouds drained of their fluffy white as they tried to make like the universe and expand to eternity only to break apart into smaller scattered clouds turning a plum-gray in the departing light. Chris toasted the sun, I toasted the sky and we, in turn, got nicely toasted. Our guitars joined the party and we sang until it got in the way of drinking and drank until the buzz requested a song. Soon the sky went dark and we fell silent as the ocean said, Shhhh. The waves' white caps could be seen through the night although I don't know if that was due to the moon, light man made, or by virtue of the water's contrast within itself. The white grabbed at my eyes before every collapse into the sand. I felt myself rise up off my heels leaning toward the shore then settle flatly back with every incoming and disappearing cap. I couldn't decide whether the sea consumed the land or if the sea had been simply absorbed.

I'm guessing it was my idea to run into the ocean. Chris, I'm sure, drank enough to be more than a willing participant. Still we agreed to do it in shifts so that one could keep an eye on our stuff. Chris went first—if something were to go wrong he probably wanted it to happen to him. We took several turns each. The salt immediately swarmed my lips, as I wasted no time testing the temperature—I attacked it. The heat had bathed in the water all summer long and had left it quite welcoming. I reminded myself that this was the kind of thing one read about in the paper: DRUNK MAN DROWNED IN OCEAN. But once I got the feel for the current, and I settled on a comfortable distance from the sand, I let the world go and the sea have me. I submerged myself wholly only to explode from the earth's womb over and over.

I woke up in the middle of the night in a damp sandy bed to hear Chris muttering to himself as he climbed in the back.

"If you take a piss out there be careful; I just slid down that hill. The first time I tried to make it on foot and fell on my ass; sliding is funner."

We had parked near an empty lot that slunk down off the pavement.

"We got all the guitars and everything," I said, as the evening started to present itself to me in pieces. I remembered the water and everything before that, but the trek back to the van was an assumption at best.

"Yeah, it's all here," Chris grumbled his answer.

"I gotta piss."

I slowly eased my feet down to where Chris laid and he turned to make space for me. Once I felt that I had futon beneath my feet and not Stopher, I crouched off the bed, leaning on the van's wall with my left hand and whatever boxes were stacked under my right, and inched my way to the back door. I fumbled with the sheet that held the outside world's view to get my hand at the latch then opened the door. Sliding the sheet out of the way completely, I stepped to the ledge, tucked my head down until it was clear, pivoted on my feet as I turned to face the back of the van, then gingerly lowered one foot to the ground as I clung to the lip of the roof. This procedure would get smoother but at first it was just another physical example of the mess I had become—an old man at thirty-five. I stood on the sidewalk barefooted at who-knows-when-in-the-morning, hung over and totally out of my element. I saw the pathway amidst the brush and approached cautiously. I hesitated as I glanced in both directions. The narrow walk crowded me encouragingly down the hill. I took a couple steps then considered pissing on the sidewalk. No, the last thing I wanted to do this early in the game was get busted by a cop for pissing in the street. I continued on with a miniscule shuffle as I leaned back with my hands behind me. I stopped as soon as I felt out of sight and had good enough footing to stabilize my position. I pissed, crawled back up the hill, climbing back into the van as decrepitly and gracelessly as I had exited.

"Ouch."

"Sorry."

And I was back in bed.

The next day a line came to me and I wrote it down: *I didn't drive two thousand miles to get drunk and run into the ocean, but it felt good.* Around that time another line came to me and I wrote that down too: *Reasons try to justify actions but actions act alone.* The former never found its way into a song; it simply sits, a crumpled piece of paper from a long-gone notebook, attached to a clipboard buried in a pile of other papers, folders (I got a play I wrote in there somewhere), other notebooks, maps and songbooks in the van between the engine's doghouse and a box (the size of a 12-pack container, maybe a little bigger) that is crammed up against the cooler that serves as a counter between the two front seats; the crammed box holds a checkbook I almost never use, varying cooking spices, which I use constantly, and a miscellaneous collection of knick-knacks, meaningless mementos, important documents—van's registration, etc.—a circular, tin box full of pennies and business cards I would come to collect over the years—all assuredly meaningless—and a business calendar containing record of all the gigs we played on our trip out west as well as not recording all the gigs we failed to get afterwards. I remember how much it meant to me when I put the line to paper; like so much of the other trash that built up in the box, meshed in with the papers against the doghouse and thrown out amidst yearly spring cleanings over time. It wasn't that I thought it profound or even clever; it placed me were I was at a time when uncertainty haunted me step for step; it confessed myself to me and gave absolution.

 The latter line sat untouched for a few weeks, maybe a month but it stayed in my mind and once in a while I'd play with the concept of its meaning. I remember sitting in the back of Steve's car reading it out loud to him and Chris. The line provoked an interesting discussion. Chris liked the line but didn't necessarily agree with it, not holistically at least. Steve said that it gave one pause but, like Chris, didn't know that one could act without reason. I argued that that was the point. Yes we involve ourselves with reasons, to the extent of making it the focus over what we actually do. The line for me encourages us to, once the act is done, let it stand alone on its own merit void of the cushioning benefit of some rationalization. I'm all for having reasons but at some juncture the act has to speak for itself. The conversation showed me that there was a good song in that line, one of those songs that might actually clue a listener in on an aspect of their humanity yet uncharted. I know that is a bit self-important of me but it is one of the REASONS

I write. The two lines were related to each other in that I had guilt over getting drunk and indulging myself when back across the two thousand miles I had a daughter that would rather I be driving a truck in Nashville. And what did I say about the act:...*it felt good.* (No reasons to make it okay, no fancy footwork to give it any dramatic purpose. I did what I did and it felt good.) So even though that line is nothing but ink on an unread piece of scratch paper it played a part in the birth of an idea that apparently meant a great deal to me. The song it became never generated the response that I thought it warranted but Chris and I would continue to have good conversations about its subject matter and recently he said, "I think you be right about that line."

Oh, and the song totally fucking rocks.

CHAPTER SIX

The Unurban Café' was a cozy little joint on Pico and Thirty-Third in west L.A. Through the front screen door a small room held the counter to order food and drink which I nor Chris ever would; immediately to the left was a doorway to the next room where the stage stood with its back to a plate glass window draped with a curtain to keep the Pico pedestrians from viewing the performers asses; the thin rectangular room had four rows of auditorium benches centered in front of the stage and a few stools placed under a couple of tables against the wall and a small aisle in between; once you got beyond the benches there were more stools under tables on one side and a long couch on the other with a love seat lined up next to it; at the back of the room adjacent to the side screen door entrance was another love seat; next to that was another doorway that led to the back room, which was filled with various tables and chairs that could have easily gone to the local thrift shop. That was the motif in general: thrift store casts offs. It had a pleasant, artsy effect. I thought maybe we had found a new home; a place to be that place we came from.

Steve ran the show well, keeping it moving while making the crowd laugh and feel a part of something cool or fun. In order to a get us a couple of extra songs, Chris and I signed up separately; I'd play sideman to his two songs and vice versa. The order of who played when was determined by drawing three names at a time from a hat as the night went. Steve asked when we wanted to play—we said about nine-thirty—and miraculously our names were drawn in tandem at nine-twenty. I had seen that kind of favoritism a million times over in Nashville but had never experienced it first hand. I liked it.

A typical writer's night ensued: Some talent, mostly just good enough to be annoying but all in all a good thing for those at that level to have access. Good for them. Not for us. Chris and I had reached the point by the time we left Nashville where this got to be kind of an insult. Not to say we were better than this, but, WE WERE WAY FUCKING BETTER THAN THIS. Preferential treatment was not going to make this palpable. Again, there were some good writers that even deserved to be on the same stage with us; not on the same night but…Chris and I had paid these dues.

I had Steve introduce us to the manager and booker of the Unurban so that he would check out our set to approve us for a gig. After we played I talked to Lee and he gave us an hour slot on a late October Saturday night. No money, but hopefully it would be the beginning of our legend. The night went nicely enough, we talked to some people and met a few of Steve's L.A. friends. I'm going to assume we had vodka in water bottles to help the night go down but I can't say for sure. We did try to cut down on the drinking; part of the trip's mission, and all that: Go west, live humbly, lose weight, get in shape; take world by storm. Before leaving we asked Steve what he knew about the promenade and he said that he and his partner, Jacob, had played there once. They even bought a special four channel, battery powered Carven PA amp for that very thing.

"I couldn't get Jacob back out there again," Steve smiled.

"Was it that bad?" Chris asked.

"I didn't think so, but then I have haven't gone back out there either."

"Chris and I are thinking of giving it a shot."

"Wanna use my gizmo?"

"Wow, thanks. But no, we'll try it with just the acoustics and see how that goes."

Chris nodded.

"Are you sure? Well let me know if ya change yer mind."

In bed Chris and I softly spoke within the walls of the van, afraid to alert the world to our presence. We parked along side Marine Park on a dark street that borrowed what little light it had from the sky, houses and the spillage of the distant main street's glow.

"I'd really like to make this work without bothering Steve," Chris declared under a hushed breath.

"He seemed happy to do it."

"I know."

I could hear a knowing tone in Chris' voice. I didn't know what he knew and I doubt that he did either.

The next week filled itself with us getting a permit, me working with Steve, and alone with my charts, and the daily chores that accompanied our new life. In the morning we went to the public showers at Memorial Park on fourteenth near Colorado with the rest of the van dwellers and truly homeless. The first weeks found me feeling like a nine-year-old going to the YMCA except without my Dad. Being naked around other men was not much of an obstacle; I had long since come to terms with my obese body and the very average penis that dangled not near as much as my belly. I felt like an intruder. I was an intruder. The thing about being from a close, big family is that your formative years are so self-contained that when you venture out into the world its like walking into the filming of a movie where everyone knows their lines but you. You only get one home and my dance card had been filled; balance must be served. In other words I was so at home growing up that I could never feel at home anywhere else. Even when I was paying rent with my wife and daughter I probably thought, on some level, that home was where I grew up. Wherever I have gone in my life, in whatever situation, the others in the room seemed more at home to me than I felt. Then of course every social dynamic or scene has etiquette. I'd come to find that when your existence is subjected to a never-ending influx of nomads, etiquette go bye bye. But on the day I was the influx I saw it as my duty to bow to my hosts out of respect to those who had come before. (I am my mother's son.) The other thing I learned was that, because the majority of these men were either clinically insane, drunks, maybe a criminals or two, and generally those who had been qualified by their families, society, and even themselves, unfit to live with, etiquette was whatever they wanted at the moment and decorum was gimmie, gimmie, mine, mine. So I was left with being the person

I was taught to be my family. And home at this point was still in Chicago. As the years talked to me and I them I would find home in the last place I looked.

On one crowded morning I placed the tin box (a blue and white recipe box that our Chicago friend Steve had given Chris and I as a care package. We each got one but Chris lost his on the trip west. In it he supplied us with bandages, a sewing kit, the hundred dollar bills we bought the blow with on our last night and few other things, all of which got spilled and lost amongst the van's other rubble) that held my soap and razor along side my toothbrush, etc. on the bench and saw that some of my clothes were touching someone else's things. There was no space for me to move the other way while on the other side of his things I saw a tiny bit of room. I carefully nudged his pile over.

"That's my stuff; don't be touching my things!" A voice boomed from the showers. A naked middle-aged, balding black man came toward me with his substantial cock waving disapprovingly like a pendulum out for blood.

"You move your shit, not mine."

I contemplated explaining my actions so that he would know that I had considered the matter thoroughly, but all I said was, "Sorry."

He walked back to finish his shower and I got ready for mine. He was no taller than me but had a good build and seemed fit. His willingness to fight made him formidable but more than any of that he felt at home and that not only fed my timidity, it made me feel wrong. That man was one of the handful I still see to this day—in the showers, on the promenade and such. Now when our eyes meet we acknowledge our common existence with a nod. It took more than a year or two, but he had seen me play and apparently had yearning to play himself. I'd see him walking with an electric guitar now and again over the years hooked up to his headphones. I could tell by looking at his fingers on the fret board that he would never learn to really play; he liked fooling with it; he liked having his hands on it; the way it looked with them there. Once he said something to me like, "I seen you on the promenade." That was all he said but he smiled, nodded his head and mimed the guitar with his hands as he spoke. The guy became a fan of sorts. At the very least he respected me.

The showers were full of characters, some amusing but most annoying. One guy Chris and I called Loser boy. He had seen our propane tank on one of the rare days that we cooked at that park. We cooked there maybe once or twice and then never again. It had nothing to do with the way this old guy mocked it though. Our philosophy came to be, don't cook where you shower; don't get greedy with one place. If they were gonna let us shower there we decided it best not endanger that privilege by making camp there too. Anyway, one morning we did set up our stove with the little quart-sized tank screwed into its hose and started to make some rice. When out of this pint-sized camper comes a ragged little man in pink sweat pants and powder-blue wind breaker zipped up half way exposing his bony, frail white chest with his wild, mostly-grey-partially-clinging to blonde-strands, unkept mane trying to escape his head, decrying our harmless tank.

"That's a loser tank!" His voice had a quality of having been shouting all day at a concert or ball game; tattered yet forceful.

Chris and I looked at him with puzzled faces.

The old guy cackled, "That's a tank for losers."

He approached in increments never quite closing the distance, wanting his voice to carry the message. There was an insane wizard quality about him as if he had seen one too many king fall for not heeding his word.

One of us said something still unable to ascertain his gist.

"No, No, you're wasting your time with that; it's a loser tank."

He mumbled some other things in his gargled, gnarly, warbled throat that I could not say for sure were directed at us because his manner scattered elsewhere. The word food found our ears and his finger seemed to be pointing at the stove. Then he went to his camper and pulled open his back door for us to better see inside.

"That's a tank" he said satisfied that his gravely, hoarse voice had shone us the error of our ways.

Through the rubble of papers, pots clothes and who knows what other debris, the coot managed to clear enough space to open a cabinet door and reveal a five-gallon propane tank.

"Oh," I said relieved to have the puzzle solved, "the propane tank."

The old guy approached again, "That's a loser tank."

"Yes, yes it is," Chris, agreed happily.

The old man gradually wound down mumbling a bit more about other matters than tanks that lost. On other occasions he would appear at one of the van's windows to complain about the police or profess his love for baseball. He said his name was Jim but to call him Rogers Homersby because he is great in the field and can hit for power.

"If you ever wanna play catch I'm in," he once told me.

I had seen him on the diamond once pitching balls to the backstop and his form showed talent. I bet he was a hell of a ball player. In the early years I'd see him in the showers regularly but now I only see him in the parking lot. Chris and I started ignoring him after the first year because he was one of those people that talked at you, not to you. He got the idea and stopped bothering us for the most part. I felt bad at first because I knew he just wanted to feel alive, to know that all that shit rambling round in his head had some place to go once in a while. Life in the streets and on the promenade paraded these people who needed someone to, if not listen, at least let them talk, into my life by the barrel full. The ones that allowed me a word in edgewise were the ones I tended to indulge. Loser boy's aggressive venting got progressively worse so we cut him loose. I'll say one more thing about Loser boy: that short little guy had the biggest cock I'd ever seen on a white guy and maybe as big as any I'd seen in the showers period; I'm just sayin'.

After the showers we usually went over to cook at Marine Park. In the beginning we would just set up on the bleachers by the baseball field just off the parking lot. That lasted a few weeks, maybe less, until one of the park rangers told us that it was against the fire laws to use a propane fueled stove in a public park. The park had a picnic area to the left of the basketball courts that could not be easily seen from the parking lot so we started cooking over there and no one ever bothered us about it again. The key here is low profile showing the proper amount of fear and respect. No one wanted us there—us being the van dwellers and the homeless—so it behooved us to blend into the woodwork whenever possible. Our schedule had us heading toward the promenade by ten and we wouldn't be back at Marine until after four, and we would soon be sleeping regularly in Albertson's parking lot so we were able to spread our unsolicited burden around quite nicely.

The first time playing the promenade we went strictly acoustic—may have made a buck and some change. We tried for an hour or so then agreed that we would have to work something out with Steve. The first time we played with the gizmo (Steve's Carven) didn't fare us much better. Our schedule had not yet been defined so it was an early October evening when we set up shop. The rules of the promenade state that you have to rotate spots every two hours on the even hour and that you must allow forty feet between each performer. The tourist's season had ended but the crowds were still hefty enough to bring performers out so Chris and I found a spot between Wilshire and Arizona. It was on the north end of the promenade and seemed to be the least busy. It was just before five when we got there so we waited for the six o' clock slot to play. When the time came we set up, got the sound levels adjusted and began to play. During the second or third song we were introduced to Geronimo. Geronimo played the buckets. The buckets were empty ten gallon pails of which he had roughly six, and Geronimo arranged them with their bottoms facing up around him like a drum set. He also had a few of pots varying in size to spice up his percussive options. Forty feet away a thunderstorm of pounding beats rained down on our music rendering it an after thought to the evening air at best. He was good; I couldn't say that he didn't have talent. The folksy novelty of it along with the pure volume drew a crowd around him quickly. The fact that he would play for ten to fifteen minutes and then take a break made it possible for Chris and I to endure it long enough to get our two hours in and make a couple of bucks.

It was our first time out there so I don't think we made too much of a fuss. I'm sure we asked him if he could move a little further down the street or if it was possible for him to play a bit softer.

"Gotta take the good with the bad," was all he said in response to our plea.

As life on the promenade unfolded Chris and I would each display our righteous rage to the inconsiderate and selfish with results equal to futility. That night we pretty much took our lumps and agreed to start coming out during the day. By mid-October we were playing noon till two usually on the center street at the northern tip of a dinosaur's tail Wednesday thru Friday and then finding another spot for the two till four slot. Saturday and Sunday the spots got harder to find and we usually had to wait two hours in between sets; for five days a week we played fours a day.

I'll get a technical fact out of the way here: The battery in Steve's gizmo gave us one set's worth in the beginning so, with Steve's permission we paid to have an extra battery installed. That solution didn't stand for long and we soon began a collection of batteries designed mostly for jump-starting cars. They looked a bit like a small cooler with cable clamps on the side. Within the first six months we had four of them. Steve graciously permitted us to re-charge them in a corner of his already crammed living/working space. The first year and a half saw us going in and out of Steve's on a regular basis. Chris and I tried to get on a consistent schedule that got the least in Steve's way. Of course his schedule changed constantly with every new project. If he was doing sound for a play he'd be gone most of the time, or sometimes he'd be on the road doing his stand-up. On those occasions, Steve was good enough to leave his keys where we could find them. For security purposes alone I had wanted to suggest us having our own key made, but I think that that was a line Steve didn't find comfortable crossing so I let it dangle. We did our best to stay off his toes and there were times when we did get too familiar with the coming and going. I will say here and later on repeat that without Steve, Chris and I would not have survived long enough to build the life we currently enjoy. (If

I never say it again: Thanks, Steve, I owe you more than I'll ever be able to repay.)

The money leaked while the boat stayed a float. From the start of our journey out of Chicago we saved every receipt to keep track of where the money went. Also we thought that if we ever started making any real money—HAHAHAHAAAHHHAAAAA! —that it would be helpful when doing our taxes. Oh, the hopeful. Every month had a standard white envelope with the receipts from that month stuffed inside and the total expense of the month written on the front along with the month. Those envelopes we slipped into a large manila one. I started out with roughly five grand and the trip coast around fifteen hundred give or take. It took until after Christmas for the money we made on the promenade to sustain our day-to-day life. As much as we tried to live close to the bone by eating off of the twenty-pound bag of rice and ten-pound bag of beans, we are weak, gluttoness people, Stopher and I. Then of course there is the booze and weed. We stuck with the rice for quite a while but by spring we pretty much turned to the cheap and easily cooked Ramon noodles for our starchy desires. The rice just took too long and was too much of an iffy task to get right, particularly in the windy rainy months. I can see Stopher huddled around the stove's second burner trying to keep the wind from belittling the flame while I chopped the meat and vegetables into the big stew pot. The beans we gave up on almost immediately. I made some chili one time and used up a whole propane tank just to get the beans ready for the sauce and meat. And most days we didn't have that kind of time to spend on cooking. That was another weekly sometimes bi-monthly expense, six to eight dollars for a two pack—two for four on the weeks when they had specials—of our propane tanks. Each tank cooked three to four meals, depending on the length of time it took to cook, which was greatly effected by the wind and temperature of the park. Then of course we discovered George's diner and the tank expenditure became less of an issue—good food at reasonable prices and in healthy portions. They had a hefty burrito for five bucks that you had to unroll to eat it with a fork before you could rewrap and pick up with your hands. Then there were the chili cheese fries for three-fifty after taxes. For seven bucks we could both be stuffed, and hey isn't that what eating is all about: Feeding your face until breathing becomes uncomfortably difficult. There were the fast food chains gunning for our money with their dollar sandwiches and it all added up. If a place didn't accept my debit card all we had to do is buy a stick a gum at Albertson's and we could get up to a hundred dollars cash back. So the money leaked while the boat stayed afloat.

When I wasn't thinking too far ahead I really liked my life. In that first month I worked hard at my charts whenever I could: In the morning by Marine Park, or over by the showers at Memorial, on the promenade waiting to begin our noon set and at Steve's with the other musicians for the show; for the first time I felt like a musician and not an artist of my own work. God, I was slow but I made up for it by working my ass off. After a few weeks I started to think that I might actually get it all down well enough to fake my way through. Steve kept saying that as long as he didn't hear the bad notes he could live with the ones I glossed over. It all worked in with my playing at the promenade because the rehearsals at Steve's were in the evening as were the ones with the actors at the theater. I had done musical theater in school and always loved seeing the way a show came together. (I played Henry Higgins in my Fair Lady to rave reviews thank you very much.) Having the actors sing to the music I was helping create, seeing the scenes build up to each song and just being around theater people; I am theater people. Oh, and there were hot women around.

Sukey's music was great stuff too. The dialogue at times got a tad sitcomy but the story was powerful. There is a certain constructional style to a song in musical theater that challenged me in all the right places. The chording is more inherently orchestral and demands specific fingering from both hands. When I got something right it juiced me to my core. When I got it wrong I cursed my lack of discipline for a proper education. It got to the point that when I played with the band or at least just the piano I could make it work. The problems that nagged were the two songs that I had to accompany an actor all by my lonesome. One of the songs was a love song sang by a gorgeous redhead. Sukey approached the guitar with a piano's mentality but the piece would not have been a real problem if I had written it. I had written pieces a hell of a lot more difficult but they came from an organic place that set me up not to think. Oh, thinking is a drawback. In two weeks I learned twenty songs.

    The dress rehearsals started up and the shows director expressed concerns to Steve about me. The funny thing is that not a soul in the production, including Sukey and Steve, had a clue as to the many deer-in-the-headlights moments I experienced throughout the show; I am the plow. They only noticed it during the redhead's ballad and another song that featured my guitar. The second one I knew I'd get a handle on and had in fact played pretty well in spite of their worries. At the end of the second to last dress rehearsal I played in I had forgotten that the director wanted the song pushed; he felt it dragged. To me it was probably the most moving song of the night and the push that the director had asked for deflated the raw emotion of the piece. It was also one of Sukey's favorites and I remembered her being very specific about the tempo of it whenever she coached me on it—Steve as well. So that night when I started the song I, not consciously, couldn't remove it from the groove that had been burned into me by the writer. I think being a writer myself and just plain thinking that the director gave a moronic order based on the show's running time, made even more stupefying by the fact that the song he decided on pushing was the big finale, had me subconsciously unable play it any other way than that which I, the author and the shows true band leader, Steve, (the official musical director was the pianist but to me Steve was the man) knew that it should be. I started the song and everything would have been fine—the director wouldn't even have noticed—if the actor I accompanied had not started fighting my tempo. This kiss-ass, of a wanna be, hack pushed out ahead of the music. Now I know I should have followed him and I knew that at the time, but some part of me got caught under the wheel. It probably had more to do with nerves than any loyalty or affection that I had for the piece. I wasn't going out of my way to defy anyone, I simply could not rise myself out of the pocket that felt so very cozy and right. At first I thought, Oh he'll come back to me, but by the time the clarity of his intentions seeped into my brain I was kinda helpless. After the first verse Steve cued the piano to come in early to take over the unfolding train wreck before it wiped out the station.

Luckily the director thought me unworthy of words personally so I didn't have to hear about it from him. Steve did. Steve was very understanding and patient with me at every step since offering the chance to be a part of the show. Well, there were a few sessions that he seemed to not understand that I was way out of my element, but for the most part he was a saint. He came to me after the director had unburdened his displeasure over my performance into his lap.

"Could you not hear that he was a measure ahead and getting farther and farther away?"

"Why didn't he stay with me?" I complained weakly knowing that it was my job to stay with him.

"Because he is an actor; you make them look good, not the other way around."

I knew Steve had a soft spot in his heart for hating actors.

"I know." I paused. "But I did play it the way you taught me."

"Yes, you did. If the two of you were on different stages, in different cities it would have come off great."

The next rehearsal was my last chance. The show didn't open for another two weeks, and one of the lead actors still needed a script on stage; there were a million other things that needed more than just a little tweaking but this was my last chance. Chris boiled over about it.

"The fucking lead actor is reading from a goddamm script! You are the least of their problems. You'll get those last two songs by the end of the week let alone in two."

"Yeah, but there's a ton of things I'm doing wrong that no one is noticing."

"If they're not noticing then you're doing your job."

The next run through came and I had worked those two fucking songs to perfection. Every waking free moment I gave to playing them over and over. I sang them in character for christ's sake. The night came and as the redheaded ballad approached just before intermission my nerves bubbled beneath my skin. The rest of the songs went pretty well aside from a few chords I passed on or reformed, as I blew by; all in all no one died. The moment of the redhead's song lowered itself before my eyes, and I think for the first couple of bars I had it, then, poof, my brain and fingers had a lover's spat. To be fair to me, it wasn't a disaster, but the second the song ended I knew that I had failed. I've performed in all kinds of situations and worked my way out of nerves before. If I could have put on a red wig, slithered into that turn of twentieth century wardrobe, not a dry eye in the house. I was a singer, a player, a performer—not a pure musician.

Chris would argue and he had his point but I know what I mean. (Of course, if I were offered that gig today I'd nail it.)

The second act went well and I played the last number at the proper tempo but I knew that wasn't enough. When the show ended I headed out through the side stage door into the courtyard with Steve at my heels.

"The director wants you out."

"Good."

"I told him that you worked way too hard and that you were getting close; you just need some tutoring. So the director said if you work with me over the weekend you can have another shot."

"No!" I was done. "I know that song inside in out. I played it perfectly all day. There is nothing you can show me this weekend to get me to play right under those lights."

"He won't give you the chance unless we work together." Steve wanted this to work out. He felt bad about all the time I had put in.

"It's over," I pleaded. "The whole charade. I don't know what I'm doing out there. You have no idea how many mistakes I've been hiding between the drums and piano."

"That stuff-"

"This is not me, Steve; this is not what I do."

"You're a great guitar player."

"I'm a great me."

"I just want them to see how good you are."

I don't know why that was important to him. Did he think I cared what they thought of me? I guess it would have been nice to have them know but at this point the emotional exhaustion from the pressure of trying or pretending to be more than I was proved too much. I could feel the relief spray down my spine and tickle my toes. My chest crumbled over the laughter that never reached my mouth. All that came out was a giddy scoff. (I was in a band called Giddy Scoff—A tribute to Joe Jackson.)

"Thanks, Steve. The whole thing has been a great ride and I'm glad it's over. I'm a better musician than when I started. Thanks, really."

"Thank you for trying. I appreciated your company on all the drives back an forth and having someone around besides all these theater jerks."

After all that I almost ended up playing in one of the shows. A bit into the shows run the drummer took ill and wasn't sure if he'd be able to play. The understudy for the drummer was Steve and the understudy for Steve couldn't make the last minute call so the drummer said he'd try and tough it out. The day of the show I went to Steve's to go over all the songs, which I hadn't played since the fateful firing, but they were very much still hammered in my head.

We ran through the show and Steve said, "Why did we fire you?"

I answered by overstatingly crunching the soft, gentle intro to the redheaded ballad.

"Oh, right."

Chris and I had been to see the show a couple times already and we liked it for the most part but not enough to sit through it again. Steve had pleaded with drummer to at least survive the first act so that I wouldn't have to play my Achilles' heel. Once the drummer got going he went ahead and finished the night so I never ended up playing. But Steve insisted I be paid fifty bucks for showing up and I got it. Woohoo!

The drummer by the way was named Dave and through our hanging out at rehearsals we got to jamming. Chris was there a lot so he'd join in and Dave started talking about getting us a few gigs. Steve being a top-notch bass player made us a damm fine band in the making. Alas, as was to be our patterned fate (I was in a band called Patterned Fate—Heart) it never amounted beyond a few practices and a lot of talk.

One more tidbit that came out of the KITTY HAWK saga that I found amusing involved Chris hanging out at the rehearsals. Remember

Chris is a tall imposing reddish haired man, fury-faced and sparsely mustached. His beard did not curl up like, say a Santa Claus' would. It fell almost straight from his cheeks and chin like an unkept tangled beaded curtain. Back then he wore black suspenders over sometimes green, black, or maroon tee shirts and almost always navy-blue dress/work pants. He would occupy himself quite often in the lobby of the theater with the laptop our uncle Bob gave of us before we left Chicago to keep up on our writing. Chris sat in the lobby typing away while I helped Steve with some set up or other before the rest of the cast and crew arrived.

One night when the show's producer came to have a look see on how the money had been spent, he walked into the theater and asked Steve, "Who's the Amish guy on the computer?"

It became a theme for the evening. The first thing that struck me as so funny was that the bozo didn't seem to note the incongruities of an Amish man using a computer. The second one was that I had never noticed how much Stopher had come to resemble one.

Through all of that Chris and I got familiar with life on the promenade and in the van. Our niche developed out of a routine carved from trial and error. James Mitchell, the old black guy singing on the milk crate went out of his way to make us feel welcomed. Mel, his lead guitar player, gave a well-meaning smile in the morning but kept more to himself. In time Chris, with all his praise for Mel's grace and style on the fret board, helped form a relationship based on the mutual love of guitar and of music in general. Mel was not without compliments for us, he knew a player when he saw one, but Mel remained his own favorite subject. Mel and I had that in common. It's not that Mel and I didn't share Chris' appreciation or respect for other players, we just guarded our place in our own eyes. I can't speak for Mel on this because I don't think he had any insecurities stemming from a lack of formal education; when it came to music I slipped in through the back door. Today I think I have dislodged the better portion of that particular chip from my shoulder. Chris is a self-proclaimed born spectator while I grew into the role of spectator-hobbyist by comparison. (My songwriter's chip still burrows in deep to the bone's marrow and shades my eyes from the sun. Chris, I think owns one of those too, as he should.)

James Mitchell would greet us every morning the same way.

"Praise God, Chris and Dave."

"Morning, James."

"Well, better go get my spot."

As our lives intertwined the conversations bulged. The daily grind soon became part of our morning hello.

"Some folks coming by, taking our pictures, leave nothing; ain't right. I understand if you wanna hear some music and you got no money, but taking a picture? You dollar up."

James and Mel had a sign testifying to that very fact.

James would sometimes take a break from his set down at the south end of the street by the shoeshine stand and have a smoke while he listened to Chris and I. He'd smile with his head nodding knowingly. The man didn't just love music, he loved those who loved it and gave love to it. James saw the blood in our music.

Usually he only stayed for one song and if he could spare it he'd tip us a dollar.

"I love those harmonies, Chris and Dave. Dave here has a beautiful voice, but when you both sing together: Praise, God."

Nothing that has been said to me before or since has meant more. James Mitchell was a genuine article of his times and he saw that we were that very thing to ours.

The weekdays had other performers but few as consistent as the brother's Smith along with James and Mel. The weekends held a whole other hosts of regulars that during the busy seasons came out more often. They'd start coming out on Thursdays and then Wednesdays. Like I said before, the evenings were a different beast. Ned Timms and his wife Layla were the kings of the weekend. He was a short, white, balding, mealy, little man who could drill the fret board into sawdust. His wife, Layla, a pale South American woman, played the keyboards that also contributed percussions. She had a mic in front of her that was only used to pitch the CDs. They played flamenco music that while having some pretty melodies and a few interesting chord changes mainly relied on the blurred fingers of Mr. Timms traversing up and down the board at warp speed. One couldn't help but be impressed, not to mention that growing up as guitar player who loved Al, John and Paco, it had been my goal to achieve such dizzying heights. On days Chris and I did not play if we were on the promenade to catch a movie we would always stop and take in one of his twenty-minute sets.

Again Chris heaped on the praise as I begrudgingly conceded his phenomenal ability. There was actually something besides egocentric defense or envy at play in this case. The man had so little soul. His beady eyes darted about the crowd (he always drew a big one) between flutters, nervously seeking approval through the duality of his pompous air. I could hear the on going monologue going on inside his squirmy head:

"How about that? Hey, you in the red vest, you couldn't do this. Do you love me? Fuck you, I don't want your love! Your love isn't worth my desiring it. Oh, this one over by the tree liked that. Here watch this. I really am incredible. What! This old lady in the polka dots looks bored. Who cares? I don't need her—I didn't my mother's love; I sure as hell don't need hers."

A fucking great technician who knows more about music theory than I could pretend to imagine.

Pat was another guy who we'd see on some weekdays and every weekend. The guy looked like John Denver and sounded just like James Taylor. He wore buttoned cotton shirts, usually a light shade of blue, beige or khaki pants with a same colored baseball cap. The cap owed more to a tennis player than baseball; deflated dome over a weak bill—a truck driver would just as soon wear a bonnet. His bit was taking four or five of Sweet Baby James' most popular tunes and play them over and over. Financially it made sense; the songs made money and it was a rotating crowd. The people that worked the carts and in the restaurants grew to hate him. Like Chris and I, Pat tended to play in the same spot whenever he could, about eighty feet north of our home at the dinosaur's tail by the Criterion movie theater.

Pat befriended us by way of offering up an inclusion to a philosophy that created an atmosphere exclusive to that section of the promenade.

"The Timms and I have made it a rule of discouraging more than one performer at a time playing north of the center square."

Chris and I were all for that. I had never realized just how close forty feet could be until I played the promenade. At first I thought we had fallen into a friendly little niche with Pat and the Timms, they seemed reasonable on top of their being talented. The one down side was that they got out there so early that both the noon an two slot were taken so Chris and I would have to fend for ourselves elsewhere. Some mornings we'd get out there by seven am and still not beat the Timms or Pat. Rich Smith was a third that coveted that area. He played classical/Gershwin piano. (He called it neo-classical.) A tall good-looking man in his late twenties with short curly brown hair and a knowingly shy smile, Rich came out in black tails and tie playing an electric piano on wheels. Actually what he did most Saturday mornings around five or six is chain his box on wheels without the piano inside to a light post or bike rack, and then go back home to sleep until past nine. A rule on the promenade stated that if you played the noon you had a right to stay without rotating and play the same spot at six. So between Rich, Pat and the Timms, our favorite spot could be booked from noon until midnight. But we respected the unwritten rule of not having two performers in that area and played either at the head of the third block, the same block just on the other side of the center square by another dinosaur's tail, or down on the south end by the shoeshine stand where James and Mel played during the week. We usually did the former two because we felt that the shoeshine stand spot belonged to James and Mel. If they didn't show up by eleven and no one else grabbed it, then we did.

On the days we beat the Timms or Pat they at first respected their own unwritten rule but not always. The Timms started playing more consistently on the first, most southern, block by the Lowe's cinema during our first summer so that opened things up a bit. But when push came to shove the Timms would set up on top of us blowing us out of the water. So I was happy when they started fishing at another hole. Pat for the most part seemed happy with the two spot so Chris and I settled in on the noon leaving the four to Rich.

When Pat quit his day job and started coming out during the week we started to see the squirrel of his nature. One afternoon he said he would take the noon. He beat us fair and square so we accepted the two. He played a few songs before the rain shut him down and then he informed us that he would start up at two. Pat would change his mind even without the rain forcing his hand; if he said noon and at that hour the crowd seemed small he'd beg off until two. That was fine with us but it got annoying. I remember watching him do a set while the Criterion Theater was doing some remodeling. Pat could have set-up down the street but insisted on his usual spot. Now I understand the frustration of wanting your music to be heard free from the accompaniment of a jackhammer, power saw, etc. but these guys were just doing their job.

"I'm trying to do my show!" Pat complained into the microphone.

His indignant tone shamed him. Here we are, getting to play music in the street for money while these poor sons of bitches have to slave away doing real work and then on top of that, endure the amplified, verbal abuse of some pompous dweeb who confuses the privilage he's been given with some sort of entitlement. I worked in the manual labor world for most of my adult life and if I were them I would have inserted a wrench up his nose to get at that screw lose in his head.

The thing about life on the promenade is that there were a lot of regulars, from the people that worked there to the homeless that didn't. If you played there, hell if you sat there, your ear was gonna get bent. Pat had installed a defense mechanism against that by pointing at his throat to indicate that he had to save his voice for his sets. At first I bought it as genuine because four hours of singing five days a week had gotten to me already. I could hear it in his voice on some days, but then there were others when he sounded fine. He didn't just do this with the rabble hounding anyone that might give them a quarter or at least a momentary reprieve from the isolation that their lives had become, Pat would pull that shit with me, even when I was trying to communicate on our daily business.

I remember one Thursday night—Chris and I had been playing there over a month now—we were playing near the Criterion because of the threatening rain and the construction around it offered a bit of protection. Pat was waiting for the eight and in the meantime had been really getting into our set. When Chris went into the Sheryl Crow tune, IF IT MAKES YOU HAPPY, Pat got excited. He jumped from his chair and grabbed one of his speakers and hooked up to ours to give us a fuller sound. He moved about in a kind of prowl around us to show any passersby that something cool was going down. I remember his smile having a tone of menace. Pat had a clean-cut image while Chris and I were the slovenly, tough looking guys from the seventies. Our shirts were clean as were we but there always has been something inherently dirty about us. I have my uniform much like my Dad did. For more days than not, Dad wore a blue work shirt, blue denims, and yellow construction shoes. I wore a black-buttoned shirt that could pass for a dress shirt but had a deliveryman's quality over a black tee, black jeans and the construction boots—the same that I had worn when I drove a truck. Chris sported his customary Amish outfit. We could have traded clothes and Pat would still be the clean-cut one. Our mutual respect had been previously established but on this night Pat had a gleeful envy for what we were about.

"That is so cool," Pat, said when the song ended. "Two big guys singing this tiny girl's song."

"Well," I responded not knowing quite how to take it.

"You should record a whole album like that."

"That would be cool," Chris said.

"Thanks for the speaker," I added.

"I just had to hear it better."

Pat's excitement began to settle as he walked off a little in around us before finding his chair. I never saw him like that again and in fact that would be the peak of our friendliness. Pat was like most people who spoke of high ideals in casual conversation; rearranged them the instant they conflicted with any immediate desire of his own. He weaseled in and out of his own words like the empty hot air they were. As time went on we talked less and less and played against each other more and more. Only he against us though because other than a couple of times before we got a sense of the place, Chris and I never set up near another performer; we'd just as soon wait for the next set. Pat started playing elsewhere after the first year and half and then left the promenade altogether. Now and again you'll hear some one say, "What ever happened to that guy who looks like John Denver but sounds like James Taylor."

One day during our first few weeks of playing, Chris and I met the Raven. She was a hostess at George's Bistro, a restaurant that sat to our right as we played at the dinosaur's tail. Bravo sat next to that, the food court beyond that and across from George's Bistro was Johnny Rockets. That was what I liked about that spot: all the people sitting at those restaurants. For Chris and I to be truly appreciated you had to spend some time with us and having lunch while we played afforded us that time. So we were playing a song, lyrics by Mom, music from me, called HARDEDGE BLUES. (I had asked Mom way back before the Nashville years to give me something tough. She responded with a verse and I said, "I'll need a second one, lady." It became a riffy little jam that Chris and I always had fun with.) This woman in front of George's clapped for it more than the others if anyone else clapped at all; she was the first hostess to ever clap period. All the girls that stood in front of their eateries were pretty but the Raven had something else going on entirely. They were girls, most of them, and she was a woman. On that day she had her long, wavy, dark hair up in a bun but for the few strands strategically strewn down the side of her face dancing on her cheeks, tantalizingly dangling about her sleek, tanned neck. I acknowledged her applause graciously but avoided gawking at her overwhelming beauty. I did catch the mischievousness that emanated from her brown almond shaped eyes but I lingered not. Her smile showed her teeth effortlessly framed by trim sensual lips that rose and dipped in the middle. Her high cheekbones protruded from her face like chestnuts warm and edible, helping define the graceful slope down toward her chin. She wore a long black gown that draped about her curvaceous body, clinging in all the right places. She had something like a half-sweater or jacket that wrapped around under her mouth-sized breast putting them on a pedestal for all to wishfully marvel.

After our set as we broke down she called me over.

"If you can play bluesy guitar like that, why do you play anything else?"

"It's just the way we are." Our diversity was our curse and I thought better of getting into it.

"Well, you guys sound great."

Her cleavage sounded good too.

"Thanks, it's nice to play for someone who welcomes it."

"I love any music that's good."

"Hey, wait a sec." I walked back to the equipment and got a CD to give her. "Here."

"How much?"

"Let's just call it thank you."

"No, let me give you something."

She disappeared inside and returned with a five-dollar bill.

"Where are you guys from?"

"Chicago. We've only been out here since late September living in our van."

"Really?" Her face lit up then quickly narrowed as her voice hushed. "I live in a camper too, but no one here knows." She put her index finger to her lips. She looked around to see if anyone had heard. "Where do you guys hang around?"

"Marine Park off of Lincoln and here mostly."

"I know that park; I'm a dog walker. Maybe I'll come by sometime and show ya my camper." ("Show ya my camper," is a phrase never construed with lasciviousness or innuendo; it gave me chills anyway.)

"Well that'd be nice."

I said see ya around and went back to help Chris. When we left she went out of her way to say hey to Chris as well. I knew that she was a friendly gal who loved music. I did not entertain for a millisecond anything beyond that had transpired. Having a beautiful woman like our music was more than I had expected when I woke up that morning. I told Chris how she lived in her camper and we both thought that very cool. Not to mention her ass so perfectly round that Columbus would have sailed around'er twice.

"She seemed to like you," Chris offered as we loaded up the van.

"She liked us; she likes music."

By the time October came to an end Chris and I were still tinkering with our daily routine; had met a beautiful Raven; and I had turned thirty-six and been fired from my first gig as a musician in a musical. Sukey's music did leave a mark on me as I used some of what I had been exposed to in writing the music for the lyric that started with the line about reasons and actions. Particularly in the way I structured vamp riffs to connect the chords.

Reasons try to justify actions but actions act alone
"Whys" simply fall to the side to lie at the feet of what's been shown
I have reasons but they escape me when I'm at my best
Or is it that I set them aside to put what I've become to the test?

Waves crash; questions on a beach
Wiping away footprints: answers as to who was there
Rolling in to recede
Afraid being told when it go or where

All my life I've been afraid of it ending—my consciousness rolling away with the tide
Not tasting the salt water or hear the sweet sound it's sending—just another set of footprints the sand couldn't hide

So I move to be moving for the joy that it brings
So I sing to be singing the songs that are me
I lay quiet and still to let all that has come in go free
Reasons are for those who need them to be sure of why and where
Me, I'm going, to be where I am, making friends with my worst fears

All my life I've been afraid of it ending—my consciousness rolling away with the tide
Maybe I'll taste the salt water and hear the sweet sound it's sending—still just another set of footprints the sand couldn't hide

CHAPTER SEVEN

    Although we didn't cook as much as we should have we still cooked enough to stem the tide of our growing financial concern—a tad. On top of that there was the benefit of an intimacy with your own survival. In an apartment there is a room designed especially for the mundane chores to be executed, storage area for the supplies, all contained under one roof. Doing dishes in our world required stacking the pots, bowls, utensils, etc methodically as to be able to traverse through the park without dropping things and calling as little attention to your intentions as possible. The towel draped over your shoulder, the sponge and soap all informed on lookers as to your agenda but the preparation in arranging these items on your person with the pot holding all other dishes minimized the mark it left on them. If one is stealth enough the impression you may give from a distance might be of one going to brush their teeth. And that is just the cleaning up after the cooking. In the beginning it felt as if Chris and I had to communicate constantly to coordinate our every move:

"You got the stove?"

"Wait, no, I'll take this."

"Did you grab the salt?"

"I think I did?"

Many trips would made back to the van.

    But through it all we got better and then worse and better again. The point being that nothing within the process of preparing a meal to cleaning up afterwards came to pass void of connection to the act. You had to be involved. Aware. Once I gave myself to the life, as soon as I coaxed myself into embracing the detail of things it all became very Zen; I am one who washes the forks—the forks are clean because I washed them. I have always been big on systems. From my days running the stock room at Marshall's I learned not only the value but the necessity of limiting your movements and the movement of the objects involved to the depth of a cosmic flow. All things were washed in the pot and the pot's refuse emptied into the toilet; I didn't want to be accused of leaving a mess behind; a good neighbor is a good neighbor whether he lives in house or not.

When we were good there was not a movement wasted between us. I passed the sudsy things while he rinsed and dried. If he fell behind I'd take up the rinsing until he caught up. We both moved evenly and steadily. When we were not good it was best that only one did the washing while the other listened to the radio in the van. In fact only one doing the washing came to be the norm. We did enough together. But during the first year it was more shared chores than separate ones. And yeah, we argued a lot.

As for the promenade we evolved into our roles there as well and probably even more quickly. I'd drop off Chris with all the equipment but for the guitars. That left him with the gizmo in one hand and the maroon gym bag with the needed chords, mics, pedals and metal, microphone stand, platforms inside with the unattached stands slid across the top in the other. He had to muscle all that no more than a block while I, after having parked six blocks away if I was lucky, walked the Martin and the Strat to whatever spot he had attained. When the sets were done and we had packed it all up one of us would get the van to pick up the other with the equipment up. We took turns walking for the van but it's my guess that I went more often because Chris walked like molasses on a sub-zero morning. All of that, like the cooking, evolved and you'll see how as this burgeoning epic unfolds.

Our first one-hour set at the Unurban went well enough for us to get a second. Only two or four people showed up to see us: Steve, Jacob and Steve's other friend Burpo. (I know that's only three.) Chris and I drank as hard as we played and I think we sounded damm fine. Steve said some nice things, as did Burpo and Jacob.

We booked another set for early November but Chris knew that this was not the way we would be going. I knew it too even though I talked as if it still might lead somewhere. The street began to feel more like home and I loved the aspect of not having to worry about the responsibility of filling a room. At this time of year the weather continued to play nice so every time we played the air carried an atmosphere of gigs at a summer carnival. On the down side: Money had yet to solidify into anything we could hang our hat on; the distractions of other musicians in my ear; the miscellaneous noises from crowds and construction; the homeless blasting their boom boxes, banging on bongos or garbage cans—yelling at each other, both in jest and fury, about and alternately at God in earnest, at the masses, vulgar with raw, wounded rage (I was in a band called Raw Wounded Rage—The Henry Rollins Band) and those weren't necessarily the schizophrenics.

Chris and I sat in the van in the parking lot behind a closed bank that sat across the street from the Unurban. We were an hour or more early—we were always early. (There are two kinds of people in this world: Those who hate to wait and those who hate to keep people waiting.) Chris and I had been to so many general admission concerts in our time that waiting had become a skill then an after thought. Over the next four years that ability to let time tick came in handy.

We had decided to play sober because we knew that Lee, the manger, had a low threshold for being around drunks; reformed drunks hate be reminded of their former selves. So we sat with radio on, talking more than listening. I wish I could remember what we were talking about, probably the promenade or the set we were going to play. There are some moments that are thrust into your life with such force that when you look back on it, the moment before that moment holds an importance that otherwise it would have not. I'm making too much out of it all I assure you. I had never once cared to consider what was being said before the event until this moment when I am about to write it down. I just wish I could because I do remember feeling relaxed. We had been in Santa Monica well over a month and for all my apprehension, all the uncertainty, I had begun to notice a tingling of knowing something about what my life was becoming.

I looked out through the windshield from the driver's seat to the left and saw a middle-aged man walking from the ATM machine on the street side of the bank. The street was thirty-third and just beyond that was the main street Pico intersecting with it. Across Pico I could see the plate glass window of the Unurban boasting its name. As early as it was Chris and I had just recently talked about grabbing our stuff and heading over. There had been a couple of teenagers, they looked like teenagers, mulling about in the peripheral of the parking lot to our right. Chris said later that he noticed them and felt flash of uneasiness. I noticed them but thought nothing other than, God, I hate teenagers. As the man passed through our immediate field of vision the teenagers encountered him and ceased his movement. I only half noticed at first, Chris stiffened next to me and then my eyes focused on the one man flanked on either side by two boys. The boy with his back to me wore a black shirt and pants. The pants hung below his waist hugging his cheeks as the current fashion had ridiculously dictated. The boy facing us had a grey hooded sweatshirt, which was too warm for the weather and equally fashionable but also served a function to his endeavor; I couldn't see his features very well. The boy in black probably had hooded shirt as well but all I remember is a black baseball cap worn with the bill down and to the side. The man's face went disturbed as his hands rose from his side as if to say, I ain't got nothing, and he stepped awkwardly between them as they each gave him a shove. The man bumped to the other side of the boys and turned to keep their eyes in contact as he slowly backed away. They moved hauntingly toward him.

    I grabbed the door handle and opened it ajar before pausing. Do I really want to do this? The grey hooded kid was short and not all that stocky, the other stood tall with broad, but let's be honest, boney shoulders; Chris and I could take them—I had a sledgehammer and an ax. Chris' left hand shot out at me as his eyes darted at my door then back to the scene; do you really want to do this? his motions asked. The man wore a green flight jacket just like the one I wore when I was twenty. His dully striped buttoned shirt revealed a beer belly and his faded Levis fixed at the waist indicated that he was neither current nor fashionable, and probably not all that rich. The boys advanced with a lunge and the man tripped over a parking stump falling on his back. I began to push the door when I heard Chris squirt out as I saw the taller one grabbed at his back pocket, "He's got a gun." I looked at Stopher, I looked at the man on the ground—I turned the key that, bless all that is holy, was already in the ignition. The engine that had not so much as had a sniffle or a hiccup since that day in Albuquerque, suddenly whined and sputtered like a child wanting to stay in bed instead of going to church on a sub-zero morning. The usual click and respond from my faithful Ford companion stuttered, mirroring my panic. The boys had crouched themselves over the balding man, who for Christ-fucking-sakes should've just given up the goddamm wallet in the first place, hovering above their completion when they heard the van's graceless attempt at fleeing. The punks (boys become punks when they carry guns; so do men for that matter) looked up, and for the first time became aware of the television drama that they had been performing for us via the windshield.

There was a moment before the engine collected itself when the punks stared from their crouch at the van. It was a short moment. It was a question mark for both parties: I didn't know the van would start; the punks didn't know what they would do if it didn't. In that moment Chris, me, the punks, all waited to see what we would do when the next moment arrived with an answer. The balding, middle-aged man, wearing a jacket I wore when I was twenty, didn't look or think. If he had any contact with his brain whatsoever at any point amidst the whole affair he would have given up his money, ran, taken a swing, shouted for help, something—anything other than being the empty vessel adrift helplessly in an event in which he was the star.

The van did start.

I decided to forgo the usual five minutes it required to warm up and as I simultaneously—as humanly possible from the instant the engine turned over—rammed it into reverse (clunk), hit the gas (screech), barely touched the bake before shoving into drive and hitting the gas again (screech, clunk-clunk, screech). Out of the corner of my eye I thought that I saw the punks running but I couldn't be sure; I was too fucking scared! As soon as the van's tires found thirty-third heading for Pico guilt and shame doused my soul.

"We shounta left."

"He had a gun!"

Luck held the green light long enough, just long enough, for us to make the yellow and we headed west on Pico toward home plate. The second I turned I had decided to go back. A Trader Joe's sat directly across from the bank parking lot so I turned again immediately into the Pico side entrance to double back to the bank's lot. Coming out of the thirty-third street side of Trader Joe's driveway I stopped just long enough to see that the punks were gone. Middle-aged guy's brain saw enough of the light to lift his petrified ass off the ground and now had four or five concerned citizens around him hanging on his every word.

"They took off as soon as you got'er in gear," Chris said, as if having just run a race.

"Yeah, " I agreed, "I thought I saw that too." I looked at Chris as I eased the van out of the lot towards Pico. "I had to make sure." I smiled wearily.

"No, you're right. Now let's get the fuck out of here."

The faithful Ford passed to the left under a fleeting yellow light only as steadily as my singed nerves could maneuver. The dusk had only just now given way to night so the headlights that blew the red light behind me caught my eye. All I thought of it at the time was that there seemed a heightened urgency in the manner of its turn.

I mumbled something to that effect. "He's in a hurry."

We drove a couple of blocks and as relieved as I was, as over as it was, the weight of the moment had not completely let me go. I can't say that it was one thing that made me pull into the Wiener Dog parking lot; a chance to collect myself surely had been in my mind. Along with that sensible reasoning rode a spooky, intangible realization that this might not be over. But that sensation wasn't even in the shape of a full thought. It hung like a cloud outside my head trying to get in. Practical things needed addressing so with the van in park and the engine still running I sighed.

"Are we still playing?" I asked.

"Doesn't sound like me."

I had heard a screech come from the street as I approached my spot. My mind fumbled with the connection of the screech and the car blowing the red light. Someone had been in hurry at my tail twice in the last minute. It didn't come to me in any clarity but I felt prodded at. Chris was talking and I wasn't listening. I kept staring into my passenger-side mirrors, one to the other. Headlights shined into my field of reflected vision as the light's source moved hesitantly forward. The nose of the car peeked out from behind the van and stopped.

Chris was still talking when I spoke to the driver's side mirror. "Alright, keep moving."

"What?"

"What's this guy doing?" My right hand settled on the gearshift while my foot hovered a whisper above the brake.

"What guy?"

I stopped talking as I thought about getting out to see what this putz was up to, which if I had a clear understanding of what my senses were telling me would have been the stupidest thing I could have done. The car began easing past the van's rear and my eyes widened as if they knew what they were expecting to see without cluing in my brain.

"He's wearing a ski mask," I blurted out.

"Who?!" Chris' jumped in his seat as he looked back into the van filled with our life then to me for a crisper depiction.

The ski-masked driven car began to pull along side me thinking himself undetected. The second he left me the space I had the van in reverse and then moving in the direction from whence we came. As I moved toward the street I checked my mirror to see if he would follow. He followed. I turned east on Pico before I reasoned it to be the right move. If I waited to turn west I could have got stuck waiting to make a left hand turn through four lanes of traffic. Although that could have worked to my benefit if he got stuck while I slipped through, if we both got through we would be headed toward what Chris and I considered home. Something about a man in a ski mask knowing on what dark street by a park you slept at most nights in a big white van with a tire strapped to the roof seemed less than prudent. All of those things crossed my mind but only after I had been driving east for two blocks. As I passed the Unurban I accelerated through the intersection just in time to make the light. The celebration died before we could start it because ski-mask boy simply blew another red.

By this time I had caught Chris up.

"Is he still there?"

"He's two cars back."

"He is a serious fellow."

"He must have been watching those kids."

"So we basically walked into the middle of some gangland initiation."

"Pretty much."

Traffic got thick as we sat under the freeway. The ski mask changed lanes in an attempt to come up on our passenger side. For a moment he had the room but then a car moved in next to us from the far lane. In that brief instant I almost pulled into the on coming lane because I'd be dammed if I was gonna sit there for him to throw bullets at us. His lane backed up but he managed to slip in behind us. Traffic loosened up enough to get out from under the freeway, which relieved me a little; MEN IN VAN GET SHOT BENEATH OVERPASS, seemed like very viable scenario. Chris started shouting out his window to people on the street corners or with their windows rolled down when we were going slow enough to be heard and answered, asking where the nearest police station was located. We had gone a couple of miles when I saw our man pull a u-turn. I turned right at the next main artery and encouraged the van to gain me distance. My heart remained swollen in my chest afraid to let go of the fear that had kept me aware to keep us alive.

"He's still not there," Chris said to me with his eyes focused on his side mirror.

"I don't see him either."

Our eyes met with a communal, "Well what the fuck do ya think of all this," that bled into a careful laughter. I continued to head south until Washington Blvd. and then proceeded to turn west toward our neck of the woods. I don't think that either of us would stop checking our mirrors for the next month let alone the rest of that night. When Washington found Lincoln I took a right and headed north.

"I'm not sleeping by the park." Chris allowed absolutely no room for discussion.

The park, at least in my mind as we were defining our existence in Santa Monica, was the place that best fit our needs for sleeping. It was dark, unassuming, and at the eastern tip across the street was an electric company power station. The goal to me was to not be parked in front of someone's house. The bathrooms in the park stayed open past eight so that was an added bonus. Up until the ski mask event we tried to sleep by the park as much as possible. A couple of drunken nights were spent in the northwest corner of Albertsons parking lot because of the twenty-four hour bathroom access. On some nights we would start off at the park but around three or four in the morning I'd hear Chris bumping about trying to get out of the back without shitting his pants so he could drive over to Albertson's. That whole period was short lived but I do remember carefully stumbling about Chris' limbs, making my way to the back door, moving the curtain, getting smoother at easing myself out on to the ground and standing by the twenty foot plus fence that held the ball fields to piss. The quiet dark stayed dark but the water streamed out of me through the fence on to the grass with a hollow wet drilling that, despite the absorbing earth, seemed to echo to all ends of the park while retaining the intimacy of having only one human being there to listen.

The first thing I did on arriving at Albertsons after our adventure was take the tire off the roof. The white van had a better chance of melting into being one of countless white vans roaming about void of the calling-card-tire standing up for all to see, advertising, "Yep, that's right; it's us. Put on yer ski masks boys, it's open season on traveling musicians." (Of course I still had Illinois plates.) Secondly I called the Unurban to explain our absence. I had two numbers to call and got machines on both. I did all I could and knowing bar owners and bookers the way I did assumed that it wouldn't be enough. I heard from Steve later that Lee thought we made the whole story up. Can I get a whatever!?

In my active imagination, somewhere in a back alley garage, a basement cellar, or in the bowels of an old abandon warehouse a group of young Latinos (I didn't mention they were Latino kids but they were) vowed their revenge on the two fat gringos in the white whale; we were their Moby Dick. I had terrible dreams all through the night depicting the van as a fort under siege. In everyone I committed an act of cowardice to rival my worst opinion of myself. One had me leaving Chris behind somehow. Even the next day the dreams were a cloud smoldering in piles of rubble leaving a single remnant of what my psyche had been saying about me behind my back. Today the dreams are further gone then the days themselves could number. In bed that night before sleep for the sleep was a long time coming, Chris and I both revealed how the thought of leaving Santa Monica that very night crossed our minds. No, the thought was never seriously considered by either one of us, but yes, I felt that scared, that alone. I saw myself as an exposed nerve, raw and vulnerable. I barely noticed that car blowing the first red light; it could have all gone so many different ways; I could have gotten out of the van before noticing the gun; we could have gone inside to the Unurban five minutes earlier and avoided the whole thing. But the remnant that ruled each dream was not what happened during the events, it was how shaken it had left me, and how quickly the thought of running home to Chicago popped into my head. I don't think I voiced to Chris just how badly I wanted be able to go. I knew it not to be an option, and I knew that I could not put the words in the right order in my head to convince myself, let alone to rise out with a voice to speak them. What bothered me most was how long and hard I searched to find the words. It always amazes me how quickly things get processed in the mind in comparison to the ticking of a clock. I battled life and death, intellectualized pros and cons, stretched every rationalization beyond their workable capacity, and scoured the bottom of my philosophical soul in search of a loop-hole all in the matter of moments, maybe minutes, maybe seconds. T.S. Eliot saw through time and when I go into the mind I start to see his point.

The one compromise we made was that we were not going anywhere near the Unurban for a while, at least not in our van. We did try to sleep by the park again but when he heard a group of teens burning rubber around the parking lot Chris announced, "On weekends we sleep at Albertsons." Weekends became weekdays the very next week and home had been claimed.

I wouldn't say that a welcome mat was thrown out in our honor but their acceptance held grace as their humanity took a stand. Some of the younger clerks, part timers who worked after school, I'm fairly certain shared jokes at our expense but to our faces offered friendly smiles. We helped our cause by buying all our groceries there. Chris and I tried to stay away until the evening hours mounted but as the sun started falling earlier we found that increasingly difficult. Following the second set at the promenade we would shop and head over to the park to cook. If we didn't cook we'd go to George's diner, or McDonalds, or whatever, and then go the park with the intention of staying there until eight or so. As Christmas neared the park got quieter sooner because the soccer season was over and it'd be months before baseball started up again so the bathrooms got closed up considerably earlier. It got to the point that if the sun was down we'd head over to Albertson's.

We weren't the only ones to park and sleep there but the others would come only three or four nights a week and not get there until nine in the evening the earliest. Chris and I went out of our way to be good neighbors by putting stray carts away on our way in and out of the store, adjusting the unevenly stacked baskets while we waited in line; the little things. One time Chris saw some guy pouring liter fluid on the hood of a car and lighting it, so he told someone at the service desk and they called the police. Another time on his way out of the store well past midnight one of the cashiers asked if Chris wouldn't mind accompanying a customer to their car. Home is where they let you park your van.

Keeping up on writing letters home and to Aubrey didn't suffer the first six months to a year. Once a week one of us usually got off something to someone for a while. My letters to Aubrey were, in the most well-meaning way, self-serving. I expressed guilt over having left but backpedaled just enough slip in how offers were given and choices made. I went on and on about how anytime she wanted to yell at me I would listen without argument and take my lumps. Oh, how fucking gracious of me—I'm a goddamm prince. It all came from a good place. What I wanted most, given the situation, was to make her feel as connected to me as I could; I'm not there but talk if ya need to talk and scream if ya need to scream; let's just not let the years pile up and fall away without knowing each other. Along with the art of writing letters I did buy phone cards and early on worked a deal with Steve that I would use his phone and give him a twenty at the end of each month. He'd keep track to let me know if all that turned out equitable. That arrangement came and went throughout the first year as needed. Catching her on the phone the first year or so wasn't as consistent as it would become. We worked with what we had and God knows I would've had more money for phone cards if I didn't spend so much on booze and such. But I did manage to call every ten days or less—catching her at home was the hard part.

To the folks, Chris and I sent tales from the road, snapshots of words for which to offer a slice of our life. They returned the favor and together we ventured to be the good company on the page that we enjoyed so very much whenever in the others company we found ourselves to be.

I don't remember exactly when I formulated a way for the folks to call me but I know that it happened on the promenade. Countless of times I'd be sitting around waiting to play and a pay phone would start ringing. On one occasion it rang on unanswered, others it got picked up mid-first ring, and others still you could hear panicked steps race from the center square to heed the call. One day it hit me all at once: I get the numbers off pay phones from selected areas, like the promenade, Albertsons, George's diner, and give them to the folks along with a name that is code for a specific number. Then I call collect from a phone, give the operator the name that represents the phone I'm on and the folks will hear the name, know where I'm calling from, refuse the charges and call me back. Not all of the phones I tried received incoming calls, so trial and error ensued until I had a couple of phones on the promenade, one by the showers and another at Albertson's.

I didn't write Angel because I was able to call her on a one eight hundred number at work. We talked a few times a week for a while and that would dwindle down to once a week and then less—by the second year hardly at all.

So that was the framework of our life: Wake up at Albertson's; hit the showers, stop by the park; go to the promenade to play two sets; get something to eat, hang by the park until it's time to park for the night at Albertson's. Meshed within all that were days of drinking before going to the movies instead of playing or parking near Venice beach to walk amongst our partners in societal drop out. I don't want to gloss over the drinking nor do I want to beat it to death. In our time out here Chris and I have had few good stretches that lasted forty-days plus, once over fifty, but for the most part we averaged twice a week maybe more. We've hit pockets of five-day binges and others where we only fell twice a month. The thing is that it was, and always would be, an issue, a constant battle, full of victory through compromise, and abject surrender.

In the beginning getting weed was not something we could count on. The small time dealers that hung on the promenade and around the nearby bluffs of Palisades Park were weary of new faces; their faces changed all the time too so it got hard to find some who'd trust you. I met a few guys that knew me, one from the Unurban another who played on the boardwalk in Venice, that trusted me but only sold minimums of eighths for sixty bucks. I was, except on one or two rare occasions of extravagance, relegated to the shoes of a nickel and dime man. Five bucks would compliment a nights drinking and in some cases ease the withdrawal of the next day or fuel more drinking and another nickel. I had something Serpico about me that took dealers a long time to let go of and sell me my fix. No matter how many times they saw me playing on the streets, or showering amongst the large-cocked homeless, they thought I was a cop. I am an authoritative kind of guy apparently.

In this early period Chris discovered the true drug aspect of cigarettes. One night, grumbling as he drunkenly lumbered from the Albertsons' bathroom cursing another night of alcohol void of the sweet bud of our youth, his eye got drawn to the ashtray stand outside the entrance. The butts ranged from thumbnails to those that had barely a few puffs dragged. I think his first thought had to do with satisfying the oral fixation. I was laid out in my bed when Chris arrived very much in the middle of his experiment. His focus drew me from my stupor just enough to sense, not the essence of the quest, but that indeed a quest was afoot. I rolled my hefty bulk to gather myself above elbows while trying to stretch the sleepiness from my lids and shake off the otherworldly state that one starts out seeking in distilled grains. Stopher sought out a lighter and laid out butts arranged by size. There were three or four which indicated the seriousness of his commitment to the experiment. Through the haze of my sleepy, drunken distance I slowly grasped the facts before me but without really understanding of what they told.

We did a lot of self-indulgent, destructive things to our bodies but cigarettes never once held an appeal to either of us. When I was eleven I smoked one from a pack my friend Jerry had stolen out of his Mom's pantry and I absolutely hated it to the core. Since then I may have had a drag at a party to make fun of who ever the cigarette belonged to but it held zero appeal. Well, I had a couple of girlfriends who smoked, and I have to say that tasting the smoke on their breath when we kissed did something for me. Other than that cigarettes remained the one vice never to grip me.

Chris picked up a half-smoked cancer stick and got out of the van. I lost, momentarily, the battle to stay with the chain of events. The sleep conspired with the booze drifting me into limbo; awake but not there. In my absent place the smell of burning nicotine wafted around my senses, changing the ambience of my concocted reality. It was one of those moments when the content of your mood changed before becoming aware that a physical influence had dealt you that hand. My elbows collapsed and had already swallowed my head when the distasteful aroma came creeping. I tossed without getting away, I turned to still be found and finally returned to the van, and the realization that someone was smoking a cigarette.

The passenger door opened and Chris climbed in with his usual drawn out motions and hitches that were both a necessity to his accomplishing the feat and servant to his O.C.D.

"Who's smoking?" asked the comatose.

Stopher's head hung from his neck without speaking. It rose briefly and intimated at turning my way, then bobbed forward once again.

"Wh-"

"Me," he huffed.

"Oh," I said. "That's funny."

I fell asleep and had a dream of Stopher on a steamboat rolling down the Ole Mississippi dressed like James Garner in Maverick, playing cards with a cigarette dancing in his mouth.

The next morning Chris drove us to the showers as I bounced in bed. When he killed the engine I let the silence speak first.

"Did I dream you smoking a cigarette?"

"No, this is the dream; you're still back in the cell."

"Fell off near Brighton," I Pithered my Python response.

"Yeah, and I'm telling you it was great."

Chris went on to tell me how he discovered the heroin in tobacco. According to his theory, he believed that with the right mount of alcohol, combined with the lack of tolerance by virtue of not being a real smoker, one could go from drunk to seriously drugged in a couple of puffs. I remained uninterested. I don't know how long it took for me to succumb and test the theory but I know why. The next few times we drank I witnessed the transformation. I heard his brain go, slumk, to the back of his head. I know what it is to have your eyes roll away from the world, finding more appeasement in viewing the underbelly of where the forehead engages your skull, than watching the meanderings of hominids so agreeable with the institutional format on their plate, prance and lollygag their way through life outside my van.

"Okay, then," I said one night, "let us go get some cancer."

For a month we'd scout the ground and eye the ashtrays when we were drinking, or had decided that drinking would be the evening's primary activity. On the nights we got a hold of some weed we either had no tobacco puffs at all or only a few. The day we actually bought a pack of Pall Malls, my grandpa's and Kurt Vonnegut's brand, I saw a line get drawn in the sand and stepped over. I never once considered or even remotely craved a cigarette when sober. In fact the hangovers took on a whole new nauseous turn from the tobacco. The smell of someone smoking had always bothered me in the past but now it crawled up in me, wrapped up my intestines and tried pull them up through my throat where my mouth could taste it, feel it surge but not evoke or swallow.

The whole affair may have lasted three months but I think less. Whether Chris and I had established a more reliable relationship with local merchants of our preferred substance or not (oh, we did) the smoking of tobacco would have stopped. It was not us. But Chris, ever the buzz-chemist was right on the money with his conclusions. On those nights, we drank to where the drink could take us, and with the balance of a walker on wire, the precision that is a technician, and the inspiration of an artist, we inhaled our demise until the substances tangoed their way over our frontal lobes.

CHAPTER EIGHT

Our first visitor was cousin Aaron and his girlfriend Laura, an independent filmmaker who came up through the ranks of the Sundance Film institutes' workshops making some L.A. connections. Aaron is one of the east coast Jungels who formed a dance troupe with my aunt Dorothy. He had a roof over his head but if anyone was living as close to the bone as Chris and I were, Aaron would credit a mention. Aside from the government grants that the dance company received for working with inner city kids, they would also get booked in art houses on the east coast and sometimes further across the country. Aaron also did some handy work around the building he lived to help pay his rent.

While Laura was in meetings Aaron spent a day in our world. It was a short visit but good to see him and be seen in our new life by someone who had played a part in the old. During the day we hung around the park and shot some hoops. Chris and I, as part of our half-assed attempt to get into shape, had started shooting games of horse with the occasional game of one on one. Chris, ever the better shot, would always kick my ass in horse unless I piled on with trick shots that involved actual physical moves. I tended to stay away from shots that made him jump so he won most of the time. In one-on-one I won most games because as terrible as the state of my health and shape had come to be, I moved with the grace of a deer compared to Stopher. Now Aaron has always been in great shape. He wrestled in high school and then got heavy into modern dance, which the way the Jungels go at it is extremely demanding physically.

I say all this to set up the one-on-one game I had with Aaron. It came to be the great victory of which only Chris and myself saw the beauty.

Aaron's older brother Mark would laugh at my pride because Aaron could shoot a ball off a boat in the middle of the ocean and it'd stay dry. My Mom patronizingly soothed me, her subtext clearly indicating that Aaron, being the perfect male specimen that he is, would have won had he tried.

I was a jock and for all my fat, tormented joints and organs, my heart still beat strong enough for me to remember that I love to play. As bad a shot as Aaron had, if he got close often he'd lay the ball in sooner or later. We weren't out for blood but both played competitively in one sport or another throughout our lives and got off on the challenge of playing the moment better than the other guy. I started out by hitting a few from the outside. When he tightened up I drove. Aaron tried to back me up so I put my fat up against his muscle to make him work for it. We played up to eleven but it took a while because not only did he have a weak shot but we both poured on the defense. No it was not a clinic in the grace of the game but it was a testament to sheer effort and will. When Chris and I played it was understood that we'd take it easy. Aaron and I slashed and bruised our way to the last shot made.

What Chris saw is what I felt: We can take a punch; once our hearts are in something, that something becomes us along with the best and worse of what we entail. I don't mean to make more of the game than I should. I was at the beginning of a long haul and I had always had a kind of inferiority complex with the Jungels kids. They were all tall, fit, smart, talented and gorgeous while us Smiths—though definitely attractive and talented (to me)—in the eyes of the outside world we would always be out shined or overshadowed by them. It wasn't something that haunted me or even bothered me all that much. They were sweet, wonderful people who were always glad to see me. I guess it comes to this: Despite how wonderful I think I am, as I get older the role of loveable loser fits me more and more. (Loveable and occasionally viciously bitter loser, depending on the day.) I am a better basketball player than Aaron and I should beat him. But that is not what people get from the visual of us facing off at the top of the key.

Aaron and I had a great time laughing at each other and ourselves while playing hard. When the game ended he looked as tired as I felt and that was enough of a victory for me right there. I could see Chris' pride; I won one for the fat guys.

Later on we parked by the ocean in Venice and caught the sunset. I have a picture of Aaron and I laughing with a postcard sky at our backs, and from our smiles you can feel the genuineness of the moment. I liked who I looked like standing next to him. We were family in blood but there was something more to it, and I would experience that feeling a few months later when his brother Mark was in town on business—we were family in life.

That night we took Aaron with us over to the Unurban on a writer's night. This was before the ski-mask incident. Chris and I drank cheap vodka from plastic Albertsons' water bottles and Aaron had a few beers. He seemed at peace with the evening but I sensed that he'd rather be with Laura. When I look back on his visit I think of how I was beginning the process of getting to where Aaron already was on that night. He had carved out the place he wanted to be, what he wanted to do there, and whom he wanted to do it with. I'm sure he has the doubt we all have, the anger we all harbor, but he seems to indulge it less than the rest of us. I began the process but it is like the weather, sometimes it rains; sometimes it shines.

Eric arrived in California just before Thanksgiving. Back in Philadelphia he had slowly rebuilt himself into a less broken man. He worked a meaningless job, fell for a girl who only fell so far, dabbled in community-theater, then decided he wanted to try living somewhere else. Acting was one reason he chose California, but I think it had more to do with the weather and having friends there who would take his side. Music, who had been his dearest friend and fiercest foe, came with him but they spoke less and only, for the most part, played at parties. (I am being cute of course.) While in Philly he barely touched his guitar and stopped writing altogether. In the company of Steve, Chris and myself he played but it took another year for him to more freely release himself to his love of guitar.

As far as acting, he did get a bit part in a play that was directed by Steve's friend Jessica. He had no lines but looked natural up there. Eric took some classes but didn't stick with it because that's Eric. No matter what anyone does there will be huge downsides: The people you have to endure, poverty, in-house politics, giving your time and emotions to a specific thing that you don't believe in to get closer to what you do. I have issues with institutions. I have my vision, compromises I found myself unable to make, and others I couldn't get around—enter poverty. That was my major concession among a few miscellaneous ones. Eric would never take the leap Chris and I did nor could he succumb to the alternatives. In the world of art, like any other world, something has to give. More often or not that something is you. Eric ended up getting an office job, renting a room, and doing his best to make the utmost of every second of free time. He always liked to hike and there were ample places for him to discover in the area. Either way it was good to have him around.

Our first Thanksgiving in Santa Monica was spent in Marine Park with Eric. I made my cayenne chicken while we chatted away as we are apt to do.

"What do you do for bathrooms?" Eric would spend the next few years trying to wrap his brain around our life.

"There is always a bathroom somewhere." I said.

"But in the middle of the night?"

"Albertsons is open twenty-four hours a day." Chris took a swig from his vodka.

"What if they kick you out?"

"Why, have you heard something?" I mocked concern.

"Seriously. You know they won't let you stay there forever."

I should have thought that, and deep down I knew it, but like with death my present peace of mind was better served by not pondering it too long; I took a swig from my vodka.

"There is always a twenty-four hour place somewhere. Worst-case scenario me and Chris would just have to eat earlier and not quite so hardily. Obviously taking a piss isn't a problem anywhere we park."

"We should be eating less anyway so maybe getting kicked out would be a good thing." Chris took another swig.

"Doctor perspective has arrived," Eric laughed in concession. "Well I'm just amazed. You are better men than I."

"We're better than a lot of men." I took another swig.
"Have you any insecurities?"
"My weight and women."
"Ahh, the women," Eric sighed. "They are an elusive bunch."
"They're soft." Chris took a swig.
"Soft." I took a swig.

A pause settled among us to give our thoughts time to themselves.

"I remember once when I was in the cafeteria at high school and it finally became too much for me," Eric said. "The women; their curves, their smells-"

"Their softness," Chris and I chimed.

"Their softness, and they are everywhere. It all became too fucking much so I jumped up on to the table and shouted, 'All right, God, I promise to procreate. Just give me a moments peace'. There were a few laughs, some applause, but I was mostly ignored."

"To be fair to God, you never did reproduce and if I'm not mistaken, you have no interest in doing so. You, my friend, lied to God," I said.

"Ahh, but he never gave me the much sought after moment of peace."

"He's got the big guy there." Chris declared.

"Okay," I yielded begrudgingly, "technically. But between us who actually exist, Eric, you were never gonna have kids."

"Probably not, but God didn't know that."

"God knows everything," I countered. "He knew you was fibbing."

"Does he also know that he doesn't exist?" Chris inquired wryly.

"Before anyone." I pouted smugly.

"You're an atheists with the logic of a born again Christian," Eric observed.

"Mind-boggling ain't it."

The cool of the day grew a few teeth by the time dinner was served. A better meal in the park could not be imagined. I didn't miss the turkey, stuffing or the mashed potatoes and gravy. I missed the family back home but this was our Thanksgiving and we were grateful for the food, the company, and the feeling that our lives really did belong to us. Freedom is a relative concept. I was free from direct institutional confinement but their shadows remained a watchful eye on my movement. The one institution that did still reign supreme over all I did was the institution that is me. I had traveled all those miles, and all the back roads the country could muster would not provide me with enough twists and turns to lose all that I found wrong with who I was. Chris and I wrote letters home talking of the efforts we put forth to eat better, drink less and exercise more regularly. The work involved with getting us to and from the promenade and the four hours we played there became very consistent, and that was a world of difference in activity for us, particularly for Chris. I at least had days working in the warehouse when there were no deliveries to be made. The drinking and eating…I guess we did better with it. At least it was just booze and weed now.

"You are out of that dark basement walking in the sunlit world," Dad would say over the phone. "That alone makes it a healthier way to live. My guess is that you are playing more music than you have in years."

The old man has never struck me as a cheerleader but he has never seen the point in leaving the good in something go uncherished either.

I did feel good about the direction we were going but I couldn't stop needing. Desire has pushed to me to create words with and without music while also creating a need (an overtly misused word I know, and here it is so again) that I have never been able to satisfy beyond a handful of moments in time; each moment of satisfaction births more need. Food and alcohol only ask that you purchase them. They are not love but they deaden the emptiness of love unfulfilled. When my marriage ended I had set aside romantic love in my mind. I had been so blessed already where love was concerned that I had come to believe that maybe I had caught my limit. My parents are very specific, enlightened people. Growing up and beyond I never met anyone with as good a relationship with their parents as I had with mine. They are the only people I know who beam with pride about two sons living in a van. One could argue that as a flaw in their parenting. Instead of going into an in-depth analysis of why that is a crock of shit, let me cut to the chase by saying: Eat a sandwich, and fuck off and die.

I don't mean to suggest that I think that they are perfect there by implying that I have been raised to be perfect. We are, they and their offspring, as flawed and fragile as any other except for having a solid grasp of our collective and individual humanity. I am a greedy, gluttonous, self-indulgent, self-destructive baby prone to volatile displays of righteous rage. I don't know where all this need came from. I do know that it has pushed me to perform and work towards being a great songwriter.

On that Thanksgiving I didn't think much about my shortcomings. I would eat, drink and be merry.

I love to cook for people; I am my mother's son. Mom keeps telling me how she is done being in the kitchen. Maybe she has hated cooking for her family but she always did it with such care that my eyes translated it into love. Last time I called home Dad said that Mom couldn't come to the phone because she was cooking for the grand kids. I am sure she is tired of it but whether she ever loved cooking or saw it as her duty, what came to the table was lovely.

I love to cook for people so when Steve asked me if I'd make pizza, my specialty, for a party his friend Jessica, the stage director, was throwing I said sure. I had brought some of my pans, a rolling pin and cutter along when I left Chicago in case a pizza emergency broke out. Cooking for family had been the impetus for my affection toward the task but as I got better it became a craft, then an art form, and from that it grew into another venue for performing. (I am an ego driven guy.) That being said, it all does start with the love of the act; the intimate action of putting things together combining what you've been taught with the inspiration of your own sensibility.

Of course Steve, Eric and Chris were there, as they would always find a way to be whenever I made pizza, all the others in attendance where theater and musician types. It was nice to be among them hearing their stories of auditions from hell, or how excited they were about the part they just got. The evening was centered on watching a video of a play Jessica had directed, which Steve shot, and a short film that Jessica's downstairs neighbor had made, which Steve did the sound for.

(Steve did a little of everything.) Most of the goings on took place in the living room while I toiled away in the kitchen, eavesdropping on the conversations, and looking in over the counter or from the doorway when I could. The obligatory, "Hey, get out of the kitchen and come join us," was hurled from the other room but when I make pizza I only know how to make a lot. Once the factory picks up steam it has to keep on rolling until all the dough is flattened, in a greased pan topped with the last shred of cheese, and in the oven. The tomato sauce is never a concern because it last forever without spoiling, even in the van, and can be used on anything from a sandwich to rice, or just drank down straight as Chris has been prone to do. There has never once been a left over topping—not on my watch.

There were a few actors who worked on KITTY HAWK at the party and Steve wanted to set it up where I got to sing a few songs so they could hear what I was all about. It never happened as the night went its own way, and that was fine with me. As much as cooking food connects me to the center of a gathering, like performing, I feel distant from the crowd. As the food gets consumed people ooh and ahh their compliments or ask about how I do it with untamed fascination while offering tales of their own gourmet coos; then like turning to another television show they move on to the next topic. It is all very organic and I'm happy when the attention has shifted. It's the same with playing a song; I'm starved to be loved only to be embarrassed by praise.

As Christmas approached I was asked to make pizza at Sukey's. I eagerly accepted thinking that cooking for a large group on the holiday would help me think less about being away from home. Angel had already planned to be in town for that week so things were looking up: I had Chris for family, Steve and Eric for friends, Angel a friend for sex, and cooking a big meal for us all on Christmas.

Angel arrived a few days before Christmas and rented a room at a local motel. I felt guilty sleeping in a bed that night with Chris in the van but I did it anyway. It was good see her and I definitely enjoyed the sex, but felt unsettled. When we started up I explained that I'd be leaving, that it would be a fling. I sensed her getting attached to me and I too had formed some affection. I was not all that attracted to her.

She was a short fleshy girl with long, frizzy, brown hair and a nose that had been broken as a child and never healed quite right. She did have a friendly smile, full lips and, as she was fond of pointing out, a big rack. Don't get me wrong, I was lucky to have her be attracted to my three hundred pound bulk, alcohol soaked liver, and I knew it. Her eyes were like a pair of brown beach balls, and they said, Look at me. They were the pretty eyes of a little girl in a women of twenty-three. I point out the physical because it was there but it was more than the physical. Angel was a good kid whom even if she had lived as many years as I did would have seen them very differently. I did enjoy her company in limited time frames. That's how we did it in Chicago, a few quick moments around the work place, half of the weekends in a motel, sometimes a little more, and sometimes not at all.

I was in the middle of redefining my whole life and every time I called her on the phone over the distance she talked like a girlfriend. She listened well enough, and had concern for my well being, but there were moments when I swore we were in the middle of different conversations.

Anyway, she came and it was good to see her. Angel fit in all right with the boys. She had the same affinity for parody songs as Steve; they both loved weird Al. Eric found her a bit abrasive but then Eric can be a bit soft. We had a good old fashion Nashville round where we'd take turns singing a song while the rest followed along in whatever way they could. Angel, who trained in opera, sang along on the few she knew but spent most of the time filling in the beat with a sneer drum. She did a hell of a job on that actually.

On her second day she and I walked over to the Albertsons lot to meet up with Stopher. The plan was to show her a day in the life on the promenade. The van had in the recent weeks showed signs of having the water pump going—an occasional engine rumbling. The good news—it wasn't the water pump. The bad news—the timing chain went. Luckily it went after the van backed up about two feet out of the parking spot. Of course when the van's engine sputtered not to be restarted, we had no positive notion other than our guess at the water pump. Our guess was based on a previous sound made by a previous car in a previous state when we were living a previous life.

I had a triple A gold card, YES! Sometimes I do practical things.

The tow truck came and the driver went through his usual check list to make sure we weren't just idiots who forgot to put gas in the tank, oil in the motor, or oxygen in our brains. I had yet to establish a relationship with a local mechanic so the driver recommended someone that was on a triple A approved list.

The bad news—the chain would cost just over a thousand dollars. The good news—I had it.

For two nights Chris got to sleep in a motel and I didn't have to feel guilty.

The bank took a hard hit from the timing chain, which wasn't helped by the two nights in a motel for Chris, or the fact that we weren't playing much because of the van going down and the holidays. I'm sure all of that had an effect on me at the time but it's not what comes to mind when I think about that Christmas. Angel being there corralled me into being a host, a boyfriend. I had guilt over being a bad father; I was a son who missed his Mommy; an adventurer who set aside both only to be in a position of concern with the social amusement of a girl whom, no matter how well I thought of, meant nothing to me by comparison to those I neglected.

On Christmas Eve Steve and Burpo had organized a musical get together at the Unurban for those with nowhere else to go. It would have been the perfect, if not antidote, then combatant for the unsettling stir of emotions that groped at my breath, tugging words back down my throat until I lost their intentions inside the hole expanding within.

"You know I love the guys," Angel said, unaware of the sword she wielded. "Last night was fun and tomorrow will all be together at Sukey's; tonight will be for us."

She flew all this way to see me, bought Chris and I a couple of meals, had been good company, and gave me sex. I never wanted her to come, I quit being responsible to others—just ask Aubrey. She had no idea what any of this was to me, not a clue as to the gamble I had made with my life; she was on vacation. Angel couldn't have been happier to spend a Christmas away from her family. She was twenty-three with no one counting on her for anything. She worked her job well, saved money, and would never gamble on a dream. Angel wanted to be in radio but the thought of working for nothing until she paid her dues, and all the uncertainty of any pay-off at all sent her running to hide behind a desk with one drawer for her pay check and the other for her health benefits, and still another holding a 401k. None of this was her fault: her coming to see me; the squirrelly wrench in my gut; or wanting to spend one complete evening alone with me. The only answer would have been to tell her not to come when she mentioned it on the phone in late November. Of course she never asked; she assumed I'd be grateful; she thought I was her boyfriend. It was good to see her, and we did have a good time despite the inner rumblings that would have tormented me whether she was there or not.

    Chris had this big lime green sweater knitted by our Chicago friend Steve's mother. It hung on him like holy a cartoon emblem. Whenever he wore it ones eyes were drawn to it and faces could not suppress a smile. Put the sweater on anyone else something would have been lost. Chris' big pumpkin head and round, baby face covered in his strawberry blonde hair and whiskers, with his John Wayne/Steinbeck soul emanating his duel gruff/gentle loving disdain draped in a homemade glow-in-the-dark Christmas ornament was destined to create a legend. I don't know who said it first but it started out innocent enough.

    "My, that is a big green sweater."

    Then came the greeting when he entered a room with it on.

    "Hey, it's, Big Green Sweater."

    On that Christmas Eve the greeting became a chant, and the chant has echoed down through the years. There were a series of performers getting on and off the stage all night. Chris had already been up once blowing the crowd away. When he returned later in the evening the chant rose from the crowd.

    "BIG GREEN SWEATER, BIG GREEN SWEATER, BIG GREEN SWEATER!"

    I got the story second hand the next day. As much as I wanted to go the night before, as much as I knew that was where I needed to be that night, the next day the stories I heard—of which the big green sweater was the topper—not only confirmed my wishes as a kind of necessity, but also fed the emptiness whose true source ran deeper than any good story.

On Christmas day I made pizza. People wouldn't start arriving until three with dinner to be served at four so I had to get started by noon. The beginning of the dough is similar to that of laying the foundation of a building: Ingredients are mixed with water then observed by a solemn increment of time wherein the elements of nature converse void of human intrusion. Once these elements merge the hand of man plunges their fruits and things get all higgly-piggly. Flour settles like soot from a backed up chimney on the kitchen counters and floor; garlic sautés with basil and oregano in oil permeating the air; shards of onion skins trickle off a knife's blade while the seeds of green peppers sprinkle in and around the trash can; tomato sauce splatters on the stove and the surrounding walls as it engulfs the oiled spices. The kitchen is mine.

As people arrive they ask to be of help but I am a one-man show. Chris does play the prop man, although his service has been fulfilled once the show is well under way.

"Hey, Stoph, I need the soy sauce from the van."

"I'm ready for a drink."

"Stopher, I can't stand this can opener, can you bring me ours?"

And so on.

(For those who care, I use the soy sauce to help prevent the spices' flavor from being swallowed up the acidic nature of the whole tomatoes and paste.)

I started drinking a little earlier than I usually would at an affair such as this; usually waited for the prep-work do be done because that required the most thought, and because it would be a long day. I felt unusually thirsty. The fact that it was Christmas inspired a bit of my recklessness but that was the tip of the iceberg. There had been plenty of nights lying awake in the van after Chris had found sleep (up until that time in our life I pretty much always fell asleep before Chris) for me to attempt at coming to terms with my actions, and even more long-winded conversations in the light of day with Chris to exorcise my guilt.

All that had been achieved was pacification, a seduction to dormancy in a comfy corner for my guilt to rest quietly. Chris had his guilt too. Aubrey always said that she felt like she had two dads. But Chris' guilt was more on line with the guilt I suffered over Madison, which was no small torment yet more easily rationalized. The holiday was one thing but I had already missed her birthday, and Thanksgiving. It had more to with the collection of days mounting on days, the illustration of reality taking root and telling you in no uncertain terms what you have done. Plus I missed my Mommy and Daddy.

If I truly believed that what I was doing held no importance, had no bases in anything but pure folly, and that I had simply run away, I probably would have packed it in, or simply pled guilty to the crime and colored myself a selfish asshole with a hardy heartfelt wave goodbye to my self-respect. There would still be guilt but without the conflict. I did believe in what I was doing but that was of no comfort at the time. All those considerations filled my interior while the exterior beamed with a jovial relish: I cooked and drank; I laughed and sang, all with genuine zeal. I recall being aware of a forced nature in my tone, an intensity in the fiber of my movements, a kind of urgency in my humor. Although it wasn't until the next day looking back that I saw myself and made the connection of interior struggles to exterior actions.

I make no bones about my being a drunk. I make no apologies either. I am usually a well-behaved drunk; I don't knock things over, piss my pants, pass out on the living room floor, or pick fights. Eric has always marveled at how sober I appeared to be when drinking. I won't go so far as to say that I am the life of the party but I do my share of being entertaining, my wit remains sharp even as my words begin to slur. On that night I was a downright cliché. I don't think I could have talked louder if I had shouted, I constantly told Steve and Eric that I loved them as I tried to squeeze the life out of them with bear hugs, and grabbed their asses quite a bit (never did that with them before or since; "Paging Doctor Freud, paging Doctor Freud"). I did knock over a bottle here and there, but controlled my bladder and bowels while not starting a single fight.

Steve had been a bit offended by it, and Eric too was a tad annoyed after a while but they both humored me. Angel endured me with a few cross looks and rolled eyes. Fortunately for them I fell asleep during our traditional viewing of Bill Murray in SCROOGED, so they had the rest of the night free of my obnoxious prattle.

The next day I heard about it from all parties and smiled my acceptance of their friendly condemnation. My initial reaction was to feel stupid and be embarrassed. Underneath though I had an unsettling notion that something had been over looked by everyone. I was nagged by the fact that I had acted so out of character to such an extreme. When I saw clearly how much pain I was in and how it affected my behavior, I have to admit I was hurt. Eric and the rest had seen me drink a million times and I had never acted that way before. They know the facts of my life—we have had plenty of conversations about my guilt and the gamble that is my life. Not one them expressed any concern or even acknowledged that the previous night's display had been out of the ordinary. It was as if they perceived the whole affair as just another in a line of countless disreputable actions on my part. It is understandable that they could not see beneath the surface of the events, but I thought I had earned a little credibility in the area of being a professional and tolerable drunk. If I didn't drink a drop I could have easily made every bit the spectacle of myself, or even worse. Hell if I were sober I probably would have picked a fight. I eventually brought it up with Eric in a casual conversation weeks later. I was making a point in relation to something we were talking about, how narrow the scope of the average person's compassion is because of a knee-jerk dismissiveness.

"All anyone could see was that I was being an obnoxious drunk. No one took into account that I never acted out like that in the past. I was in terrible pain, and then had to apologize for it the next day."

"I did think your behavior unusual," Eric admitted. "But you are right, it never occurred to me that you might be upset."

"And that's my point: You are a good person, one of best I've ever met, and you dismissed me despite knowing better of me than my specific actions on a given night."

"I'm really sorry."

"It's not a big deal. I only bring it up because you were being so precious about some woman mistreating you. Which is actually bullshit because I have wanted to say something about it since the day after it happened. And still, it really isn't a big deal."

"So basically, we all suck."

"You are a bright lad."

New Years Eve Chris and I hung out at Steve's by ourselves. Steve had a gig and Eric a date. Steve left the key for us under the welcome mat as was becoming our routine. Of course we smoked weed and got drunk while watching a few of the live videos we brought from home. We had Stevie Ray Vaughn live from Japan; Billy Joel, just before the Stranger made him filthy rich; some old Bruce; Jackson Browne on Soundstage; and a little known act by the name of R&R CROSSING. It was just another night for talking about quitting drinking and losing weight, getting Chris' many scripts out into the community and being the guys we always wanted to be when we weren't busy being stuck who we were. At the midnight hour we stood outside the back door of Steve's studio by the edge of the swimming pool. The evening air spoke more of June than January to our Chicago senses, but we rolled with punches. There was a smatter of jubilation heard, a firework or two painting the sky, but nothing compared to the explosion of a side street in Chicago. In the biting air that seized Chicago's front walks and back alleys, children banged on pots and pans, adults whooped and hollered, and some over zealous drunk unloaded his twelve-gauge shotgun into a telephone pole. Standing by the pool inhaling the joint's reward, my mind's eye saw the pajamas of ten year olds rustling in the wind from under their unbuttoned winter coats as they shuffled in front of their houses in untied boots. The middle class down to the poverty line jumped on every calendar's offer to let the regular order slide. Dad had always found it unfortunate our need to elevate one day as more important than another.

Living in our van among the million dollar homes with swimming pools I understood their lack of desire to exalt one day over the next. Most of them sniffed their brandy, mildly saluted their daily privilege, and watched the fake fire glisten off their silicone breast. Soon I would be asleep in the van knowing that the next day I would have neither the security enjoyed by the rich nor be forced to carry the responsibility of the working class. I wouldn't even be playing on the promenade until next week when we picked up our new permit. Chris and I both knew that we had to stop spending the bank money. The promenade held enough to support our day-to-day existence; the bank had to be spared for emergency. The embryonic transition had come to an end; enough questions had been asked and answered.

Steele Smith was a tall lanky man in his forties with square but frail shoulders. His long ponytail belonged to the sixties, not to be confused with the short pretentious tails sported by the gimme, gimme sect of the oily suited eighties. His mustache and goatee were neatly kept, even dignified. He wore faded blue jeans, dull colored sweatshirts or a windbreaker over tee shirts and plaid colored, flannel button shirts. He had been graying for years but maintained as much pepper as salt. When he spoke, his tone, as casual as his dress, carried a confidence in his words that reflected an unforced authority. Steele had been a court reporter in Santa Monica for years so he had a solid working relationship with the beat officers. That was the main reason he had been offered the position of artist liaison for the promenade. The other being his even-tempered, mild manner, and the fact that he looked like he could relate to the artistic element. So the former hippie, ex-court reporter walked the line of authority and free speech holding hands on either side.
"Happy New Year," Steele greeted us.
"Well it's new, I'll give ya that," I begrudgingly conceded.
"Happiness awaits to be allowed," Steele returned.
"You're an up beat fellow," Chris observed.
"Someone got laid over the holidays."
"I was simply going for a philosophical optimism."
"Alright, just don't let it happen again," I warned.
"I've been hearing some good things about you two, but I'm guessing it hasn't translated into tips yet."

"Oh, we're getting by; we just need to quit drinking."
"You're playing the noon?"
"Yup."
"Okay, I've got you down." Steele started off then turned back. "It takes time for the regulars to warm up to you. The tourism will be down for a while, so until the spring you'll have to rely on the regulars, the people that live here. You've been here since October; they should be coming around soon."
"Thanks, man," Chris and I said in unison and equally weary.

"Hey, Chris and Dave," James Mitchell greeted us in his usual manner.
"Morning, James."
"Praise, God."
"How was your holiday?" I asked.
"Oh, my sister and her kids came to visit, and it looks like they'll be staying."
"How many kids?"
"Two girls, one in high school the other is just eight, and one boy who should be working for his own place."
"Well it is good of you to let them stay," Chris sympathized.
"Well, Chris and Dave, I prayed on it a whole lot."
"And ya let'em stay anyway," I joked.
James gave that soft chuckle of his that just as soon let the last word be a smile. "I best be getting to my spot."
"Good luck, James," Chris offered.
"Praise, God."

The Raven showed up a couple songs into our set. She was only ten minutes late for work—according to her time frame five minutes early. After getting her bag put away in the back, wiping down the empty tables and the menu display in front next to her perch, then adjusting the awning to her liking, she settled into her real task: Telling us what to play.

"I been here all of ten minutes and I don't believe you two no-goodnics have played me a lick of blues." She paused. "Chop, chop."

"You heard the lady, " I said to Chris.

Chris always took the lead vocal for the first hour leaving me the second.

"Well my baby told me to take one step at a time…" and so forth.

When we finished the Raven clapped and encouraged the few people sitting at her restaurant to clap as well. "What's that one about the Black something or other?"

"THE BLACK MESA," Chris told her.

"Yeah, play that one."

"Or?"

"Or else!"

"That's more like it," Chris said.

"Yeah," I agreed. "What's the point of being bossed around unless you throw in the threat of violence?"

"Oh, your points are less," she confirmed.

The afternoon sun weakened by the end of our set giving the air a chill.

"That's it for us, we are R&R CROSSING and we have to move on down the line," I spoke as if an audience actually had cared. "We tend to mosey when on lines we are moving but today in honor of the New Year, I think we shall saunter."

"How about some sashaying," the Raven shouted.

"Sashaying is really more of east coast thing, but never let it be said that R&R was one for turning down a request."

"That was no request." The Raven pounded a fist into her palm as her head bobbed to the beat.

"Okay, Knuckles, whatever you say." I mocked a shiver.

"Yeah, yeah, sure, Knuckles." Chris shook like Cagney himself gave the order. "We don't want no trouble, see. We'll sashay, we'll sashay all ya want."

"Okay then." She ran her sleeve up under her nose. "Get going. Nice and friendly like."

I finished packing up the gear while Chris grabbed a mic stand and guitar to go claim another spot. As I started off the Raven came over from her perch and assaulted the hair on my chin with a hefty tug.

"Good set."

"Thanks."

"Did that guy buy a CD? The old one with the cane."

"Yeah, we sold one to an old guy."

"You owe me a commission on that one."

"My dear, I owe you my life."

"No thanks, that decrepit bag of bones ain't worth the canvas you'll be buried in; I want cash. You going by the park after the next set?"

"Yeah."

"Maybe I'll come by."

I smiled; she tugged at my beard and returned to her perch. Walking away I flung my hips to and fro over elongated steps as her cackle followed me down the street.

Chris and I sat on our bench in the corner of the park, he keeping a watchful eye on the rice and me finishing off the last of the cutting. I waited until the vegetables softened to the heat of the tomato sauce before stirring in the paste. I added some more garlic and basil with a hint of oregano, then a few dashes of soy sauce, stirred again then covered it up to let the heat regain its momentum. Chris gave me a thumbs up on the rice and I slid the cubed chunks of London broil off the cutting board by the blade of my knife into the pot, stirred and covered for a twenty count. On twenty I mixed in the rice, covered for a thirty count, stirred—thirty count, stirred—ten count and turned the stove off. The pot immediately went into a doubled plastic bag, was tied, then covered by a third and placed in another double for carrying. We broke camp, loaded up the food, stove and tank into the van, cleaned the cutting board and utensils in the park bathroom, and retired to the van where we ogled the pot stewing in its plastic cocoon for at least ten minutes before eating. The early evenings were getting cooler so we ate in the park less and less. On top of that we realized the benefit of a lesser profile by getting in and out of the park as quickly as possible.

In doing this we found that the meat kept cooking once removed from the stove so it became quite the art form to achieve that perfectly pink texture without it being too chewy. I had always been a medium rare guy, Chris too, but we both developed a bloodier disposition as on one occasion we erred on the red side of our delicacy quest.

"Next time let's just show the meat a picture of a flame," I said.

"A low flame," Chris agreed.

Since that day the experiment to achieve the perfect balance ensued. Some men tilt windmills, others cross oceans; we sought meat at its rarest, while maintaining a modicum digestibility.

The batch on that day had been well played.

The Raven's face beamed through the windshield of her camper as she pulled into the parking lot. From our windshield across the street I could tell that she relished in being seen behind the wheel of, what she considered to be, chic ruggedness on wheels. She hopped out and bounced over the black top to our window.

"Howdy, boys."

"So that's home," I said.

"Nice little camper," said Chris.

"That is no ordinary camper; that is a genuine Phasar; domicile worthy only of the original Macho Princess."

"Indeed." What else could I say?

"Come on over and check her out."

The Raven waited for no answer, unaccustomed to being refused. I went to follow when I noticed Chris offered no interest.

"You coming? It is a genuine Phasar after all."

"I see it."

I paused with a puzzled face.

"She wants to show you."

I shrugged thinking that Chris, as usual, wrote in his own meaning over people's intentions. I climbed in the passenger door where I found her smile opening me up and shutting me down all at once. Beauty, in its purest form, has a way of defeating all attempts at explanation. Her hair fell down around her shoulders as her eyes narrowed in on mine giving me a sense of importance.

"This is control central. Note the space age dials, the sleek gearshift and luxurious captain chairs. I added the coin operated dash feature myself."

I looked on top of the dash in front of the driver's side and saw a metal coin slot sitting unattached. It had button for coin return and could have come from any kind of older model of machinery, from a washer or dryer to a candy dispenser, but appeared very much at home on her dash.

"I love old junk," she said, taking it into her hand and passing a coin through it.

I could tell that it was an older, heavy metal by the way her arm drooped as she held it. She it put back on the dash.

"Wanna see the back?"

"Sure."

The Raven pulled a curtain, stepped through and I followed. The path way was limited by the debris of her possessions: clothes were strewn on either side of us, a stack of three full size, glow in the dark, red/pinkish parking cones sat in front of the back bed which was covered with clothes and a few duffle bags. On the floor near a drain that I assumed was for the shower, laid a pile of rocks, some of which could have been classified as small boulders and a couple of twisted, knotted branches that were maroonish in color and over an inch thick.

"It's a mess but I manage," she said standing near the side exit door. "That's the shower." She pointed to what looked like a closet door opposite the side door. "It pulls out over the drain. Those two tables you're standing between fold out into another bed. It has a stove and sink under the rubble on this counter but I never use it."

Above and around the back bed and along both sides of the camper were cabinets, no doubt filled with useless clutter I began to suspect. It was then I saw the shame creep up on her excitement.

"It is all quite impressive."

The Raven's shoulders rose to frame her nodding head. "It is The Phasar."

"Not 'a' Phasar."

"No, 'THE' Phasar."

"I'd expect nothing less from you."

"Thanks."

She liked that.

We returned to control central and conversed about our previous lives. She talked about living with her last boyfriend, a marketing designer of some sort. I told her about my marriage, and we both were very much at ease with each other. We had goofed around on the promenade over the last few months, and she had come to the park a handful of times, but this was the most intimate our conversations had become. I had already told her that I was an alcoholic, divorced with a daughter and that my current existence was in the midst of a last desperate effort to salvage a shred of my torn and tattered dreams. Those concepts were so large and dressed in my best self-effacing humor that they obscured any real depth. Talking in her Phasar, we focused on the mundane things that, little by little, paint a bigger picture.

"When we started having our own blankets, I slept a lot better," I told her.

"What about the accidental sex?"

"Accidental what now?"

"Accidental sex! You know, you're both laying there all mingled every which way, and then one wakes up but only a little bit, then a hand tumbles unintentionally into a crevice of arousing tendencies, or breath steams into an ear; you know: Accidental sex."

"Okay, I hear ya. Like when you come back from the bathroom and trip and say. 'Oops, sorry dear; I fell on your cock.' Then you try to get off but it just gets harder, and the next thing you know, boom! You are having sex."

"Come on, you know what I mean."

"Yeah, I do. It does sound nice the way you put it. I guess I'm always wanting sex so it's never an accident."

I was taken with her ease, and how that put me at ease. As knockdown gorgeous as she was, romance didn't interfere because she was too beautiful, too hot. Three hundred pound men living in their vans tend not to attract women like the Raven. She liked Chris and me; she thought we were really talented; and that's all there was to it.

Because I knew I'd never have a shot at her, and she knew I knew, we got down to the business of simply enjoying each other's company. We both loved to play with words so that is what we did. Along the way information flowed and we liked who we were getting to know.

In some ways, a lot I guess, we were polar opposites. She was an only child who never knew her real father. Her mother married a couple times and they moved all over the country. She even lived in a Chicago suburb during the winter of '79. Always being the new kid forced her to be out going and make friends. One of the reasons she befriended the musicians on the promenade, besides loving music and art, was that they were usually from out of town and didn't know many people. She saw herself as an adoption agency of sorts.

I went back to the van and as I watched her drive away it had occurred to me that she didn't make a single comment about Stopher not coming over to see the Phasar.

The drinking continued as did the arguing, all the more so when we were drinking. Chris had in the past been an angry drunk, and though he had mellowed with age, any lingering issue he had suppressed under the influence of sobriety held the potential to boil over in a stewed state. I, as has been previously mentioned, was usually an easy going drunk. That being said and true, alcohol exposes any live wire and we all got'em. Also, when I'm good and drunk, especially with weed in my system, I become dense and slow. My brain is flying with words, thoughts and high concepts, but when delivering these to my mouth the train gets derailed. The transferring of facts in a conversation, whether it be intellectually lofty, or retracing the chain of events from that day, or simply moments ago, get muddy. I can be infuriating and annoying as hell. Then throw in the personal assaults that always enter the equation, drunk or sober, and the alcohol will intensify ones reaction. Intensification is what alcohol does best. You laugh hardier and shout louder. It also dulls the senses of proportion and perception. A fury of fists won't hurt a bit, but a single word can wound you to the core.

Of course a good deal of my favorite moments in life were, and are, when Stopher and I get good-n-smashed. Back in the basement we had turned our heads into crock-pots. The meat was the brain; the alcohol sauce; for spices we had weed, coke, mushrooms and acid. (There had been varied combinations.) It should be said that we never argued on coke or hallucinogenic no matter how much we drank. Well never is a big word, but if we did it had to be weak and short-lived. When you are that far gone your humility surrounds the ego and embodies all thought. We have argued under the influences of weed alone but let's face it, if you are high and yelling, then you are just plain fucking angry.

One January weekend we stumbled upon some acid. It turned out not to be that potent but it added a little something to the stew. The top of my scull did not get ripped off letting my brain pulse openly in the atmosphere, as I had been accustomed to, but it was a nice break in the reality. It was a Sunday so we were able to park on Broadway near fourth because the meters didn't have to be fed, and walked down to the shore near the pier. In the shadow of the fairest wheel and rollercoaster, within faded earshot of the crowds, and lightly scented reach of the hovering smells of spun sugar, various meats soaking in spicy grease and warm salted pretzels, we dug in for the day. Armed with water bottles, water bottles with vodka, a couple of joints and two acoustics, we set up camp by a wooden pole close to the shore. I remember a wire looping over the sand from an empty lifeguard house to a pole that sat just east of it, then from that pole to another further east still but then to no where else, and I couldn't imagine its purpose. The day, owned by a clear sky offering a warm sun, saw little traffic on the sand. A handful of scattered groups sat on blankets, even fewer ventured into the water. I left the Martin in the van in favor of the three hundred dollar lesser-named blue guitar that Joel had let me have for just this kind of outing; to be in the world playing and not worry about losing or doing damaged to my prized Martin. Chris had the Ovation, which I bought from Joel twenty years previously, and had served me well. The Strat and Martin were our livelihood, the others were for the woods around campfires, and drunken excursions on the beach.

We had dropped by the van knowing that whatever transpired from it would not do so for roughly an hour. Once settled on the beach we drank in earnest to encourage the chemical's bidding. A few songs got sung before the first tingle emerged.

"Let's smoke one to open'er up." Chris suggested.

"Let's."

The alcohol and weed danced in our brains swirling about the floor knowing the room well. The acid sat in the corner like wallflower unsure of its worth. When I felt my brain heating up and dumbing down I set the guitar aside; remembering lyrics and chord changes got in the way after a while. I asked Chris to stand guard on the camp, removed my socks and shoes, rolled up the cuff of my jeans, and headed down to the water.

With the cuffs of my jeans up around my knees I stood where the water could build its rhythm around me without swallowing me whole. The sun, although warm, did not beat on my skin, but instead caressed it with sensual, friendly hands. It was then that I felt something at work, and it was not the acid. The acid may have been working just enough to open me up to what the earth had to show, and in fact, I think I would have missed it otherwise, though one never really knows. It began with the whoosh of waves as they crumbled down around me like a beggar, pushing the water in and pulling it back out; water grabbing at the earth, giving and taking, pulsing and receding. My feet once a top the wet sand, slowly, in accordance with the rhythm of the ocean, sank; first only creeping over my toes then the feet and soon my ankles, until finally sucking around my shins grouping for the knees.

I had stood there for over an hour, sipping at my vodka, observing the surf and its intentions, on the way to revealing a single-minded purpose. The ocean interacting with the land was no coincidence, and it was more than conversing. It was the earth breathing. The moment of realization had been built up to so meticulously that I refused to deny its conclusion. I smiled, I laughed, I roared as I buckled. When that subsided I looked down to see my legs being sucked on by the earth, and roared again.

I knew that instant that this was something to be written about. Luckily I was in the middle of writing a play called, THE LINE. It chronicled a group of friends waiting in a line for two days to see

Frank Marino at the Aragon Ballroom in Chicago. Chris had been so productive cranking out screenplays that I felt I had to write something just to have anything to talk about. Every Monday and Tuesday he'd be in the library with the laptop Uncle Bob had given us. After a month or so of being shamed by him, I remembered that I had this idea for a play running around in my head for years. That coupled with the fact that, through Steve, I had a connection to the local theater scene made it seem like the perfect project to work on. I had even cooked pizza in the house of a working director. I gave my "earth breathing" bit to a character in the play in the form of a revealing speech about his place in the world, and it worked perfectly. God bless acid.

When I returned to where we had made our camp Chris was sitting up against the pole with a goofy, drunken smirk on his face.

"I discovered the earth breathing, what's your excuse."

He sat there as the smirk turned superior, and his shoulders raised his arms with open palms facing up. He dropped his arms looking around innocently while suggesting that I take a gander as well. I noticed some markings dug into the sand that surrounded the pole. There seemed to be a pattern of some kind.

"Is that supposed to be something?" I asked.

Chris climbed up on his feet and walked west of the pole, over the markings there, then about another twenty feet, stopped and turned around. I inferred that he desired to be followed, so I did. When I turned I saw his creation. Stopher had drawn a big face around the pole so that it looked like a cigar being smoked by the earth.

"You discovered it breathing; I got it to smoke."

"You created the illusion of it smoking."

"Okay, you win, but mine's funny looking."

"Agreed."

Chris then went in search of another pole to draw a face around. I sat by the original artwork with my back to the cigar and began strumming a few chords. I could see Chris due south digging his heel into the sand, backing methodically around the new cigar giggling to himself. I closed my eyes and sang a song I had written that had been inspired by hanging around Portage Park's playground in Chicago with Aubrey when she was two or three. It was called SPRINKLER'S CHILD—still is one of my favorites. There is a peace in the picking of the alternate roots as the melody cascades the lyrics down around them that no misery I feel at a given moment can out run. If I had to pick one of my songs over all others to be the one that the world would hear, on most days, it would be that one. The song ended with my eyes still closed as to protect the magic from vanishing for single moment longer. I closed my left palm over the fret board and slid it softly with an affectionate linger in tribute to the gift to myself I had just given.

"That was beautiful man," a young man's voice said. "Did you write that?"

I opened my eyes and shaded the sun to see his young face, his unwashed long, thin hair wrapped behind his heads in a ponytail tucked under some sort of knit Rastafarian hat, and not much else.

"I did."

He sat crossed-legged in front of me. "I'm James."

"I'm Dave."

We shook hands, he weakly, and I in customary, Irish fashion.

"I wanna write too. I can't play like you but I know I can write."

"I'm sure you can."

"How do you know what to say?"

I took a sip of my vodka and smiled, then took a bigger swallow. "Every song is different. Sometimes it's just a feeling that you follow until you figure out where you're going; others, it's an event you want to re-create, or a story you want to tell; or a person that you are talking to."

"Right, right."

I drank some vodka and thought about the next song I would sing to myself.

"Yeah, I have all these thoughts that I know would make a good song," he said wistfully. "The kind of songs that would help people, ya know? I just can't get started. I'm never sure what the first thing to say is."

"Trial and error. Just don't it; decide what's good later."

"My mind is so crowded," he began to sing. "So much to think about, so much to say. I-"

"Not here," I instructed, firmly while trying not to be hurtful. "Over there," I pointed toward the shore, "but not here."

His face turned wounded eyes falling to the sand.

"Hey, I'm just out on the beach, getting drunk and strumming a few chords to songs I already know. Creating is better left to solitude."

"I just thought maybe you could help."

"I ain't here to work, and when I do, I work alone."

"Sure, I understand." He smiled, at first limply then assuredly. "I just needed to make a connection."

"I do know the feeling but I'm not in that place."

"Cool." James got to his feet and walked off humming toward the shore.

I would see James on and off over the next few years and hear a little of his story. He was raised out east, didn't think much of his folks but loved his sister. After battling depression during his teens, at the age of twenty, he swallowed a double-edged razor. He spent time in an asylum, and when they let him go he was eligible for SSI, (Social Security Insurance) which paid him seven hundred dollars a month. Out west he discovered heroin, and spent more time shooting than writing. Nice guy though, usually good for an interesting conversation about life, and existence in general. James, at times, had the gift of self-awareness…a rare quality in those I'd come to meet.

I love being drunk. I hate waking up having been drunk unless I know that I'll be drunk again soon. Days gloss over themselves smiling, slurred by their own brilliance. Night lays in velvety contrast while retaining that friendly fluffy hue of forgiveness, even more so because the day is done. I usually don't see the sun as forgiveness but when the chemicals conspire, sunbeams relinquish their reticent, yet judgmental, glare, and all that they have been holding becomes empathetic; a soft glow, yielding certainty of joy. A binge becomes a symphony of watercolor over a thirsty canvas. Anyone on the outside would see only the sludge on glazed eyes, like cherries topping a sundae of man melting into a mesh of his weakest instincts. On the inside a voyage ensues that takes on a monumental importance towards soothing an aching soul. Sounds grand don't it? If it were a weekend or a month of a life, I would say it is the stuff of a great coming of age story, placed in the backdrop of a struggle towards defining one's self. In the context of my life it is simply another nail in the coffin. Pretty nail.

One Saturday night in the midst of a drinking frenzy, we discovered Albertsons closing at one in the morning because of construction. (No, they were not building a new store; money needed to move, and this was how some suit in a conference room deemed it be done. Corn would move to aisle twenty-one while the butcher remained in the southeast corner because exercise had been served by moving the corn.) We drank as if we meant it because we did. Before passing out Chris drove over to a twenty-four hour Jack-in-the-Box just south of Pico on Lincoln, and found a parking spot on Grant avenue in front of a closed bar across the street. Going straight to sleep would have been the smart thing to do but Chris had visions of tacos. Earlier in the evening we had fried chicken, so tacos seemed like the next logical step in testing the limits of our constitutions. Two for a dollar garnished us six tacos each. My eyes were slits upon a face that could have not been dopier looking if one had found a way to extract every point of I.Q. from my liquor soaked brain. I stumbled out of my boots and groped along side of the van until I found the back door. It took several long breathy sighs before mustering the strength to fall into the van, and crawl up to my bed. I fell asleep somewhere along the way because I don't remember my head hitting the pillow. The sleep was deep as death without a hint of a dream. No brain waves would have registered if someone had ventured to measure. It was good to be gone, shut down, wiped clean of anything related to thought.

A few hours later my stomach shook me awake. There was no gradual build up or friendly conversation about it whatsoever. It shook, the bowels shifted, and I knew instantly trouble to be afoot. I made for the back door forgetting that Chris slept beneath my steps. Out of pure luck, or from some repetitious programming, I managed not crush any part of him. Every movement was a question mark as to whether I'd shit my pants or not. Aside from the body moving and the mind's ability to hold fast to a single objective, crediting me with consciousness would have been presumptuous. Keeping the cheeks of my buttocks clenched demanded all my attention. Before each movement could be agreed to, I had to consider the ramifications in relation to my butt. Could they remain clenched if I stretched my right foot that far ahead? Would bending my knee open the floodgates? What clenching power will be lost by reaching my left hand for the door? Would it be better to use the right? Poor Stopher had no idea how close he had come to being shat upon. When I set my feet on to the ground the momentum of the small jump almost caused me to lose control. I flexed my entire body straight as if that would pull back the shit that seemed so determined to come out. My stomach groaned, my intestines knotted, my sphincter bulged, and I prayed. The surge had been endured as the pressure lessened to the extent that I could move my legs just enough to attain a forward progress that generous eyes might consider a distant cousin to walking. I inched to the van's driver door, fumbled with my keys, got it open, and stared in wonder at how I would get my boots on. I loosened the laces, pulled down on the tongue widening the boot's mouth as much as possible, then with a slight bend in my back I dropped the boot to the ground in hopes of it landing on its sole. Each boot now sat waiting to accept my foot, and I was able to slip them far enough in void of leakage. I shuffled toward my salvation making necessary pauses along the way. One of the boots almost came off, but I stabbed the foot back in. On arriving at the door I felt my stomach trying to push its burden out, begging me for release. I closed my eyes and mumbled for the strength. A cold, grimy sweat glazed over my forehead; I felt feverish. The surge relinquished, I moved through the door and towards the bathroom. I smiled weakly as I took the knob in my hand and was all but defeated when the knob refused to turn. Locked. I was asleep and drunk, I couldn't think clear. I suppose that I should've asked the manager for a key or tried the women's door. The journey from my bed, and the constant clenching, had drained whatever clear notion I may have had. My brain pulsed like the surge in my bowels; the doorway to rational thought was full of Stooges in the midst of a bomb scare. I stood there like an exclamation point, shouting its warning of a runaway train.

Something in my head popped. I began shuffling away. I made it back to the van, grabbed a roll of toilet paper from the front seat, and headed for the alley. At this point I said to myself, "What? You're going to shit in the alley?" I stopped, and wiggled my way back to Jack's bathroom door where I stood in silent torture, resuming my wondering how long I could hold out. There seemed to be no life on the other end of the door, nor in me to call out and define the circumstance—probably another drunk passed out on the pot. I can't believe that I never once checked the woman's door. (In fact, that's the first thing Chris said when I revealed my struggle the next day: "I just assumed that the men's was out of order and used the women's.") Being that I resembled more Zombie than human, that my mouth and brain no longer remained aware of one another, and that I couldn't really ascertain whether I might still be in bed amidst a nightmare or not, I ended up finding a dark spot between a dumpster and a recycle container. I stood there for a moment looking both ways. It was if I were watching it all through a foggy, thick lens. None of it seemed to be happening to me as I pulled my jeans down and crouched. I remember doing some wiping but when I woke up in bed the next morning, it wasn't until I got out of the van, and saw the shit stains on my boots and cuffs, that I relived the chain of events. At that moment I remembered being stricken by panic as I realized that the bathroom was locked. I even remembered that after I grabbed the toilet paper I went back into Jack to check the door again before I headed for the alley; I remembered the relief, but that is all of the alley I could recall; I had no visual memory of squatting and shitting; there was a good deal of shame and embarrassment, but that was immediately dwarfed by the relief of my insides being freed. The next morning saw the shame and embarrassment return in a big way.

The alcohol, fried chicken and tacos, along with a sleepy state and a locked door, conspired against me. And it was the best summer vacation ever.

The Raven had a way about her that helped you set aside her beauty without letting you ever forget that it was there; she raised her shoulders to take a tomboy stance in lipstick and gown. The Raven liked to mix it up with the boys, but still waited for doors to be held. "I'm a glorious dance off dichotomy personified," Quoth the Raven.

She had been trying to get Chris and I to attend one of her picking parties. We liked her but our anti-social nature won out over her first invitation.

"Listen, motherfuckers," she cursed, playfully. "When I say Friday at eight, I expect to see you waiting at my door at seven fifty-eight with one grimy paw hover over the doorbell, and the other holding a clock, while you wait with baited breath for the bitching hour."

"I believe that's witching," I offered.

"You'll believe," she said taking hold of the shrub on my chin, "whatever it is that I'll have you believe, cocksucker."

"I'll believe anything you say, just keep saying cocksucker."

"Yeah, I gotta cut down on the swearing." The Raven released my chin and sat on the park bench placing her forearms on their respective knees. "I've been getting carried away."

"Not so's ya'd notice."

"I let one slip talking to a customer at the restaurant the other day. Some guy was flirting with me as he lit up a cigarette, and I hate smokers. So I said something like, 'Keep your cancer to yourself, motherfucker.' I did say it in a friendly-flirty kind of way, and he liked it."

"Of course."

"But it's a bad habit; it could get me into trouble."

"You'll manage."

"So you and your no good brother will be in attendance this time."

"Yes, dear."

"I told you that this place I'm house sitting is for some record executive."

"It is the closet I'll ever get to having an actual meeting with one."

"That's what momma's been saying."

"That's what daddy's talkin'bout. If you are going to insist on stealing my bits, you could at least show the proper respect and steal them accurately."

"Darlin'." she rolled her tongue lusciously over her upper lip. "Mamma does what mamma wants."

"Indeed, momma, indeed."

We flirted, but she'd flirt just as soon as breath. She told me that once in high school a girlfriend she had made started to avoid her. When the Raven confronted her, the friend said that she was tired of all the flirting—she was strictly into guys. The Raven laughed hard telling that story because she knew how much of her nature it revealed. So I knew it had been her way, and put any hope of romance out of my head while enjoying her humor and beauty. I was never much for female friends. There were Josefa's friends when we were kids. As I grew older my sexual drive ceased allowing me to see new encounters as anything but another women who would not have sex with me. I guess I had gotten so fat, and fell so far down the economical ladder, that accepting my lot in life widened my perspective. Besides, the Raven was good company. She loved to play with words; had that knack for taking what you said and twisting it around in some clever fashion. She and I entertained each other, Chris too. He had less patience with her grabbing of the beard bit, but his affection for her started to grow along with mine. Slowly she became someone whose visits we looked forward to.

There were few others who had tried to befriend us. Nice enough folk, just not worth the extra weight of humanity on the boat. This one guy, Prometheus Patience, had a son that he delivered and retrieved from the daycare center at Marine Park a few times a week. He played guitar, saw us practicing, liked what he heard, and came over to hang out a bit. I got the impression that Prometheus was a kept man; his wife worked, he took care of the boy. He looked to be either a young sixty or an old fifty, (I guessed the latter) and had a beaten quality about himself, which he was either not aware of, or deemed undetectable by others. His five-eight frame, with lose skin sagging apathetically off its skeleton, somehow maintained a certain confidence. He had lived and done interesting things, been around great men, and lent a hand to projects of merit. Prometheus claimed to have worked for

John Cassavettes. It was one of the few stories I believed. First of all, Cassavettes is not exactly a household name; it's the kind of name that will only impress a small and specific group of people. I think it surprised Prometheus when we knew of whom he spoke. I'm sure he got a lot of, "John Cassawho?"

Like most folk we came across, Prometheus liked to talk. You could sense his hunger to be heard on all the subjects that fascinated him, to once again traverse the terrain of the life he no longer lived. I must admit that if I had ever worked for someone in the ilk of a John Cassavettes, I'd never tire of telling anyone who'd listen. He told us about some authentic looking English castle up in Malibu where Cassavettes had his crew staying for months at a time during a shoot. I wish I could remember the film. Prometheus mostly ran cable and adjusted lights, but said that John always had an ear open to the crew for ideas. His tired eyes grew young when he tried to recall a moment sitting around the table drinking, everyone offering up something of worth to enhance the project. Standing in front of us with his hair, grey, thin and fading, Prometheus spoke in low cool tones, and said things like, "I remember this one cat…"

When he ran out of those stories all that he went on about was the studio he was building in his garage. Now Prometheus did play guitar, and he came out with it a few times. His singing voice was a whispered talk that held a tune; his picking also soft, but good; his lyrics, pedestrian. He could seem so excited yet weak and beaten at the same time. I didn't dislike him but he wore on Chris and I; Prometheus talked but did not converse. Like so many he took the moments you spoke as an opportunity to gather his thoughts for his next monologue. The worst times were when he talked about sound and sound systems. I am a musician not a technician so all, the BXM Digital transformer with a QGT Compression unit bypass system talk, not only fell meaninglessly on my ears, but may have killed a few hundred brain cells; I was saving those to be killed by drugs.

"But those quarter inch bullshit chrome ones, ya know, man." His thin eyes reveled in his own story.

"Yeah."

"No, exactly, that's why I'm waiting until I can afford to get the three pronged brass; those are smooth." The pasty white foam in the corners of his mouth bubbled and multiplied.

"Yeah." I wiped the corners of my mouth with the index finger and thumb of my right hand.

"But when I get it all together, my studio is gonna shit velvet, man." Some of the white foam evaporated but more bubbled up too replace it.

"Velvet." I wiped my corners with the other hand turning away from his mouth.

"It's like I told this cat who tried to sell me that sub-standard crap: 'Hey, man, I'm too old to be pulling on my Johnson; I got a kid, my fucking around days are over.' He found out real quick what I was about." A bit of spittle shot through his teeth while talking so he licked his lips, entirely missing the foam in the corners.

"About." I looked at the ground.

Chris and I took turns being the one who pretended to listen. When I had KITTY HAWK to work on, I always had an excuse to be elsewhere.

Prometheus kept talking about coming out to the promenade to play but his sound system always needed tweaking. I did hear a demo he recorded in his studio, and it did show a level of talent. I hate to have to say it: I didn't think much of the sound. I kept that to myself in favor of smiling while nodding. It was nice that he had his world to play in, but he searched my eyes for justification. He wanted to wear the badge that was my life, and I was too petty to let him. After we had known him a few months he started opening to us his personal struggles. His wife nagged, then threatened, that he had to grow up.

One night he showed up at the Albertson's parking lot drunk. "I love my son so much. You guys know that, you see how we are together."

"You're a good guy, Prometheus."

"She doesn't understand what it is be a musician, an artist, like we do, ya know, man."

"We are all very specific people." Chris could generalize in the middle ground with the best of them.

"I know she makes all the money," he sobbed. "I am still a man."

Take it Chris.

"She's probably just venting her frustration."

"What about my frustration!" Prometheus proclaimed as if he had been cut deeply.

Nice going Stopher.

"Well that is something you'll have to sort out with your wife at home, not with us in a parking lot." Chris' soft pretentious hands were not working quickly enough for me.

"I'm sorry. I shouldn't be bothering you guys with this."

"You just had to blow off a little steam." Chris consoled.

"You'll be alright."

I had no fucking idea if he'd be alright. To be truthful, if I had placed a bet, money would be leaning towards seeing Prometheus at the showers any month now. Prometheus Patience was just another lonely soul who saw the sun sparkling off our head mast as we sailed diligently towards impoverished anonymity, loudly into the night. We saw less and less of him as I'm sure his wife screwed down her thumbs on his will into his soft kept belly. Our logistics changed as time went on as well, but Chris and I crossed paths with him once in awhile, for as briefly as we could manage.

Chris and I pulled the van into a spot near the address the Raven had given us, and each took a pull from our special water bottles. We were both a little nervous; social butterflies we are not. With guitars in hand we walked up the steps of the swanky condominium, and rang the bell.

"We don't want any," said a voice from above.

I stepped away from the door and saw the Raven looking down, smiling through her dark, wild mane.

"I'll give ya a buzz."

The door buzzed, we entered, and took the elevator up.

"Did you ever consider the irony of an earthquake hitting at a time like this?" I asked Stopher as the elevator began to rise.

"Explain."

"Well, in our current living situation, I'd have to say that we are fairly impervious to harm from such a natural disaster; we're either in the van at Albertsons or outside on the promenade, and etc."

"No second story to be crushed by."

"Exactly."

"And you bring up this after the elevator doors close and we are moving."

"It just now occurred to me."

"Thanks for not waiting for us to get out of the death box."

"No charge."

The doors opened, I waved for Chris to go first. The Raven was not in sight, but pulsing funky music called from an open doorway, so we followed our ears.

"That's not irony; just bad timing," said Chris, as we walked through the open door.

"What if we were on our way up to the top floor of huge skyscraper to sign the record deal of our lives?"

"Eh, that'd just be our Smith's cursed luck."

"I was in a band called Cursed Luck."

The Raven greeted us in mid-exchange from the kitchen. "Ah, you were not neither."

"Yeah huh, a tribute to Def Leopard."

"How ya figure?" Chris inquired.

"They hit it big but then the drummer loses his arm."

"I'll give you points for creative association; interesting but weak."

"I can live with that."

"Who shot the leopard in the what now?" The Raven leaned against the sink squinting her eyes over a wine glass.

"Oh, just a word game we play," I said.

"Some radio guys back in Chicago used to do it," Chris informed.

"Who did it first?" I queried, sensing, but ignoring, the Raven wanting to jump in, "Steve Dahl or Kevin Mathews?"

"I like words; I like games." Her eyes widened like a kid hearing that there was a chance of going somewhere neat.

"One of 'em? Both? They stole from someone else?"

"I think Steve did it first, but Mathews did it more."

"I like words; I like games," the Raven repeated with all the zeal of her first attempt

"It starts when in the middle of a conversation someone says an interesting phrase. Like I just said 'cursed luck'. Then someone has to uses said phrase as the name of a band that is a tribute to a band or performer that is famous."

"Cursed luck, huh?" Her wheels turned.

"The phrase can be reminiscent of something in the bands name or like in my case the bands history," I instructed.

"Like if I said, Virginal Slut." Chris paused. "Madonna."

"Well played," I congratulated.

"I actually thought of that one the other day and had been saving it."

"Cheater." I turned to the Raven. "The whole point is to be quick; off the cuff."

"I'm still working on cursed luck."

"Have a few drinks, mull it over, and get back to me."

"Who did that song, Born Under a Bad Sign?" She asked.

"One of those old blues guys, Willie Dixon or Muddy," Chris answered.

"But that works too if the phrase connects to a song that someone was famous for."

"Jailed fowl," Stopher snapped.

I paused for a beat then shot out, "Lynnard Skinnard."

"Bingo."

"Oh, I get it," the Raven nodded slyly. "They did Free Bird so, yeah I get it."

"Of course jailed fowl is not all that interesting of a phrase," I pointed out.

"I started with the band, then their most famous song, to come up with a phrase to give her an idea how that aspect could be applied."

"Look at you with the teaching on your feet."

"You two put an awful lot of thought and energy into a silly word game. No wonder you both live in a van."

"Sounds like a toast to me," I said, raising my bottle.

Stopher and the Raven joined in and all was well in the world.

"Blue Oyster Cult?" The Raven finally ventured.

"I'm not sure about the content, but I like the sound of it," Chris said.

"Thanks for playing." I smiled.

The Raven smiled back and I felt something pop in my chest.

As usual Stoph and I were the first ones there. Soon others arrived, mostly musicians from the promenade: Splash, a homeless conga player; Bill another conga player (the Raven likes her percussions) who played with a few different acts: a saxophonist who played with Bill; and another guitar player who I had not met. Derrick was an old friend of the Ravens who D-jayed in the clubs, and there was another couple of civilians, a guy and a girl who I don't remember much about because they didn't stay long.

The Raven had some dips and chips set out along with some Indian food on a table on the first level. (Oh, there were two levels) As people started showing up Chris and I settled in the living area on the first level. The majority of people mingled on the upper because that had a balcony, and most of them smoked. I talked with Splash a bit, and he seemed even more uncomfortable than Chris or me.

"How ya doing, Splash?"

"Just trying to stay dry and fed."

Splash was a sturdy five-ten black guy with a full beard who usually smelled as homeless as he looked. We talked on the promenade once in a while and got along.

"How did you do out there today?"

"I made enough to eat in the morning then tried an earn me a ticket into the movies in the afternoon."

"Right, you were waiting on our spot."

"Yeah, I played for about twenty minutes after you and your brother left when the Timms set up on top of me exactly forty feet away, pointing their speakers directly at me. Wasn't much point in staying after that."

"Really? What the fuck is up with that?"

"They don't like me. They've done it to me before, and I asked if they could at least not point their speakers at me, the dude said, 'The promenade is for real musicians, why don't you get a job at McDonalds?'"

"What a prick." I had not yet discovered the depth of that for myself.

"He's just one of those people that thinks he's better than everyone else."

"Well so do I, but at least I'm nice about it," I joked, but Splash didn't smile.

"You ain't like that."

Splash had a vision for a utopian society that was built on an agreed love of oneself through the light of a true God. He described it on three large pieces of cardboard in black marker, and laid them out on the ground in front of his conga to be read whenever he played. Splash believed in it completely. I once told him that people will never agree on anything universally let alone a vision of God.

"They'll believe this," he said plainly, void of feeling challenged.

I liked Splash when he was on his medication, soft spoken, unconcerned with convincing you of his convictions. He saw himself as an idea certain to find its way into the hearts and soul of humanity. The words on cardboard echoed each of his steps and nothing else was required. Off his medication he rarely played but instead stood on the curb talking fast and randomly to no one. No longer a man of a larger picture, all he had to say pertained to the persecution of his sexual will.

"Just because I want a white woman they send me men trying to seduce me, clawing for me to desire them; just because I don't want a black woman I have to be gay. I ain't gay, you can't make me want a man, you can't stop me from wanting a white woman; you can't stop from wanting what I WANT."

The first time I saw him like this he didn't even respond to my hello. I was nothing but a smear in a collage of a faceless force conspiring against him, and his only defense was to abstain acknowledgement. During the first year on the promenade I did not often see him off his medication. (Today we are pretty much strangers. I don't see him much, and when I do he doesn't see me at all.)

Splash left the party once he had some food and felt ready to sleep.

"I better go get to my spot for the night."

Chris and I drifted upstairs with guitars in hand once the live music began. Bill and the saxophonist were riffing off each other, and then the other guitar player joined in with a few chords. They had all been playing together on the streets for only a couple of weeks and it showed. The three men were loving themselves beyond reason as the initial jammed bled into another, sounding pretty much the same as the first. I was tired and a little drunk, but jumped in after about ten minutes. No one was quite in tune so I picked my way carefully. Chris sat back with his bottle and nodded encouragingly like a visiting uncle who could leave at any time.

In one of the transitional lulls the Raven said, "How about a song?"

I smiled my relief, which unfortunately gave Bill time to chime in.

"Earl, play that song we were working on yesterday."

Earl, the guitar player, proceeded to play some quasi-political tripe that my eyes couldn't roll far enough into my head to escape. Throughout the evening each man in the trio took their shot at eyeing the Raven into submission, and during his tour de force journey of sub-mediocrity, Earl sultralized his eyes upon her in comical proportion.

When Earl finished, Bill beamed. "That is great song, man."

Earl oozed his humble concurrence.

"Hey, let's do-"

"I wanna hear one from the boys," said the Raven, cutting Bill off. "How about some blues of a hard-edged kind."

Chris and I laid down Mom's tough lyric in our riffy-way, the sax jumped in, as did Bill on the conga; I gave everyone a solo but brought it home before it went on too long. It was then I noticed that the Raven had a bit of the bubbly bouncing around in her head.

"I wanna dance," she slurred.

She went to the stereo, put on a smoky little beat and started to move. I felt instantly uncomfortable being in a room with all these guys, and one drunken woman dancing. Chris nudged me to join her, but besides the awkwardness, I was drunk, and felt clumsy. Bill took on the task, and though the two of them moved smoothly enough, they looked to me separate. Billy smiled while the Raven closed her eyes to the sway of her body. The fact that Bill was an older man in his fifties tempered the tension of any advances. Which was probably why he got up while the younger wolves hesitated licking their chops. Age gave him the ability to enjoy the offered present, as youth contemplated a way to turn it into a future conquest. There was little room; I felt grateful to be on the couch. When the song ended, and the Raven opened her eyes, she looked a little woozy.

"Whew, my tummy is getting a little flighty." With that she went down the stairs.

A moment later we all heard her throwing up. Bill called after her; she said that she was fine.

She reappeared a half hour later as we were all getting ready to go. Chris and Bill were talking on the couch while Earl and the saxophonist were having a smoke on the balcony. The Raven waved me over to the stereo.

"I wanted you to hear this song, I can't stop playing it. Did you ever hear of Shawn Mullins?"

"Yeah, that Rock-a-bye song; he sounds a bit like a friend of mine from Nashville."

"This is a different one, and I just love it."

We sat on the floor in front of the stereo and listened to the song. It had a waltzy kind of feel with a wistful, melancholy melody. There was a great line in there about being lonesome but I can't remember it now.

When it ended she looked at me like a child with a snowflake on her tongue. "Don't you just love it?"

"It's nice."

She played it a few more times, smiling at me on occasion, wanting the song to be for me what it was to her. I liked the song, but not as I much as I liked her wanting me to like it.

CHAPTER NINE

The promenade began to feel like home. Still, I couldn't completely shake the feeling of being an intruder. They all got there first, the workers, the performers, the homeless. Ironically I didn't feel as much of that for the people that actually lived in the neighborhood. They didn't have to be on the promenade, they had options. The center kids, some of whom were older than me, exuded entitlement. It is not so hard to understand that those with nothing, having given up on everything a civilized society deemed basic requirements for inclusion, lay claim to a spot in the middle of what was built for and by those who went the other way. Who else would be walking or lounging about the streets of an outdoor mall but those who have more money than they can spend, and those who have absolutely nothing. The answer: Those that work to serve the "haves" while enduring the bitter spewings from the peanut gallery of the "have-nots". The square between the two large dinosaurs of the middle street had the most space to lounge in, and the most foot traffic to beg from and scorn to. It was the same reason performers coveted the area, well except for the scorn part.

They gathered in numbers ten to twenty every morning as the workers arrived at their jobs. The homeless are early risers for the most part. By the sun's first glint the night's cool has seeped into their bones and the dew through their sleeping bags. In the mid to late afternoon on the bluffs of Palisade Park under the shade of a palm or spider tree they can retire for an hour or two nap, then return to the task of begging, rooting around town for recyclables, peddling dope, or just conversing with their voices. Those that make money mostly do so to achieve one kind of fix or another. The crazies sleep longer for their needs are less. When they walk the streets of the promenade it is usually to scavenge the trashcans, or sit on a curb listening to whatever free entertainment the likes of Stopher and myself provide. To me the true crazies are the schizophrenics, the rest, be they manic depressive, bi-polar, addicts, or just broken souls from a life of abuse, self or otherwise, are a different beast altogether. Being that my brother Joel is a schizophrenic I obviously have a soft spot in my heart for them. Most out here stay to themselves, and the only way they put upon the rest of us is by forcing us to hear their one sided shouting matches with their voices. That's not to say that some don't lash out to those of us existing in this agreed upon reality that the rest of us share. There are levels to everything.

Old Horace is one of the true crazies for whom I had come to have affection. We never once exchanged a single word in four and a half years. His face had tough sunken cheeks that were perpetually smudged; a trim but not skinny, long, strong nose; and full brown eyes that said more than he did. Horace stood around six feet, his thin but unmistakably solid frame dressed in a dirt farmer's attire: Baggy trousers, two sizes too big, with a crackled, worn belt that owed as much to rope as leather; checkered flannel shirt, always tucked in though never neatly; a soft-domed, flimsy-billed, beige, baseball cap; and torn, tattered work boots that were always tightly laced. His prominent cheekbones told a story about him that I could never put a moral to, while his mustache and the scruffy whiskers about his chin portrayed a quality of being kept when you know damm well that he barely ever washed his face with soap let alone running a razor across it.

Horace ambled down the street with a stroll that placed him in another time, a day that saw Woody Guthrie conversing with Steinbeck about something other than a social cause. The two literary men would buy Horace a beer eagerly, and not even ask a question for their notes. I have seen Horace pensive with thought and shouting his rage, never once betraying dignity. His words were hard to make out; barks and growls with content. The name Wyatt Earp came up several times in both his rants, and those rare times he spoke warmly to something soft and beautiful.

Over the years countless homeless would sit on a curb and watch Chris and I play. Some would come back daily for weeks and months at a time. I could tell when they sought us out—whether they were crazy or not—if they listened to the words, or just like to use the music in their thoughts. I could have been wrong about every assumption or none at all, but most likely somewhere in between. In that first year, Horace was one who sought us out. He'd sit on the curb with his back to a trash can, stand up against a tree, or be off in the doorway of a nearby vacant store. There were weeks when he listened every day, and even reappear after we moved to another spot; sometimes it'd be a month before he stopped again, choosing to keep moving instead. Whenever he stopped, especially when he sat, I felt the purpose of being who I was overwhelm me. If you had told me before I left Chicago that those moments would be the total sum of my rewards—now knowing what it was to have, in some way, been of service to the Horaces of the world—I'd be, and have been, honored to accept. A sparkle entered his eyes from within as if a valve long shut had been opened. It did not gush or even ooze, it simply appeared as if always having been there. When he smiled it was not at us, but the distance. I think the music took him somehow. Not necessarily to a home he had known in this life, but a place he knew more intimately about than any other that he actually had. Horace dragged on a cigarette freshly rolled for the moment and rode the peace. A few times I looked directly into his eyes knowing he would not notice, and sing to them, and the places they could take us both.

If it seems too grand, it was, if I sound full of romance, I am, if you think I am revising or overstating the truth for some cinematic purpose, I assure you, I am not. I had hoped for a lot of things when I loaded up the van, mostly a modicum of financial success, a little to a ton of hot sex, and the respect of the writing community. I could say that I'd settle for the moments that Horace and a handful of others have given me, but that would be a lie. Though I am truly honored by them I still want everything I started out for and more. I am greedy and full of desire, though as I get older, I am attempting to detach myself from those facts because I am so very fucking tired of the pain they have and continue to cause me. I guess all that this passage exists for is to tell you, and remind me, that I have been blessed.

Now back to the curse.

A section of the homeless exists that are restless and resentful. Part of their resentment comes from defensiveness against those that assume the worst of them. Another stems from knowing that some of the worst assumptions about them are true. People from all walks of life, educated professional to skilled laborers and janitorial technicians, have found a way to fit, or at least accept where they have been stuck. From those that thrive to those that simply eek by, each of them has found it in their will, desire and or ability, to apply themselves to the machinery of society. The homeless on the other hand, for various reasons ranging from mental illness to self-destructive addictions, have found themselves to be disenfranchised. They were not all crazy or addicts to begin with though. Some were broken by the inability to find or reside in a niche handed down by a world that doesn't give a flying fuck what that individual feels or thinks about what it is they want to be handed. I am not only talking about the ballerina wanna be that weighs three hundred pounds, or the kid who dreamed of the big leagues despite being cursed with an arm that should have gone to the ballerina. A portion of people walk the earth not seeking a grandiose destiny, and are still told to flip a burger, drop fries in the fryer, then grab a mop. The choices for the middle ground fade more every year. Work with computers or dig a ditch, and that is if you are lucky. Don't me wrong, the homeless are complete with miserable assholes having only themselves to blame. But as my Dad might say, "Plumbers are miserable assholes too." In other words, every walk of life has got'em.

One day, waiting to play on the south side of the center square, Chris and I watched on as Layla Timms sang a song from the top forty. Her husband Ned made plenty of dough with her on keyboards, but she fancied herself a singer—tunes she could carry but that don't make you a singer. At the moment she, with broken english in tongue, (she was Brazilian, Ned was as white as bread) sang Jewel's, I WAS

MEANT FOR YOU, well enough albeit a tad clumsily. During the first chorus a hip-hop beat intruded upon her melody in the form of a boom box sewn into a backpack over the shoulder of one of the center kids called, Clown.

Clown was tall, fit and muscular with wide shoulders, bulging biceps and a barrel chest. He was a cliché' of a young black youth designed for the playing field. Full lips, rock hard jaw with a prominent forehead sporting a protruding bone structure around the eyes wrapped in skin as black as coal. He wore blue coveralls unbuttoned down his chest, over a white tee shirt. His steps bounced to the music as he and a diminutive, olive skinned sidekick strutted purposefully by, skateboards in hand. They circled in front of Layla slowing down to annoy her with their boxed music as they headed back to the center square. As Layla began the next song, Celine' Dione's, OUR HEARTS WILL GO ON, the boys returned from the other side and stopped in front of Layla's tip bucket.

"You get out of here," Layla shouted, at them off mic.

The boys smiled innocently then pretended to look at her CDs as if interested, while the obnoxious beat bled from the speakers in Clown's backpack. He had the volume so loud that the speakers themselves pleaded for another fate.

"You," Layla stuttered with anger, "you, you little assholes."

Clown, who had been crouched, looked up placing a palm over his mouth shaped in an "oh my" expression. The Italian looking kid stood behind him grinning, but gradually backed away.

"You are fuckers," Layla raged. "Nothing but asshole fuckers."

Clown stood, took a couple steps back, then began thrusting his pelvis in accordance with the beat turning in a full circle until he again faced Layla head on. At that point he thrust harder, pounding his fists on his hips, lifting himself on to his tiptoes with each gesture, all aimed directly at her. Layla's eyes boiled, Clown smiled, and the little sidekick giggled. Suddenly Layla took the far end of the, abruptly unplugged, guitar's neck into both hands and started swinging it like a baseball bat at Clown's head. The first swing came close enough for Clown's smile to take a break while he ducked, dropped his skateboard and scooted down the street. The boys laughed riotously once they achieved the proper distance from the guitar's violent heaves. Clown even stepped into each swing to further taunt the exasperated, and tiring, Layla. Once she saw that he had regained the advantage she turned back toward her stage. At that point she saw his skateboard and dashed back to scoop it up.

"Hey, that's mine." Clown momentarily lost his sense of humor.

"That's his," the runt echoed. "You can't take that."

Layla turned on the smaller one and chased him down the street, holding the guitar secure to her side with one hand while wielding the skateboard as a deadly weapon in the other. It was then that Clown took notice of the money in the tip bucket. This all happened in a matter of a minute, maybe two. Chris and I watched from the curb assuming it to end quickly enough without our getting involved. We worked there too, and I didn't want make an enemy of the center kids unless left no choice. Clown snickered to himself with his hands mulling over each other at his waist as he slithered toward the bucket. His head turned side-to-side wondering how much attention he presently garnished from the public eye.

At first I thought, he wouldn't dare. The moment his eyes widened and his steps quickened I got between him and the bucket.

"No," I said, firmly without trying to challenge him. "You are not touching her money."

Clown stopped walking but his eyes were in the bucket. The equation formulated in his head faster than any math problem he got wrong in school: The bucket—two feet behind me holding fifteen maybe twenty; five feet between he and I; I being a good two inches shorter but no push-over. Before he could decide for certain Stopher's voice entered the equation.

"You had your fun."

"Not the money," I added.

Clown smiled as over his shoulder I saw Layla toss the skateboard after other boy, who's ass I'm not sure couldn't have been kicked by Layla, skateboard or not. With a shrug of the shoulders, Clown fetched his boarded wheels and howled with glee at all the fuss he made. A job well done, he howled, a job well done.

Layla returned and I asked if she was okay.

"Fucking assholes," she huffed.

She plugged her guitar in and went back to work.

I am sure that I expected some change in the weather for winter out here, but when the rainy season came it took me by surprise. There were weeks where it felt like it never stopped raining, or getting ready to rain. An ever-present threat permeated through our collective senses. I always loved a good midwestern thunderstorm when the winds shoved you around like a playground thug after your lunch money; trees moaned to its gospel, whooshing to the will of an unseen God; bowing branches collapsed earthbound in a gathering clutch only to be spread out wide, lunging at the sky in a plea for forgiveness; rain came down in a slanted sheet diving under shelter, attacking without remorse; lightning flashed the sky's brilliant anger, a precursor to the roar that followed. When it stormed in Chicago, nature's tongue lashed you like a southern Baptist preacher on Sunday hell bent on retrieving every single last sinner from Satan's blood-soaked tooth. Of course these were spring and summer storms because in the winter, things in Chicago, got nasty.

The rain in Santa Monica wept gently, almost apologetically as if the sins belonged to nature and not us. I'm not saying that it never rained hard. It did. Even then I was unimpressed by its force; no crash, no more than I hint of a whoosh. There were winds and shoreline Palms did turn to fists, but they did not seem to belong to the rain. The wind came from the ocean, or was born of the desert, while the rain fell separately as sole property of the sky. The rain's power grew out of its incessancy. Like a boy with no friends, lingering over a crowd that had no use for him, the rain remained until its sorrow emptied.

During our first rainy season we tried to play as much as we could. The majority of the time the rain trickled into a drizzle, rose to an actual fall, then subsided to a mist. Chris and I had a six-by-ten foot, plastic tarp for the equipment but it couldn't cover everything while we played; it only served as protection when all was neatly stacked together. Desperate to play, we would set up under cloudy skies only to have them turn wet then dry up after we broke down our stage. The gizmo belonged to Steve so we had no right endangering his amp. Pat, the James Taylor guy, played on unless the rain got heavy, and I hated him for being the one toughing it out while I cowered in a corner.

On the days we relinquished the battle, in the van I took comfort in being defeated. I lay in my bed listening to jazz on the radio, sipping charcoal-filtered, vodka from a water bottle smiling my submission. Chuck Niles rasped his way through stories about some small-time jazz great between sets, and laughed heartily on the edge of a smoke induced cough at the wonder of all he had been blessed to have played the witness. Chuck was an institution on the airwaves. Dodger baseball had Vin Scully, the Lakers Chick Hearn, and jazz radio in Los Angeles had Chuck Niles. Hearing his voice talking about who played what on a given track, or how lefty Ramirez was a righty who always left his band mates with the tab, made me feel like I was back in Chicago sitting in the dining room while Dad steamed vegetables in the kitchen. Chuck Niles loved what life had become for him, or so it seemed from my bed in the van. His thick baritone lived in every word.

On one occasion when the sun peeked through the clouds to say hello and the day's work had already been excused, I said to Chris, "I have found the basement in my van."

"It's a nice break in the day, isn't it?"

"Indeed."

On an evening that Stoph and I challenged the weather, we stood on the south end of the dinosaurs of the middle street with wind wiping mist in our faces. I knew we wouldn't make much but felt better for trying. With forty minutes to go a large black man stood smiling in front of us while we sang Van Morrison's MOONDANCE. He had to be almost six-four with a substantially round belly that seemed like less when related to where it was housed. His forehead slanted out over sunken but sharp eyes perched atop a chubby, flat nose with permanently flared nostrils. He listened intently with a well-meaning ease that, ironically, only this bear of a man with wide uneven teeth could manage. The song ended and he laughed rhythmically as a dollar dropped in our bucket.

"I been out here on and off for years, and I ain't ever tipped no one before," he declared, cheerfully.

"We are grateful," I said.

"I'm Roger, I come out here from Vegas most weekends when I need a little extra money."

"I'm Chris, and this is my brother Dave."

"I don't think we've seen you play out here yet."

"I mostly play on the north end where there aren't as many performers."

"Or as many tippers," I added.

"I do alright," he chuckled. "You all are as good as I have ever seen out here; you gonna do fine."

"That's what Steele and James Mitchell keep telling us, but we consider ourselves lucky when we make twenty," Chris admitted.

"Oh, you met James and Mel?"

"Yeah, we play a lot of weekdays."

"You keep it up and you'll be making a whole lot more than twenty. Last Sunday I made a hundred dollars in one hour."

"Wow," I said, although I did not believe him in the least.

"You'll get there, you two are the real thing. You can play that guitar," he said pointing at Chris. "If it doesn't get better soon, try playing some Motown, that'll get'er done."

I'd run into Roger Ridley like that a couple of more times before I actually saw him play. Chris and I both assumed that he exaggerated about the money he made—we were absolutely wrong. Roger had a voice as big as a church bell. He was a genuine good ole' Georgia boy who sang songs that might as well have been written specifically for him; Sam Cooke to Smoky Robinson, fitted him like a tailor made suit that he owned like his skin. He had a train whistle of a falsetto that cleaned your ears out, and a bellow below it that did the same for the soul. His eyes closed, the mouth opened, and his body rocked gently to and fro while the songs poured out of him. Roger was in his fifties somewhere close to sixty and he belonged to the time he sang from. People loved him, and would warmly shed themselves of their money as if the word of the bible proclaimed them to do so, void of thought, full of joy.

Roger and James would never understand how the money eluded us. They loved music, they adored those that honored it with skill and inspiration, and when they saw us, that's all they could see. I soon developed theories as to why people held their money from us, but at the time I tried to trust the word of the men I had to come to respect, and whose respect had been bestowed upon us so graciously. James, Mel and Roger were genuine articles of a time and culture that provided a generation with a soundtrack, and that soundtrack was seen by the masses of third street as the birth right of those three men. Chris and I are genuine articles too, but that of a young white class from a self-indulgent era not quit far removed enough from the present day. I couldn't manage too much bitterness about their good fortune on the promenade. Roger and them were older, had paid dues that would never have been asked of me, and therefore got a reward I couldn't possibly earn. James and Roger saw us as brothers, and Mel too, although as wrapped up in himself as I was in me. That was the first badge of honor Chris and I garnished out on the promenade, maybe the most meaningful. Two men who had lived life according to the music saw our worth, and gave their blessings.

The rain kept falling through the season, the ocean threw its winter winds at the shore, and we played our songs to them both when feasible, hiding in the shelter of our van and the comfort of a bottle the rest of the time. With all the rain, I kept meaning to get an umbrella but my money always ended up elsewhere. We did get a grey, hooded, plastic poncho, which doubled as a tarp, from the parking lot at the showers. Someone pulled up and opened their trunk to distribute blankets and such to the homeless. Good people. Still I knew that we needed an umbrella and I never sought one out. Every time the rain caught me running from the van to the bathroom at the park, or going into Albertsons I thought, I should have an umbrella.

The subject of desire versus need sparked another song. The music I put to it had a driving, bluesy pulse that let up during the bridge. It was my attempt to have the music rain over the words, which were as follows:

When the rain finds me I never have an umbrella
The sky is everywhere and you can only hide so long
A river of shit flows; yeah I've always got something to tell ya
Words won't keep me dry but they steer me clear of ever being wrong
I'm deeper than the average fella but when it rains
I never have an umbrella

I don't think of it 'till I need it, I don't believe in it 'till I see it
Though I've seen it all before
There's always something in between putting desire in front of need
So no matter what I need I want something more
I don't have an umbrella. It's a raining and I don't have an umbrella

An umbrella won't save my feet from the holes in my shoes
It can't hold back the cold or keep the rain from turning to snow
My heart will break when it's breaking; the sun can't stop the blues
But rain ain't just a metaphor when water's wet and hard winds blow
So it's clear I'm a clever fella but it's raining
And I don't have an umbrella. It's raining and I don't have an umbrella

Let the days make the years
I'll figure out the rest as I go
Today it's raining, this much I know
I don't have an umbrella—it's raining—I don't have an umbrella—it's raining

The folks came for a visit somewhere in February but luckily no rain fell during their four-day stay. They took us out for meals, caught a few sets on the promenade, and offered to rent us a room at their motel for a night. It was great to be spoiled but we refused the room.

"Save the money for more food," I suggested.

When Dad saw our life out here first hand he said, "You two are my heroes. You are living as close to the bone as I could have ever hoped for—and the music-."

He broke off as his eyes liquefied. My Dad the hard-ass had turned into a sweet, old man. The truth is that he was always sweet, and still could cut you off at your knees if he smelled any bullshit on you. No one loved life more than him. It never failed to touch the fiber of his belief, or stir the base of his soul when he saw someone giving them self to anything that required skill, passion or even mild curiosity. The search for life in oneself as expressed through a physical act always impressed him. If he saw a man tinkering with child's broken toy, or an elbow joint under a sink he wished them a good, and hopefully a fruitful, journey.

Mom loved the new songs so much that she lamented our not being able to record them. By this time I had written three and Chris had at least that.

"I know you have lots of wonderful songs but these are so connected to what your lives have become. When you sing them I can see them jumping out of your chests."

The recording talk started Chris off on one of his Steve tangents. Part of our coming out here was fueled by phone conversations with Steve offering up studio time on credit. Of course he would have expected to be paid eventually, but over the distance he seemed unconcerned about how long it took. On our arrival the subject never got off the ground, it was Steve who directed it so. He feared being taken advantage by friends, so all offers made over the phone shrank into a former shadow of themselves. Chris and I realized early on that he was no longer comfortable with any loosely open-ended transactions. We both took that hard at first because making another CD was one of the big reasons we thought to come out here. Chris is a big commie at heart: He had envisioned a gaggle of artists helping each other create and bring their work to light. Steve had made a lot of friends, but Chris felt that the years in Nashville with all the phone calls from Chicago to California had added up to as much in Steve's heart as they had in his. On top of that none of the others that Steve referred to were even remotely close to being in our league genius-wise. Whether he had the right to be or not, Chris had been hurt. I felt it too but not as deeply as Chris. He took Steve in a little deeper so the cuts ran deeper as well.

Of course no one did more for us than Steve when we got there. If not for Steve the whole thing would have been a mess. Love is a funny thing when left in the hands of a human. When one hurts, the specificness of that hurt can't be healed by a separate act of kindness.

"He is not here for you," Dad stated dryly.

"But wouldn't it be nice if he was," Chris said dreamily.

Dad laughed and Mom smiled, but I could tell that she bore our wounds. Mom can be a hard ass too. I remember when I worked in the stock room at a Marshall's for five years. I started there at eighteen, and by the end all I did was complain about the lack of respect and appreciation I received. I'd come home frustrated to tears and after offering much empathetic support Mom had had enough.

"Why do you keep on letting them do this to you? I'm starting to think you like the righteous anger. There are other jobs but even then, chances are that you'll never be loved by anyone that you work for."

"I'm not asking to be loved."

"I think you are."

She was dead on, balls accurate. Chris and I both wanted to be loved in everything we did the way our mother loved us. She got tired of the fruitless drama that I seemed to thrive on, and simply couldn't shoulder the pain that I kept handing her. The folks are a couple of sweet hard-asses.

Sitting on a patch of grass between the Venice boardwalk and the beach with a guitar in my lap leaning against a Palm tree I took hold of my mother's eyes. She sat on a bench with Chris next to her, Dad stretched out at her feet on the grass with his grey, hooded sweat jacket serving as a pillow, and a baseball cap tilted to his sharp, long nose; I saw her wanting for us against her better judgment as the hard-ass turned sweet. Guilt tingled down my neck. I wanted so much for once to solve a problem for them. At the very least I wished to cease being the one in need. It doesn't matter that neither Chris nor I raised the question of our recording another CD; we existed to be helped.

"You boys have a beautiful beach," mom said soothingly.

"We like it," I agreed.

In that instant I saw Mom taking care of herself. The troubled look turned into ease as she set aside what wasn't and embraced what was. Her round smooth face opened to a smile as a few wrinkles gathered about her eyes leaving her cheeks even smoother. The sky called to her, and for a moment or so she left her man and two boys behind on the land to be with herself in the blue day. On returning she still appeared a tad gone.

"How about another song?"

On their last night Mom bought a half-gallon bottle of Ten High, so we all sat around their motel room sipping and talking, talking and sipping. They gave us the Chicago scoop on Grandma's health, the turbulent downward spiral of Art's marriage, and the story that Mom was writing. Soon the conversing transcended the specifics and flew over the vast terrain of breathing on a spinning ball in the middle of space.

"I remember complaining about something to your father and he said, 'Life's a struggle, Barbara.'"

"He so wise," Chris cracked.

"Ugg!" Mom exclaimed. "I said, 'I know, Bob, that's what I'm complaining about.'"

Dad laughed at the sound of himself with a knowingly, shaking head, as his face went red beneath his baseball cap. (He had assumed the same position on the bed as he had on the grass in Venice.)

"How do you endure me, Barb."

Mom reached from her chair next to the bed and rubbed his belly. "You're a fine straight-man and a good sport."

Chris and I sat in chairs on the other side of the bed by the window.

"I guess Mom is the funny one," I said.

"Yes," the old man concurred emphatically.

"Yeah, but Dad's taller," Chris pointed out.

"Your father is a saint: To Saint Smitty," Mom called as she hoisted her drink.

We all joined in grateful for the excuse to have a drink.

"I gave you both those pins, didn't I?"

I removed the beat-up old grey fedora from my head to study the railroad sign of a pin I had inserted into my hat.

"I put the other one into Stopher's black hat but he doesn't wear that much."

"I just wanted to make sure I didn't forget."

After we saw the folks to the train I felt even more determined to make something out of all this struggling. That being said I knew even then that I had begun to give up on a few of my initial goals. Back when we were living in the basement, preparing to make this journey I had done something similar. I accepted that I would forever be a fat guy drinking himself to death. Of course at the time I knew that my life had a major change in the works. Returning to the van from the train station I realized that the major change in question had taken place, and any transitional period had been indulged. Fat and drinking myself to death remained the course. Chris and I both tried on the trip out and continued to try in the ensuing months but failure blew our sails. Still we tried and would try again, but even in the midst of the vow I heard myself making in honor of a mother's love and a father's faith, I detected a hollow ring. I knew my heart was no longer in any effort to stop drinking and eat right. Something inside me searched for a platform to announce to myself that continuing to write, and play music, was the only guarantee I could make. More than that I tired, to the point of boredom, of pretending that I even wanted to quit drinking. FAT, DRUNK, UNKNOWN, BRILLIANT ARTIST FOUND DEAD AT 52—Eh, at least it spoke of a life ventured. I got sick of fighting my natural tendencies. The next few months would be my experimentation with really giving up on that fight.

In the month of March Chris and I had another visitor. One weekday afternoon during our second set, down by the shoeshine stand near Santa Monica Blvd., I looked up from the guitar and saw my cousin Mark standing behind a video camera. When the song finished I gave a nod to Mark without saying anything to Chris, curious how long it would take for him to notice on his own; Chris rarely looked out into the crowd whether in a bar or on the street. He was playing the acoustic and singing lead so paused to consider his next song.

"BLACK MESA?"

"Sure."

Stopher went into the song so I put Mark and his camera out of my mind to let the warm mesa wind travel me across the necessary state lines, and into the land up on to the mount where a hawk waited on our music. BLACK MESA came to an end, Chris looked to me for a request.

"How's about, WHERE ARE YOU?" I waited a beat, then added, "First let's tell this deadbeat with the video to drop us a buck."

It was an unwritten rule among performers that anyone taking pictures should tip a buck. Some performers had a strict policy of no video whatsoever regardless of tip. Chris didn't bring it up much unless we were in a bad mood our simply dying a terrible death, as we were that day.

"I'm too tired to give a fu-"Chris had started to say wearily until he noticed that I had been referring to Mark. Stoph immediately mocked an angry old man's face whose lawn had been trampled on by the neighborhood boys yet again, and shook his fist at the camera. Mark kept rolling while throwing Chris a wave. We did a couple more songs before stopping to switch guitars. Mark took that opportunity say hello.

"Can I buy you boys diner?" he said as he dropped a twenty into our bucket.

"I believe you just did," I answered slanting an eye toward the mostly empty tip receptacle.

"What time do you finish up?'

"Four."

"Then we have to load up the van," I reminded Chris. "So more like four-thirty."

Mark had been to Santa Monica on business before and probably knew the area better than us so we told him where we were parked, and he met us there with his rental car. That night we dined like kings in a place coincidently called The King's Head. It was the kind of place that my folks couldn't afford to take us to.

"The food is good, but I really come here for the beer," Mark informed as we sat down.

At Mark's insistence we tried various imports as he dismissed any concerns about the money. He told us about life in China and how the factory he ran would be closing down within the year.

"What then?" Chris asked.

"Back to Providence, although I wouldn't mind getting work out west."

He had to get up early for a meeting the next day but before he dropped us off by the van we had arranged to meet at his hotel around ten the day after. On our arrival, Mark had the camera hooked up to the television so we could get a look at the footage he shot of us. It had been the first time we had seen ourselves on camera since we had been out there. Chris cringed but I was pleasantly surprised how good we sounded.

"Do you think you boys can handle a little hiking?"

"I'm sure Dave could keep up well enough but I don't mind dragging behind."

With that Mark drove us up the PCH to Topanga Canyon road, and up into the mountains. The trail was mostly open fields surrounded by trees elevated in the distance. Chris held true to his word and fell behind telling us to pick him up on the way back. I, in work boots, held my own against the Nordic figure that is my cousin Mark, who fashioned his feet in what he called the ultimate scandals.

"I play full court basketball in these."

During our walk he chastised me for taking anything resembling pride in being victorious over his brother Aaron in basketball. I submitted to his ridicule while holding firm to my personal triumph. The trail ended on a majestic boulder hoisted up by the land to look down into a green valley, and out across to an equally green rising peek. I sat on the edge to take in the wondrous view.

"Leave it to me to be taken sight seeing by an out of towner."

"I try to get out here whenever they send me to Santa Monica."

"Do you like running a factory? You never struck me as the corporate type."

"I like the people who work for me, I like being in China." Mark let a breath empty out over the valley. "The money is great, Annie loves all the help, especially with Silas—it's a good life."

"But?"

"I've always been the odd man out in my family. They're all artists who have been able to make their work their life. That's what I want; a job I don't want to retire from."

"My Dad can't wait to retire."

"If I were a writer, or a painter—but I'm a worker."

"Hey, you don't have to tell me. I've been around you when work had to be done; no one worked hard enough for you."

"Do you know my family?"

"I saw how you rode Aaron getting the house ready for Rachael's wedding."

The look in his face argued my point but he let the words fall unspoken.

"You work harder than most, and are disappointed when they don't maintain your standard; I'm the same way."

"Maybe."

"I bet you have a book in you."

"I don't have the patience."

It felt strange to see Mark as a man with any doubt, or questions untagged to an answer. We all got together for weeks at a time, sometimes on consecutive years but we did grow up in different families, a thousand miles apart. His hair had been blonder and his face not so drawn. I knew he still loved his life, and what he had built of it with Annie; I guess I never saw him as human as I should have. Mark Jungels was easy to idealize.

When he dropped us off that day he said that he'd be in meetings for the rest of his trip. We said our goodbyes, and looked to our own maps. Naturally Chris and I got cheap vodka and chili fries. Drunk and fed we dosed off sitting up in the front seat, I in the passenger, Chris behind the wheel, and the night aged without us. Somewhere after ten a big hand repeatedly appeared knuckles first on my window. My eyes opened but I heard the flesh and bone pulsing through the glass before my eyes considered the sound's source. I lifted my head away from the window while the blur outside the van began to resemble Mark. Stopher made sense of it all within moments, I heard his door open and saw Chris through the windshield talking to Mark. I got in the back seat of Mark's rental still unclear as to why I wasn't getting in bed. I then noticed that I had an Albertsons water bottle in my hand with a good couple of swallows in it so I emptied it of one of them.

"Should I be awake for this?" I asked.

"I'm taking you to my favorite place for Mexican food, and some good beer."

"But I already got drunk and stuffed once tonight."

"But this is free," Chris smiled.

"Oh."

"I just got out of the last meeting, and realized that it could be years before we tipped a few beers together, so.'"

I took another swallow. "Mexican, huh?"

At the restaurant Mark kept ordering beers, before the food, during the food, and after. Chris and I decided to have our mostly untouched dinners wrapped up to go. At first I tried to keep up, but Mark was thirsty, and way fucking behind. He had such a joy about him. I had always found Mark to be a positive, warm person with a mischievous twinkle, but I saw the steam being released behind his eyes. Here Chris and I with nothing but the van, the music, and the accessorizing doubt that came attached, crossed paths with the well traveled, well educated family man in Mark, who had doubt every bit as ensconced in the fabric of his life choices. I think he felt good about being in a position to treat us so well; I think that for whatever reason, he saw a moment where he could reconnect with an isolated, but much glorified, part of his past; a past that we were too young to see in one piece until now; I think Mark wanted to down a few beers in the comfort of familiar souls that had little to do with the next day's responsibility. He paid the bill, seeming the more grateful one.

When he pulled up along side the van he pulled out his wallet and handed me five twenties.

"I talked to Annie last night, we both agreed that you should be able to take Aubrey to California Adventure when she comes to visit you."

"Aubrey and Mom won't be here until June."

"I guess you'll have to save it."

We shook hands, and Mark left. I looked at the money in my hands, and felt terrible. I knew what would become of it: weed, booze and movies. And so it went.

Somewhere in that period Chris and I broke down, and bought a five-inch television for like forty bucks at a radio shack. We had since discovered that Savons, Circuit City, and sometimes Albertsons, were cheaper places to look for them. We got along well enough without one. I remember watching the first half of the Ravens and the Giants Super Bowl in a bar; we left to get money off the card from Albertsons. While I got the money I bought a little food. I returned to the van; Chris had the game on the radio.

"Do you really want to go back to the Bitter Red Head and waste all our money?"

"What, and listen to the second half on the radio?"

"Watching the Ravens play defense or listening; excitement has never been more grunty."

"Okay, I'm just about drunk enough not to really care."

We listened to the game there, got a few beers, and had a good time. In the ensuing weeks, or the next month, we started talking about buying a television. The first thing would be to get the lighter in the van fixed so that we would have something to plug it in to. Once again Steve helped us out. It didn't take much, all we had to do was take the screws out of the dash's face, and connect the grounding wire from the lighter's insert piece to something metal. It took roughly ten minutes, but I would have been too intimidated to remove a single screw myself for fear of blowing up the transmission. I sat there mirroring Steve's screw driver with mine, and watched as he looped a wire into a hole that was part of the insert piece, then observe him take the metal clip that was on the other end of the wire, clipping it to some part of the dash's framework that was also metal.

"And I just thought those things were for smoking joints all the way down," I said.

"Grounding a wire, frying a brain cell; it's all the same," Steve replied.

I don't remember if we had the television during the folks or Mark's visit. I'm thinking it was late February or early March so we probably got it in between the visits. What I remember for sure was putting it on the card. In that same time frame our back brakes went out on the van; the shoes, master cylinder and something else I can't recall, all had to be replaced. The card money was below five hundred but by April it would get a two hundred dollar plus shot in the arm from my tax return. As long as something on par with the timing chain fiasco stayed out of fate's way, we could keep the van on the road.

The promenade was being more consistent in supplying us with our daily needs. Chris learned from Mel about applying for food stamps but we weren't in a rush to do so, yet. I still couldn't get myself to stand in the various food lines we came across. On Sunday and Wednesday at seven in the morning by the showers there was food provided every week. Wednesday offered beans and rice, most times with a slice of ham; Sunday had meatballs with mixed, canned vegetables in a red sauce over rice with a tiny chocolate donut on the side. A slight, old Irish man named Martin supplied the beans and rice on Wednesday, and the rice on Sunday, as he returned with a middle aged man who brought the meat in sauce, and his little daughter to hand out the donuts. The kid's body-type and a bit of her face reminded me of Madison.

It took me longer than Chris to stand in the lines for food. I just felt like we should leave that for the ones who really needed it. Before the first summer ended, I realized that I was one of them.

There were other lines with hot meals being offered in parks or bag lunches handed out at churches, and places like the O.P.C.C. (Ocean Park Community Center) service building. I would patron them all in time, some more than others, but Martin still sticks in my mind as someone special. He had an understanding or acceptance about those he served that exceeded others on a day-to-day basis. Martin, with his slumped shoulders, thin arms, and coke bottle-bottom glasses, had either gathered wisdom from his years or had been born with an innate sense of his own humanity in relation to those both stronger and weaker than he. I know very little about his life—family relations, the career that occupied his years—I only saw the manner in which he spoke, the tone of his eyes when he listened. The middle-aged man who came on Sunday, or the elderly doctor who brought the ham most Wednesdays, were both calm in the face of the obnoxious, and patient with those who weren't. They are good men who set aside their time and money. On occasion I'd catch a glint of disgust or disdain in their eyes, with good reason: Beggars may not be allowed to be choosers but they complain constantly, and are often vulgar, ungrateful, and contemptuous—they don't always smell very perty either. Nothing that either of these two kind gentlemen had ever done in my view had shortchanged their good nature or name. Martin simply had disarmed himself of any judgment; Jesus had fewer cheeks than the guy.

Some days a breeze blows just so, and the next moment it is gone or has changed. It still carries the sweetness of a season, but it somehow no longer understands you. There was this breeze that blew a lot when I was a boy coming home from school on a September afternoon, or on a Saturday morning before a baseball game at the park in early May. It touched me like no other, warming when I felt cool, soothing when too hot. Once in a while a breeze will feel that way to me again, and I don't know why, but I am certain of its' importance. Martin has a perpetual breeze inside him to share where others have only enough wind to blow their own sails.

Each morning when Martin was ready to serve he asked the crowd, "Would anyone like to say a short prayer?"

When I first started waiting in the lines there was a dumpy, aging fellow who appeared to be somewhat articulate, and educated, that always offered to do the deed. His words were weighty and winded in a meandering scope with all the main buzzwords in place. I always enjoyed Martin's simple take on the ritual.

"Thank you lord for this food, and help us to be truly grateful."

Sometimes he would add "beautiful morning" or something to speak toward a specific holiday. "Help us to be truly grateful," was a sentiment I had a great deal of respect for, an act that seemed to elude most of whom I encountered, and myself, on a daily basis.

Chris and I had been in California for only a month when I exploded on him about his sensitivity. We were on the corner of third and Arizona by the AMC theater, I had my head in my hands with elbows perched up on top of one of the four paper machines lined up on the curb's edge. Chris was hurt by something I said, did, or didn't do, during our set. The equipment was piled against the wall, and one of us was supposed to be walking for the van.

"You have no idea how you are; you don't see yourself." The heat behind his eyes measured his words.

"None of this, even if you are right about every little thing, should be this big of a deal." I couldn't look at him; I kept my face hidden in my hands.

"You make it a big deal by being so fucking obtuse, and denying how you treat me."

"Do I really treat you so badly?" I said, turning to face him. "Steve called you the most defensive person he knew last week, and I agreed with you about how ridiculous that was. You are the most self-aware man I know, and make more fun of your faults more than anyone else. But these last few weeks you have been so fucking, incredibly, sensitive. Yes I have been impatient, demanding and inconsiderate, but Jesus-fucking-Christ, not at every single turn I haven't. When did you become so frail? When did all our disagreements grow into this monumental fiasco where all requests upon you are taken as harrowing demands, and all words razor sharp daggers intended to cut you down? I know I can be an asshole, but it feels like that I either have to do it your way or I'm a cold-hearted prick."

"When do we ever do things my way?" Chris' eyes watered with the heat behind them.

"Please tell me you don't believe that."

He stood silent and I knew that I had been answered. All he knew was all I could see for that moment: he was hurt. Not by a solitary remark, not by any specific person. Inside him was a leader that no one followed. Back in Nashville Chris envisioned Ty, Steve, and Eric joining forces with us, and forming the next Eagles. Here in California I formed a habit of taking control once too often. I knew he was right about some of it, but lately he had taken it to an extreme. His wounds had surrounded him leaving the outside world no other choice but to hurt him. I knew that my point had been made, so I was quite surprised to hear myself continuing to rage at him.

"I can't take it anymore. 'Steve said this; Steve should do that; Dave doesn't listen; Dave only cares about himself.' My God, you are a fucking Martyr crucified by his own fucking cause. I don't know what to say anymore, or how to act."

SHUT THE FUCK UP! You don't have to say anything, look at him—I've never seen him so beat. Stopher waited with his mouth softly closed. His lips rested against each other, not anticipating a single word to pass through. Those big round shoulders dipped into his spine as if waiting for the head to be lopped off.

"I just-"

For the love of all that is pure and good in this Godless universe, leave the guy alone. I couldn't

"I just think you need to not be so precious about what you think we should be for you. If nothing else-"

At least I had begun to lower my voice to a sensible tone, offering something gentle rather than the previous vengeful venom I had spewed.

"If nothing else cut us some slack, and know that we love you even as we are failing you."

Finally I stopped. Chris turned away for a moment while I tried to investigate the parameters of turning back time. My eyes pleaded with the back of his head to seek out the good in what I said while dismissing all the extra bullshit I piled on top of it.

He faced me, and as he spoke anger grew ever so slightly beneath his words, but not to the point where his meaning or understanding of his role in what was wrong got lost. "You're right. I see people trying to take away my reality, and I get precious. I'm a big baby who thinks he is right. The thing is that somewhere between some of the time and most of the time I am right. But you are right that that is all beside the point."

Chris raised a hand in a gesture usually accompanied by words then turned away and let his head drop. I wanted to say something soothing but figured I had said enough.

"You are right, Dave. You are right."

He said it, meant it, and never did the words mean less to me. Being right at that moment left me empty of satisfaction, full of remorse.

After that day not much changed but that was okay. It helped to know that the other guy understood a little more than he did before even though he could do little to change what he understood to be wrong with him or the other guy. The arguments kept coming up, and we sorted through them as best we could. A lot of them started on the promenade during a set. On some occasions we suppressed the real meaty volatile action for the van. On others it became part of the floorshow.

Chris and I had different mentalities and sensibilities on stage. I was the plow; keep it moving, let it flow no matter what, and soon we'll get it back on track; something goes wrong, don't worry because odds are that we are the only ones who will notice. That served us well up to a point, but Chris always felt that if you knew you were out of tune within the first bar of a song it would be better to stop, fix it right then and there; too often I regretted not having that ability. Stopher also had that kind of rock-n-roll, Pete Townsend attitude that declared, for all to suffer through, "I am here, this is what I do, and whatever antics I display to get me where I need to be to do what I do, that is how I will behave." If Chris felt frustrated with a lead he played, or was in the middle of playing, he would bend the strings obnoxiously, run the fret board up against the mic stand, throw up his arms in disgust, or a pen harmlessly behind us. I hated it when he did these things between songs, but when he did it in the middle of one I wanted to kill him. The thing is I came to understand how he used those tantrums to get at the best part of his performance. It didn't always work, but it was his way of trying, of caring.

These differences had surfaced in the past years as we played in bars and such, but in our new life we played five days a week, two sets a day, as opposed to the weekly gigs to which we were accustomed. We had sets that went relatively smooth; sets that tickled our frustration or tested our limits; and a few that, once in a while, to some, might indicate that maybe one day we might kill each other. Looking back I see many things that I could have done differently, and others where I was as wrong as I could be. Of course there are those where Chris was a complete asshole. Most I would say were a combination of one having a rough time, and the other missing out on the opportunity to show perspective or compassion, thereby taking a fleeting flame, and trying to suffocate it with a gallon of gasoline.

Discussing missed parts, off notes, and mistakes in general, proved to be our most consistent mistake. On days when both our moods were light, or when a song was new, Chris and I made great teammates in the way tinkered with a loose screw to make a given part tight. Those were the days void of personal baggage, shared and otherwise. Some days you were hungry to get it right even if you disagreed with the other's assessment. On others it was "That cock-sucking, tone-deaf know-it-all is purposely trying to make me look bad."

One day when the winter rains had ended and the sun shined through a clear blue sky on to an April afternoon, Stoph and I were both battling our own ears. We had days where we could tune strings made from the gut of a rat, in wind tunnels, with an orchestra playing the 1812 overture on bagpipes, and then there where the days when the opposite rang true.

On days like the latter you attempted to keep a sense of humor about it, making jokes to the good folk of the promenade.

"We tune because we care."

After a couple of songs the tuning still isn't right so you offer another friendly quip.

"We tune because we don't know how."

We were having one of those in April, and the sound wasn't quite right either. The lead vocal had too much bass, the acoustic was weak, and the Strat sounded like it had been wielded inside a tin box. We fiddled with the EQ but our ears were of no help, they couldn't tune, they couldn't EQ and, in fact, the only thing they were good for was to tell us just how bad everything sounded.

We soldiered on.

A half-hour into the set Chris muttered in between songs, "Are you going to do something about that B string?"

"Give me a D."

"I said B."

"I know, and I said D; none of it sounds on."

"I can hear it, it's the B."

"Do you want to put me out of my misery and tune for me?" I offered him the Strat. "Give me a D."

A couple of songs later Chris gave me a dirty look during one of the chorus' in response to one of my harmonies. (The thing to do here is let it go.) I waited for the song to finish to make things worse.

"What's your problem?"

"We're out of tune and sound like shit."

"I meant that look."

"You're flat."

I shook my head as if he were nuts. You see, in my warped mind that was not being argumentative because I didn't say anything. The ballet of animosity built on itself look-by-look, glib remark by glib remark. Soon I was on the acoustic with Chris taking the Strat.

He tuned as I impatiently stared and critiqued in my mind. (Flat, flat that's got it.) He sharpened. (You had it dumb fuck.) On the next string the same unspoken conversation ensued between my stare and his tuning hand. String after string the tension in my eyes glowed brighter until finally he hit a chord that sounded good to me.

"Ready?"

I hit the first chord to Searching.

"Hang on."

"What?"

"I never said I was ready."

My eyes rolled, my head tilted, and I stepped off the mic: More tuning begat more staring, as if I had been the perfect tuner everyday in my life, let alone earlier in the set. I felt like a crowd drooled their hunger for our first note, screaming for blood or, even worse, for a refund any second. Of course the shoppers walked by unaware as those dining perused their menus.

Ding, ding ding—the string rose in pitch. Dung, dung, dung—it slipped back down. My face tightened as I imagined my hands wringing Stopher's neck. (Pick a pitch you insipid putz.) A full chord strummed announced his concession.

"It's the best I can do."

Finally I sighed and began the song. Then a few bars in I realized that something was off but being the plow I drudged on while sprinkling my resentment righteously behind my eyes. The civilians could not tell, but on some level, I'm sure I went out of my way to make certain that Chris could. Halfway through the song a part of me realized that it was in fact my guitar that was out of tune. I had one thought, Stopher must never know. In the battle to be found correct in each other's mind, truths must be arranged accordingly.

Stoph struggled with his lead work throughout the set thereby shitting on my songs with his mini-tantrums. I did my part by acting superior, and pacif-aggressively doing my best to breast-feed him shame. No big whoop; just a couple of self-involved baby-slash-assholes sorting a few things out. At the end of a song I wrote called, ROAR ON RORY, (A tribute to the late, great Rory Gallagher) the arrangement called for us both to hit the last chord and hold. To vent his frustration, Chris went on a blipping tangent with the Strat that if I were watching from the street would have blown me away. In fact, of all the antics he had displayed, that was one that made the song work for the better. Though I did have a specific reason for wanting the song to end the way I arranged it, that was not why I responded the way I did. On any other day the most I would have said was, "Cool ending riff, but don't forget the way I want it."

"God, you're a prick," I said softly, but loud enough for him to be stuck by it.

"What?!"

"You know fucking what!"

"All I know is that I finally played something that resembled good rock and roll and my supposed partner turns on me."

"I turned on you?!" My eyes boiled, my arms flailed, and I looked upward for a witness. "You haven't been with me all day."

"That's right, you are a perpetual victim; the epitome of loving support failed upon."

"At least I don't shoot you with daggers for every tiny miscue."

"The whole time I'm tuning your burning a hole through my skull."

(Oh, he noticed that.)

"I'm just staring into space."

"What fucking ever!"

This is where I submit my calming influential, superior voice to show that I am above the fray, and capable of pulling back my anger as to bring peace.

"I know you're having a bad day." I am such a sweetheart.

"Here comes the choo choo train," Chris mocked shoving an imaginary spoon at my face, "with yummy patronizing, peach, mush for little Stopher."

"Well that is the most accurate perception of yourself I could conjure; you're a fucking baby."

Our voices engulfed the street and people looked on to see who would kill whom. I could see his face stretch, as eyes seemed prepared to explode out of their sockets, knowing that I looked the same. (We are our father's sons.) My fists clenched, and deep inside I wished that I were capable of beating him in a fight, but my anger fell short of that delusion. Moments existed in the middle of it where I saw the folly from a distance; knew in a vacuumed part of my brain exactly where I had gone wrong; exactly where Stopher stepped out of bounds. Useless knowledge isolated from action lounged in its disappointment of me while the train picked up speed. Curses flew on wings of personal attacks that targeted buttons only a loved one could know.

"Being calm for an instant doesn't make you right, it just makes you deceptive and manipulative."

"Being hurt and wounded only makes you more pathetic."

At some point I grew tired of trying to decipher the specifics into an assignable blame we could agree on, and the folly found me to call a truce.

"Your right, I'm sorry."

I can't say if Chris knew the statement to be pure, to be completely sincere, but he was tired as well. We ended the set early, and started breaking down with a few minor eruptions whenever one of us made the mistake of attempting to engage the facts of the events under the guise of an intellectual discussion. By the time we had the equipment in the van Stoph had a low boil going, and I just wanted it to be over. For all of Chris' accusations of me having to be right it was he who had the hardest time with agreeing to disagree.

"Let's get drunk."

That eased the tightness in his face.

The van sat by the park as the sun weakened, and we vacantly looked out our perspective windows, I behind the wheel. The alcohol flushed me of the desire to ponder beyond the hum of the burnt wires in my head. Chris on the other hand had a steady flow of unresolved anger permeating the air.

"Let's play catch."

Stoph opened the door so quickly that I momentarily remained uncertain if he had heard correctly, and was getting up to retrieve the gloves and ball, or if he thought I had challenged him to a duel and went search of the sword of his choice. He got the gloves. As we walked to the field I sensed in him a boy whose father's will had once again been forced upon him. It felt good to throw the ball, and see it glide under the park lights that melted into the still blue but darkening sky; I loved the sound of the glove being popped by the ball; I loved the motion of my arm delivering, and the delicate technique of the gloved hand receiving; the body turned and swiveled in obedience to both movements. At first I didn't care to notice Stopher's stubbornness in letting the day go; I wanted to feel good, I wanted to feel forgiven. In the end, my joy could not ultimately stand up to his pain.

"Can't you let yourself enjoy this?"

"I am still angry," he said too evenly to be even, and then threw the ball back.

"Baseball and booze, Stoph; what else do you want?" I threw the ball.

"Look, I'll play catch, and I'll be angry." He threw the ball.

"Fuck it." I caught the ball and walked toward the van. "This could have been a moment worth having," I said as I walked past him.

Stopher always came around in one way or another; he was and is a self-aware man. Unfortunately awareness does not influence control, or the lack thereof, it's only a witness.

For all the bickering about music, or the asshole verses obtuseness ratio ranging between us, Chris and I spent the majority of our time making each other laugh and think while filling the promenade with tough, beautiful music. Not all of our fans were other musicians, homeless or hostesses. First of all there was Al, a large, round middle aged black man who showed up every Saturday for our noon set. He bought our first CD one week, and came back the next week asking when we would make another. Al didn't talk much about his life, and in fact shied away from any direct questions. I know that he was an Angels and Lakers fan, but had no interest in football; he loved great guitar, but more so when laid in the heart of a good song; and he loved horror movies (the old ones) and professional wrestling. (I'm pretty sure that he knows that it's fake.) He had the powerful shoulders and the chest of a sweaty, angry lineman with the soft full cheeks of a lost child at the circus. Mostly, his tinted, seventies-round, glasses hid his eyes, though on occasion I would see them, circular and a little vacant. One thing remained evident, he liked watching Stoph and I play, both old classics and songs written by us. I loved watching Al standing on the curb in between songs when he caught our attention to make a request.

"What's that one called that Chris wrote with the line about mechanics?" Al asked, with his usual tapping of the right index finger on his chin while his thumb caressed its underside. Sometimes he rocked back and forth on his heel to help jar the memory.

"Up beat?" Chris tried to clarify.

"Kinda bluesy, but it gets a little rocky."

"Oh, BUILDING A LEGEND," Chris remembered.

Al nodded his agreement raising his finger in the air then touching to the side of his head in way of noting the title for the next time.

I kept waiting for Al to tire of us, and find another act to support, but every Saturday he'd be there. It got to the point that if I ever knew ahead of time that I wouldn't be there the next week, I'd let him know. Also, if Chris or I felt too hung over to play on a given Saturday, at least one of us would always make it out for Al.

People I didn't recognize would start saying "hey" to us on the street. One time coming out of George's diner on Lincoln someone driving a Ford Bronco, stopped by the traffic light, held our FINAL CALL CD up against his window while the two other guys in the truck screamed, "You guys rock." It very well could be the fullest extent of celebrity that we would ever come to achieve. At the time it started happening I probably thought of it as just the beginning, but I think there was a part of me that assumed it would be all we ever got. Therefore I took great satisfaction from each moment.

The Raven started asking me to write things for her to read on her perch. I'd be waiting to play usually having anywhere from an hour to four hours to kill, and she thought that I should put the time to use by amusing her. She had these advertising post cards that she carried around with her. Each month Yahoo.com had a different ad that they printed out on these three by five cards. Sometimes they depicted an up coming movie, a bottle of Absolute vodka, or the MTV awards. One Saturday, after we played a noon set by the dinosaur's tail, while waiting to play again at six, she, for first time, wrote me a quick note on the top card of three she handed over that threatened me in her flirty fashion:

Write to me white boy or suffer my wraith.
Please! Tell me a story.
Lest your hiney taste the tip of my boot!

I knew better than to write anything romantic although poetry was the first thing to pop in my head. As much as I knew that she was too fucking far out of my league I still had an awfully high opinion of myself. As Bukowski (a writer whom I would not discover until 2004) was known to say, "I'm hot with words." I thought better of it even before I actually considered it, and decided to stick to the literal request of a story.

I knew she had a thing for Persian men, and far away, exotic places, so sat with pen in mouth considering the aforementioned things. I looked around the promenade searching for a beginning, and then began:

When last we saw, dogs played, she smiled and the world seemed at ease with itself.

Meanwhile...

The sun beat mercilessly on the Sudan desert floor as Telhan sped along parting the sand at his wheels. He alone knew the powers loomed, taunting the peaceful present with a fearsome future. He also knew where the key to destruction dangled. Days in the middle of nowhere meditating and praying beneath the sun and moon under the influence of just the right combination of drugs (mostly hallucinatory with some heroine, a tad of cocaine, all drowned in a couple bottles of bourbon.) Through blurred eyes and a pounding head, his journey of indulgence had shown him the way. A long way indeed—to the other side of the universe and back. Now on the move once more with another trip ahead, not quite as far spiritually speaking, but this time he would need an airplane to Santa Monica, California in the U.S. of A.

His visions weren't totally clear but he saw bubbles floating over a map bursting in Santa Monica. So he would go there and take more drugs to learn the rest.

That took up the time I had to kill, and or, the creative energy I had to spare for that day. She read the story as soon as she could; I watched her read while setting up my stage. I knew my handwriting to be indecipherable to most eyes, but she seemed to be getting it, and liking it. I'd lay out a chord from the gizmo to the mic stand, and see her smile at a phrase. During the untangling of a few other chords I heard a cackle, and quickly looked to see her teeth revealed, her nose scrunched up, her eyes sparkle with amusement. It warmed me to see her take joy from the words, but I did my best to remember my place, and keep her laughter in perspective. Just as Chris and I were set to start the Raven shot from her perch with a bounce to take a tug at Stopher's beard, then mine. She circled us, headed back, but stopped to look at me. A few seconds ticked while I spent hours watching her take a brief moment to look into my eyes. I could see that the story made her happy, that I had done something right. The fact that I wrote about a drug fiend with a beyond worldly purpose instead of trying to seduce her, I think, kind of seduced her. I took her somewhere without being obvious or typical, and in that pause before returning to work, her smile told me all of that. I smiled back slightly sheepishly as if to say, "I'm a writer—it's what I do."

"I really liked my story," quoth the Raven, after our set was done. She started to leave then stopped again. "I-thanks."

Enjoy it bucko but don't even dream about it, I told myself.

Within the week we were in a similar situation, she asked for another installment:

Telhan's plane landed on a misty Santa Monica Saturday night. Once through the luggage carousel he had one thought: find a reliable dealer and head for Venice beach.

He hailed a cab, jumped inside, and was shocked, but pleasantly so. A countrymen behind the wheel, he thought, what are the odds? As this new best friend drove off, Telhan told of his miraculous mission and urgent needs. The countryman peered into his rearview mirror, disbelieving yet sympathetic.

"I will not doubt your words, crazy as they are," he said. "Venice beach will have all you seek. Go to the skateboard pavilion and ask for Skippy."

Tears filled Telhan's grateful eyes.

"Thank you, thank you," he said laughing through watered eyes. "You have been sent to me, this is true, but it was you who took heed to the call. Bravery and wisdom you possess beyond your own comprehension. For that I thank you."

The cab pulled to the curb, Telhan poured out, found Skippy, dropped several hits of orange sunshine and plopped on to Venice's darkened shore. His brain disengaged, reality got over itself and all became clear: Bubbles were not bubbles, but a woman—Bubbles Fontaine. He saw her in the stars outside the realm of consciousness. Her smile graced a carnival where dinosaurs of green stood with no intentions of moving, animals of ballooned limbs succumbed to the whims of children and music filled the air.

Did such a place exist? He wondered. Maybe this was all a code to be deciphered? Why did all these images come in threes?

Still in the throws of a warm sensation, compliments of the sunshine, which is orange, Telhan stumbled northward along the beach. He felt compelled to do so. Night owned the sky for hours to come. He would walk for as long as he could.

I had to stop there and get back to my day job.

It would be a week or so before I saw the Raven on the promenade. There was a visit or two in between at the park. On one of the occasions she had decided to take me for a ride.

"I'm taking your brother hostage," she informed Chris matter-of-factly, speaking to him past me.

I sat behind the wheel of my faithful Ford immobile for a moment, watching her standing in the street with the park over her shoulder. The word "no" held little in the way of a specific meaning with her. I had in the past rejected her commands so she knew me to be capable of resisting the charms that beamed through a beauty deep enough to shame an ocean into drying up. At first, I said no because that is how I am with people I don't know; later I refused, to remind myself that I was, and would remain, alone; she liked my company—that's all. Through our time on the promenade, and her continual visits with Chris and I at the park, I came to feel true friendship bloom, so I knew where my feet were to step, and where they never would.

"Well," she smiled, "are ya gonna sit there or get up and hug like a man."

The Raven had hugged Stoph and I in one instant or another. She was a friendly girl with a lot of people so I went out of my way not to write anything into them. She was soft, warm and genuine, so I enjoyed them on their intended level. I got out of the van and wrapped her up in my arms. The Raven liked firm handshakes, and even firmer hugs. The lists of things I liked about her grew.

"Let's go walk a dog."

I loved the way she said "dog" with a strong D followed by an O sound that rolled around her over exaggerated lips to come out of her mouth almost like an echo, but with a low solitary tone befitting a cartoon gold miner; the G came from the back of her throat a solid after thought.

"Oh, you'll need a guitar."

"Of course."

I grabbed the blue one—Joel gave me—from the back of the van, and we were off.

Coco, a chocolate lab-pit-bull mix was the Raven's main client. She shook her behind, yearned with her eyes, and sniffed at us from the back seat of the black Neon as we got in the front.

"Coco!"

The Raven leaned toward the back grabbing the dog affectionately round the snout, bringing it to her lips.

"Yes, Coco, I know," the Raven cooed. "It's make-out Monday. I missed you all weekend too."

I watched happily as the two bitches said hello extensively.

"Lotta love in this car."

"And you ain't getting' none of it."

"Ouch! That hurts in places were even soup don't feel good."

"Ha, ha, ha, "she cackled throwing her head back. "That's funny; I like that. Did you just come up with it?"

"No, it's something a great songwriting friend of mine from Nashville used to say."

"That Steve or Eric guy?"

"No, he's still back in Nashville, although I think he's headed for Austin: The great Ty Hager."

She drove us to a dog park where balls were thrown for Coco to fetch, and songs were song at the Raven's request.

"Play me something I never heard before."

I offered up a few songs I wrote in Nashville that never made it into the act—she loved them.

"I love that twangy shit."

The time came for Coco to go home so she dropped me off at the van first. We had only been gone an hour but it felt longer.

"That was fun, huh?" She looked at me with a wide expression that didn't look needy, but in its own way was.

"You are good company, kid."

In the van Stopher grinned.

"I'm telling you she just likes hanging out with us."

"She didn't take me hostage."

The next time we saw her on the promenade was a weekday, our set had already started by the time she showed up for work. No stories for the Raven today. The more I got to know the Raven the harder I played when she was there, and Goddammit, I always played hard. It turned out to be one of those days that convinced Chris and I that we were as good as it got. The harmonies meshed, the guitars soared, and the songs hit humanity on the nail. The Raven seemed convinced too.

"Ya done me proud, boys," she said as we rolled our equipment away.

Yes, by then we had broken down and got one of those hand trucks (in mid-March or early April) that can be assembled easily into a four-wheel cart. The gizmo, chord bag, guitars, mic stands and mic stand platforms all fit quite nicely.

Having had a good day, musically and financially, Chris and I picked up some cheap booze for a gentle evening's demise by the park. The sun gripped longer and longer to the day, but the clocks had not yet been sprung, or had only done so recently. The trees across from the park cozied over the van like a mother nestling her young, and we sipped our medicine in the hearth of her cool womb. It was at that moment I saw coming down the street from Lincoln the sleek, dipped hood of a black Neon Plymouth cruising in our direction.

"The Raven doth approach."

I got out of the van to meet her where she parked in the lot by the bathrooms. She seemed excited.

"Boys! Mamma has come to take you to the House of Blues."

Stoph too sniffed the excitement in her approach, and had stepped out of the van to cross the street when the announcement was made.

"What?" We both had an uncertain notion of where it all might be leading.

"I have two V.I.P. passes to the House of Blues to see Shawn Mullins. You remember that song I loved so much? Well there are two other bands, or maybe just one, and he's the opening act, or he could play between the other two—if there is even a third—but I think it'd be cool all the same."

Chris searched my eyes, and I his, for a graceful way out.

"Why don't you and Dave just go?"

I shot him a, "Hey, nice stab in the back; knife-wise," look.

"You're both coming—I'll be right back to finish telling you what's what." The Raven rushed to the toilet.

"Thanks a lot, Stoph."

"She doesn't want to take me, she wants you."

"I am telling you, she just likes to hang out."

"This will be perfect: An evening on the town, she's dressed to the nines, V.I.P. passes at the House of Blues. What have you got to lose?"

"I know, I know. Just come."

"I don't want to."

"Either do I, well mostly…I don't know."

"You guys will have fun."

"Still, it feels weird. I think she might want you to come so bad just so I don't get the wrong idea."

"I am getting drunk here."

"Here she comes."

"Alright, this is not a discussion. This is one of them there things where I talk, and you move your big tushies."

Chris and I exchanged glances, "Tushies."

"That's right, motherfuckers: tushies. I got it all figured: I buy a regular ticket and you two can take turns checking out the V.I.P. room."

"Let's just do it Stoph. When else could we afford to go to the House of Blues?"

"I really don't want to."

I could hear the patience being tested in his voice, and draining from his face.

Chris and I talked about that moment recently but neither could pinpoint exactly how he finally agreed to go. In the end I am sure he did it for me.

"Okay," the Raven said, breathlessly when Stoph consented, "I gotta make a couple of phone calls before we go."

She walked off.

"Thanks."

"It could be fun. Oh, and I'm not going in no fucking V.I.P. room. You go with her; I'll get drunk and watch the show. Just do me a favor."

"What?"

"Don't be a complete tweeb; make *some* kind of move."

"Are you sure about the V.I.P. room? It could be cool."

"I'm positive; you two go your way, I'll go mine. We'll just pick a meeting spot and time when we get there."

I stood facing the ball field running a pick through my hair. Chris and I both put on our double-breasted, black suit jackets in honor of the occasion.

"Don't comb your hair," the Raven said impatiently. "You'll make it all frizzy."

"I like frizzy."

"I don't-"

"And that's all that counts."

"That's what Momma's talkin' 'bout."

The Raven had said something about me combing my hair on the promenade once before. At the time I thought she referred to the bad edict of grooming oneself in public. It sounded like something my Grandma would say, so I complied.

"You have such great hair and you're ruining it." The Raven slid her fingers up into my hair and gently fluffed it. "Wait here."

She went to the car and pulled a big black canvas bag out of the backseat. From it she retrieved a couple of eight ounce spray bottles, one red the other white.

"Come here," the Raven ordered in a motherly tone.

She started spraying around my head with the red bottle first.

"And you are?" I asked void of fussing.

"This water, the other is my own personal concoction of water and various conditioners."

"A taste from your personal stash as it were."

"Yes, in drug-speak."

She finished spraying and fluffing, walked around me touching lightly at some here; squeezing other bunches into curls there, as she saw fit.

"Okay." She walked back to the car and started rearranging the mess of bags and garbage in her backseat to make room.

"What? No lollypop."

"I'll give ya a pop." Her head remained in the back of the car while her voice and ass floated above the fray.

We arrived at the House of Blues late walking into the main room just as Shawn Mullins was finishing a song. The three of us stood toward the back of the room but saw the stage just fine. He did two more songs, and that one of them was the song that she loved so very much. When he started that song her eyes darted at me while her hand took hold of mine, warmly with purposed affection. (I was in a band called Purposed Affection—Poco.)

"He had a single mic with a guitar, and the sound man still fucked it up," Chris said when Shawn left the stage.

"Yeah?" The Raven didn't let the remark disappoint her enthusiasm. "He did my song."

"Right on cue," I said, like a father grateful to see his child happy. She had a dangerous way of making you feel like a daddy—a daddy who wanted to do unholy things.

"Lets go upstairs." Her hand got tighter around mine.

She has been holding my hand practically since we'd been standing here, I realized with a strange sense of delight.

"You kids have fun," Stopher smiled.

The Raven began to drag me off, but I slipped my hand away to come back toward him.

"I'll come check on you in an hour."

"No. I have my bottle." Stopher stopped to survey the room. "When it's all over I'll be by those stairs that lead to the bathrooms."

"Are you sure?"

"Positive."

The Raven had already drifted toward the stage left stairs that led up to the V.I.P. room. "Come on," she shouted.

I looked at Chris with an appreciative nod, then flew for the Raven.

The upstairs room was just another bar with some televisions for viewing the stage. The people there all had a vibe of belonging while casting aspersions on anyone else's presence. They dressed well in silky eveningwear that matched the colors of their eyeliner, and spent more money at the beauty parlor then I did on liability insurance for the van—that was just the men. Of course there were some who wore jeans, or at least draped a bandana around the neck to say, "Rock and roll, baby. Now pass the sushi." The Raven wore one of her long dark gowns with a multi-colored, rabbit fur vest. I am not a fan of the whole fur and leather thing but I was still a fan of hers, so I bit my tongue, on that evening at least.

She bought a glass of wine and we sat at the end of the bar near a television hanging off the wall. The band was called the Honeysuckers, Honeydogs or maybe it was Old 98. I had heard Angel talk favorably over the phone about them. We listened a little as they plowed their version of rock and roll, which came out to me as rehashed from the stuff that went before just not as good. The Raven seemed even less interested in them than I did, so we started talking.

"Tell me something about your family," she said, taking my vodka/water bottle from in front of me.

"We've covered all the highlights I'm sure: Great, artistic parents; blue collar, lower middle class—financially speaking; oldest brother Joel taught me how to love playing guitar then, went crazy. Say, are you gonna have a drink of that or ya just keepin' it company?"

"Never you mind; it's in good hands."

"Have a drink and slide it this away; nice and friendly like."

She had a pull and I followed suit.

"Whenever I hear you talk about your family I think about how I wish I had grown up like that. Yet I don't think I could have stood sharing things, like toys, food, clothes; I AM an only child, ya know."

"But if you were born into them you would have been different."

"See, that's what I'm saying, I was born to be an only child."

"You mean spiritually speaking you have a soul that is destined to be alone?"

"Well not to that extreme, but some where in there," she said, holding her hands out parallel, left above the right, in front of her face, her eyes searching the space between them.

I laughed at the exaggerated tone in her voice.

"You think I'm funny, huh?"

"Yeah, I do."

"I had a friend who said that we had sitcom-banter. We have that but…"

"Only more sophisticated."

"What he said." She spoke to an imaginary audience behind the bar as she shot a thumb in my direction.

"Okay, I have a question."

I paused as she turned to face me.

"I know that you are this friendly only child who likes to adopt orphans away from home. Throw in your love of music and words, and that pretty much sums up our time together."

"I likes you guys; you're good people." The Raven's voice went Brooklyn with a touch of twang.

"I know and I understand my place: I'm a fat, drunken, middle-aged, brilliant failure. The thing is that Chris seems to think that you have some kind of attraction to me beyond a friendly-persuasion. I guess I've been feeling that too. A little bit."

"I told you how I had a girlfriend in high school who thought I was flirting with her, didn't I?"

"Yeah, believe me, I know how you are. No, I have taken that into account and just thought there might be something going on between us. Obviously you are a knockout, and I'd do ya in heartbeat. Literally."

The Raven's eyes crinkled with laughter as her smile beamed a breath of shyness while not betraying her slyness.

"You talk real perty like, I'll give ya that."

I sensed that things were not going in the direction of romance. Oddly I didn't feel embarrassed, or all that disappointed, because it was worth knowing for sure, and not even in my highest expectations, did I really, think much of my chances. If I were seventy pounds lighter she might give me a shot, but who could blame her.

"I just don't think that way about you."

"I understand. Believe me I understand." I thought that was all I had to say on the matter but I kept going. "I do think there is some kind of attraction on your part that you're not copping too though. I may be a slob but I happen to be a very sexy one. I know you love my hair." I gave it a bouncy toss. "I'm a good looking guy with a hell of a lot more talent than fat, and that is saying something. On top that I happen to be a dynamo in the sack."

"I can see how you might have gotten the wrong idea, but you asked and I answered. "

"What about the way you look at me when I'm playing?"

"I do that to help you get tips. I figure someone sees a pretty girl gazing at you they'll listen a little closer and see how much you've got going on. Besides, I look at Stopher too."

"Not the way you look at me."

"Well, you are kind of cute, and your voice is damm incredible." She thought for a second. "Your voice does get me tingling once in a while but that's not enough."

"Once in a while; aren't you the coy one."

We sat silently for a few minutes, each us sipping from my bottle, exchanging glances.

"I will tell you what." I announced.

"Oh, I am sure you will."

"Kiss me once right here and now."

"I'm not going to kiss you."

"Why not? What's a kiss between friends? I promise you that at the very least it will be pleasant. Come on, I went out on a limb here tonight. We're sitting here in this high-falooten joint, out on the town, had a few drinks; it seems to me like the right thing to do."

"Alright, I'll kiss you."

"I knew I could con ya."

The Raven got off her stool to stand in front of me. We leaned toward each other slowly. I kept my eyes open until her lips touched mine, then opened them once for a milli-second during to see if it was actually happening. Now I have a rule about kissing someone for the first time. I part my lips slightly to envelope the upper or lower lip, or to receive the tongue, depending whichever is offered. Once contact is made I am in a position to play off whatever lead the women in question has laid down for me. I had suffered the awkwardness of sticking my tongue into someone else's teeth enough as a youth. Her warm breath spread over my lips then disappeared into my mouth. At first I readied myself to receive her upper lip when her tongue graced the outer edges of my lips on its way inside. It did not lunge nor slither, it merely appeared, becoming instantaneously a part of me. The kiss maintained a subtlety while gently pulsing beneath the thinning boundaries of passion. Our jaws gingerly guided the swirling tongues that mingled between us void of exaggerated folly.

It was a very good kiss.

She pulled back hovering over the event. Her mouth still hung before me, tenderly open, so I considered myself cordially invited in for another whirl.

"Eh, eh, eh," the Raven pulled back, "just one." The distance now placed between us withdrew the invitation while taunting of the party to be had.

I knew she felt what I felt about the kiss, but she downplayed it as nice. We sat for a little while longer until we noticed that the show had ended.

"We better go find your brother."

Outside the door a few steps down the trendily conceived, rickety stairs she turned abruptly and grabbed my face with both hands.

"Okay, one more."

She planted a kiss on my lips, minus the tongue. It happened quickly holding none of the previous sensuality that the first one captured so eloquently. I took the second one as a validation of the first. Deep down I think she knew that kissing me would stir her blood, just not as much as it did.

By the time we found Chris and got to the car, I realized that I was quite drunk. I had started drinking at five in the afternoon, but paced myself when our adventure with the Raven had begun. I think from the moment she doused any little hope I had for an extended romance I must have started pounding because from the time just before we kissed to getting in the car, my bottle went from over half full to pretty much empty. I squeezed into the back seat grateful the night would be over soon. The rejection apparently was having a delayed effect on me.

The Raven began our trek home with a reckless u-turn out of the parking place only to make another u-turn a few blocks later and park again.

"I have to show you guys this place," she blurted.

If I hadn't been so drunk I would have been in a better position to see how drunk she had been. The details here get murky. I remember walking into a fancy hotel. The hotel had some affair going on, we were crashers. As we were doing it I remained unconcerned because number one, I didn't give a fuck, and number two, Stoph and I were but henchmen for the Countess of Frivolity, all questions belonged to her. Who at any kind of party would object to the presence of a beautiful woman? On top of that we only floated through the outskirts of the gathering on our way to the women's restroom. The Raven had dined at the hotel with one of her many wealthy suitors, and I guess the toilet made a substantial impression on her. Oh, and she was drunk. Actually I think she was getting a kick out of roaming among the glitz and glam of Hollywood with a couple lowdown beastly scruffs like Stoph and myself. She dug the contrast of walking between us anywhere, the added hoity toity atmosphere only made it more so.

The Raven practically dragged us into the bathroom. We still hung close to the door as she spread her arms out in the room's center lapping up the ambience for us to drink.

"Here, this what I wanted to show you." She walked to the mirror and leaned on the counter. "I love luxury."

"I love not getting arrested," Chris chimed in.

My head bobbled to and fro in lieu of actual words.

The Raven leant further on to the counters with her elbows. "I can see my ass."

The ceiling had a mirror, the opposing wall had mirror; reflected images ran rampant.

"I don't know exactly why, but there is something so chic and sexy about the way these mirrors are arranged."

"She wants you to go over there," Stopher said, nudging my shoulder.

"She doesn't see me that way," I mumbled with mockery to the memory of her in the V.I.P.

"Look at that ass," he whispered. "She wants you to grab it."

I mumbled incoherently. Most of this part of the evening was re-told to me by Stopher. During our little private conference, she lounged over the counter, staring into the mirror, no doubt conjuring up princes on Harleys who bought her minks and diamonds, served on platters with racks of lamb. Stopher tired of my drunken indifference, and offered her ass his hands. She indulged him politely, but ever so momentarily, then escorted us back to the car. Stoph has never forgotten what heaven felt like, and if one wants to make him happy, they only need ask about the night he groped the Raven fair.

She delivered us back to the van. All I can tell you about the ride home is that the car shook with speed. Chris got us to Albertsons, and I began to rouse from my stupor. I don't know how long it took from that point to realize that Stoph was angry. I believe that I relayed to him my attempt with her, and the ensuing failure, at some point before his anger. He even congratulated me on the kiss, relishing in my detailed telling. So when his anger found me I couldn't have been more shocked.

"You left me."

"What?"

"You ran off without a thought or concern for me."

"You said I could; you told me I should."

"You could have checked on me, made sure nothing happened to me. I could have been beaten in an alley, or rotting in jail for all you cared."

It all escalated rather quickly, and I lay that at my feet. He was being absolutely ridiculous, a historic revisionist about the evening, but I could have defused him with the right approach. Instead I attacked him.

"You fucking, mother fucking baby!" I screamed. I started out confused only to arrive at furiously-righteous by the next breath.

"Right, I'm a baby, and you're a goddamm saint who abandons his own blood at the first whiff of pussy!"

"You have got your head so far up your ass that I couldn't possibly scream loud enough for you to hear me!"

"Go ahead and scream, that's what you're good at!"

I was drunk, sleepy and fed up. A little bit more sober and maybe I could have seen how gone he was; how far off in his very own liquor-soaked pain he had been. It would have been a long ugly night, but not as ugly as it got.

Once it got going all I did was scream: "YOU FUCKING BABY!!!"

Oh there were variations on theme but that holds the gist.

Finally a switch went off on Stopher's face. Never mind that he started it, forget that he was about as wrong as he could be—I had gone too far. I dismissed him completely and viciously. The wrong that he saw done to him, the due kindness he felt deprived of, would not be shouted down.

"That's it." His voice turned cold. Not soft, not loud, but final and decisive.

The van's driver's door flung open and he got out.

"I am kicking your ass."

I saw him through the windshield stomping around the front of the van. Amidst that moment I had a few thoughts, all related to the same end. He had snapped, I had snapped him, and I could not unsnap him. I had no delusions about winning a fistfight with Stopher, yet as seriously as I took him, I remained unafraid. It could have been I was that angry, thought him so wrong, or that I was *that* drunk. The sheer insanity that he could feel righteous about something where all the facts stood clearly against him, left me out of the moment, a spectator; a spectator whose door had just been opened by a large, angry man.

Stoph leaned into the van clutching at, and tearing, the collar of my t-shirt. His nail tore at my skin, he may have swung a couple of fists. If he did they damaged the air not me. As he came at me I managed to turn to face him, still seating, and pull my knees in to place my feet on his waist. I unleashed the strength of my legs forward sending him flying. The big man hit the cement hard, but agile as he was, got back to his feet before I thought to get out of the van. There was an instant when I saw him on the ground and believed, "I'm going to kick his ass." When he came at me again he brought a resounding truth with him: "There is no fucking way in all the world that I can kick his ass." The scary part was that I was damm well going to try, and he was damm well going to make it an issue of me having to do so.

Then the cops showed up.

Four cars pulled up from different directions. I don't remember flashing lights, and I definitely heard no sirens. Stoph had resumed his attack position when the cliché' called out:

"Freeze!"

I think someone said that, I mean, it certainly would have been appropriate.

"Out of the van, both of you!"

Stoph backed off of me and I slid out of the passenger's seat on to my feet.

"Sorry to drag you out here officers," I said, amazingly calm, I thought. "Just a couple of brothers sorting a few things out. Loudly."

"On the ground." His voice settled substantially.

There must have been a gun pulled somewhere but I can't see it in my mind. Cop cars parked every which way with doors flung open colored the moment in white and black. Two officers sat Chris by the front tire, cuffing his hands behind his back, while two others laid me face down with my forehead on the running board.

"This isn't as bad as you think," Stoph offered.

"It's bad enough," an officer replied.

"We really are good neighbors," I added, speaking directly to the ground.

"Any weapons inside?"

"No," Stoph answered.

"Well, we have an ax and sledge-hammer just inside the front door, for camping; chopping wood." I didn't want them finding it and think us liars.

"Any drugs?"

"Just a little booze," Stoph sighed.

I could feel his shame, his utter disappointment in himself. I wanted to say something like, "We couldn't find any weed today" or "If we had weed none of this would have happened" but instead I looked at an oil spot on the pavement, and hoped it came from some else's car. I heard Stopher's voice plead with them to allow me to remove my face from the pavement.

"Get'em up," one ordered the others.

With that Stoph and I were helped to our feet and we looked each other in the eyes; I smiled, while he shook his head then looked at the ground.

"So, what's going on here?"

I recognized the questioning officer, and a couple of others, from the promenade.

"Just a couple of drunk brothers blowing off steam," I said, then quickly continued. "We're musicians who play out on the promenade. We live in our van and sleep here a lot. The store manager knows were here, up 'till now we've been quiet, respectful neighbors. Ask Steele Smith from the promenade, he knows us, he'll vouch for our character."

"He knows Steele," one of the backdrop officers, whispered, into the ear of the man in charge.

I glanced at Stoph and he mouthed wordlessly, "Good one."

The officers conferred, ran our licenses, asked the usual questions: Any outstanding warrants? Are you a member of a gang? Any scars and tattoos? Etc.

The best thing I can say about the whole incident was how Stoph and I responded to the arrival of the cops. We calmed them down, spoke with respect being immediately apologetic. It took a while but they decided to trust us that we would go to sleep and not cause any more trouble.

"If we get called back, you are both going to jail."

"We understand."

"Thanks so much."

"Again, we are very sorry."

"Have a safe shift guys." Chris always said that when bidding farewell to an officer after an encounter. He always meant it.

As they pulled away relief sprayed down my spine. It all could have gone so very badly.

"We dodged that bullet," I said to Stoph empty of all anger or resentment.

"You can still go fuck yourself," he said in hushed but harsh breath.

His previously contrite face melted to disdain before the cop cars left the lot. He walked back to the driver's seat in a huff. At first my head filled with hot raging blood. Even if I had been the cause of this fiasco, his own good would have been better served by shutting his mouth, and going to bed. I stood dumbfounded in the lot unable to let air out of my lungs for fear of forming a word or creating an action.

Go to bed, close your eyes and keep your mouth shut, I ordered myself.

Once in bed the covers took me in forgivingly. They understood how much I needed them.

"You can blame me for the whole thing, and I know you will," Stoph fumed from behind the wheel. "Dave doesn't ever do anything wrong. I know what I did, I know who I am!" As loud as his rage scowled the parameters of the van, they felt confined to our walls. The venom in his voice however, seeped on to the ground, cracking the surface that held our wheels, with pure hatred. "In the morning I'll be sorry and you won't own a thing. Fuck you, fuck you, fuck you, fuck you!" His throat hissed each "fuck" and oozed each "you" minding the outside world while thundering an apocalyptic storm in his chest.

The lids of my eyes squeezed themselves, holding off their surging desire to bulge, my lower lip crawled between biting teeth that demanded silence. There was no rational discussion, no harmonic conclusion that words could arise, only fire and gasoline, gasoline and fire, begging to burn, crying for fuel.

He ranted and I held myself from head to toe, beseeching silence, a world where no one had anything to say. It felt like he burned for hours, and that sleep would never let me in. When I finally let the flames engulf me, when his rage overcame that which burned inside me, I was freed. Once I no longer had anything to suppress, and conceded to the heated winds, his words simply became heavy music, and I slept.

In the morning I woke with a hoarse throat. The yelling had taken the toll of singing a twelve-hour rock and roll show. The liquor's remains pulsed in my head, and the night's rage awoke inside me. My lip, sore from being bitten for so long, loosened and the very act that allowed sleep had also acted as a storage facility whose walls no longer stood firm. It needed only for Chris to speak.

"Sorry abo-"

"Don't you dare," I rasped. No police would be called for, I could barely hear myself. "I don't care what you have to say, or how you feel. We almost got arrested and you, instead of licking your wounds, counting your blessings, and going to bed, you chose to attack me, belittle me; my arms were down and you kept swinging. You think last night was my fault? You are as wrong as fucking wrong could be. You told me to go, and I went. I gave you every chance to take it back, and you didn't. Then at the end of the night you cry like a baby acting like a big man. Fuck you, fuck you!" My throat screamed out its shadow of a former sound, I dug deeper and deeper with each muscle from head to toe. "You think I'm a shit who never sees his end. I always see my end! I'm I taking away your reality? Well that's because your reality is fucking full of SHIT! I have always come around to seeing my part and 'fessing up. Last night you were as wrong as wrong can be, it was all you, all fucking you. I'll never say any different, and if you don't like that, I'll buy you fucking bus ticket right fucking now! I don't care what you have to say, I don't give a shit how you feel. I had to lay here and listen to your endless, whiney shit for hours biting my lip, keeping quiet so we wouldn't bring the cops back. I'll buy you a bus ticket right now! RIGHT FUCKING NOW!!"

I coughed and whizzed while Chris sat silent behind the wheel where he had slept. I laid in my bed behind the curtain, the steam of my spent rage, wafting from the blankets.

I don't know how we settled it but we did. We gave each other space, talking very little over the ensuing days. I'm sure some things got talked about for that was our way, but not as much as they usually do. For my part I have never hated him as much as I did that morning. Of course now I do see things that I did wrong that night even though he *was* about as wrong as he could be. We are all silly, needy animals who know they are going to die. It is too huge an object, this business of existing, to be precious about the whole thing at once. So we pick a moment, or an event, or a feeling, and try to pack all our preciousness into them, and demand others to take heed. Chris is as precious to me as the word will allow. See how we are?

Life settled back into life, and we played a Saturday noon set on the block north of Arizona by the smoothie-fruit stand, Al looked on. Stoph sang ALL ALONG THE WATCHTOWER, and I gave it my utmost funked-up attention, as my way is apt. Al had requested it, which boosted its meaning for Stoph and I. During the last verse when Chris came up on the line, *"Two riders were approaching…"* he had long ago formed the habit of holding two fingers to phyiscalize the lyric. On this day Al joined in on the ritual, mirroring Stoph from his position on the curb. Chris got the biggest kick out of that.

"Great set," Al said, as he approached us extending his hand while we broke down the equipment.

"Thanks, Al," I said receiving his limp-fish.

Al held out his hand, soft and passionless. It appeared to be a pleasantry he indulged while not fully understanding its purpose. To look at him was to suspect an almost mythic strength stirring beneath a dormant hulk. Taking his hand revealed Jell-O in Jell-O-skinned clothing. Seeing Al every Saturday warmed my heart, and lit a fire under my musical soul; shaking his hand afterward was a meaningless encounter, like a breeze that doesn't lift a single hair out of your eyes. To be clear, I am not one of those who expects a Roman-knuckles challenge to define who the real man is, with every handshake. A hearty grip to exhibit a notion of goodwill was all I sought. I guess it's one of those things you get from your elders or you don't. My Grandma Mullowney (my Mom's mom) insisted we understand the value of a firm handshake. A good deal of her edict fell on deaf ears, but the firm handshake found its mark.

Al said goodbye to Stoph, I could see him looking at his hand searching for the point as Al walked off.

"I'll get this, you grab the Martin and a mic stand, and go see if you get the six at our spot," I said.

Stoph had already picked up the guitar, grabbing the mic stand, before I spoke.

I rolled into our favorite spot at the tail of the dinosaur to find Stoph off to the side watching Ned Timms flying up and down the fret board. I looked around for any other equipment or sign claiming the six'o clock, as I'm sure Chris had already done. In my search I came upon the Raven flirting with a would be customer in front of George's Bistro. Her laugh, genuine, her eyes, sparkling; the man and his friend had no choice but to want to be near her; they took a seat and hoped for her return. As she scanned the walk for another body to seat she saw me and smiled. This smile had less energy then those that shined before. It settled easily on her face like bird on a branch after a long flight in the wind. Her eyes dimmed the sparkle, darkening with penetration. I had seen her by the park a couple times since the House of Blues, and played for her once on a weekday on the promenade. We mutually, without discussion, decided to not re-live the kiss, and I never told her about Stoph and my fighting. By the park she did make a comment about the tear in my t-shirt.

"Nice skin, sleezeball."

"Oh, Stoph was just putting an exclamation on a given point."

Nothing else on the matter was said.

A family walked in front of the restaurant and the Raven chirped to their hunger. Twenty minutes passed, I settled in for a long three-hour plus wait before I could play.

"I'm gonna take a walk," Chris informed me.

"Take your time."

I sat around the side of the dinosaur's oval home on the cement ledge, leaning my head back to watch a couple of palm trees wave at each other. I enjoyed feeling a bit more at home in California, like I belonged in the streets of Santa Monica. The transition from intruding guest to established presence eased ever closer toward completion.

"Here ya lazy bum; get to work."

The Raven had placed a pen and some cards in my hand, and fled back to her perch before I could pull my eyes from the sky. By the time I returned from my reverie all I saw was the back of an elegant creature in a long, red, spaghetti-strapped gown; long black boots bouncing away like a schoolboy who had just pulled my pigtails. I looked at the top card and read:

Now write to me white boy...WRITE

Go on & make up sumthin

Don't just sit there!

ORELSE (This threat of violence brought to you by the number 8)

Do I need to give a boost or can you do it by yourself?

If you need a start...make up one about this jewelry for instance

I looked to see her sly smile and cocky, swaggering, impatient stance. Her necklace looked Native American or maybe Aztec. I remembered the story I had already started and asked the Raven if she had it with her. She told me to wait, then ran it over to me ten minutes later. I looked over where I had left off, and took a moment to think.

More time had passed then Telhan could account for.

"Where am I?" he asked the wind.

The sun answered by beating his brow. "Under my rising force," it boomed.

Telhan rose from the sand, stumbled up the shore and landed on the street in a heap of confusion. The street told his knees that it was not soft like the sand.

With the pain gripping his knees, blood rushed to his brain with its message. The blood also carried a memory.

"3rd street," he shouted at the traffic light.

The traffic light said, "Walk."

He did.

Music played, balloons squeaked, dancers shuffled and Telhan's eyes went a blaze, his ears popped and his mouth gaped.

"Such a place," he blurted.

Then he began down the street mumbling one word over and over, "Bubbles."

Two blocks pushed beneath his feet before a voice answered his chant.

"Yes," she said, smiling.

"What?" He spoke as if awakening from a deep sleep.

"You called me," she laughed.

"I did?"

"'Bubbles,' you said 'Bubbles'; that's me."

"You?"

"Disappointed?"

"No," he replied heavily.

"I should think not," she said, striking a pose while flipping her majestic hair. "So, whatta ya need?"

Just then, Telhan saw the necklace around her neck.

"The necklace!" he shouted.

"Slow down my little puppy," she said completely unthreatened. "I'd like to help you, and you sure look like ya could use some, but that's taking it too far."

"You don't understand," he implored, "there is certain danger—forces you could not possibly comprehend."

"Well I'm sure these forces will comprehend my knee-high boots up their ass," she said unimpressed.

"You are brave, I can see that," he surmised.

"Brave enough," she countered, through a curious squint.

"May I ask where you received such a necklace?" he asked cautiously.

"My mother," she responded. "It's a family thing."

Suddenly music exploded from across the street causing Telhan to jump.

"Relax," Bubbles said, "those are my boys blowin' some steam. Don't worry, they're good for what ails ya."

"Indeed," he whispered before continuing with his questions. "Then you are of blood with the necklace?"

"Yeah, you could say that."

"Then there are no worries. But if that is the case, why the spiritual journey and visions of travel? Why was I submitted to dire chemicals and organic herbs of hallucinations?"

"I dunno," she shrugged. "Did you ever consider that maybe you have too much time on your hands and a serious drug problem?"

"That would explain a lot," he confessed.

"There ya have it then."

"Hey," he said, changing the subject, "these guys are good."

"You bet your ass,' Bubbles concurred. "That's R&R CROSSING, and they ROCK!"

THE END

I handed it over knowing she would get a kick out of the whole "Bubbles" connection. The Raven had a thing about making up alias names for herself. One title? A single name? These were hardly sufficient for the Macho Princess. One of her pseudonyms was Bubbles Fontaine. The funny thing is that I think I wrote the part about the bubbles popping over a map before making the connection to her alias. The mind holds and distributes information like a jazz musician on heroine.

We had been using our hand truck only a month or so when one of the two small wheels crumbled beneath the pressure of our musical weight. The ball bearings inside the right castor bunched up in protest before spitting out like teeth at the hand of a barroom fist. Our initial reaction was simply to go to the Home Depot where we bought the hand truck, or maybe a neighbor hardware store, and buy a replacement wheel. Of course if the one went the other, in theory, would eventually follow. It had been over thirty days, ever so slightly, but never the less, slightly enough to prevent us from any free exchange or replacements.

"The curse of being us," Stopher proclaimed.

I believe it was also Stopher who observed that the wheel we were in need of held similar dimensions to those found on shopping carts. Our wheel functioned just barely enough to buy us a few days to lure a cart away from its flock at a given supermarket. Albertsons was eliminated from consideration because you don't pull shit like that where you sleep. We did however research the worthiness of such an endeavor while picking up some food there. I pushed the cart through the vegetable aisle while surveying the nuts and bolts compatibility with the hand truck concluding that such a transplant would take. Though I had never been especially handy with tools the operation seemed simple enough, even for me.

"It shouldn't take too long to get them off. We just need to find a cart on the skirts of the lot by a Ralphs or Vons, and slip into the nearest alley undetected," I slyly conspired.

"I doubt you'll have to be that risky, Dave. You can't walk down a side street or alley without seeing an abandon shopping cart. The homeless live out of them for God sake."

The next day on the promenade I walked out into the alley on my way to the restroom in the parking garage across the way, waiting as if on special order, sat a shopping cart turned upside down with its wheels seductively prone for harvest. I ran back through the foyer in the office building that led back to the promenade without even using the restroom first.

"Stoph, I found a cart."

"Okay."

"Watch the stuff, I gotta run back to the van and get my wrench set."

"We can always get it later."

"Someone might take it by then."

"Oh, no."

"I want to get it now."

I ran the six blocks to the van. (Well, for me it was kind of like running.) I returned to the alley with my trusty set of socket wrenches in tow ready to do mischief. The cart was where I left it, and though I had to struggle a bit, soon I had the wheels in a bag. The perfect crime. I couldn't wait to see if they would work so I unloaded all the equipment off the hand truck, detached the broken wheel, and the other puny-soon-to be-broken wheel, then attached the larger-broader-stronger-more-robust-certainly-more-manly-wheels, of my recent heist. On finishing I gave the truck a few tests spins gleefully. The wheels ran straight and true, stood tall and muscular, ate big bumps and small curbs for breakfast. So excited was I by my apparent victory, I immediately loaded the equipment back on, strapped it down with the black, hooked, bungee cords that I kept from my trucking days, and gave the wheels another whirl. I had hunted, I used tools properly, and I saved money! Aside from sports I had been pretty much useless as a man, so this felt pretty damm good.

"Good to have that out of the way," was all Stopher managed.

He was probably even more useless than me when it came to such masculine tasks, but not so much so that he failed to see the insignificance. Over the next week I took note of the countless times I saw abandoned carts all over Santa Monica. I could have performed the operation over and over again, had a fresh set of wheels every day of the year. Within a month of that, one of the two larger inner tube wheels went flat. Fixing them cost more than replacing, and all the shopping-cart wheels in the world rambled on meaninglessly to my quandary. It cost us ten bucks at The Home Depot to by a new one. Ever since, those have been the wheels that rolled our music to and fro to this very day.

Mom decided that we needed to record another CD. Nothing fancy, no big arrangements, just Chris and I doing what we do everyday on the promenade. Her hope was that some of the new songs that she heard on her visit would make the cut.

She had started to ask how much it would take then thought better of it and said, "I have four hundred dollars."

"We'll make it happen."

Chris and I made a list of about ten songs each, ranging from the songs recently written to songs that simply meant the most to us, or we had the most fun playing. We had Steve set up a couple mics for vocal and one for the acoustic. The Strat was plugged into the gizmo with the chorus and overdrive pedal we used on the promenade, so a mic got set up in front of that too. The idea was to recreate our street act in the studio. Chris started on the Martin with me on the Strat. The Studio tends to leave us both feeling restrained, fearful of the finality of it all; where as live the moments come and go. If you felt good about something on the street the feeling went unquestioned. In the studio, running tape challenges every moment. Enter cheap vodka. Being too subjective is as bad as being too critical or precious, but our budget forced us to toward the former. The plan was to play for three hours and use the rest of the time on the cover's artwork and burning CDs.

Since arriving in L.A. from Nashville Steve had expanded his operation into video editing. Burning CDs was usually something he did for his own projects, but he agreed to burn fifty or a hundred for us, charging us thirty or forty (he changed his hourly rate at some point) an hour for his time. That was the good and bad about working with Steve. No matter what he did the fee for his time stood pat; whether curing cancer or twiddling his thumbs, the fee remained the same.

The first couple of songs went smoothly. I forget the order but during an old Fred Neils' song called, EVERYBODY'S TALKIN' AT ME (the theme from Midnight Cowboy) Steve picked up a conga and started playing along. On the recording you could here the squeaking of his chair as he put it between his legs. The conga was recorded from the other mics in the room. After we were done Chris and I agreed that he should go ahead and mic it, but that before each song, whomever was singing the lead vocal, would either tell Steve to jump in or leave it alone. The whole project by, at first necessity, then design, was to represent life on the road with all its unexpected shifts. The less you have the more you have to allow for.

Stoph did another cover, THE YEAR OF THE CAT, by Al Stewart, giving Steve cart blanche and we plowed onward. When we came to Stophers, TWO KINDS we hit a tuning snag. The other tracks up until then were done in one, sometimes two takes, no punching. TWO KINDS was stopped and started numerous times because of some lyrical flubs, but most of the time on that song dragged because I couldn't get the damm third position chording to sound in tune. On certain songs, when Stoph played in the open chord position, I found a real homey sound playing the same chords on the board's high end. I have a decent ear, but it is day-to-day with its quality. The age and miles of the guitars didn't make it any easier; wood breaths and frets wear down. On that day I was having a hell of a time. Unfortunately, Steve, who has a good and more consistent ear than mine, didn't fair much better. Finally we got sounding close enough and made it through. No congas though, Stoph wanted no distractions.

    Meanwhile we were both getting a nice buzz on. I handled the day's frustration, and the general stress of being in a studio, a little better than Stopher, so he got a bit more hammered than I. After an hour we switched guitars and I sang my songs, which included one I had written with Mom, called PILGRIM. It was something she started writing after being flipped over in a car with my sister Josefa on a highway in Michigan. The theme of being on the road and heading home, then almost being killed, felt right for the album. On top of that it had a driving beat. Most of my songs had congas because I trusted Steve, and was more adventurous than Chris. There were a couple like REASONS, which had too many subtle changes to wing your way through.

    "Okay if I step out and leave the tape rolling while you do this one?" Steve asked.

    "Sure, in fact, I'll d o a few in a row that I know you won't play on."

    "Cool. Call me you when you need me."

    (I keep referring to tape but that is only me showing my age. It is all on computers now. "Leave the hard-drive on," zero romance compared to, "the tape is rolling.")

    After I had gotten through enough songs to sort through for the CD, Stoph had a few more to sing and we were done. It all went well enough; I wished I could have tuned better; it would have been smoother if Stoph wasn't Stoph; and I think Steve could have given it a bit more love. Of course we approached it with a, "let's crank this sucker out," mentality because of the money issues. That is not to forget or dismiss the way Steve felt inspired enough to pick up a conga, or when Stoph and I went into what we called "the game," how he started grabbing any percussive thing in reach to add to the madness. No, Steve gave love and talent. I guess as the session wore on his excitement waned, and maybe I felt that, sound-wise, he could have looked out for us little better. That said, I loved the final product, and I love Steve for his important contributions.

A word about the game. The game is an improvisational jazzy thing where Stopher and I talk back and forth on guitar trying to break out of our normal patterns. It was something we started doing consistently during our drug-fogged years in Chicago between coming back from Nashville and leaving for L.A. We made two attempts at it in the studio that day: The first with me on the Martin, and Chris on the Strat, the seconded the other way around. The second came out the best, becoming the final track of the album.

Unfortunately songs like SEARCHING and REASONS and a few others didn't come out well enough to make the cut; the CD came out this way:

STEADY IS THE COURSE—A song I wrote before I moved to Nashville about my struggle with being a good father, and following my artistic path.

UMBRELLA—Rain in Santa Monica, self-destruction in my soul.

THIS LAND IS YOUR LAND—The original folk-hobo, Woody Guthrie spreads his communistic dream.

DUST BOWL—Stopher melts down one of the essences to Steinbeck's THE GRAPES OF WRAITH. (Some of the lines in the song are taken directly from the book.)

TEXAS, I DON'T WANT TO LEAVE YOU—Chris wrote this lying on sister Josefa's basement floor in Michigan. We had spent the day helping her, Ross and their two boys, Guthrie and William move in. It depicts Will and Guthrie as two well-meaning cowpokes on the run from a misinformed posse.

SMILES IN MY POCKET—A song I wrote for Angel before I left Chicago.

SPRINKLER'S CHILD—As I've said before, the song I cherish most.

MY FATHER"S HOUSE—A song Chris wrote years ago about a grown son with his own family who in troubled times stands outside the house of his father in search of solace.

TWO KINDS—Stopher's travels over land by way of his soul. Written in Marine Park in the company of cheap vodka.

THE BLACK MESA—An ode to a moment in the middle of a country so vast you can't help but find yourself.

PILGRIM—Another travel piece to show you who you are.

SO EASY TO DIE—I wrote this after teaching Aubrey to ride a bike when she was five. First bicycles then drugs; it is amazing anyone lives past eighteen.

THE MOON WILL FOLLOW—Another one of my favorites. I was walking with Madison outside my apartment in Nashville by a little man-made lake there. She looked up at an almost full moon and said, "The moon is following me." I used the moon as a metaphor to tell her that no matter where I am my love is with her.

EVERYBODY"S TALKIN'—The creaking chair reaching for the conga, Chris' lilting interpretation, and my soulful yearning guitar, made it perfect fit for the CD. Oh, and Fred Neils wrote a great song too.

THE GAME—If we die tomorrow at least there is evidence of our musical bravery. My advice: have a drink or a toke, or both, and let it noodle your brain.

That was our first CD recorded in California. The title, IN A VAN DOWN BY THE OCEAN, obviously takes from the old Chris Farley bit on SNL, but more than that it was who, what and where we were. The songs all speak to the road, and or, the people we love; a journey that takes us to and from them, but starts and ends with who we are. That where we go and whom we love helps define who that is, is no coincidence. The sound of the CD is a bit shabby; some of the vocal and guitar performances most definitely could have been better, and have been any given day on the promenade. To wish for the power to go back in time and fix it would be to miss the point and elude the beauty. The CD stands as a record of that moment. When I give the energy to take it as a whole, it…in its way IN A VAN DOWN BY THE OCEAN is as important and as large as SGT. PEPPERS, or BEETOVEEN"S FIFTH. At least to me, because the songs were served and the songs are great.

Al went to pay for a copy but we told him that he earned a free one by coming to watch us every week. All the songs on it were part of our regular sets so he was familiar with the material and had already made a habit of requesting songs from it before it ever existed. Songs like PILGRIM, UMBRELLA, and TEXAS.

"I just wish you could have gotten BUILDING A LEGEND on there, or that one that Dave sings…" taps his index and caresses with the thumb, "…you told me the title before…BALLAD, or something."

"BALLAD OF KENT AND DONNA"

"Yeah, you should have recorded that one too."

"We actually did record both of them, but neither version was up to snuff."

One of the cart workers became a big fan of the IN A VAN…CD.

"Whenever I put it on my girlfriend insists that we listen until the end. 'You have to follow it all the way through; it's a journey,' she always says."

He loved the first one, FINAL CALL, and would sing back to Chris one of his songs from it, I'M ALIVE, whenever Chris walked past his cart, but there was something magical about the VAN CD for him, and his girl.

Another who bought our first CD back in January worked in the movies. He was a safety inspector on movie sets. For two weeks we kept seeing him after he bought it and he always stopped for a few songs, and tipped well.

"I just don't know what you did in your past lives to be stranded out here like this." He used to say.

Then he disappeared until one June afternoon.

I saw him leaning against a pole smiling with a sort of sad disposition. I finished the song and gave him a subtle glance before going back to our set. It was near the end so he came up to us when we were done.

"Do you remember me?"

"Seth?"

"Joth."

"Right, how's the movie business."

"Keeping our stars safe," Stopher added.

"You guys have a great memory. I can not believe you are still stuck out here."

"Well," I offered, "at least we have another CD you can buy."

"Hand it over."

We exchanged some more pleasantries and he went his way. A handful of days later he came by during our second set one weekday and dropped a sawbuck ($10) in our bucket. He stood staring at us waiting out the rest of the song occasionally shaking his head almost as if we had offended him somehow.

"Is that ten-spot a request for us to leave?" Chris joked.

"I listened to your new CD and right off I was captured, engrossed; the imperfect sound, the driving emotions. Then the beat falls off, and I feel the spaciousness all around me, and I feel like I'm in a trance, not really even listening. The next thing I know—in the middle of MY FATHER'S HOUSE—I am weeping. I mean heaving; absolute weeping."

He shook his head and seemed close to tearing up there on the street.

"So you liked it?" I smiled.

"Yeah," he recovered from the reverie. "You guys are amazing."

He shook our hands and walked off; haven't seen him since. But man, he loved IN A VAN DOWN BY THE OCEAN.

CHAPTER TEN

I had my bouts with guilt over Aubrey. Time's passing soothed some of it, as is its way. After a while, the continuing of an action takes hold, and what has been set aside is shifted even further to the side. Her birthday was tough, but that had been way back in November just before Thanksgiving, Christmas followed and then the New Year. Aubrey and I tended to spend most of the big holidays together, but not in this life. It had been ten months since I had seen Aubrey when she arrived by train with Mom and Keeley in early June.

Back in early February I had my most dramatic melt down since leaving her in Nashville. As I said there were lots of a little moments; heavy sighs; deep breaths extracted in an attempt to relieve weight from my chest. The moments, pass into others built for tasks, or are simply over taken by pleasure, organic and induced. The moments multiply on top of one another and soon life insists on being lived, you find yourself moving on from surviving to thriving and then tumbling to where your fingertips clutch to survival. The multiplying starts all over again, you ride the waves paying closer attention to the consistent thoughts, and more profound ones.

Chris and I went to see a film directed by Lasse Halstrom starring Juliet Binchot called, CHOCOLATE. I think the spelling of the word was represented in another language. If you saw it you'll remember that it chronicles the arrival of a woman and her daughter to a small European village during some form of olden days (1930s or 40s or something like that.). They face the obligatory struggles of fitting in as they set up shop selling chocolates, and dispensing a more opened minded way of looking at life. The mother has a mystic side owning something to witchcraft. To be truthful, most of the film's scenes and message are vague at best in my mind. Except for the scene towards the end where the mother, feeling her gypsy roots yearn for the road in the face of local controversy, packs up her pre-pubescent child and attempts to flee in the night. The child revolts because she is tired of the life her mother has chosen for them; she likes the town; has made friends and feels for the first time a connection to the concept of home. I am a fan of Lasse Halstrom's work and did love the movie that I was seeing. Yet what began rumbling within me, as I saw this sweet, kind-hearted child being dragged about according to the whims of a parent lost in her own fears and agendas, transcended the story on screen. All I could see was Aubrey begging me to be with her in her world of choice, to stop needing more than being anywhere other than with her. I felt physical pain ripple over my shoulders and sink in under the collarbone on its way to wrenching my chest in a vice. My face shook, heat seared in and around the temples as my eyes prepared to be engulfed by hot salty water. My stomach knotted, breathing stilted, I instantly knew I was about to be over come. The scene ended within minutes and moved on to the film 's eventual happy ending. The actors smiled, the music danced beneath the visual joy, and the sound of a child's agony was all I heard. Aubrey's flushed round cheeks raged with despair, her soft-growing-out of-being-a-buttoned nose ran wet with an unrelenting plea to be considered. My eyes and mind, saw and processed, the film's good intentions, but could not block the horrors of my soul. They existed equally within me until the credits rolled and the happy ending was gone. In my seat I turned into a mushy pool of muscle spasms struggling to find air. The crowd trickled out as I bent into myself hiding my face.

    I waited for a break in the storm. As soon as I felt the energy to contain the flood in me I made for the front door, head down and a hand clutching my brow as if in deep thought. The only thought I had being, stop thinking about her long enough to get out of here. Outside the sun burned painfully bright as if in accusation. I momentarily felt the pressure in my chest relinquish, as I was able to take a few deep cleansing breaths. I took in air to let it spread within me, building up my strength before exhaling my shame. Chris walked ahead of me to the corner of 2nd and Arizona. I must have noticed him as he passed me by. He certainly noticed me.

"You okay?" He smiled.

I began with a grin that crumbled more and more under each word. "It all hit me at once, all I could see was me breaking Aubrey's heart in two."

That did it; I was off again. One or twice I tried to speak and that only made it worse. Finally I cleared my eyes just long enough to see Chris loving me with a look of compassion and sympathy. He seemed to say, "It hurts but you are a decent man and a good father." His lips never parted, and were no longer smiling. They simply stretched mildly over his chin acknowledging that the time had arrived again for me to suffer. Helplessly he raised his arms and shook his head. As I walked by him I heard myself laugh through the tears just a little.

"I gotta walk," I said barely audible, over my shoulder.

I crossed Ocean Avenue to stroll along the bluff. Every so often I'd lean against the thick cement fence unable to see beyond the profusely draining, steaming, salt water that had by now become the color of my eyes. I didn't walk far but had been gone from Stopher for about a half hour. He waited on the corner where I had last seen him, pacing and looking at various parts of the sky. He saw me coming and laughed at the sight of my brokenness. I chuckled weakly.

"So you're a selfish asshole—now what?" He kindly shouted over the remaining twenty feet between us.

"I'd like a break please." Tears still clung to my eyes but production was close to an end.

"I guess that's up to you."

"It always is."

"Yeah it is."

I stood in front of my brother grateful to have him on my side.

"What was I gonna do, drive a truck in Nashville the rest of my life?"

"Fuck no." Stopher's voice retained the humor of the scene while adding a serious edge of support.

Tears built up again, I laughed like a fighter bitterly amused to find that he could take such a beating; that he could lose so badly yet think of no other option other than answering the next bell.

"Oh, I'm getting drunk."

"Of course you are."

I had other days of remorse but nothing like that afternoon. June came, and in a week, I'd see her again. Her voice on the phone during our time apart had been strong but void of any certainty. She didn't hide anything, it held more of a, "What is there really to say?" quality. We would talk about our lives but not in any depth. This was the beginning of that time in her life where we would drift apart regardless of the space and time between us. We were alright though. I could feel it.

On Friday, the first of June, our favorite spot had been usurped so we moseyed down to the shoeshine stand near Santa Monica BLVD. Chris was in one of those moods where the sound didn't bother him and he barely notice the buzz on the Strat's twelfth fret-fourth string. On those days the music flowed easier and we made each other laugh between songs or during. When he set the world and himself aside, Stopher was a lot of fun to play with.

We were doing our version of the Stones', CAN'T ALWAYS GET WHAT YOU WANT, which Chris sang. He turned it into this gruff, blues song that made you feel the holes in your shoes, taste the dust on your throat. I, without a single doubt, consider myself by far the better singer of the two, as does Chris. The thing that Chris had over me at that time was his ability to take other people's songs, and make them sound as if he had written them. This was no longer the property of Keith and Mick; it became the story of Stopher and his plucky, funky, picking sidekick, Vuma, the boy wonder. He put the words forth while I danced and jabbed around them for punctuation. Like a lot of covers he sang, I preferred his rendition. I would come to own covers the way he did, but only because I paid close attention.

At the end of the song Chris announced into the mic, "That's little Billy Watkins out of Cleveland on the guitar. Thanks for coming out tonight, Billy."

I gave the nonexistent crowd a wholesome, hardy salute.

A few songs earlier Stoph had me as, little Lenny Crenshaw, from Toledo; I don't think he consciously targeted the state of Ohio; it had more to do with ring of the towns. In the past I had been from New Orleans or Baton Rouge, Pittsburg or Scranton and not necessarily grouped together in a given set. It was a charming way for him to point out my guitar work on a given song, and it never failed to tickle me to no end.

"Hey, guys, excuse me." A voice came from behind us.

We turned to see a middle-aged, balding man of some apparent means.

"I've been seeing you guys out here for a while, and again just now I was watching. I see people walking by and," here he paused to draw us in, "they don't get."

Stoph and I smiled gratefully understanding his drift.

"It goes right past them because on the surface it's familiar, but they don't get it."

"Thanks," Chris said.

"No, I mean it; you are simply too good for them to see."

"Hey, I stand next to this guy everyday when he plays guitar." Stoph pointed to me. "Like that Stones tune we just did. Mick had Keith, and I got Stevie Ray Vaughn."

The man laughed, and abruptly stopped for fear of losing touch with the weightiness of the moment.

"That's exactly what I mean. They hear a couple of guys doing a Stones tune and that's it. The varying influences you mix in with your own obviously original flare means absolutely nothing to them. Anyway, I just wanted tell you both that. Keep it up."

With that he handed us a five-dollar bill and went on his way. Chris looked at me and I him.

"We was just sayin' that," he scolded me, slapping my shoulder.

"We say it all the time."

We played a few more songs then switched.

"That was nice," Chris said.

"What?"

"That guy going out of his way to say that."
"I liked the specificness of it."
"Exactly; shows he's been paying attention."
"It shows we're fucked."
"Explain."
"Paying attention is paramount to thought, a.k.a work."
"Uh huh."
"The general public doesn't work to understand entertainment. These are the same folks that made "Three's Company" a smash."
"Not to mention Urkel and Madonna."
"Madonna is a freakin' genius compared to some of the crap they glorify."
"Oh, we're fucked."
"Yeah we are."

The set went well putting twenty plus into our bucket. More than that we let the music be us and us it—not as simple to do as it sounds, trust me. The words of that passerbyer solidified the smile we had begun the day with. We packed up and headed to the north end of the center square to see if our spot in the shadow of the Dinosaur's tail was free for a two o' clock dance. Chris went ahead with guitar and stand in hand while I finished up getting the gear together.

"It's about time," the Raven said tapping her foot on her perch and pointing to a watch on her wrist that never got her anywhere on time.

"My sincerest apologies, madam." I bowed ceremoniously.

"Come bow over here and I'll give ya a tip," she said lifting the hem of her dress to reveal the narrow end of her shiny, black, still tapping, impatiently, boot.

We set up quickly to serve our most sexy and beautiful master. On the heels of our first successful set we built another. The Raven called them out, we laid them down; someone took a picture and she hawked a buck out of them; a woman on the patio of her restaurant commented on my voice, the Raven talked her into buying a CD.

"They're out here singing with all their hearts, it is the least you could do." Always friendly, forever charming, but in the end dead serious.

We made another thirty and our cup bubbled over.

"Here," she said running from her perch as we packed up. "I wrote this when I got to work today. " She handed me one of her post cards.

Dear David Dear,

As I turned the corner, my eyes searching the sidewalk ahead. I did not find the sight which I sought. What they did find was a blight of sight, sound and senses. Surely this specter was not to replace the splendid sound of, R&R CROSSING?

SHIT!

This message brought to you by the letter "S"

P.S.

This is why I am cranky

I read as she watched from her perch and she bashfully cackled, if such a thing is possible, when I smiled.

That night we drank to the day's good fortune, from the money to the stranger's kind words, and of course the chance to play for the Raven again.

"She is definitely sweet on you."

"Hey, I gave it a shot. I think she digs what we do, and if I lost, oh a hundred pounds, then maybe."

"How about that note?"

"She missed our music."

"It wasn't addressed to me or even us. *'Dear David Dear.'*"

"I am a sexy, brilliant man. No doubt."

"No Doubt."

"So she has a thing for me, it's not going get any where past all this fat."

The next day we, again, got beat to our spot by George and Cool Breeze. They were a couple of black fortysomthing—maybe fifty—musicians that played Motown with some classic rock. George had a fine voice and Cool Breeze was a hell of a player. They also had bass and drums on backing tracks piped into their sound system. A very professional act, well dressed, no originals, but very smooth. They had a big board on an easel listing thirty or so songs people could request.

It was a good shtick, because when someone would ask for a song, a request of a dollar would echo back, and how could one refuse after just asking for something from them?

Chris and I crossed over Arizona to play the frozen fruit stand. Al showed up as usual and we had good time playing for him. Like the Raven, playing for Al became a mission: Don't let him down. Getting a two o' clock after a noon set was impossible on a Saturday so we settled in by our dinosaur tail and waited for the six. The four was usually taken as well but on top of that there would be a good chance of the Raven working the evening if she wasn't there for the afternoon shift.

At five-fifteen she showed up, by five-thirty I was given a post card. I looked down on my assignment then up and across the street to my assignor. I knew that I'd never be more than a friend to her, and I knew that she held some sort of attraction for me. I didn't want to write a story, I didn't want to pretend that there wasn't something going on between us. So what if it would never progress from where it was, it was still there. I eyed her pink top accentuating her ample breasts and she caught me staring. She smiled warmly, almost lovingly.

I wrote.

Pink was more than her color.
It was her attitude.
Gripping her shoulders, raising her flag...If you what I mean.
Her black hair, her sly smile;
the night could learn a thing or two from her.
The stars gazed
The wind played
Dancing on my face
If they were poetry what words would they say?
So if pink is just a color and poetry only words,
Then indeed
Words and colors exist to serve her

She couldn't read at first; too many people insisted on being seated for dinner. By the time I looked over as I plugged the last chord into the gizmo, I saw her eyes on the card. Did I go too far? Would she be creeped out? I cared and I didn't. She started all this not me. I never had an intimate friend as woman unless romance was involved; I had enjoyed that aspect of us, yet I wanted more. She wouldn't be able to see muscles flex for all my fat, I couldn't afford flowers; words were all I had.

She looked up and saw me watching. Her smile grew slowly holding a hint of sadness. I had moved her and I think that gave birth to the sadness. Gradually, the melancholy faded into the warmth of her appreciation. Soon her smile, while maintaining a subtle posture, began to beam. Or maybe it had been her eyes taking over. Either way I felt surrounded by her, I felt her surrounded by me; I felt us.

She turned to her duties and beyond a few curious glances between us we kept to our work. At the end of the set Stoph and I packed up, and headed for the van. As we passed her perch at George's Bistro she momentarily hid her eyes. I started to wave goodnight but she was going out her way not to look.

I said to Stoph, "I think I crossed a line."

Before he could answer the Raven's hands were on my shoulder, "Good set boys."

She ran over to Chris, gave his beard a tug and did the same for me. With that she stepped toward her perch but stopped to come back, looking me in the eyes with a purpose that she seemed to rather be rid of than nurture:

"Thanks."

"For what?"

She looked down then up at me with that purpose she couldn't shed.

"You're welcome."

I saw her the following week when Mom bought Aubrey and Keeley into town. After that she'd work a split shift catching two more sets. It'd be a month before I saw her again.

Chris and I picked them up at the train. All the guilt, distance and fears of awkwardness washed away the second Aubrey rushed into my arms: She had grown a few inches, in height and around the waist, but still fit perfectly—didn't really have to bend but did anyway; I stood to swing her around, her feet barely left the ground. Hugs went round and round then we piled into the van to go see an ocean. The sun had fallen so it was a short visit. Of course Aubrey wanted to disrobe and run into the water right then and there.

"I have my swimsuit on underneath."

"Tomorrow, after my set, I promise."

The next day we set up south of Arizona by the frozen fruit stand and played our set. Al showed up but I could tell that he would rather forego any introduction. When the folks were in town the first time he suffered through it timidly—I took note not to put him through it again.

The kids sat through a few songs with smiles and applauses. Aubrey had to live with my music from the very beginning; at every family gathering, we played; rehearsals for the trio in the living room; "Not today, sweets, I have to rest up for a show tonight." My music and her formed a civil, adversarial relationship. She liked the idea of her dad being a writer/musician, but the nuts and bolts of it cluttered her life.

Of course she loved hearing me play songs that were inspired by, or written for, her and got an added kick seeing other people hear them. So I did SPRINKLER'S CHILD, AUBREY'S MOON and STEADY IS THE COURSE while slipping a couple non-Aubrey songs in between. Chris did Jim Croce's TIME IN A BOTTLE with both Keeley and Aubrey in mind:

"But there never seems to be enough time to do the things you wanna do once you find them. I've looked around enough to know that you're the one I wanna go through time with."

In his introduction to the song Stoph mentioned something about some of the favorite women in his life being in attendance, so the chorus choked he and I up each time we sang it. Because it is true that time is short, and even though you know whose company you want through it all, other desires, events and practicalities get in the way. Up until that day I always thought of that song in terms of a man loving a woman. Now I usually think about Aubrey, and all of the nieces and nephews, whenever I sing that chorus. So much life being lived outside of my grasp, and not just any life but the lives of my brother's and sister's children. I have gotten to know some of them better than others over the years but they all own a part of me. If I never saw one of them again their place within me would remain the same. I have distance from my siblings that I thought I never would, and I don't just mean in space. It has all been very natural, they are living their lives and I am living mine. It would be that way if I had stayed in Chicago. Each of the six Smith kids has a separate relationship with the other and a collective one. Every now and then it hits me: Eileen, Art and Josefa all have kids, and I have loved them since the day they were born by virtue of who their parent is to me. We have spread like wild fire and the heat warms me as I need it to.

"...But there never seems to be enough time..."

The girls got restless so Mom took them for a walk to look around, do some shopping.

"Don't run her ragged, Breeze-child," I told her before she left.

"I know, dad."

She could be a handful but has a good heart, using it most of the time when it counted.

Chris and I decided to have them meet us on the middle block by the movie theaters after we had loaded the equipment into the van, and *then*, we'd head down to the water. George and Cool Breeze were there singing an old Smokey Robinson tune, and Franz was selling his balloons nearby. (Franz was an interesting character that we had met in the beginning and is still out there to this day.)

"Hey, Franz."

"Good to see you, sir."

"How about making me look like a big shot in front of my daughter and niece, and comping me a couple of your finest animal figures."

"Why of course. What would you like girls?"

That made me feel good. Aubrey had pretty much grown out of that sort of thing, but I guess, for me, it showed that I was part of a community, even well liked and respected within. It was a small thing but it meant something to me and, I think, Aubrey.

"Dance with me, kid."

"No, dad!"

"Come on; let's show'em how it's done?"

At that moment I saw doubt in her eye—maybe bashfulness. Or maybe she'd come into that age where all the things we used to do were now corny. I could still see the three year old in her, the one who, no matter how many times we did whatever game we were playing, shouted, "Do it again, Daddy, do it again." We had so many bits between us. There was the one where I had her cower behind her hands pretending to quiver with fear, while I attempted to coax her out of the agreed upon shell.

"Come. Come, child, look at me." I spoke with a crackly pseudo-Transylvanian accent, kindly with an underlying hint of menace.

She would peek ever so cautiously through her fingers only to withdraw.

"Come, child. Come. Look at me." I'd fan my fingers near my face crookedly in a come hither gesture.

Once again she'd venture a glimpse and recoil.

"Come. Come, child, come. Look at me."

Her face crept out from behind the safe fortress of her palms, peeking over the fingers, trembling at her own courage. Still unsure she paused, her protective hands hovering just below the chin.

"Come."

Finally she released her apprehension in a sigh, smiling relief.

"DON'T LOOK AT ME!!" I would scold.

He face, with terrified eyes, disappeared into her hands instantly to shake and quake until the game began a new.

"Come. Come, child. Be not afraid. Come, look at me."

It would go on all through breakfast, and up to lunch if she had her way. My favorite part would be when we switched roles. To see this small face with skin so new, untaut, untested; eyes bright and circular, completely unable to not sparkle with keen interest; and a button nose so enticing that not biting it off seemed unreasonable; to see that face turn deceptive and somehow resemble an aged villain luring the innocent into her web, and hear those soft, puffy, pink lips try to emulate my made-up voice; preciously precocious only licks the tip of the iceberg lollypop. She even mimicked the fanning crooked fingers gesture like a pro. There was theater in her blood.

We also had the simple bit where I would sing, "Hey, Aubrey!"
"Hey, Daddy!"
Or:
"Hey, Breeze-child!"
"Hey, Vuma!"

She actually tired of that at an early age. But being the good sport she is, whenever I put the call to song she would play along, albeit somewhat unenthusiastically.

"Hey, Aubrey!"
"hey, daddy."

The dancing we took turns tiring of from year to year.

Donna used to spin around the room with Aubrey as a baby in her arms, so she was Aubrey's first dance partner. (To this day, Donna is probably the best dance partner I ever had. My first being sister Josefa. In fact it was Josefa that taught me the moves I passed on to Aubrey.)

It's a typical routine where you start holding hands at arms length with your partner and step into one side of them with one hand stuck between at the chest, and the other arm stretched straight out together to the side. Next you step back to the original position then step in to the other side; then back out and in, but this time with the smaller partner spinning around and underneath to be wrapped up in the other's arms. From this position Aubrey, being the smaller one, would be spun out by me to the right where she'd continue to be spun like a top in one place as I moved around her. After a bit I'd reverse her spin so that she'd return to my chest facing away wrapped in my right arm. At this point a dramatic pause is served followed by a collective backward lean. The lean should have hint of tango in it with a dash of dip. Here I spin her out and we join hands resuming the original position. All steps get repeated until at the end when she is spinning back into my chest. Instead of holding my position I take one step back as to allow her an extra spin that leads her perfectly into the final full-fledged dip. Ta da.

I looked at the taller, thicker version of the kid I used to dance with standing on my knees with a half-pleading glance; the other half said, "Don't sweat it, kid, I'm just glad to be standing here with ya." Aubrey bowed her head taking a few steps past me then turned to face me as if the lights poured down on a rising curtain. Her arms reached for mine, I caught them and we stepped, spun, twirled back over the years effortlessly.

"*I know you wanna leave me, but I refuse to let you go,*" George sang.

The movements were effortless, but in the underlying essence of her smile I detected an unresolved awkwardness. It wasn't that she merely indulged me; she came to the moment of her own desire; Aubrey had always been one to seek out life at its most theatrical, I had hambone in my blood and passed enough of it along for it to be coursing through her veins. Another trait I had was talking every happening or emotion to death. Aubrey tired of that bit long ago but had always been kind to let me drain myself, as I required. Not that she ever really had a choice, but she grew into being a good sport about the exercise. I wouldn't classify her in Madison's league of buttoning up. More accurately would be to say that she dwelled in the normal verbal range between Madison's and mine polar opposites.

All in all it was a beautiful moment for the both of us, and Stoph and Mom got a kick out of it as well. Whatever specifics Aubrey carried aside, there is always that thought in one's brain that tickles the self-conscious during acts of exhibitionism, "Do people think I am a dork?" I simply beamed with pride and swung her to the music.

On that day we took the girls down to the ocean by the pier. Mom and Chris sat on a blanket in the sand while I waded among the waves to keep the girls among us and be of some service in the form of fun. As big as Aubrey was getting I could still lift and throw her about in the water. She had those hefty Smith bones but so did I. Keeley, a couple of years younger, was smaller though still sturdy, could have been thrown further if not for her wishes being otherwise. I wouldn't categorize Keeley as timid, but in the presence of Aubrey, even armored soldiers paled by comparison. Years and the events within them would temper that, though never completely. Forever unchanged would be that the water and Aubrey were the best of friends. On land she plodded, in the water she sailed; where solid ground and gravity conspired to be keep her slow, water parted to her cutting whims. She is the egg man; she is the walrus; goo, goo, ga, jube.

At first Aubrey contented herself splashing around where Keeley felt comfortable. The waves were peaking at four feet, which gave us an ample target to dive through, as well as a formidable challenge to try and jump over. Neither kid had a real shot of clearing a single wave but I mustered all the Walter Payton inspired remnants of my youth to tickle my way over a white cap or two.

God, I loved Walter Payton.

"Payton clears the line and into the end zone," I shouted my theatrics.

"Payton cl-." A wave swallowed Aubrey's attempt to emulate.

Aubrey soon tired of the limits on Keeley's courage and started easing out further little by little. At first I stayed by Keeley to keep her company and give Aubrey my faith. When Aubrey had put twenty feet of ocean between us, I inched a bit her way. Keeley, meanwhile, inched toward the shore. Finally I found myself symmetrically between them. They both were very well entertained in their respective positions. Kids can be so in need of the company of other kids, or incessantly demanding of an adult's creative supervision and affectionate attention, then turn on a dime to be absolutely content in their own self-sufficiency. And there they frolicked in their own worlds on their own oceans while I—the catcher in a wet, salty rye—looked out to sea to see that Aubrey saw the shore again, then landward to watch Keeley seeking out an adventure on her terms. I don't know if they thought they needed me out there. The more I watched the more they peacefully bobbed up and around like buoys tied to nothing but going nowhere; safe, unsinkable, and pleasantly alone.

I wrote one of my best lyrics because of that moment. It was me encouraging Keeley to test greater and scarier depths, while understanding and appreciating her reserve. They had only been back in Chicago a week when I wrote it. I titled it, A CALL TO KEELEY:

Buried beneath a wave; hidden in a breeze
Clouds carve a message in the sky piece by piece
Wet sand clings, salt air seeps
The world squirts through the toes of her feet
A call to Keeley; a call to arms

Dreams need vacations; heroes indulge caution
One-way streets are an illusion
Trains not found on maps aren't necessarily off track
If the engines blow and the wheels roll, it's moving
The unknown says, "Boo."
Harm smiles, "Hi."
No I'd never say that fear was in need of proving
A call to Keeley; a call to arms

The world is already conceding
But even winners take a beating
Not all chances are worth taking
But there are some moments in need of making

Buried beneath a wave; hidden in a breeze
Clouds carve a message in the sky piece by piece
A call to Keeley; a call to arms
A call to Keeley; a call to heart

I am an honest to goddamm, fucking poet. Oh, I'm aware.

When Chris and I drove them back to their motel after that first day at the beach I laid in back with the kids singing some old traveling songs. Songs that Aubrey, along with Madison, knew by heart, but that Keeley had to learn. It was a short drive so the lesson didn't go too far. In the instant that Chris pulled the van to the curb Aubrey's face drained of all joy. It was as if the rolling wheels were directly connected to her heart. I couldn't say that she looked sad because she had no expression at all. One moment her smile beamed, her eyes jumbled with life and her cheeks bloomed, in the next it all shut down. Her mouth sat limply under nose, her eyes looked unplugged from her brain, and those cute, chubby cheeks sank into themselves like a turtle into its shell.

"What's wrong, kid?"

Her eyes filled with water, her upper lip trembled with the words she couldn't find.

Mom felt the change without having to turn toward us from the passenger seat. She and Chris quickly collected Keeley and their things, and headed for the room.

"Take your time," Mom said to me.

Aubrey and I stared at each other in silence, me lying on the bed her sitting up. I placed a hand on her bent knee, beginning to put things together in my mind. I had a bad habit of talking too much in these situations, speaking to both of our thoughts, in such a rush to show her that I understood. I bit my lower lip.

"Let's go for a walk."

She nodded her head as her eyes filled up again.

The night's warm breath settled on the back of our necks in well-intentioned whooshes. We didn't actually walk so much as meander around the rear of the van; up on the sidewalk, into the street—each move physicalizing our respective search for the words that contained a chance at corralling an accurate essence of our collective and separate pain.

"I don't want to complain."

"You have every right to complain."

"But it's not what I want, it's not how I feel. You should be here, I want to be in Nashville."

Aubrey lifted her arms in surrender as her face collapsed in a soundless explosion of tears. She left her arms out as her head bowed and shoulders shook. I didn't want to crowd her, I kept saying to myself, be patient, don't assume what she needs you to say or do. My arms ached to wrap her up and absorb her pain and frustration. This was her moment to run, not mine to cheat her out of what she might need it to be.

"Mom and I don't talk the way you and me do. She doesn't listen or care, she just wants to be with Larry."

"She cares."

"I know she cares!" Aubrey's voice rose with anger as her arms dropped. She turned away. "I just need more than she's giving."

I tried to suppress my Dad's wisdom and failed. "You won't get it. This is who she is; all she'll ever be."

"God, I know! I just want to complain about it."

I laughed.

Aubrey took a deep breath, wiped her nose and eyes, sniffed and faced me with a smile. She stood apart from me distraught and haggard.

"I was feeling fine, having fun. I don't know what happened."

"Kid, your parents have put you through a lot, it catches you when it catches you."

"Aren't you supposed to say, 'Life is hard,' somewhere around now?"

I moved toward Aubrey with open arms and sang, "Life's a struggle, come on and huddle, give yourself cuddle now."

I put my arms around her tucking her head under my chin and began rocking gently.

"You wanna keep sleepin'," she sang weakly to my chest, "but the world keeps keepin', tearing at your dreamin' now."

I kissed the top her head. "You remember that one, huh?"

"I remember everything."

I placed my hands on her shoulders and she looked up at me. "Do you? My greatest fear is that I'll be gone so long that you'll forget what a great life we've shared." My eyes and nose liquefied. "I loved our life, I loved being with you; you know that, right?"

"I know, Dad. That's what makes it so hard."

"I know, Breeze-child."

We held each other for time in silence then gradually slipped from each other's arms into our own space, our own thoughts.

Aubrey stared off into the leaves of some tree. "She acts so fucking surprised when I tell her how she never spent time with me growing up. She just goes on, 'I did this and I did that,' and I can see she is so full of shit that she doesn't even know it." She faced me. "I remember last month when I got in trouble at school for arguing with a teacher, and she said, 'I didn't raise you to talk that way.' And I'm like, 'You didn't raise me at all—Dad and Chris did.'"

I had always felt that way but tried to never let it show to Aubrey or influence her perception. To hear her say it, to know she felt that way, almost hurt me with pride. It cut into me with the realization that my truth and her truth were the same, but it was a painful truth for us both. My wife—her mother, it is not something you want to be true about them. I dealt with it years ago and Aubrey was now coming to the same conclusions. So she said it, and while I hurt for her it filled me with pride. Pride that she could sort through the bullshit, and the fear of what that truth entailed, and also pride that, in her eyes, Chris and I had done the job we thought we did.

My eyes steamed over and the words barely came out of my mouth in an audible form. "Thanks, Sweets, it means more than you know to hear." I gathered myself a bit. "I'm sure your uncle would enjoy hearing it too."

"Well, you'll have to tell him, 'cause I'm spent."

We laughed through our mutual tears and headed back to the room with nothing changed or solved. I put an arm around her as we strolled.

"Whenever you need to vent I'm a phone call or a letter away."

"Okay, okay, but can we be done for now."

"Hey, Aubrey!"

"hey, vuma."

"You're not supposed mix nicknames wit-."

"I know, Dad, I know."

"Fucking with the old man, eh?"

"You *are* quick."

I had previously confessed to both Aubrey and Mom that I had spent the money Mark gave to take Aubrey to California Adventure on, "other things." They forgave and offered no surprise. (Oh, they know and accept me.) Mom announced on their arrival that she could swing the expense of renting a car for me to take the kids while she and Chris hung out in Santa Monica. But after the first full day by the ocean Aubrey and Keeley said that they would prefer to spend another day at the beach, and spend the evening on rides provided by the Santa Monica Pier as opposed to driving out to Pasadena for the day. I did manage to have around forty or more dollars to spend on her while she was in town as some small token gesture towards making up for the C-note that I and Stoph had indulged in. (Father of the year or what?)

I'm just glad that Stoph and I had a good couple of weeks on the promenade that lead up to their visit. Of course the days they were in town we died terrible deaths. The Saturday and Sunday sets put together barely cleared twenty. In fact, whenever someone had visited us, be they family from out of town or local friends, on the promenade, it always seemed liked we had a bad money day. The Raven laid witness to some very good days (of which she obviously took credit for) but only because she worked there. I would have especially liked for Aubrey to see us do well, if only, to give her the tiniest of hopes that her dad had a glimmer of a shot in hell of actually making a dime in this business that he could share. At least she wasn't going to get the impression that I was living high on the hog—more like in the crevice of a hoof.

On that Sunday I introduced Aubrey to the Raven. Aubrey knew of my affection for her and that we had kissed, so I held some of the nerves involved with my daughter meeting a girlfriend. I wanted them to like each other. In the two to twelve seconds that they shared an approximate breathing space, I guess, I got a watered down version of that. They were awkward and pleasant, and glad when it was over.

For our second ocean excursion we took the kids to Venice beach. It mirrored the first day although Keeley seemed more confident, and I spent a little less time in the water. As the sun sank we went out for dinner—Mom paid for everything—then on to the Pier. By that age Aubrey had already achieved amusement park veteran status. The rides on the Pier were toys to her, but she still liked toys. I think there was a part of her that settled for the Pier over California Adventure because she thought it would be easier on everyone else. It saved Mom money, me from the shame of Mom spending more money, Keeley the challenge of facing bigger, terrifying rides, and Chris, well Stoph was pretty much unaffected. I do think that Aubrey wanted more ocean time, and that she liked the idea of skipping the long drives. She also, I believe, preferred us remaining one group. Particularly Stopher, she wanted him around, even if he wasn't on a ride or in the water. Aubrey is an only child whose mom had an identical twin and a father who came from a big, close family. She had a sister like relationship with Madison, but they didn't live together all the time, and they grew up ruled by different authority figures. Groups of people meant something to her, she liked being one of many. And as I said, Chris' presence, in any context, meant more than most.

I rode the mini-roller coaster and ship that pendulumed to and fro, climbing closer to either extreme but never turning upside down. The other two spinning turning rides they had there I was unable to fit into. On those Aubrey went on alone because Keeley needed an adult to allow her to believe a safe return possible. Keeley would wait with me or find a smaller ride near by to tackle on her own. As with the water I stood in the middle ground keeping a watchful I on the river of people flowing between us, making sure that one of them didn't take the hand of either of my dears, leading them out to sea. Mom and Chris found a bench in an opening where we could easily find them. Stoph had his trusty "water" bottle while Mom sipped from inspired plastic of her own. Wine I'm guessing; she saves bourbon for bedtime.

The kids and I went back, forth, all around, separate and together, hands intimately intertwined, and held together by my careful eyes. I stood on the ground watching Aubrey giggle at the heights and the speed at which to them she sped; I listened to Keeley tell me about her friend's new dog and took in the feverish fury of words that zoomed between them as Aubrey moved on to the next event, without trying to understand them. Towards the end of the evening when Aubrey had extracted all the excitement from rides at her disposal, I sensed, for a solitary moment, regret in her voice at not going to a real amusement park. She mopped it up the instant she let it spill.

"We haven't hit the fairest wheel."

I hate fairest wheels. The relative stillness of them gives me the willies. Twist me, jerk me, turn me upside down, hurl me to and from the earth, but for god's sake do it with tremendous speed; wrap me up in gravity and push me in my place. The haunting, lilting rise of a big wheel that gingerly sways offering your physical being no limitations; gravity releasing its pulsing palm from my chest, in favor of hanging on my dangling feet like a lead weight, smiling slyly, "I'm still here."

That being said I climbed aboard and let the wheel roll me up into the night. Other than death most of my fears can be transcended by opening my perspective. Even death has lost some of its fangs. I looked at the wonder rising up from the colors below dripping out of Keely's eyes. She was nervous too, just not as much as she was excited. Aubrey looked a little bored yet the beauty of it all crept through a crack of her lazy smile. The three of us sat quietly, sinking from the sky into the hullabaloo of squirming flesh as the individuals within moved one way or another in search of a moment they could talk about later. The lights became pedestrian on descent as they meshed into one with all the different colors and sounds. Down in the midst of the cultured chaos, engulfed by its urgency, we became them, but only for as long as it took for us to come out on the other side. There we would push away upward where the dark sky waited, indifferent but open. Once again the mulling below gave birth, by contrast, to our heightened peace; not a single word broke through the collective drone; every face a dot on the brush of Monet; while lights, with the distance, gained definition through separation and each sang its own song, forming a visual, choral harmony.

"Thanks for this."
"It was really my pleasure," Mom said with an eased sincerity.
"I know-. It meant a lot to me."
The train station wasn't empty only sporadically decorated by a handful of travelers. The kids were running through the aisles formed by the large old wooden benches that could have easily once been used as pews for a church in the land of giants.
"They've been very good company, and well behaved girls."
I felt shame turning to heat, and guilt to water as I listened to Mom minimize what she had done for me by dressing it up as a kin to a selfish act. Her round face and deep eyes had the talent to take you in, rinse you off and fill you up; get too tall and they'll cut you off at the knees.
"It meant a lot." I held back the water but the heat raged.
"I know."
The time came for them to go and I gave Keeley a hug while Chris said his goodbyes to the others. When Aubrey came to me she was

already on the train. Her adventure awaited—together we had played out more than enough tearful farewells.

"Love ya, kid." I told her under a heavy breath.

"I love you too, daddy." And she was gone.

I had her in my arms and she was on a train. Life went on.

Knowing me I got drunk and stayed drunk for a couple of days. Life did go on, and life for me was playing the promenade and working on my play. In fact I finished the play during that time and got it to Steve's director friend Jessica; another iron in the fire—a line in the water. Dad always said, "Just show up." By this time in my life the words came to define the best that I could do; be the only promise I could keep so the only one I made. As much or little hope as I had back then, and that varied from day to day, I remained consistent and I would surprisingly come to find how little those words, leading to that action, meant to others.

Angel arrived for a second visit a week after Aubrey left. It was good to see her, nice to have sex again, but I couldn't shake an ill-at ease feeling about her presence. I'm sure the futile crush I developed on the Raven had something to do with it. Not that I thought, for a second, that Angel being there hurt my chances with the Raven, because I knew very well that I had none whatsoever to begin with. The thing about Angel is that she came from my recent past. Not the long in depth past that formed so much of what I had become, but simply that small interval of time where I had floundered in a drug induced limbo and drove a truck until I had paid enough penance to get out. I liked Angel, which is the only reason I kept up contact in the first place. But I also felt beholden to this sweet girl who saw around the fat and found me interesting, and sexy. Mostly I didn't want any confusion about what we had and where I was going.

For instance she had once told me over the phone about a guy hitting on her in a bar. She made him sound worthy enough but subtly intimated that she restrained herself out of loyalty to me.

"You know you are free to do what you want?"

"I know."

"I'm no one to plan a life around."

"I know."

She may have known it, but she sounded like she felt something else. Because of that conversation I held back telling her about the kiss with the Raven when it happened. Not that there was much to tell: Knockout-dead, hot babe likes my music, thinks me smart and funny, so I start thinking about her when I beat-off. It is an old and tired wrist—I mean story.

All that said it was good to see her, I trusted her to take care of herself.

We had a lot going on during her visit. Chris and I had just begun to jam with a drummer who played on the promenade. His name was John, a tall skinny guy around thirty, who wanted to front his own band, but should stick to the drums; he's probably the best all around drummer I've played with. Like most of the folks I'd come to know on the promenade he was a social misfit. Somewhere along the line these expectations, whose validity or reasonability are constantly contradicted by life, infect us all. The guy had major issues with any kind of authority; stemming no doubt from the hatred he had for his father whom he desperately wanted to impress. And I mean impress, not prove wrong.

We had seen John playing by himself on the promenade and also run across him at the Albertsons parking lot. He lived in an old beat up blue sedan. I don't know who approached whom. My guess is that it came up in a conversation organically. Of course Chris and I made so little money we warned him that he probably did better on his own.

"Oh, I have hundred dollar nights all the time. I'm just tired of getting hassled by the cops. They see a drummer by himself and all they hear is noise, but if there is a song going on around it, then they see it as different."

People have told me all sorts of stories about how much money they make and very few of them are true. I had my doubts about John but had long since grown weary of challenging causal acquaintances realities; him fitting in better on the promenade with a band up front made complete sense.

"Well, you'll be lucky to walk away with ten or twenty playing with us, but it could be fun, and maybe lead to some gigs," I offered.

"I like you guys, and I think your playing is quite excellent, and you have solid originals. But I have my own vision of where I want to be, and of course, my own songs to sing."

"I understand completely," Chris said.

"Sounds like you make a lot more without us, but if you ever wanna hook up for the fun of it, just let us know."

Steele Smith, our artist's liaison with the city, had actually been the first to suggest that John and we hook up.

"John would definitely blend in much better around here and I would really be interested in seeing what you three could accomplish together."

Steele genuinely wanted to be of service. He started out to be a writer and a poet, the only thing he ever got published was who got arrested for what, in the local paper. The thing about people like Steele is that in the end he is just another struggling artist with no real connections. But he did preside over an institution that saw a couple more than a few get good work from being seen there. Whenever he told of those instances his smile betrayed a trace of pride about it, although he knew that it had nothing to do with anything he did or said.

"I have heard some real good things about you two." He told us once. "Someone described you both, the kind of act it was, and said, 'Those guys from Kentucky are amazing.'"

"Did you tell him we were from Chicago," I asked.

"You know, I didn't have the heart."

"Good," Stopher said. "I've always wanted to be from Kentucky.

One day John came up to Stoph and I and asked if he could jam with us that night. We said sure. The first time is always rough especially when you are playing originals that have timing changes or nuisances. We stuck to as many one beat covers as we could, throwing in a few of ours to see how he'd handle them, and aside from being a little stiff and uncertain, in parts he did real well. I think we had previously given him a CD to check out and he said he gave it a few listens, (From my experience no one really does prep work—for us anyway.) At the end of the set there was thirty bucks to split between us, which left twenty for Stoph and I (that's toward the high end of our quota. Quota—WooHoo!).

John looked disappointed, but then he pretty much always had that type of scowl at the ready; he said he'd be willing to do it again. We set it up for the following Friday because things got their wildest and loudest on the weekend nights so we had a shot of standing up to it with the drums. I decided to see if Steve was game to join us with his bass, "Okie-dokie." (Yes he literally says that.)

The night came and we muddled through it all together. The sound was a bit of a mess; Steve knew some of the material and was good at improving—but our stuff tends to take unexpected turns; and John had followed some of the songs better the first night. All in all it was frustrating, invigorating, a headache and fun. Hell, we even moved on after our two-hour set and did another one down the street.

John had a problem with the split on the CD sells. My first leaning was to give him nothing so I thought a dollar per sell perfectly fair. We only sold a few over the four hours so it didn't add up to much anyway.

"John," I told him, "we invested over five thousand dollars in this thing."

"And I'm helping you sell it."

"And I'm giving you a ten-percent commission."

"A band should be all or nothing."

"If you are telling me you want to make a commitment I'd consider it, but we'd have to let some time go by."

"If you're saying you're in, I'd cut you in for third right now, " Stopher said encouragingly.

"I just think a band is not a band unless every member is equal."

"Do you want to be a member?"

"No, Chris, I don't."

We ran around in those circles for about twenty minutes, each of us gave up trying while surrendering nothing. We gave him what we thought was fair and he felt slighted.

When I asked Steve what he thought of the music that night he said, "He seems kind of angry, but he's as good or better than anyone I've played with since coming to L.A."

When Angel hit town she witnessed our last night playing with John and Steve on the promenade. I think we played a total of four times maybe five spaced over a month. Steve only played twice.

Earlier that afternoon Stoph and I did a noon set with just the two of us. Angel sat in with me for two songs. I had learned MISTY from some sheet music she had left behind on her last visit. Mostly I looked at the paper, and then said to Steve, "What's that chord?" I got a version that suited me and had fun with it. Playing it for Angel without singing it was a bit trickier, but we made it through unscathed. The other song was one that I had written years before, for a friends wedding. I wrote it as a duo for Josefa's childhood friend Kathy D. and myself. The friend in question was her brother Tony, and we had already begun working on being a trio with Stopher, it was all in a friendly, family kind of thing. Before I left for California Chris and I were asked to sing at the wedding reception of another childhood friend, since Angel was my date I asked her if she wanted sing Kathy's part with me for the event.

So we sang our songs and Angel's voice was a perfect fit for the somewhat schmaltzy love song. The Raven looked on from her perch and came over after both songs were finished.

"You have a beautiful voice, I can see why Dave loves you."

What a crock of shit! I don't know if the Raven was just being nice or was nervous being around a girlfriend of mine because of our growing intimacy; she knew damm well that the last thing I wanted anyone, let alone her, to say to Angel, was that I loved her. The Raven and I had talked more than enough about our personal lives for her to know of the line I sought to maintain between Angel and I. She was probably just being nice, but there was an edge in her voice, and the tip of a glint in her eye when she looked at me before returning to her perch.

That night we rocked the promenade with the band. The sound was still rough, Steve continued to miss the same notes he had in the past, but John did a better job of following the rhythm guitar as opposed to the bass. In most bands the bass and drums feed off each other, but since neither the bass or drummer had a full grasp of the material the over all good was better served by the drums feeding off the rhythm. What made that night better than the others was that a group of people came along that wanted to get rocked. Some sixteen-year-old girl was out celebrating her birthday with friends and felt like dancing in the street. Enter R&R CROSSING. The second someone stands opened armed and minded saying, "Please, kind, sir, will you rock me? And if it is not so very much to ask, could you rock me hard?"

We answer, "YYYYYEAHHH, BABY!!!"

We hit'em with JOHNNY B. GOODE, bitch-slapped them with RUNNING ON EMPTY, and funked them good with our take on, ALL ALONG THE WATCHTOWER. Once we had them we slipped in a few of our own up beat-tunes before falling back on an old blues standard called, ONE STEP.

Angel got to see us be loved, the first out-of-towner to do so. The Raven worked a double shift so she laid witness as well. In fact when she saw folks taking pictures of the happening she quickly handed them her business card and requested a few snapshots be sent to her P.O. box.

The tips were many, at least for us, and even after paying John and Steve their share Chris and I cleared forty easy.

The next day we set up camp at the Malibu RV state park for a few days; it cost a third of getting a motel. Returning to the first place Chris and I slept on arriving in California gave our time here scope. Although a shape of our life had been formed, if not yet completely defined, we were still an incomplete test. Being back where we had started left a bad taste in my mouth. Officially we had not lived out west for a year but for all intents and purposes we had; we certainly no longer could be confused with, or be accused of being, tourists.

Having to drive the thirty miles to the promenade was not something we could afford so Angel (who obviously was already paying for the campsite) had to help out with gas money. I didn't have to ask for it because she had a fairly clear concept of our pauper's existence, and for that I was grateful. Still my guilt over accepting her offer danced with my resentment toward her for putting me in the position to need it, and they had a lovely time. During the first year, up to that point, a part of me began to resent visitors in general, more and more. Living in a van required us to adhere to a specific routine of the showers, food lines and promenade. At times it came to be a burden but it was my burden, and it was based on something I wanted to become. Even on the days of raging against it, the burden never ceased being a badge reflecting honor; a journey holding salvation.

"I'm in the middle of something here." I would complain to Stopher, sitting in the van when we were alone, separate from our intruders. "I love seeing them, I appreciate the good times and free food that they bring, but..."

Yet I enjoyed being perched on a bluff inside the tent that I loved so well, and I took pride in the definition being back there gave to our first year.

On our way into town to play a late Saturday set on the promenade we pulled to the side of the road to take some pictures of Stoph and I standing by the van near the ocean. It was to be the cover for the CD we recorded the previous month. Angel had a good camera and the talent to use it well. We took some shots of us holding guitars on the passenger side looking out at the ocean, pretending to sing or staring pensively. Some shots saw us at the back of the van with the doors open to reveal our world, and others had us seated up front and hanging out the windows. The shot we ended up using was taken with Angel shooting us from the other side of the PCH as we leaned, holding nothing, against the side of the van toward the rear. Chris actually stood upright, squaring off with the camera, looking half unconcerned and half ready to fight. I stuck out a hand leaning on my home wearing an easy, partial smile.

(A quick side note about the photo: There wasn't enough ocean in it but Steve, with his enchanted computer, was able to take the shots Angel took of the ocean all by itself, and make it the backdrop of us by the van. Also there was a single bird caught gliding above us in the original shot. When we were sitting in Steve's den of evil, where reality is but a suggestion to be expanded on, Chris made an off the cuff remark about wishing there were two birds. Not only was Steve able to copy the original bird, but he also made one bigger than the other and positioned them in the sky over our respective heads—the bigger one hovering above Stoph of course. They held the sky while we soared firmly on the ground; freedom abounds; oh, it's symbolic.

Steve got paid his usual hourly rate for his efforts while Angel settled for the kick of being involved. They both did great work and the cover that was born of said work harmonized perfectly with the music it represented.)

Stoph and I returned to duo status and had a good time as Angel alternated between supporting us and checking out the rest of the scene. The noise of a Saturday evening on the promenade, with music bouncing off of music from every direction, bothered me more on some nights than others. How it affected me could sometimes be traced back to how desperately I needed money, or how badly I wanted the love of strangers. Some nights whatever song I sang, or every note I, with my black Strat, bled, kept the surrounding cacophony at bay; who heard, cared or tipped stood irrelevant outside the moment in which I created my womb of self-sufficient worth. On others they were swallowed whole, leaving me empty and bitter, battered and beaten, shaking my fists and licking my wounds. On that night I floated in the middle although closer to the former.

Back at the camp, lying in the tent alone with Angel, cuddling to a soundtrack of the ocean's whoosh, I thanked her warmly and sincerely. I was glad she came. There was a lot we didn't have to talk about, sensibilities that even similar years couldn't mend together, but she was a trooper who wanted the show to go on. I held her close kissing her soft and deep. As arms sent hands in search of pleasures, and mouths sought other flesh I closed my eyes to let my senses be served. Her skin, tender and silky, her breath warm and wanting, called me out and took me in. But in the moments approaching ecstasy, as I pulsed inside of her, my brain wrapped me around the ass of a red headed girl who regularly worked the cart near where I usually played and had, in fact, worked that night. Up until then I had been with Angel, but with the feverant rise of my passion the vision that was beyond me in reality became as real as the woman who was in my arms and no longer the focus of my passion. It was with that vision that I spent my desire. With the orgasmic rush subsiding in my veins I heard the ensuing guilt hissing in its place.

At least my mind had the decency not to call the Raven up for recollection. If my heart had been involved, surely it would have.

On Sunday we actually had a gig in a bar. Up to that point the only bar we played, in L.A., was within our first couple months out here; nothing more glamorous than a midnight slot on a Wednesday; the other two bands have played so that makes you the headliner, right? So what if both bands have run late, and it is now closing in on one a.m. It doesn't matter that the only people in the club to begin with are either in one of the bands, work for the club, or are here to see one of the first two bands because they're all in their twenties thinking they are going some somewhere. Be they in the bands or in the crowd, those lucky few that manage to misconstrue their participation as being connected to that which can be confused with an actual event, are not going to hang around to watch a couple of fat, middle-aged, never-wases. Oh, there was no money made.

Hence the promenade.

We took this gig because he promised gas money, which added up to a twenty, and free bear. On top of that it was in a small town north of L.A. called Chatsworth or Chadwick or whatever, which was both good and bad. The long drive there and back probably ended up eating more than the twenty—the van's mileage began to get ridiculously bad—but we at least had a shot at finding some folks who might be hungry for something good, instead of other jaded, artist/musicians or brain-dead zealots unable to fathom a thought not previously regurgitated into their mouths. You never know where you're going to find your crowd; the people that have been waiting on you.

I pretty much have taken to standing in one or two spots, letting them find me, but once in a while I venture out. More so then than now. At that time I entertained my own certainty a great deal more, now all certainty entertains me.

It was a neighborhood bar more than a club; they served burgers and hot wings. It had a couple of rooms and even a backstage dressing room. Chris and I got a quick sound check before starting up and I felt extremely lose. The house lights dimmed to further accent the lights on stage that stood a few feet above the floor. I started out singing lead vocal on the Martin to a meager gathering that consisted of Angel, the guy who booked us, a tender at each of the two bars, a waitress and a handful of leftovers from happy hour. I wouldn't say that they were happy but their conscious time left in the evening might succeed an hour. The sound system embraced the room warmly. I knew even then that this night would lead me nowhere but back to the promenade, but I liked stages, I respond well to lights, and I abso-fucking-lutely love a good sound system. It was all dress up, the illusion of professional show biz, and at that moment in time I loved how it loved me. The happy hour drunks rattled on in a far off corner finding each other alternatingly hilarious and despicable.

"Ha-ha, aahh, ha," one roared. "No way, did she say that? that's priceless."

A sip later: "You are a fucking liar."

Their exchanges bounced, bottles clinked, and the entire world floated outside their circle as a collection of murmuring bubbles.

Unless one of them grabbed a guitar and started singing into a mic I was more than happy to be a bubble. The promenade felt very far away, farther than miles could measure. As the night wore on people walked in and sat down at a table in the main room, shot pool in the back, formed drunken bubbles at the bar and set courses for the evening all their own. They came into a bar and Chris and I were the entertainment, take it or leave it, angrily or apathetic. There was one stage and it was ours.

I don't remember his name but let's call the guy who booked us Ted. Ted set us up with a couple of beers each replacing our empties as needed. Ted was alright. Gradually more people gave their attention to the stage so I started talking to them and engaging them more. Soon I was introducing songs as Christopher Walken.

"This next SONG, is a good SONG. It's true, I wouldn't lie."

Some laughed at my impression.

"Look, laDY, don't get me started, NOW. Christ, FUCK. I put my best friend DOWN like a sick dog, so consider your knee CAPPED cause it WILL BE. Sorry."

Then I started singing a few lines as Walken. Plenty of people, as the place began to fill up, offered little interest in our being there, but soon four or five tables were taken up and being entertained. At one point Ted shouted from the crowd, "You should be doing Vegas."

Once I established that the folks knew who Barney Gumble from the Simpsons was, I started having conversations between him and Walken. By the time I had Barney doing an imitation of Christopher Walken the laughter at the tables blocked out the miscellaneous goings on in the rest of the bar. (Unfortunately, you'll have to imagine what Barney doing Walken sounds like because there are no keys on this board, or punctuations in grammar that would visually illustrate it for you. Trust me; I was brilliant.) My favorite bit was when I did Christopher Walken doing an imitation of Jerry Lewis.

"NICE lady. With the good AND the FINE. Glaven, I said glaVEN, it's TRUE."

In the midst of all that we did play our asses off. Chris and I switched guitars a couple of times and had been up there over an hour. Stoph got a few laughs of his own doing his Harry Carey imitation and a voice he ripped-off from Kevin Mathews, one of the Chicago, talk DJs we dug that did the band tribute word game. It didn't matter if the crowd knew the character, or Harry for that matter; the voices were funny on to themselves.

"How about a nice cold bud," Stoph, as Harry, shouted.

"Harry," Walken responded, "I like nothing MORE than a BUD when consuming large quantities of freshly BOILED hot DOGS. It's true."

"I WOULD LIKE SOME DONUTS! YES! " Stoph switched into Eddie—the Kevin Mathews character. Eddie had only one volume, loud. It was a voice that came without wind and yet exploded from Stopher's knotted gut as rotund as the six hundred pound man it portrayed. "AND I WOULD LIKE THE DONUT HOLE TO BE FILLED WITH AN EGG ROLL, PLEASE! JUST WEDGE IT IN! WEDGE IT IN! WEDGE IT IN. EEEH HEE!" he gleefully wheezed.

We were just the opening act but the headliners were late, and when they had arrived, told Ted that they only had enough material for a forty-minute set. Ted kept saying, "Do another." Before it was all over we had been up there for at least three hours. No breaks.

Stoph and I went back stage because it was such a rarity in our careers that there was a backstage to go to. We settled on a couch as the headliner put the finishing touches of their make-up on and adjusted the bulges in their leather pants. One would have thought that they were about to embark on a world tour. On stage that fact was even more apparent. They were essentially a "hair band" playing Van Halen, Judas Priest, and the like. They may have done one original song but, no, there was nothing original about it, even how bad it was had been done plenty of times. They did rock the bar. People saw the bells and whistles; skinny bodies clad in leather, donning thick perms; the drums pounded, the bass pulsed, and the vocalist screamed while the guitar player had all the right toys. They were okay musicians pretending to be great.

When Chris and I were kids we had these western action figures. Most kids had G.I. Joe, we had Johnny West. Johnny had accessories like hats, holsters, guns, and a family too—wife, Josie, and two adolescent boys, Jesse and Jamie. We collected as much of the franchise as we could and gave them character traits. We actually had two Johnnys so we made one reckless, sometimes a scoundrel, but in the end a good-hearted sort, twin brother for Johnny. He was our brother Art's character so we may have called him Artie. We put them through all kinds of adventures, most of which we took from whatever current movie we had just seen. I guess we were around four or five at the start of playing these games. Art grew out of them first while Chris and I played with them up near our teens. At some point before we stopped, embarrassment about playing with the toys crept under our skin. We never referred to them as dolls. So we came up with the code "little people."

"Hey, Chris." I'd say in a secretive hush just in case anyone was around. "Wanna play little people."

Sometimes when the whole family sat around the dinner table Chris would make a slight gesture with his thumb and index finger while nodding his head toward our room. That meant, "little people."

As I have grown and gone out into the world it seems at times that I see nothing but supposed adults at play with "little people." The only difference is that they have set aside the small action figures from their rooms and are now at large, outside of their homes, even crossing state lines posing as their very own life-sized action figures.

The band that night was a case in point. I had seen it bars before but never made the connection as I did that night. As I sat on stool with one arm around Angel and the other reaching for a beer it hit me. And at that very moment I caught Stopher smiling from the end of the bar with his index finger hovering ever so slightly above his thumb. I did a double-take and his grin widened as his head nodded. We both burst out laughing and I buried my head into my arms. Angel smiled at first thinking that the band was just that bad, but then she sensed something more.

"What?"

"I'll tell ya later."

As funny as we had been on stage, the shared revelation from across the bar that Chris and I had without having to say a word had to be the best joke of the night. The name of the band? Storyteller. I am not making that up. Oh, they told themselves all sorts of stories.

Angel stayed a few more days and we had a good time. I made some pizza at Steve's and as usual the later portion of the evening gave way to music. I'd look across the room to see Angel banging away at the sneer with a big smile on her face. She was a music groupie in the best sense of the word. You have your run of the mill of hotties ranging from stunning to sleazy; she was not one of those. Yes she had crushes on the many cuties that she admired, and yes I didn't always see the talent in them that she did, but she did. She loved music and loved being around those who made it. I think that in her finding me, and thereby being introduced to my crowd, she found the backstage pass of her dreams. She wasn't a decoration; she got to be one of us; and whenever I think of her now she is bouncing to the moment with a sneer drum between her legs and a broad smile on her face. She kept a swinging, infectious beat.

In our song-rounds at least three or four of us had guitars—sometimes one was a bass. The idea being that each person in the circle sings a song while the others followed along as best they could. Eric and Steve were always good at picking up the chords of whoever was singing while my strong suit was lacing around the melody. Depending on how familiar the song was to the rest of us we would throw in vocal harmonies as we saw fit. If someone decided to debut a song recently written we usually laid back to listen. Most of the songs were old favorites that we'd take turns requesting songs from one another.

On that night Stopher, being the perceptive one where hurt feelings were concerned, notice Steve on the verge of a pout. Apparently my playing had begun to get on his nerves. A few quips passed his lips but since Steve lived for the quip I put little weight on them. At one point Steve started playing a riff from a fairly recent pop hit that Angel loved. No one picked up on the lyrics as we were kind of in between songs and the night was nearing its end. I jumped in on the riff by dancing around it with a few common notes and others counter melody.

"No, it's this," Steve instructed me.

"Oh, I ain't here to learn," I joked, as I continued to fool around with various patterns.

"That is your problem, Dave, you don't learn anything."

"What?"

Stoph saw this coming a mile away while I sat there befuddled.

"We're at a party jamming; I don't see the connection."

"I just thought you might want to learn a song that your girlfriend likes."

"Covers are not my specialty," I said with a false swagger, hoping that the humor of the moment would be realized.

"God for bid you should to something nice for her."

I turned to Angel; she seemed as perplexed as I.

"The only one who cares about this is you, Steve."

"Well I guess it's because that it has been my songs that you've been playing over all night."

"Now be fair, Steve, he has been playing all over everybody's songs tonight," Eric threw in as both a joke and a truth.

"Yeah, I thought we had an understanding; you guys sing and I get my rocks off," I offered.

"At least this is a party," Chris chimed in, "I have to work with this guy."

"I don't mind your playing, I just think your playing could benefit from listening a little bit more to what you are playing to."

"I listen." My voiced turned flat.

"You play."

"I do both; I can even chew gum and walk at the same time—got any gum?"

"I'm simply trying to help you improve as a musician."

"Dave is a great improve player," Chris said angrily. "I know he plays more notes than you like, and spits out a clam now and again, but this is a round, not a practice."

It went on like that for a while with Eric withdrawing gradually from the discussion, and Chris getting more upset than me.

"I'm not always in love with what he does but some of it is brilliant," Eric said. "Just tell him to back off on a song or two."

"Hey, I have no problem being told to shut up," I agreed.

"I don't want you to back off, I want you to listen, I want to help you be better."

"You want a helluva lot more than that, lady," Stopher said with the hint of a bitter, cowboy drawl.

"What?" Steve exclaimed shaking his head.

"A movie reference; Paul Newman in Hombre," I enlightened.

"It's just Dave, being Dave," Eric said, and then washed his hands of the whole thing.

"You're just being precious about songs we've heard a million times," Stoph finally said heatedly. Then he dropped his head to pull back. "Believe me, no one blames you for getting annoyed with it. I've played with him for years upon years and I'm just now starting to accept it more fully."

"It has nothing to do with my songs, I am trying to help him get better."

"He doesn't need your help, he is a fucking genius. A fucking genius that can get on your nerves."

It went round and round with no one changing Steve's mind.

I tell this story because I wrote a song about it afterwards. I tell it also because it showed me Steve in an unreasonable light. All he had to say is, "Yeah, just back off a bit." (I can get a bit obnoxious with my second guitar.) I have backed off a bit since that night in my approach whenever we all get together. Not just on Steve's songs but in general. I'm still obnoxious but less so. Steve could not allow that his intentions were anything less than lofty. He refused to let it be about him, and what he wanted; he had to have it be about me, and what I needed to change for the betterment of me. It rang of morality. Stopher saw all of this before Steve ever opened his mouth; I had to have him explain it to me the next day.

Here's the song:
There's so much that I don't know, partly because I'm lazy
And partly because I'm slow
But there is a method to my madness, a path through all my darkness
Don't try do see, just follow my lead
I'm long on shortcomings, never short on long phrasings
Busy at play—too much you say
But to think that I don't listen is to not go the distance
Give my due some heed

And follow my lead
You don't need to know where
Follow my lead
You don't need to know why
Follow my lead
It doesn't have too make sense
Follow my lead
Forget what you think you know
And follow my lead

You think so much is wrong when it's just another way to fall
You say, "Two plus two is always four." That's such a laugh.

I've been doing this shit for years; I was told there wouldn't be this fucking much math: Leave the mind behind; let your soul feed

Follow my lead
Where we're going is here
Follow my lead
Into the momentary high
Follow my lead
Break through the very fence
Follow my lead
Built by what you think you know

But don't think that I don't wish I could be more like you
I see all that you've got; you are everything I'm not;
or would ever work hard enough to be
But there is a price it seems you've paid and it tunnels your vision
There is something in your way limiting your wisdom
I can see beauty in you but you can't see it in me
Follow me lead, follow my lead, follow my lead

As I started writing the song all sorts of similar conversations between Steve and I came to mind. I remembered working on our first CD in Nashville, we were laying down some guitar part and he said, "You can't do that." I asked, "Does it sound bad?" "Actually no, but it shouldn't work with the chords you're playing." "So it sounds bad?" "No, but it should." "But it doesn't." "No" "We'll keep the part."

Steve knows the musical math behind what he does and I don't. I am the one I'd pay to see.

CHAPTER ELEVEN

My first summer on the promenade whooshed and swirled as I attempted to take it all in as a whole. Unfortunately, like the atom with its inner protons and neutrons being surrounded by zooming electrons, the promenade needs to be dissected to be digested, which invariably leads to explosions of one kind or another, productive and destructive. Day in and day out Chris and I sat waiting to play between sets as others made their plea for a buck from the flowing river. Weekdays resembled the weekends more and more without matching them; acts piled on top of each other with no regard for the over all peace; musicians threw notes back and forth over the required forty feet; mimes turned up their atmospheric music; and balloon men lent the bellow of their clowned horns to the mix. Sound became a violent tug of war with dollar bills tied to the middle of a rope.

At first Stoph and I tried to reason with the other performers and we did come across a few who, like us, couldn't see the sense of not working together. Within those few even fewer were able to refrain from being pulled into the audio fisty-cuffs. The best we could do was get to a spot before others and be the one that got set up on top of by someone else. Once there we made an effort to keep our sound at a minimum. But with so many variables, like the wind, an instant change in the crowd's size, and being powered by batteries that continually affected the output of our PA, it was hard to gauge and maintain that elusive volume of reasonability.

The other frustration we endured was watching practically every other act make more money than us. In the end I came to create my own understanding of it but at first I couldn't shake the feeling that the entire world had come to the promenade to give Chris and myself the finger. Slowly though, as I observed the varying spectacles, I began to attach specific reasons to each act.

For example: Twirly-Bird, who spun basketballs on his fingers as well as doing a bit of break dancing with them, used comedy. Granted, his jokes were worn and tired but he committed to them, and most folks will laugh at anything if you sell it properly; being on the streets their expectations were not exactly demanding the next Richard Pryor. Guys like him, which included the other break-dancer groups, Animation Man, The Bowler Boys, magicians, and novelty acts in general, knew how to attract an audience. They all had a way of convincing the causal schmuck happening along that he'll miss something if he doesn't stop.

Most of them start by cranking out some obnoxious rap song that pulses with fat bass lines, walking around their planned stage area shouting, "Showtime in four minutes; four minutes to Showtime." That gets repeated a few times with minutes lessening, although not necessarily in alignment with any clock. Sometimes they get right to the show while others it could go on for ten, fifteen minutes.

Twirly-Bird's next move would be to bounce a basketball higher and higher while appearing to be growing with an intense excitement. This excitement is cousin to that of a guy getting ready to take a swing at someone, but to Twirly's credit, it falls short of scaring folks away (he is for the most part a family show). Inevitably a child will stop to watch the ball be pounded into the ground and ricochet toward the sky. There could be not a single child in sight before hand, and then one will suddenly appear. They range roughly from seven to twelve, boy or girl. The trick is to have one young enough to be cute, yet old enough to have the physical strength to play along in his game. The game entailed of the kid mimicking Twirly's moves with a basketball, nothing spectacular—causing kids to get hurt or making them look too stupid ingratiates no one to nobody.

He starts by giving a sharp one-bounce pass to a chosen child whose name he has acquired.

"Gimme the ball," he shouts encouragingly.

The kid bounces it back; he immediately returns it to them.

"Gimme the ball, Brian," he shouts again.

The exchanges would gain momentum with each pass. Twirly, who stood over six feet with the physique of an athlete, had a way of exuding that presence while maintaining a gentle giant disposition. He was a light skinned black and that always helped in ingratiating him to the hicks, and or tourists. How long the passing went on depended on how quickly the crowd formed.

"Look, honey, a large African-American is engaging in sports entertainment with one of our country's youth."

"Gimme the ball, Bri-Bri!"

As the volume of his voice rose and the speed of the passes built to a climax, Twirly finally declared with a matter-of-factly pout, "It's my ball." And turned away from the child as if they were in the midst of a sandbox squabble.

The crowd chuckled at the adorable sucker punch and the child's confused expression. Deftly did Twirly make the transition to the next game before any actual awkwardness could be born. He'd pick up another ball and hand it to the kid.

"Okay, Bri-Bri, follow me; bounce the ball."

Here the show varied with the talent or ability of the child in question. If the kid could handle a ball, Twirly made faces exaggerating his dismay at being upstaged, if the child fumbled he milked that aspect, tickling the line of embarrassment without crossing. They bounced the ball, wrapped it around their waist, shuffled it between their hands over their heads—if you ever tried out for a team you know the drill. For the last exercise, Twirly rolled the ball down behind his head as he turned, letting it roll down his back where he gave the ball a pop by sticking out his butt. The crowds always found that charming, cute, darling or what have you. Whatever. The kid usually balked at the last bit and Twirly would egg them on.

"Come on, lemme see you give it the butt."

More endearing smiles.

The kid did it and again, whether he did it well or not was beside the point.

"Give Brian a big hand."

Applause.

"Give Brian a BIG hand.

Applause and cheers.

Of course Twirly was just trying to get them to make noise so that more people would hear and think that they were missing out on something.

The kid starts to walk away into the audience.

"Hey, Brian!"

The kid walked back to center stage.

"You did good."

The child started off again.

"Hey, Bri-Bri."

The child returned.

"Thanks, man." Twirly shook his hand.

Again another attempt at an exit.

"Hey, Bri."

The boy came back and Twirly gave him a lollypop.

"Aww," said the crowd.

The boy went to leave yet again.

"Hey, Brian."

Now even the kid was getting sick of the attention, even looked a tad exasperated at being continually played.

"I just wanted to say bye." Twirly appeared innocent and sincere.

The crowd was amused and touched in a sort of fuzzy, warm way.

"Alright! Who wants to see me break-dance with basketballs?"

Yeah.

"I said, who wants to see me break-dance with basketballs?!"

Hurrah!

At last he did something that looked somewhat impressive. But first he did a bit about putting on some old-school funk.

"This before Dr. Dre, this something George Clinton, the man of funk himself, cut his teeth on."

When he pushed the play button the theme from I DREAM OF JEANNIE blared from his speakers and everyone had a hearty laugh.

Twirly kept character by bobbing his head to the groove a few beats before acknowledging the crowd's reaction.

"Is this too main line for you all. Okay, that's cool; let's try this."

He put on some rap music and began rolling on and off the basketball on the ground. I had seen better break-dancing on the promenade but Twirly had shtick. That lasted for about two minutes, then he was on his feet walking around the crowd's inner circle with the ball spinning on his finger—a standard trick. His twist with it was the way he swirled his finger around as the ball spun atop it, and the goofy walk he added along with cartoonishly, googly eyes.

"It's like good wet-dream," he'd say to an attractive female member of the audience, referring to his wild and willy finger.

The sexual reference was vague enough for anyone not old enough not to get it, there by, not alienating his family crowd.

After a small sampling of antics he announced that before he could continue he needed a "little love". Chris and I had a hard enough time mentioning that we had CDs for sale; asking for tips was out of the question for us.

"Come on, Santa Monica, show me the love," he encouraged as he circled the crowd's inner rim reaching his basket into their midst. "Now, kids, be sure to stay in school." He'd pause in the center of the street, drop his basket at his feet and give it vague once over from a standing position with an index finger miming a count. "Or you'll be doing a show in the street too."

Much amusement from the masses; you could almost here a forty year old mom murmuring to her older sister, "He is sooo charming."

Once again Twirly mimed a distant count of his booty, then abruptly frowned.

"Come on now, Santa Monica," he'd crouch down to run some fingers through the bills, "I got no more than eleven dollars in here, and count," he proceeded to point his magic counting finger throughout the crowd as he rose to his tippy-toes, "at least fifty people getting a free ride."

Usually he had at least twenty or thirty in the basket when he said that, as for the number of folks looking on, he just picked a number that sounded shameful.

"Now I am out here working for your love, people. This ain't L.A. is it?"

Another handful of good people trickled in towards the basket to feed his need.

Twirly smiled ever so graciously as they brought forth their offerings of love. When all was given that was going to be given, he crouched, counted and frowned. This time he rose to the resignation that that was it.

"Alright, Santa Monica, some of you are gonna get a free show," he smiled slyly with his finger wagging its friendly shame. "I'm going to go on ahead and do the big finale anyway. You know why, Santa Monica? Because of the kids—I'm doing the show for the kids; right Bri-Bri."

None begged more shamelessly, or as often, than Twirly—but always under the grace of charm.

His big number was getting an adult from the crowd—sexes, age, and race varied—and had them hold a stick up out to the side over their head, wearing a platform containing two separate points, on their head. Then he'd spin a ball and place it on one of the points resting on their head, then a ball on the other, then the stick in their hands, and then one on the index finger of the civilian's other hand being held up as well. Leading up to all of that was plenty more banter and shtick with a side of a beggar-smoothie. He got a friend of the civilian to take a picture of the a event and made jokes like:

"Where are you from sir?"

"Santa Fe."

"Sorry?"

"Santa Fe."

"Sorry?"

"Sant-"

"No; I heard you, I'm just sorry to hear it."

I gave the act more pages than it deserves, but it was one that I had to endure weekend in and out down by the shoeshine stand that first summer through the next. At first I hated it with a passion, then I respected the craft of giving simple folk what they wanted while getting all that money, then I hated it all over again. Call me bitter, and you are totally accurate; call him a two-bit hack, professional beggar—right again. The guy could spin a basketball like nobody's business and milk a crowd; I'll give him that. In the end he entertained them, so who am I?

Animation Man had a similar bit, in that he had a physical talent, break-dancing, but working the crowd is what pulled down the bucks. He would get the folks to gather by cranking out some rap music and placing a helmet, open end facing skyward, in the middle of the street. Next he stalked it from every angle: First like a tiger sniffing it out for suitable prey; then like mathematician, calculating the degrees, figuring in the wind. He took a running start from a distance then stopped on a dime to retrace his steps from one side, then the other. The gathering gawkers assumed he meant to some how, from a sprint, get his head into the helmet in a physical feat of swooping motion. When he finally seemed ready, he raised a hand high to demand absolute silence. After a dramatic pause, Animation and his sculpted body, charged at the helmet at full speed.

The crowd gasped.

Just as he neared the helmet he halted in front of it, bent over, picked it up and put it on with darling, mischievous smile.

Animation was dark skinned with a natural menacing presence. He is the one that you see on the street at night coming your way and your first reaction is to cross to the other side. Unlike Twirly, he was not the comfortable candidate for Middle America, and not only did he not hide from that fact, he used it to charm them. Clever boy.

His humor played it up with such jokes as: "If I don't get what I want now, I'll get it from your houses later; your choice.

I didn't catch as much of his act as I had suffered through with Twirly's but had observed enough to see some physically impressive stuff and, more importantly, how well he understood getting people to give him their money.

He had his voice pre-recorded on a CD to, no doubt, save his voice, but also it had an affect of viewing him as a puppet of sorts. He mimed his own voice live in front of the people and that some how disarmed his overall intimidating stature. Whenever he said something that was obviously a joke, the voice on the CD would give a gruff giggle and he, in person, silently gave it physical life. The distance between his body and his voice created a child-like atmosphere revealing him to be in playtime.

One of his bits was to line up four women from the crowd with each representing a different race: one white, one Hispanic, one black and one Asian. The voice would explain how each race tended to dance and the body exemplified. Of course he played up every stereotype and had the music represent each culture. The whites were represented by homogenized pop music, he moved spiritedly but soullessly; the Hispanics a steamy salsa, he cartoonishly seduced, with a machismo to all get out aimed at the, by now, hysterical Latina queen; the black received a similarly sexually charged treatment, but to the tune of a funky, Rick James bass line; and the Asian got a proper, traditional oriental waltz. All the women blushed, hid their faces while accepting said ancestries. After taking them one by one and illustrating how they are perceived, Animation put on something you would hear on any top forty-radio station and randomly stood in front of one girl, doing the dance that classified them and they were to acquiesce in kind. As with Twirly and the children, some women got down with it, while others fumbled over their embarrassed laughter. Some of them were old or fat or both, but there would always be at least one hottie. As soon as Animation made a round or two within the first few measures of the song, with each woman only dancing as he danced in front of them and stopping when he moved on, he started mixing up cultural associated movements with their assigned representatives. The white got funky; the black turned prim in the light of the land of the rising sun; Hispanic became Barbie; and the Asian a Latin Queen. With each jump in the line, Animation switched their heritage, making the changes faster and faster until confusion swirled about his dancing concubines; before long all of the movements blurred into one uncertain awkward mess of fleeting identity.

It never occurred to me until just now that Animation did a nice job of drawing a physical picture of a social commentary. The commentary itself is nothing overtly insightful or groundbreaking, but the theatrical way in which he manipulated the four bodies was actually kind of clever. Having talked to him on a few isolated occasion I never suspected him as being a joiner of nations, in fact he probably only saw it as way of joining his pocket with their money. Still, it's there, and it entertained.

Animations big closing number was to get four or five guys from the crowd to lift him up on their shoulders while he wore an authentic Batman mask, and the CD player blasted the old TV show's theme song so they could all run around in a circle hoisting the superhero. He tended to only pick white guys from the crowd for this bit. I don't think this so much as more social commentary as I do seeing it as personal revenge by getting a kick out of having young, more than likely affluent, white guys doing his bidding. Not only are they carrying him on their shoulders as the conquering hero from their parent's collective childhood, but they are doing so under the guise of looking foolish and making him a mint.

My favorite visual of his was how he could make himself run backwards while appearing to be running forward. He employed a version of the moonwalk with lunging strides to great effect. He appeared to be doing everything in his power to speed forward into the night while flying in the other direction as if someone rewound the film.

Like Twirly-Bird, Animation knew that his physical gifts only got people to stop. It took involving civilians in their acts and inspiring laughter to keep the people there, and get inside their pockets. Yes, the jokes were tired and obvious and no, I didn't find them funny. Of course I am a writer/musician/artist, not a civilian, and I hated THREE'S COMPANY and the old LUCY shows even as a kid; I am no one's sought after demographic.

The true-blue break dancing acts offered humor as well but they relied more on the feats of their prowess. They got crowds started by cranking rap music and stretching out on the street four at a time (break dancers usually worked in groups of six) while throwing in a few flips or spins. When enough had gathered the leader turned down the music and grabbed a mic. There were three or for different groups working the promenade, sometimes less. They all seemed to know each other, even mixed and matched personal. The first group I saw was led by a tiny Italian looking guy who sounded Puerto Rican. He was definitely older than the rest and exhibited the most interest in choreography. They were all, for the most part, pretty amazing in the things that they did although only one or two actually appeared to be dancers beyond the realm of gymnastics. The best all around dancer, to me, was a young skinny black kid around fifteen years old. When I first aw him he was in the Italian-Rican's group, but he soon led his own troupe. Where his former leader tried to form a cohesive group movement, the young-skinny based his operation on individual riffing and humor. While Young-Skinny kept the opening choreograph and threw a little bit of it in at the end, none of it had ambition.

Every group had pretty much the same opening jokes, although Young-Skinny was a born entertainer who in another generation would have been someone in the mold of a Sammy Davis.

"Our show is only as good as our audience so if we suck…it's your fault."

Chuckles abound.

"At this time we ask that you to make some noise to get our energy up, and to fool everyone into thinking something cool is going down."

Their honesty gets both laughs and respect.

"Let me hear ya!"

The crowd warms itself up to the idea.

"Okay; that sucked. Let me hear YOU!"

The crowd responds to the challenge, but not whole-heartedly.

"That still sucks; one more time."

The crowd gives all they have, working together and doing their best.

"That'll have to do because I gotta hurry up and meet my parole officer."

More laughter: "Isn't that darling, Harold, they are making light of their terrible disrespect for the law."

"We have a few simple rules here: If you see something you like—clap; if you see something you don't like—clap ANYWAY; if you see something THAT YOU CAN NOT DO, give us a dollar."

At that precise moment two laundry baskets slide out from behind MC Skinny-Young to present themselves to the marks.

I won't describe in any detail the spinning heads on cement; the whole bodies being supported by one hand; the varying ways they can contort, hop, flip and what-have-you. They were all young fit, skinny, strong and put in their time working at getting better.

Another act that mixed break dancing was one Chris and I referred to as The Bowler Boys. I caught the least of their act because I don't think I ever came across them when they weren't completely engulfed by a crowd. They only came out on Friday and Saturday nights, playing eight and ten o'clock sets. They were two short little black guys in matching orange, sometimes yellow suits, and wore old-fashioned bowler derbies. From the reaction of the mob surrounding them I gathered it was mostly comedy that they sold. The few jokes that I heard could have easily fit in with Twirly's act. I know I saw one of the Bowler Boys doing a, "This how white dudes dance," bit. I hear that they sometime do warm-ups for studio audiences waiting to watch a television show get taped, and some ocean-line cruises. Yeah, they are that kind of funny. Those boys made a mint on the promenade.

Compared to the Silver Robot, the Bowler Boys, Twirly-Bird and the rest were the fucking Charlie Chaplin-Buster Keatons of their times. (Their jokes were that old anyway.) Silver man was some big black oaf who wore a Top Hat, Tux and tails that he spray painted silver along with whatever part of his body that shown through. He would stand on a platform with a boom box at his feet cranking, sometimes Motown or funk, others punk-ass rap, holding out a silver cup. His bit was to stand perfectly still until someone put a buck in the cup. Once paid he did a couple Rerun moves from the seventies, puckered his lips, pushed out his cheeks like a bullfrog and blew a small whistle, that he hid in his teeth, suggestively; that's quality entertainment. The civilians ate it up, especially the kids, teenage girls and old ladies.

If he wasn't getting enough attention, Silver-Man would stalk up behind some cute girls surprising them with his whistle in their ear to make them squeal. If I did that, they'd call a cop, but spray yourself silver and they call it comedy. (Oh, I'm bitter.) He didn't always clean up but he made a hell of a lot more money than me and Stoph. On top of having no actual talent he was one of those guys that would show up at the last second and squeeze in between two musical acts and blast his boom box until you felt his speakers distorting in your chest; like most performers on the promenade, utterly self-involved.

There was a statue act that came out to the promenade that first summer that I actually respected. He dressed as Charlie Chaplain and remained deathly frozen until he got coined. Kids would stand around shouting, wiggling their butts in his face and sometimes cursed, to get a reaction. He never flinched a muscle unless they tipped. Silver man would frown with his bullfrog cheeks, blow his whistle or turn his back. Not that I held it against him on those occasions, but that Chaplain guy knew the meaning of commitment.

Then there was the mime; a sweet Russian guy who always wore the same navy-blue and white, horizontally striped shirt and white pants. He painted his face white while lining black around his eyes and mouth. I know mimes usually make for good punch lines, but this guy was an artist. His wry frame could contort yet that played very little into the beauty of what he did. Yes he started off the stuff you'd expect: walking into the wind, the wall (which he took to another level from what I had previously seen) and riding the range of facial expressions from happy to sad, laughter to anger.

My one beef I had with him was that he played his atmospheric music too loud. In the beginning I dismissed him as an aforementioned punch line, a hack. Of course it was Stopher who appreciated him first. The first thing that caught my attention was how he portrayed a flower breaking through the dirt to taste its first morsel of sunshine, how it gradually grows and stretches, spreading and blooming under the glory of the day. The music he plays with it was no doubt a famous piece that I can't begin to remember, but I can, in mind, hear how music and movement meshed together so the story could be poetically sewn.

As majestic as the music for that piece had perfectly been, so was the humor that bombastically bounced through the next one. This piece followed a man through the perils of blowing up a balloon so big that it became a boulder that wanted to fly away. At first the man had to yank at it while being dragged along the ground on the heels of his feet. Soon he managed to corral it from the sky by getting on top of it. Sighing his victory the man smiled just as the balloon bubbled from the earth with a belch. Then another. And another. All it once the balloon lifted itself, carrying the man along for the ride, off the ground, into the air and among the birds. At first the horrified man scrambled over the balloon in some futile attempt to regain control of the situation only to resort to hanging on for dear life. The scared man with no escape suddenly surrendered the fight in favor of the wonder that floating above all he did behold. Now he became the honorary captain of an unscheduled flight of fancy.

The mime not only told a story, he told it in vivid colors and spectacular details of movement and wordless emotion. I had seen him die plenty of times, making five or ten dollars during the weekdays, but as time went on that happened less and less. Last time I heard he worked for a circus in Vegas. I have been fortunate to see a lot of wonderful things on the promenade while having to endure a great many more that were mundane at best, but whenever I see the mime in my mind, and I don't very often, I sense that fortune rising within me.

All of the above acts have something in common: they are things not redundantly fed to us through the media. Sure, you'll see a blurb on some magazine television show about break dancing, but not nearly as much as you did when it first made the scene in the eighties. A guy plays the guitar or a piano and sings their song, or one you've heard before; whatever—turn on the radio or VH1. Out on the street you see a man painted all in silver blowing a whistle; watch a gang of ill-spending youths do battle with their bodies on the cement; look on while some stranger is made to do something embarrassing by a professional stranger; or allow a mime to draw you into a world that isn't an easy punch line, but, in fact, is one of the world's oldest art forms. That is the promenade.

The balloon folk generally don't make much noise or take up much space. Some have a horn that they'll give a squeeze once in a while to get some kid's attention, and at first that bothered me. (Oh, I was a prima Dona.) I quickly learned how relatively harmless that was to my situation. There was one balloon, "artist", by the name of Sunshine that ironically cast the biggest pain in the ass of a shadow on many a performers day.

Sunshine, I don't believe, qualified as a dwarf, midget or "little person." (In my book she barely rated as human.) Imagine a fireplug stacked on top of another fireplug with legs coming out of the bottom one and arms the top, only more squat in dimensions, and much more evil in disposition. The limbs themselves held a proportion that could be likened to the spigots of a fireplug only longer. Her bulbous, round face had the appearance of being squeezed out of some unseen tube that refused take it back, and that gave the outer rims of the face a tightly cut-off quality. Her freckles seemed nervous to be there. She had long bushy frizzed-out, red hair and blue eyes that, though not beady, were small and piercing. It would be easy to say that she waddled, the way her arms swayed and hovered out from her side, but that would miss at pointing out the regality in which she surveyed as she strolled. On top of that her strides were surprisingly long and I'd have to say that I have seen sexier penguins.

If I sound mean, or if it is offensive to hear someone be berated solely on a physical basis, I accept that condemnation. To know Sunshine is to forgive me.

There are people who are self-involved and they are called everybody. We muddle by trying to get what we want, and if the occasional toe suffers an indignation or two we give our pillows an extra fluff drifting right on off to sleep. Sunshine had that stunning ability to shit all over you and complain when you don't wipe her ass. Did I mention that she works with children?

To her credit, Sunshine has a good act; she knows her market and offers it something no other balloon person does. In my time I have seen balloon blowers out there in full clown outfits with wigs, make-up and everything. Most of the regulars didn't even go that far and still made a pretty penny. Guys like Franz, Jack and Chandler—nice folk, crazy and annoying in their own special way—may give a kid a friendly, "Hello, young fellow," or "Hey there little, missy," but the balloons mostly sold themselves. Sunshine had story time.

She pulled a large red wagon stacked up with about ten or twelve tiny, plastic chairs in varying colors of pink, yellow and blue. Once she claimed a spot, rightly or otherwise, she'd set them out in rows of four and set up shop.

"Have a seat, and you'll get a special treat," she'd coo like a lizard seducing an insect.

She told stories that involved animals, making the animals come to life in balloon form. I can't say that I ever heard any specifics but assumed that the stories were the typical fare. I did hear enough to catch her making every line rhyme even if she had to use the same word.

""And I have been told, I say, that if you look carefully and truly true stay, in your heart all dreams will be, I say."

You would like to think that someone who made a living telling children morality tales would have a sense of fair play, or at least concern herself in the smallest way with being in line with the Golden rule. Sunshine was notorious on the promenade for constantly violating the rotation rules in order to hoard the prime locations to herself. Every act has to move one hundred and twenty feet from their last performance and not return to the same spot for at least four hours. That way everybody has a shot at getting a good spot at least once in the day. Sunshine would move barely forty feet for one set then shoot back to where she started on the next. To me, being a musician, I couldn't have cared less where she was, but it cut into the other balloon artists' profits. Of course when anyone else committed the slightest infraction, whether by a foot or a second, Sunshine was on the phone to the monitors or community officers in a heartbeat. Even if the essence of the law had been served, or even if it in no way prevented her from sucking the last dollar on the promenade into her greedy gullet, she'd still complain. It was as if she had an alarm go off in her head that couldn't be ignored. Things had to be set right until the next time she deemed it necessary to monopolize the center street, which was whenever she thought she could get away with it.

What made it all the more annoying was the unceasing pretentiously, polite tone in her voice, and the unflinching certainty with which she cloaked her every devious action in pure righteousness and unadulterated innocence. There is a moment when you look into the eyes of someone who's argument is obviously void of merit, and all you can see is how shocked they are at being told that they are wrong; it doesn't register. You begin to wonder if they have a switch inside that keeps every action separate from their conscious thought. Imagine O.J., in the middle of slashing those poor souls to pieces, asking them why they keep screaming? How come their blood insists on squirting out every which way, and would they mind terribly not getting it on his shoes? Granted Sunshine never killed anyone that I know of, she was infuriating to deal with nonetheless.

I knew all about Sunshine's mode of operating and had a few slight run-ins with her that I was able to deflect to a monitor or just side step on my own. I had amplification and she had balloons; no contest—what could she do me?

One night, however she got under my skin; the way she talked; the audacity with which she weaseled into a spot—the way she did business in general.

It was a Friday night, Stoph and I had done a two o'clock set in front of George's Bistro on our own then waited to do an eight with drummer-John. As much as we tried to keep our volume reasonable, Stoph and I realized that with the drums, we could only do so much. That is why we waited for four hours in one spot so that we could warn anyone with designs on playing near us, that while we would do our best, things were going to get loud at eight o'clock. As it happened, another band set up down the street from us about hundred feet away. They were a Peruvian band that consisted of two percussionists, a bass, guitar and flute. Indian Pride was infamous for blowing other acts out of the water. Something about the high end of wind instruments cut through the air. Not to mention that they had a twenty-four channels, eight hundred watt system with big monitors and even bigger mains in tow. They were going to kill us. Our only saving grace was that it would take them at least until eight thirty to set up. We were out of the gate at the top of the hour. At 8:05, little miss Sunshine rolled her stack of chairs, bundled balloons and forced rhymes on by to situate herself no more than thirty feet away from our stage. She set up shop and started hawking for children with cheerful words full of soulless tones.

We had gotten through three songs and it looked like we might make a buck or two when Sunshine approached us decked out in a brightly striped, colored jump-suit, a silly hat and bright polka dots with sparkles all over her face.

"Will you young men please make an effort to keep the noise down so I could please do my show?"

"You've got to be kidding?" It was the nicest thing I could get myself to say.

"If the children can't hear me speak, then they won't hear the stories."

I will say right off that I should have started out being calm, simply pointing out that it was eight o'clock on a Friday night in the most crowded section of the promenade; that Indian Pride was preparing to swallow us all; and that any plea for sanity was in fact insane. But knowing who she was, knowing how she treated others; seeing her show up at the last second to the most coveted spot on the promenade at the primest hour; and knowing she knew all of this, made my eyes grow large, then grow larger still. I could feel my sockets unable to hold them, and taste their heat on my tongue; heat that refused to diminish into salty water; heat that searched for words to be unleashed.

"It's a fucking Friday night; get with the program." Stopher found the words for me.

"There is no need for that kind of talk; I asked nicely." Some folk make an art form of being annoying.

"Look, I know who you are and the game you play." Stoph was having none of it.

Stopher and I seemed to take turns being the up front asshole in these matters; a sort of good cop-bad cop thing. I stood by being jealous on one hand, while enjoying the show from a regret-free distance.

"A gentleman would at least have the courtesy to speak in a civil manner."

"I ain't no gentle man, lady; I'm an artist."

"Well your mother certainly did a poor job in raising you, I am most sorry to say."

"Go fuck yourself, you little troll!" The bad cop had been tagged; it was my turn now. "You got a hell of a nerve showing up late, squeezing in between two bands and expecting any consideration whatsoever. We have been waiting in this spot all day, clearly communicating to all that at eight sharp, rock-n-roll would be served. So forgive us, my diminutive, evil friend, if pleasantries are set aside."

"Well, I-"

"And you never will as far as I'm concerned. Speaking of my mother, she warned me about little shits like you, and yes, she would have had us be polite, but direct. So excuse me for only being half up to the task. Speaking in polite tones and phrases don't make you decent, in your case it is nothing short of pretentious. You are a self-serving, hypocritical, backstabbing, trouble-making, weasel who frankly gives me the willies. I've raised two kids and for the life of me can't imagine why any competent parent would let you within twenty yards of their children, you scary little freak!"

God that felt good. Of course within minutes I'd feel terrible for having failed my mother. She never expected us to let ourselves be pushed around, but insults were the tools of the petty and weak-minded. Even Stoph was left dumb founded by my rant.

"I guess I'll just have to call a monitor and an officer to-"

"You do that," Stoph interjected, "and we'll have them measure your distance and check your rotation schedule."

"I have no problems with complying with the rules. Let me just say that, before I go, an "artist" as you call yourself, would find more suitable attire before going out into the public."

I scoffed, "Lady, that shows how much you know; this is exactly how an artists looks. That man," I pointed to Stopher, "has created more worthy and relevant work than anybody on this promenade put together."

"A true arti-"

"A true artist doesn't indulge in appearances period. Hey, you wanna call me an asshole?"

"I don't use that vocabulary."

"Well, if you did, it would be the one accurate thing you said all night. We are assholes. We have behaved badly towards you, and we will feel genuinely bad about it when the night is over. In fact I already do. But don't think for a second that you know the first thing about being an artist. Pretty much everyone on this promenade is going to make a mint compared to us tonight."

"Shouldn't you take that as a sign that you are not very good."

"Art and money are mutually exclusive. Or at least they should be. Besides, we know we're good—we know that we are great!"

"Well I feel sorry for you," she huffed with disdain.

"And I you," Stoph returned, for me, in all sincerity. He had found the calmness that should have been our beginning.

Not all the big draws on the promenade were novelty acts or physical spectacles. On the musical side there was an Argentinean quintet called Los Peqouis, or something like that, I could never get it right. They had three acoustic guitars, a bass and a box percussionist. They played the music of their homeland with precise three and four part harmonies, joyous rhythmic verve that I would classify as their country's folk music. I spent most of the first year or so hating them for making so much goddamm money, and forever being heaped upon with praise from civilians and other performers alike. They were great and obviously loved the music that they played. It simply took a long time to get over the bitterness I felt at being overlooked. They were beautiful in what they did, just as Roger was to Motown, and Mel and James to the blues. I wanted to be seen as beautiful by as many, and for the longest time it hurt in places where even soup don't feel good. To this day I can feel that ache on occasion, but not as often and rarely as deeply as I did then.

Then there were the child prodigies. Adam Ho was thirteen and played a mean electric guitar. He sang classic rocks songs like, HOTEL

CALIFORNIA, PURPLE HAZE, and BLACK MAGIC WOMEN, all to backing tracks. He also did a tune by the Police and one of Santana's more recent hits. The kid could play, no doubt about it. But here were Stoph and I, genuine articles of our time, and he got the glory due us. Roger got to own his roots, the Argentineans theirs, Mel and James as well, but Stoph and I...?

I remember after only being on the promenade for a couple months and feeling really down about having people coming up to me and saying, "That Asian kid is great!" Perspective takes a beating after a while and I couldn't feel its grip. I asked James about Adam Ho one morning, he gave his usual thoughtful pause.

"Well, Dave," he looked into my eyes; I could see that he saw the pain. "He can really play that thing. But he's just a kid who can play it; he hasn't lived any of it."

"Thanks."

Q'orianka was thirteen too and she sang songs like, SUMMERTIME, MY HEART WILL GO ON, and I WILL SURVIVE. She had a great set of pipes and a precocious stage presence. Not in the sense that she played up any sexuality, although she was beautiful and blooming, no, more like an old pro in a lounge. But she was still a kid so it had a grating quality on my nerves. Hell, even an actual old lounge pro gets on my nerves.

"How old are ya, Darlin'."

I can hear her voice gearing up the crowd, "Showtime, folks, Showtime."

And she had the plastered on smile that actually had a natural ease that made it seem all the more forced. The kid sang her ass off, and she looked like she enjoyed her gift. There were days, just before she started I could see that dead, I don't want to be here gaze in her eyes. Then her mom cued up the backing tracks and Q'orianka's eyes came alive. She was thirteen and singing in the streets was her job, and she loved to sing. All of it held truth. Sometimes the truths were at odds, while others they hung harmoniously at her side.

I think she knew that she had a real chance at making the big time. She was born of Peruvian and German descent, with smooth brown skin, long, flowing, curly hair, and deep, full island eyes. Her mom was always talking about the interest that she generated from industry insiders—I believed every word. The longer I worked the promenade the less I believed, but I never doubted that Q'orianka had star power, or that she wouldn't make a lot of people rich. I thought her mom was getting too picky about what offer she'd go for, because sooner than later, kids grow up, and then they are just one of many talented adults.

Like Adam, Q'orianka still hadn't lived any of the songs she sang, and like Adam there was one song in particular that showed it clearly. With Adam it was when he played any Hendrix tune. Every time I heard him taking one on I wanted to rip the guitar from his hand and say, "No, not yet; not in public." For Q'orianka that song was Aretha Franklin's, RESPECT. Sorry, kid.

Danny was a tall, young, strapping lad from Manchester, England. At the tender age of nineteen, he crossed an ocean. By the time we crossed paths on the promenade he had just about reached twenty-one. Danny had a smooth, strong voice, sandy brown, wavy hair, and a winning smile. One eye sometimes appeared out of sync with other, but other than that he passed easily as a budding Adonis. He sang in a folkie-pop style that suited his demeanor, and the songs he wrote reflected that as well. His covers ranged from Radiohead to Marley with a Pink Floyd song throw in for good measure. In that first year I'm pretty sure he lived in our financial realm but by the second he left us behind. Danny was young, handsome, fit and came across as someone you wanted to like when he sang. His song crafting was musically solid, and his lyrics, while not ambitious in their imagery, offered a feel-good vibe; peace, love and tolerance—what's not to groove with about that. He respected the space of other performers and immediately ingratiated himself with all the promenade regulars.

Danny was one of the few people, who when playing down the street from us, and approached about us turning down a little, we complied without a hint of resentment.

"Hey, boys. You think you could take it down just a notch. That big voice of Dave's is drifting a bit."

"No problem, Danny," I said nudging my vocal channel. "Let me know if that's not enough."

"Cheers, mates."

When he started making a minimum of close to a hundred bucks a set I muscled up a tad of bitterness, but not toward him personally. Danny was, and is, a good kid with a great singing voice. On top of that he is a very good songwriter, just not a great one.

The Raven used to tell me, when Danny started making bigger money, "He's easy on the eyes and his songs are digestible. If you'd just dumb it down a little, you'd make more money too."

"I'd rather be great."

"And poor."

"So be it."

Lilly had a mousey voice that purred, and a petite body to match. She whispered through moaning tones that angsted their way into every ear that walked by. Of the singer songwriters that first summer, she made the most. Her mouth opened and the money poured. Lilly reminded me a little of Tori Amos with out the edges. Men and women alike adored her. They all wanted to take her home and add her to their teddy bear collection. Within a year or more she garnered a recording contract and was gone. In fact Danny credited her with teaching him how to make more money.

"Turn up loud and sing soft."

Being young, beautiful and circular don't hurt either.

She seemed like a nice kid, although I have since heard that she screwed a co-writer out of a credit on her first release.

Another singer-songwriter that got off the promenade within a year or so was Little James. Stoph and I called him Little James to avoid confusion with James of, Mel and James. There was also a heroin James, whom I had met on the beach when Chris and I were tripping.

Little James was short with a solid build and good voice. He gave whatever song he sang an infectious rhythmic tone. Regardless of the cover he sang, they all kind of blended into one same sounding song. And that can be a good thing. At least for him it was. Most musical acts make the bulk of their money from CD sells, but Little James always made at least sixty plus in tips alone. He was black as coal oozing affability. He sat on a tiny stool, closed his eyes, rocked his body to that unique rhythm of his, and the bucket at his feet grew green.

    I gave Little James a copy of IN A VAN DOWN BY THE OCEAN because I wanted him to cover one of our songs. He wrote some but realized that it wasn't his forte'. He liked SPRINKLER'S CHILD a lot and talked of doing it along with Stopher's MY FATHER'S HOUSE, but it never happened. Last I heard he was on tour with a stage version of, THE LION KING. Nice guy.

    Arthur, the one-man-band, came from Japan as a young man back in the fifties. He wore a signature red cowboy shirt with white fringes, a hat and pants to match, playing Elvis, The Beatles and other acts from those eras, the occasional Hank Sr., and handful of relatively current top forty tunes. He played the guitar, keyboard, bass and percussions all at once—sort of.

    Arthur sat on a stool with the guitar in his lap, pedals under his feet to simulate the bass, a keyboard on the stand in front of him with a crash cymbal on a stand to one side and a tambourine affixed to a stick on top of the keyboard on the other. The tambourine had a string attached, which he held in his strumming hand, and he had two drumsticks shooting out from the guitars head. One stick extended straight out from the tip, used to slap the cymbal, the other, cut in half, poked out downward to clink the keys. He made a lot of sound to be sure—most of it was harmless—and mildly entertaining. Don't get me wrong, what he accomplished as a single performer, was physically impressive.

    A nervous character, not in the way where you thought that he thought there was something specific for him to be afraid of, Arthur had something more in the form of unresolved energy, or perpetual uncertainty. He came off as eager, but not as in to please, although I think, in his way, he wanted to. First and foremost, Arthur was a victim. His frailty endured untold hardships, except that they were told in great detail. It was a hardship to endure his telling of them.

"Last night the gypsy man, come with his dancers. Very loud, you know? Very loud. I ask him but he no listen; very unreasonable. And he no control his crowd."

He had the need to be up on you as he spoke. A dance developed between he and I whenever we talked; he'd step in right up under my chin; I'd nod a smile to his sob story stepping to the side and back; Arthur immediately mirrored that movement gesturing his most recent drama with his hands, hoping that their wringing would drip with the frustrations he had been forced in to soak; I'd lean back against a tree and gradually slide around it until it stood between us; somehow he always became one with the trunk and miraculously filled in the space between myself and the tree with his own body. No matter where I stepped he stood closer, as if the words he beseeched me to hear could not adequately pass along his burden alone. One got the feeling that Arthur had spent his life being dismissed, set aside. Now all distance was to be viewed as an enemy. His face scrunched to show the weight until his eyes widened with an unabashed wonder at all that continually had befallen him.

We all had a lot to complain about on the promenade with so many scratching and clawing for the same prize, like puppy dogs in a cage trying to be the one taken home. At first I saw Arthur as one who had been taken home a lot more often than we. He wasn't a great musician but he played all he played fairly well, and at the same time. There were days when he did extremely well but there were more than enough days when his bucket could have been ours. On the days I saw him cleaning up I got bitter.

"Fucking hack," I'd grumble, sitting on a rail waiting to play.

"Arthur is alright," Stoph always argued.

"Hack."

"He can play the guitar pretty well, and he adds new songs every few weeks."

"I stand by my assessment."

"You are a bitter man, Dave."

"And Arthur is a fucking hack; why can't they both be true?"

"I like Arthur."

I rose to my feet and got up under Stopher's chin, "I like him too, I just don't want to breath the exact same molecules of oxygen at the exact same time as him."

Stoph took a step back, "Arthur is a good musician."

I pretended to cough, "Hack."

Vince left Philadelphia for good in 1998 to make it as an actor two years before we arrived. By the time we did he had succumbed to managing an office building while splitting time living in vacant offices and his hard-shelled covered, pick-up truck. On the promenade he sold bumper stickers to supplement his income and, in the end, his social life. I think he made a decent buck, less on some days more on others, but whether that was all he came here for in the beginning or not, it became clear rather quickly that a world lived there that he wanted as a part of his own. Vince continued to take classes but I don't know that he went out on auditions; he never said anything about doing so. He showed me a videotape that he directed about the dark underbelly of Dorothy from Kansas, in the Wizard Of Oz. In his Mockumentary, Dorothy was portrayed as a manipulative, ladder climber. The production was cheap, but the idea and most of the performances were very good. Vince played the scarecrow.

In the coming years Vince put together an access cable show called STREET-TALK, and took up photo shop classes at Santa Monica College. Mostly though I knew him as the short, balding guy with four flimsy folding tables full of clever bumper stickers that said things like: Jesus is coming—look busy; My God can beat up your God; God, please save me from your followers; and If a woman's husband speaks alone in a forest, is he still wrong? He also had political ones: Don't blame me, I voted for Gore (oh, he's a liberal); life affirming ones: Celebrate diversity; and quotes from the likes of Gandhi.

At his core, Vince was a receptor who took the world in, then eased it back out. He had his self-serving blind sides, but ultimately he was more ear than mouth. Oh, he could rant righteously with the best of us, and challenged authority religiously, almost to a fault. The large quandaries of the day left him philosophical while the mundane ticked him off to no end.

The promenade was full of artists, and Vince liked that; it was also full of social misfits and he could relate to that. The promenade didn't just exist for shoppers, performers, vendors and the homeless; it also gave those with nowhere else interesting to be a place to do just that; people who had worked their whole lives only to retire with too little money to live on, or worked part of their lives and had even less. Guys like Bible John, who was nearing sixty and had lived in his van for the last ten years. In his thirties he worked for the New Orleans' police department as a sheriff. The corruption got too much and the system demanded he play ball. After leaving Orleans he knocked around and ended up on the promenade, drawing general relief and food stamps from the government. He too set out a table, but he didn't sell anything for money, he offered the teachings of Jesus. Hence the title, Bible John, which only Stopher and I called him. John was by no means a bible thumper. He sat behind a single small table that held a few books and pamphlets, and never once solicited anyone's attention. He had what he thought was the word, should someone come looking for it, he'd be happy to pass it along.

Peter claimed to be a cameraman who worked with John Cassevattes (I mentioned Prometheus to Peter and he to Prometheus but neither had ever heard of the other) and carried a portion of believability in his demeanor. Always wearing the same green windbreaker in all weather, sucking on a cigar and standing inside the same, not quite square, yet not quite rectangular, probably prescription, sunglasses, Peter hung around Vince's table at the ready for a conversation about anything—politics and art being the usual fare. He too was in his fifties but where as Bible John was short, stocky and affable, Peter stood around six foot, a tad thick, and at the ready to advocate the devil's side to keep the conversation lively.

Howard ranged between the two in height, looked closer than John to his sixties and although Jewish, cared only to talk about sports and films. Howard had not a limp, but an ill-effected walk with slumping shoulders under a tilted neck. His wrinkled face perpetually turned to the side as if doubting everything said, even when he was doing all the talking, yet he was gregarious. If you knew and liked sports or film, he sought you out.

All three men lived close to the bone, hadn't worked a job in years if not decades, and with the exception of Peter's long, straight, salted pepper hair, sported all gray in a short, trimmed fashion. Bible John's family was all back in Louisiana, while both Peter and Howard had mothers active in their lives. Peter lived with his while Howard's living arrangements varied between staying at sleazy motels, or with his mother, and finding an isolated spot under a freeway, depending on the day of the month, and how he and his mother were getting along.

That first summer you could find them gathered around Vince's tables with various other locals, deciding who was right about what and how the order of things were, should be and never would. Howard had a falling out with Vince by the ending of the summer and never again consorted around his tables.

(I'll go a while without seeing him but sooner or later, on some sunny weekend morning or overcast weekday afternoon, Howard will slowly work his way over to wherever Chris and I are seated, from wherever it is that he has been, and engage us.

"I have a question that I'm sure only you or your brother can help me out with," he'd announce.

The answer would be Stacy Keach in FAT CITY or Ken Holtzman from when he pitched for the Oakland Athletics, or within those realms. Like so many others, Howard has become a fact of my life. At times it seems he insists that Chris and I have been awarded—or burdened by—custody of his curiosities. Howard is alright. He is merely broken in the way that he is broken just like everyone else is broken in the way that they're broken, from me and Chris to Steve and Eric, right on through to anyone I've ever known. My fate met Howard's at the promenade, there we tickle each other's nerves and pass the time.)

Franz made balloons and worked a reception desk at a hospital for, I believe, the mentally, and or, physically disabled. He himself had the look of having once been a patient there. Yet, contrasting the simple eyes that sat tepidly in his face and the wildly crooked teeth jutting every which way in his mouth, both being features I had always associated with a dolt or someone suffering from Down's syndrome, Franz was articulate, well read, and possessed a in-depth fondness for sick and vicious humor. The funny thing about his eyes was how I had perceived him before knowing him. Once we had conversed a few times they seemed sharper and kinetic.

He kept his hair short atop his medium height, informed no doubt from his time in the navy, as was his fit shape. My guess was that he was one of those kids who grew up being picked on only to insist that his adult life would be different. The assumption came from nothing he said; I read that story into his face. What I admired most about Franz probably stemmed a tad from that made-up story, because the man would talk to any woman; the hostesses at the restaurants or the casual passerby, plain-Jane or super-model in the making, it made no difference. Unlike myself, Franz epitomized the phrase, people person. Oh, and no dog traversed his vision without being subjected to his affection. At times you'd be hard pressed to distinguish where his deeper passion resided—dogs or women. The main distinction being that he could touch the dogs freely.

He came off as needy at times but he was aware of the fact. Like a drunk who knows when enough is enough, he'd leave you be after a time. Except with dogs—the owners, sooner or later, would have to move on to gain their dog's freedom.

From Vince to Franz and all those in between, I came to know; like; be endlessly annoyed; occasionally entertained; and assisted a great deal in my own growth and self-understanding by all of them, they were the folk of my then present life. There were others, but these were my initial hosts, and all but Peter, and some of the performers, are still out there today.

Ernest lived in his white ford El Camino. Chris and I had seen him at the showers on many occasions, and over by Marine Park on a few. One day as I lay back in my bed, no doubt an Albertsons water bottle filled with vodka nestled at my side, I heard Stopher and Ernest talking.

"I'm just glad you guys came along," Ernest was saying. "He seemed pretty out there."

"I'm sure you could have handled him," Stopher pointed out.

"Oh, I am sure that I would have. I guess I've hit enough people in my life to get me through the day."

"Of course you have."

Apparently some wack-job had followed Ernest to the park after being offended by his driving protocol, or lack thereof. Ernest didn't really believe that he had upset the man so until he had parked his El Camino in the lot and was headed for the bathroom. Once inside the squat building, Ernest heard the man gunning his engine and shouting obscenities at the bathroom. That was when we drove up and ruffled the would be assailant's otherwise already quite disturbed feathers. Stopher parked across the street in our usual spot but made a B-line to the toilets. His direct path coupled with what was, no doubt, a stern and determined face, intruded upon the angry man's solitary showdown. As Stoph arrived at his intestinal salvation, the man squealed away, cocooned in his unfulfilled rage, searching for a more idyllic scenario in which he could extract the forever-fleeting justice he sought.

Their voices murmured from the lot, across the street, through the open driver's side window, tickling my tomb. The whole story would not be made clear to me until Ernest had gone and Stoph returned to the van.

Another time not long after that Ernest had been parked across and down the street from us at Marine when Chris and I were arguing—nothing major, probably over some semantical parting of the ways. Once things settled down, and I went to the bathroom, Chris noticed Ernest coming back from that same place.

"Don't let the blood curdling screams give you the wrong idea," Chris said from the driver's window as Earnest passed by, "just a slight disagreement really."

"No need to explain it to me; I have a brother."

That was all I heard from the toilet and when I got back Chris offered more.

"He's got a drum set under that tarp on his bed," Stoph mentioned.

"Yeah, I've noticed that."
"He seemed interested in playing with us."
"Did he say that?"
"Not right out."
"Well, if he has an interest in poverty, we can oblige."

A couple more meetings transpired over the next few weeks with Ernest, music being the main topic. Standing in Martin's food line, waiting for Wednesday's rice and beans, a tentative day was set for us to give it a try. Ernest could have easily come from the same 70's, Chicago, alley as us. He had that sensibility that permeated from my youth: If it's a song, strum it; if it's a ball, run it; if it's a car, tinker with it. And in all cases, if there's a joint, smoke it—a beer, drink it. He talked evenly in low tones that did not concern themselves with your being convinced. His stories about growing up all sounded familiar, from his high school football coach being a dickhead, to his getting five stitches in his ankle running from the cops through some local woods. He hailed from Minnesota and was a year older than Stoph. Unlike drummer-John, Ernest seemed like a natural fit as far as his personality. There was something about him that gave up on aspects of life that fell in with the way we had let the water run certain ambitions asunder.

Ernest could play, he had a nice way of letting a song come to him, but he was not in our league, which was okay. His biggest downside was that he had a hard time grasping musical transitions, and like the kids I grew up with, he was a bit of a buzz mind. He could know something during one set and have no memory of it the next.

"I just don't get that part," he'd complain about himself.
"You nailed it last time."
"That part?"
"That exact part."
"I beg to differ."

Dichotomy personified him, tall, well built yet a tendency towards more gentile qualities; loved poetry but was more than a bit the homophobe; read esoteric, innovative writers, (I would guess understanding a respectable portion of it) and not being able to follow the slightest sophistication in a sitcom. Ernest had enough stories of violent altercations to be firmly associated with all the assumptions that accompany them, but you could see him shifting awkwardly in their shoes. Violent things were born around him at an early age—family related mostly—so he followed the pattern to see where it lead all the while looking for an exit.

Ernest wrote a poem and entered it in a contest once; he placed well. I read and loved it; you instantly saw his love of words. When I asked after other work he took a deep breath.

"I worked on this piece for over a year, maybe two. I tweaked it a few times even after it took third place." He stood looking at his hands and had them look at him. "I like to play with things. It used to be cars; I'd take a part a healthy carburetor just to see how it worked as a kid. I'm slow but I am thorough."

"You're curious."

Ernest took a thoughtful breath. "I am curious." He paused. "I am E for earnest, and know of its importance."

We started with three chord jam songs like ALL ALONG THE WATCH TOWER and eased into original tunes with likewise simplicity. In the case of my songs even the simple ones held nuances that threw him. Still we put a solid two-hour set together fairly quickly. It was a set full of bumps and bruises but pretty enough. Practicing out on the promenade was tough on all of us. Stoph and I had developed a tight act, we had at least four hours of material down cold, and another two or three that wasn't far off the mark. It was hard to be average. For Ernest it was hard enough to have to learn so much without having to do it in front of a revolving crowd. Plus the tips suffered, and we weren't doing that well to begin with.

We tried practicing in Venice once. There were these circle cement platforms off the boardwalk (a folksy euphemism; all cement no wood) a couple hundred yards. They were on a patch of sandy grass separated from the beach by three freestanding walls, assembled in a stilted fashion—erected for the sole purpose of providing an artistic outlet for high-end graffiti—and the bicycle path.

The platforms perfectly accommodated one individual and their gear; Stopher and I with room to spear and Ernest with his drums using the edge of every curve. A cop rolled along in a patrol car with no particular agenda and told us casually to point our sound toward the ocean. It was a weekday early afternoon, what people there were ventured near the water or traversed the shops and sights of the boardwalk. Cops in Venice don't look for things to do; they have plenty thrust upon them.

We only did this once because of the parking, getting the gear to the spot, and the fact we were using precious battery juice on a monetarily empty endeavor. The power our batteries derived from Steve's outlets were spoken for by the promenade schedule—two sets a day five days a week. By Sunday we needed Monday and Tuesday for the juice to replenish itself in Steve's walls. It was a hell of visual to be apart of though. The backdrop of the graffiti walls, the beach beyond that; it was something out of a Beatle's movie.

The music would have to find itself on the promenade where we had a shot at making a buck. After the first few weeks we limited our drum time on the promenade to one set on Friday night and one on Saturday. The allowable levels on the promenade were at their zenith at those times, and even though pretty much everyone else played as loud as they wanted whenever they wanted, Stoph and I remained reasonable to our neighbors as best we could. Ernest would come by the van so we could go over certain changes with an acoustic guitar; he made some notations on a scrap of paper. I don't think any of it made that much of a difference. Sure some obvious things got better, but for the most part, Ernest responded to the things he understood at an organic level well and the rest was, as Stoph said about a lot of things, "The good, the bad, the ugly." We tailored our set to his strengths and that was good enough. Some songs that I didn't think he'd get a handle on went shockingly smooth. And they varied in style to where we didn't just play the blues all night.

The money with Ernest playing got good to the point where, after we split it up, Stoph and I were consistently clearing in the arena that we were used to, and sometimes more. It was working out and I started thinking in terms of having an actual band again.

Hooking up with Ernest had other benefits. He told us how the parking was free after a certain time in the lots that sat along the shore;

Santa Monica agreed to not own the sunset. That became a revelation for Stopher and me, to know that we could drive right up to a spot with only the bicycle path and sand between the water and us. For the next year we missed only a handful of sunsets. We had been there a year without knowing Santa Monica understood that anyone should be able to drive up to the sunset void of financial burden. When I saw that, when the example of it played itself out before me, I was touched and proud to know them; to see a community or government pull in the reins of its power and say, "No, we have no right to take your money for this." Obviously they have no right, but neither do the powers that be truly have the right to do many of things that they do. A point arrives when you are avidly grateful for being given what is already yours, or at least what should be. And it's okay. It is good to know that that small amount of humanity and humility exists in an institution of any kind, let alone a government.

So Ernest gave us that and it is a gift I still embrace, though not as often as I did then. We still catch two or three every week, but back then it became a ritual, rejuvenation station for our souls. All that was good and bad in my life over those days got laid on the salty wet sands beneath a departing light to be cleansed, disposed and glorified.

It was also through him that we got a library card. I had an Illinois driver's license and Stopher still had one from Tennessee. I had tired of reading the entertainment and sport section of the local papers, the mainstream and alternate both. To be able to walk into a room of books and pick one out became a life-blood for us. I had gone through periods in my life were I was almost always in the middle of a book, and then drifted away from it for a while. Living in a van, having to spend so much time waiting on the promenade, poured time all over my hands. The ability to take up company with minds that I had heard of and always wanted to get to know, like Dickens, Dostoevsky, and John Irving, as well as deepening my growing affection for Steinbeck, and saying hello to the dear old friends that had opened my mind to the universe of the printed word, like, Vonnegut and Salinger. In fact I had a copy of Slaughterhouse Five that I brought with me from Chicago and had recently read it again as an attempt to avoid the wasteland of the mass, vacuous gossip of the daily feedbag that people call the news. One of the first books I took out of the library, after another one of Vonnegut's, Hocus Pocus, was Joseph Heller's Closing time. It was a sequel to Catch-22, which I had read the year before I left Chicago. It had the best line in it about news papers, and I quote: "The daily paper should be smaller and come once a week." With great company like that, "…one could do worse than to be a swinger of birches." (Robert Frost)

Ernest loved poetry but hated Frost. "All that rhyming hurts my ears."

He preferred Rimbaud and Baudelaire. No doubt, two fine, innovative writers, the later of which I would spend a bit of time with myself.

When I was born, my uncle Bob gave my folks a book of the complete works of Robert Frost to give to me when they thought me ready for it. The years fell away and they forgot all about the book being for me, turning to it for their own pleasure. In my mid-twenties I stumbled across it knowing that Dad loved Frost, and wanting to consider myself, not only well read before I died, but a writer of worth to boot, I asked if I could hang on to it for a while. No sooner did he say, "Enjoy, enjoy," did I open it up to find a note to me from my uncle, dated the year and month of my birth, (October 1964.) In the note he welcomed me to the world and advised me that, "…one could do worse than to be a swinger of birches."

Ernest took an intellectual stand against Frost along with others of that ilk, and though I gave him a few points on the subject, I offered that he landed a tad on the dismissive side. Of course the thing about Ernest was that he, quite often, was not up to the task of being an intellectual. It was something more that he aspired to than he *was* in truth. Whenever I tried to point out pieces of Frost such as, DEATH OF A HIRED MAN and REVELATION or the even harsher OUT OUT, to give evidence to the vast scope of the man's work, Ernest's reply settled on one of his standards, "I beg to differ."

These types of discussions were both what I liked and found frustrating about him. He was out there chasing the written word with a fervor that stretched beyond what his formative years had laid out for him; his mind could only stretch so far and hold so much. He was like the Raven in this regard, although her pursuit of the written word contained much humility while Ernest, for a lack of a better word, had a kind of arrogance about it that reeked of incongruence. I won't say that he was a simpleton, although at times I did, behind his back, voice my annoyance with him to Stopher. I am no scholar but by comparison I certainly was; intellectuals bred me so it's not really a fair fight.

Ernest had been in the Los Angles for ten years previous to our arrival and had been living in his car for the last few. He knew the ins and outs of it pretty well, where the good food lines were, other options for showers, and of course the free sunsets. He had a knack for finding things: books, appliances, computers; fallout from an affluent world. Stoph and I both suspected him a thief when he told (and sometimes showed) us of the valuables gathered from the streets.

"I walk a lot, mostly through the backstreets and alleys; I peruse the inners of Venice and Santa Monica."

In doing so he came upon a five-gallon propane tank, which he gave to us. It was a bit beat up and we had to invest twenty-seven dollars on a hose to make it adaptable to our stove, but it turned out to be a financial godsend. He had found it empty so we took it to Albertsons where they take your old tank and give you a full one for seventeen bucks. After that we were told about a gas station that fills up you tank for two bucks a gallon (it's more like three now). In fact, we found this out from the scraggily old man from the showers who only in the previous fall had labeled us as those with a "Loser tank." Old Loser Boy had been right on target with his summation of our situation.

"Now, you've got it," he wheezed joyously at us showing him our new tank. "That's what you gotta have, not that loser, tank."

Ahh, he remembered our first meeting.

The shiny, clean, full tank we got from Albertsons replaced our five to ten dollar a week expense on the small, "loser tanks," with what came to be a ten dollar a year fee. That is how long we went before we had to fill it up again. Actually, it never emptied, it had just gotten so light that we figured we should get it topped off while we had the money. (The record is two full years without having to re-fill.)

So in Ernest we found a facsimile of a childhood friend, a drummer, a guide, a finder of useful things, a giver of books, a fellow lover of words, and a friend. Things were coming together.

Amid the early summer days the Raven ran off to New York where she stayed with a Persian, Wall Street stockbroker. It felt like months but was closer to three weeks. I had gotten so used to seeing her on that perch in front of George's Bistro; seeing her scurrying in two songs into our noon set, trying to avoid the headwaiter's glare; or spying the low-riding sleek, black hood of her Neon approaching from the unseen Lincoln avenue toward the park—toward me—with its slanted oval headlights coquettishly appropriate being that which announced her arrival, even in daylight.

When I took note of my continual disappointment at her not being there I let myself have it, void of ridicule. I knew my place with her and despite it being against my wishes, we had become friends. I was well aware of my growing infatuation. In this it helped to be a fat loser living in a van; expectations hunkered down 'neath the dirt and watched the grass grow over it.

On the day I saw her in early July, a shout jumped in my chest and felt all of me rise at once. She was actually early for work. I offered a faint easy going smile with a hint of a wave while everything hidden in my skin danced, whooped and hollered.

"Miss me, boys."

Stoph made a joke that I couldn't hear while trapping myself under that same protective smile.

She stood close in a pause that revealed her as awkward with us for the first time.

"Well it's good to see you both." She hugged Stopher then me. "Do me proud today boys," she ordered over shoulder as she headed for the restaurant. "Make it a good'n."

Half way through the set she ran up and dropped a card in the bucket. After the set we found a ten dollar bill wrapped up inside. It read:

Hey Boys!
I've missed ya. You don't know!

Call me to tell me what's goin' on and how much you missed me too.

She had given us her card on a few occasions by then, we had yet to call her.

As the summer rolled on we'd see her at work on the days we played there and by the park once every ten days or so. On the days we got beat to our spot in front of her perch she would frown at us, or tap her foot impatiently with hands on hips, to express her displeasure at our having played else where. That only happened on Saturdays and Sundays, so she caught our sets plenty during the week. Plus she worked a lot of weekend nights so she saw us with Ernest on the drums quite a bit.

"I don't know," she'd tell me by the park, "that drummer is kinda sleazy. Besides I just wanna hear you guys."

She never did take to E. (he tired of being called by his proper name so we only resorted to it when acting parental toward him.)

Steve had a get together at his place and asked me to make pizza so I invited both E and the Raven. She of course loved it and was all the more impressed for knowing us.

Hey Boys,
Sounds good! Bonfire anyone?
Thanx pizza-boy! Call me-
#15x2= smiley face Maybe we will get to hang out
FONTAINE aka Raven again soon

She wrote that the next time we played for her. #15 was the track number of a song called MAYBE YOU'RE RIGHT, off our first CD that she loved to hear, and wanted us to play it twice before the set was over; *Fontaine*, one of the alias' she liked to give herself; the bonfire was a new thing. She had asked us to her picking parties and came by the park, but this had a twinge of a romantic sound to it even though I knew better. Either way it would involve driving somewhere and neither Stoph or I cared much for that. She left her number at the bottom of the note and as usual we never called.

We went through a stretch in July where it seemed she worked during every one of our sets. The three of us couldn't have been happier about it. At the end of one set, she dropped three cards in our bucket. To read the black and red colored marker she used, you had to lay out two of the cards side by side length-wise and the third width-wise laying under the other two.

CHRIS & DAVE
AKA R&R CROSSING
LOVE YOU LOVE YOU LOVE YOU!
THANK YOU

R&R
LOVE YOU MORE WITH EACH SONG

Instead of writing the word, love, at the bottom she drew a heart; the second *R&R* was written inside the drawn heart; and beneath the *THANK YOU* and the word *SONG* was drawn an animal paw. She had a thing with paws.

A few weeks later she put a single card in our bucket with a single word written in the middle of it.

thanx

In the upper right hand corner she kissed it leaving the print of her lips.

I had not written her anything since the poem I gave her before she went to New York that I felt made her uncomfortable. After the lipstick print of her lips I wrote her this:

The sun sets the sky free (I stole that line from one of my old songs)
Light but a reflection off an unfulfilled moon

Music dances for itself
Oblivious to pounding hearts

Beats unkept
Steps misplaced
for finish lines void of a start

Poor useless words

My worthless fortune
My empty beauty

Let the sun go
Let the music play
movement will come

Days upon days
all is fleeting

I remember thinking as I wrote those lines, will she understand what I am saying? Do I? I know I was saying that there is beauty that is ours, and that which we are given. I wanted her know that the music I played was mine first, and that in fact all I had that was of worth, or of beauty, was in my words and music. My heart was pounding for her, but as I waited to play, that became beside the point, or at least only a small consideration by comparison. Ultimately, I had no chance with her. I knew it and it bothered me, but her beauty still danced with mine. The days would go by.

The fact that the poem was written on the back of a card that advertised for the movie MOULIN ROUGE was a coincidence but appropriate. Another meaning would be attached in time.

The act performing while we waited to play that night was a petite Asian woman doing traditional dance from her homeland. The music offered by the boom box and her attire both revealed her culture accurately enough. Although I don't know that her ancestors would have approved of the white, see-through skirt that only served to accent for the eyes, all the more, the way her sharply cut, tight, pink panty graced her firm shapely body.

So...enjoying the Chinese panty-dance I see.
Yes, folks, it's cultural exchange and its finest

The Raven slipped me a card as I looked on. Wish I could say that I detected a hint of jealousy, but there was none. I had not yet delivered my card to her that night so who knows what she might think of the line, *Light but a reflection off an unfulfilled moon.* She might get jealous yet.

A few weeks later, in mid-August, she dropped this in our bucket:
SO,
IF I haven't mentioned it in the PAST, I'm sayin' it now,
"THEY ROCK!" No really.
You boys really got me now! I just appreciate ya'll so much—your writing and VOICES are a treat.
And...cookin' ya do. HAPPY-From me to you.

Beneath the note she drew her paw that was the trademark of her dog walking and house sitting business, Gimme Paww.

The cooking reference of course was to my pizza. I had a momentary twinge that something might be changing between us. I think my pizza impressed her as much as our music.

We almost got a regular gig that first summer. On the Santa Monica Pier there was a restaurant called the Boathouse. Chris had been talking about going in there for months to offer our services. He had seen the guy they had playing there one night; he figured we'd being doing them a favor. In the end it was me who ended up dealing with the manager. Stopher got us the initial audition but the business fell to me there after. They were looking for someone to warm up their Sunday night band from six to nine. For the audition we came in on a Monday afternoon. That went smooth enough; we didn't get a fee but made around ten bucks in tips for an hour of work.

The manager was a scrawny little French guy. I say that void of disdain; it's just the best way to describe him. He had a thick accent that swirled and stabbed in all the wrong places. You can only say, "I'm sorry," and "What was that," so many times before beginning to fear that the man will tire of repeating himself and send you away gig less. Actually my first impression of him was positive, but only because of two very petty things:

One, he recognized us from the promenade and liked us. The second was, when discussing the promenade he mentioned the, "English kid that played out there."

I said, "Yeah, Danny, he's a good kid and a talented guy."

"Yes, him, he came in here, but no." The late twentysomething, young man shook his head ever so slightly, assuming that all the wisdom from his vast experiences needed little explaining. "No, he is not right for this." The palms of his hands were turned up and raised to survey the joint as if it were something much more.

So I guess I should have known then that I was dealing with a pretentious schmuck.

He gave us the next Sunday for sixty dollars plus tips and free beer. Free BEER!

Stoph and I were pumped; sixty guaranteed was sweet even though we had been doing pretty well on Sundays at the time. The best part would be a roof to play under come winter rains, a name to put on a resume, a place to build a reputation—and free BEER! Imports. On tap! Can I get a Woo Hoo!

The first Sunday came and we took the stage to a small but jovial crowd. They had a nice day on the beach, a good meal, (maybe?) and had moved on to happier hours. Two tables had a family feel to them while the other three had singles but mostly in their forties. By the time we got the sound together with our tuning, the two family tables vacated out into the evening's salty air.

The Boathouse had at least seven tables in front of the stage with a bar in the back of what constituted the main room. To the right of the bar was a row of tables running away from whatever the stage had to offer. Up by the stage to the right directly across was a door holding another room of tables, and slightly backstage was the door leading out to the Pier. A stairway, just to the right and a handful of feet forward from the stage, led down to the lower level.

A few more folks dribbled in over the first five songs and things looked promising. It felt refreshing to have a handful of people sitting down, even if they were talking amongst themselves using us as background filler. The best part was being the only act in the room. No one fought our music with theirs, not even a note from the Pier's many outdoor performers wafted, gently, harmlessly or otherwise in through the front door on the air; it was all R&R Crossing. That was the case until they started blaring the salsa music downstairs. Apparently they had a band on the lower level that the manager failed to mention. As the night wore on it got louder and louder, our only saving grace was when they shut the doors at the bottom of the stairs, which was perpetually momentary because someone was forever going in or coming out. I'm sure the Boathouse was making a hell of a lot more money off the salsa band than us, the lower level was packed; so I understood why they were there. I guess to the people at the tables in front of us it wasn't that bad because the stairway that led down, that all the noise bled from shot out towards the front door and, unfortunately for Stopher and myself, at the stage. We had twenty minutes or so of peace then the ghosts of the promenade haunted us for the rest of the night. We had the occasional reprieve but that was minimal. The promenade, as it turned out, was the perfect training ground for this gig; I couldn't have imagined handling the conflict of noise on the Boathouse stage if I had never played in the streets.

So we muddled through, played well, pleased more than a few drunks, made twenty in tips, and on top of that the bartender loved us. I love when the guy who controls the booze is a fan.

The strangest thing to me about the whole gig was something I knew going in. We were not to be paid in cash or at the end of the night. Frenchy told me that he paid the musical acts on the books like the rest of the employees. I even had to fill out a W2 form. Never in my life has a bar paid me that way. I've done parties or conferences that paid by check but not on the fifteenth and thirty-first of the month. We ended up playing there twice, two Sundays in row, but each Sunday fell in a separate pay period. We had to wait one week for the first check, then two more for the second. I guess if it turned into a weekly gig it would have been worth it, but alas, it was us, and it did not.

The band that went on after us the first time wasn't there the second time so we instead opened for the act that usually opened for the band. He was the guy Stopher had thought so little of, that got him to think we could get the gig in the first place. As it turns out the guy was really good. You couldn't stump him on a cover, if he didn't know the exact song he knew another one by the same artists, he sang and played extremely well, was very charming and affable on stage, and even sang an original that was damm good. There are talented people everywhere and that sometimes annoys me.

In the end we were booked to substitute for the two weeks that his regulars took off. First of all, the little schmuck should have told us, and second of all he could of at least paid us cash at the end of each night in favor of making us wait, run around trying to get the checks cashed, and again, leading us to assume that that made us in at the restaurant. I mean who puts you on the payroll for two gigs; the paper work alone couldn't have been worth messing with our minds. Well, he was French.

We saw a few celebrities that first year but not many. Mathew Perry could be seen walking briskly down the street trying not to make eye contact quite often. A couple of times I saw him with friends and he seemed in less of a hurry, not as concerned with being recognized, but still in favor of pushing on. I saw Woopi Goldberg twice; she moved evenly, keeping her eyes straight ahead of her. I understood very well their desire to be left alone. I had become a bit of a celebrity myself among the homeless and actual members of the community. I didn't mind it much but after the novelty of it wore off, I could certainly do without it.

Tim Robbins was the first I spoke to. It was a cool, gray, misty February late afternoon. I had just begun to think about setting up our equipment when I thought I spotted a tall man with a familiar face wearing a black knit hat and a navy P-coat, walking by with a distracted expression. He had the look of a family man doing a few errands away from his brew, probably for his brew, who couldn't all together achieve his tasks, or set them aside. He wanted to be alone on the street but the rise in his eyes told me he had a problem along with him for the walk that insisted on being pondered. I wasn't sure it was him at first and asked Stoph to take a look.

"Yeah, I saw him out here yesterday; that's him."
"I'd like to say hey, and maybe even thanks, but…"
"I know."
The street was fairly empty and I had a bad feeling about getting rained on; this would not be a money set.
"I'm gonna hit the john," Stoph announced.
I rolled our hand truck, loaded up on all fours, across the street from the benches were we sat to near the Criterion movie theater that we'd play next to. Just as I removed the first guitar and set it on the ground, I saw Tim Robbins coming my way with that same distracted, figuring face and I thought, leave him alone. Who are you to call a man you don't know by his first name anyway—how presumptuous.

I returned to my task and felt him passing directly behind me when he paused to check his bearings, then resumed. In that hesitation I looked up ever so casually, and in a plain, low even tone said, "Mr. Robbins."

I had hoped to be seen as a neighbor offering a simple greeting, a man sharing a street with another, two artists going about their business.

He turned sharply with a rigid contort that held hints of fear. His eyes widened and his mouth drooped open offering nothing. I don't think he ever ceased moving although his steps stuttered a bit. He turned back toward the direction he had been walking before looking my way once more, this time with a small smile; not a comfortable smile, but it was well meaning.

I told Stopher of the encounter he and laughed hard.
"You know the last words John Lennon heard before being shot, don't you?"
"No."
"Mr. Lennon."
"Yeah, but does Robbins know that?"
"It wouldn't surprise me."
"But I said it so unassumingly, like a neighbor."
"Say it."
"Mr. Robbins."
"Sounds spooky to me."
"Mr. Robbins," I repeated out loud for myself to hear. "Mr. Robbins."

"Mr. Robbins, would you mind holding this lead in your chest."

"Hmm, I guess that does come off a tad spooky."

At Marine Park we saw one film actor quite often. I say film actor because he was not a movie star at the time, but a well-known character actor. He played full-court basketball with a group of guys about once a week. I recognized one of the other players from the TV show fame, a Latino fellow, but the rest were all plumbers for all I knew. The film actor was extremely familiar to me. I had seen him in plenty of things and I even knew, from the papers, that a buzz was beginning to grow around him in the industry. He was the kind of short guy I had played basketball with a million times in the neighborhood parks and Y.M.C.A. in Chicago; good ball handler, solid outside shot and a big mouth; an on the court general. I wouldn't classify him with the jerks of that ilk, he had good sportsmanship in his approach. He encouraged and critiqued throughout the game like a coach, and where as that always came of as a bit obnoxious while revealing a big ego, he walked the line well enough to where none of the other players on the court, nor I as a spectator, thought ill of him. Well once in a while you could see a smirk on one of the player's face, or hear a grumble, but he seemed liked and respected. Actually he reminded me of me when I played.

Stopher and I both knew the face and knew that we liked his work. I knew I had liked him in something that I had seen within the last year or so but I couldn't remember what. One film popped in my head from years and years ago, HAMBURGER HILL. (Coincidentally, my sister, Eileen, had dated a Chicago actor that got a small role in that film; that has nothing to do with this story.) It was a movie that portrayed a unit of black soldiers fighting in Vietnam. The only name I could remember from the movie was

Courtney Vance.

Our curiosity finally got to us and Stopher approached him.

"Hey, are you Courtney Vance?"

The little man's eyes filled with disdain; another white man thinking we all look a like. He shook his head in disgust and walked away without a word.

So if Don Cheadle ever reads this book I apologize. I think that both he and Courtney Vance were in HAMBURGER HILL, and that's why I mixed them up, if not, then maybe I'm just a cracker racist. Know this though, I loved you as Sammy Davis Jr. in THE RAT PACK, I loved HOTEL RWANDA and pretty much everything I have seen you in. While we're at it I have to say that SWORDFISH was a piece of shit, but I don't blame that on you. Oh, and if Courtney ever reads this, I dig your work as well; you and David Morse were great in the short-lived TV show, HACK. (I'm kidding, I know that was not Courtney Vance, it was someone named Andre something or other—he's a hell of actor too.)

So that was the beginning; the first year. It had been a year since we left Chicago but our anniversary of landing in Santa Monica wasn't until the nineteenth of September 2001. By the end of August I felt less like an intruder, more a part of the scene. We established who we were and how we did business. Because of my income tax return from the previous April, we went into that September with three or four hundred in the bank. Chris and I no longer went to the bank unless the van needed work, we had finally got strict about that. The promenade was meeting our needs of food, gas and drink; we were independent, or at least damm close to it. I felt my feet firmly planted where they were and had little fear of them being shook lose.

CHAPTER TWELVE

When I say that my feet were planted with little fear of being shaken, that may be over stating things. My greatest fear at night in bed was being dragged back across the country and forced to drive a truck for the rest of my life, and I knew even then that it was still possible. Let's just say I had a few weeks there where I got a cocky about it not happening. In that first year we had put many things to test and had a few taken on us. Other than the night after the House of Blues, when Stopher and I shouted until the cops came home, we had one or two other interactions with the brave women and men in blue.

Somewhere around early spring we were sitting in the van across the street from Marine Park. (Speaking of being cocky, we assumed that everyone in the neighborhood knew and accepted our being there.) Other than one old retired navy officer, who shook his head in disgust as he came round the corner from his house on his morning walk, and then walked past our van only to stop, look back, and shake his disgust once again, pretty much everyone else gave a well-wishing smile or simply ignored us. The head-shaker, for all the vile our continuous presence filled him up with, never called a cop on us. I can't claim that as fact, but it did not seem to be his style. Besides if we were to move on he'd have one less thing to feel superior about; all that shaking must have offered some therapeutic value to his neck.

The times a cop did come by they always said, "When you park near where people send their kids, someone always notices you, and gets scared."

The first time it was a stocky blonde woman in her thirties, probably late. She passed by in her squad car headed toward Lincoln, turned left at a side street came out another, turned left towards us, went around the block, then pulled over down on the other side of the street facing us. She sat there with the engine running for about five minutes before driving our way, passing us and pulling a U-turn to park behind us. She, like all the others to come (there were just two the first year but I've lost count since), with a couple of exceptions, was patient and friendly, making it clear that she was just covering the bases in response to a complaint.

The drill began with her asking us to step out of the vehicle. In this pretty much every cop that had ever said it to me contained a controlled nervousness in their voices; they say that most plane crashes occur while landing or lifting off; for the cops the lift-off lied in that moment that they separated you from the vehicle. Even when I came across a cop that I knew had to know me from the promenade (I was a celebrity after all) that initial instant when they asked me out of the van carried that same uncertain tone every time.

Once we were seated on the curb they allowed relaxation into their demeanor. The standard questions and answers ensued:

"Do you live in your vehicle?"

"Yes."

"Both of you?"

"Yes."

"Are you aware of the laws that prohibit you from doing so?"

"Yes."

"I am not here to give you a ticket for that, but be advised one can be issued. How long have you been in the Los Angeles area?"

"About six months."

That was our answer no matter how long we had been there. We then played the, "We're traveling musicians, so we are here for a while then we're off, then back," card.

The cop would always turn politely inquisitive at this point with ranges in pretension. "What kind of music do you play?"

"We grew up in the seventies; a kind of rock, folk blues with a jazz mentality."

"That is squeezing in quite a bit."

"It is."

"How's it working out for you?"

Indicating the van, "We get by. Barely."

"Where do you play?"

"The promenade mostly, when we're not on the road."

"Huh."

Pause.

"Ever been arrested."

"Once when I was fifteen."

"What for?"

"Some guy accused me of beating him up, but I didn't and it got thrown out."

I said that the first time and Stopher stole a dirty look to me.

"Ever in any gangs?"

"No.

"Alas', nicknames?"

"Vuma."

Again, only said that the first time and got the same secret glare from Stopher. "Stop giving them reasons to suspect you. They hear you've been arrested for battery and that you have a nickname like Vuma and red flags say, 'Hello.'"

"What kind of name is that?"

"Back in the eighties I was in a band and the bass player gave everyone nicknames; I got Vuma and it stuck."

"Any scars or tattoos."

"No tattoos, but I had third degree burn on my arm in the late eighties, knee surgery in the early eighties and another third degree burn on my stomach from the early seventies." I raised an arm, a jean leg and my shirt in accordance with the list.

They were always impressed.

"That was the right arm right?" It all went into their little books. "You banged yourself up real good."

"Accident prone—yet, ironically, graceful."

I was in a band called Ironic Grace—Pink Floyd.

"Any drugs?"

"No."

The first time we luckily had none, so we didn't have to lie. On another occasion when we did and Stoph said, "Just a couple of roaches in the ashtray."

Cops in California didn't care much about pot. I remember one saying, "Hell, it'll be legal in ten years."

The other thing that I have learned is that cops, at least in Santa Monica and Venice, never look through your wallet. I don't know if it never occurs to them or whether a law forbids them. One time I was asked for my driver's license, I was sitting on the curb while he stood by the van's open passenger door.

"It's in my wallet on the dash; you could probably reach it from where you're standing."

"Why don't you come get it out for me?"

Maybe he thought there was some sort of booby-trap? But there have been other times in varying circumstances, and in all of them there was a strict, consistent refrain from touching either my, or Stoper's, wallet. We picked up on that by the second year and decided that the weed would always be in the wallet.

"Any weapons?"

"Just an ax and a sledge hammer. I thought I'd be doing a lot of camping, so…"

"Mind if I look around?"

"Go ahead. It's a bit of a mess."

When it was all done we received the same warnings about the illegalness of our life and to stay away from the park. After the first shakedown I felt a real fear of being run out of town. She was nice enough but it wasn't no welcoming committee. But like everything else that I came to encounter in my attempt at living life between society's cracks, they were just saying, "Hey, we see you." If it scared you away, fine. No one chased much further than the nearest complaint; it was all checks and balances.

The constitution of this country has been sidestepped; creatively interpreted by the corrupt; trampled on until the voting majority said, enough; it has been bent, twisted and defiled, even ignored. The wondrous thing about it is that it is still there and on a daily basis someone in power has to pay attention to it.

During the first week of our second September the van's engine rumbled as if upset with a notion that it could not explain. It was not constant, only appearing once or twice. Stopher thought, again, it sounded like a water pump going. He remembered the sound that the old Chevy Malibu made when we had first hit Nashville those many years ago. We kept a hopeful ear to it every time she started up. A few days went by between grumblings, then a few more. We had found a neighborhood mechanic we trusted over on 14th and Pico near Steve's house. His name was Ike and he worked out of an Arco gas station. He was that rare breed of an honest man who actually charged no more than the job was worth, even cut a you a break now and then with his time; a throw back to a Ma and Pa shop world; a shade tree mechanic with four stalls.

"Harmonic balancer," Ike said, then immediately added, "yeah."

The great irony of Ike was that he gave the appearance of having something to hide, as if he would eagerly change his story in mid-sentences to appease. His words held fast to their meaning, while the nervous contortions on his face and sharp turns of his tone attempted to make a liar of him. It was as if he were perpetually attached to a lie detector and the fear of buckling under the pressure made him forget that he always told the truth.

"What will it cost?"

"Well, see, that's the problem; it's so mangled I can't get it off."

His face ran a gymnastic gambit.

"It connects to the crankshaft, which keeps everything turning and if that gets damaged while I'm taking it off..." He trailed off unable to find the right words, or more than likely, afraid to.

"I'm screwed." I helped him out.

"Yeah, pretty much, yeah."

"What are my options?"

"Well, you should be fine for a few days, a week; maybe longer." His eyes searched for anywhere to look but at me. "You should be fine through the weekend, but keep the driving to a minimum; it'll be noisy but no more damage could be done, I'm pretty sure. Bring it back first thing Monday and I'll give it another try"

Ike was a decent fellow, I believed him, but no, he was not what I'd consider beyond average at what he did; replace a starter or alternator; tune up the engine; tinker about in general. Stoph and I left that Friday knowing we'd have to bring it somewhere else.

We played that weekend, driving to and fro ever so gingerly, wincing at the van's every remark and crossing our fingers. On Sunday after playing we were headed to the park. As the van sloped downward on 11th toward Marine Avenue the clunky grinding we had been subjected to for so long went silent. It reminded me of the feeling I got as a kid, pedaling with all my might to climb a hill, all the energy I spent, My muscles bulged at my skin, the heart heaved to pound and my breath ceased to be released. In my head all the effort had done something to my ears, they couldn't process sound in a normal fashion. I became isolated inside my head, everything outside it seemed compact and distant. All thought, all movement merged, leaving me in a tomb of the task of rising up the hill. But at the top breath released itself in a stunning whoosh, and as the hill pointed me away from its height I got set free from effort. Like a stout balloon untied I sailed. It always surprised me though, how the quiet remained in my head while being an all together different silence than that which suffocated me on my trek upward. The struggle was gone and it was the struggled that filled my ears; the pressure; the friction of doubt against my will. That friction caused such a noiseless racket in my head that its departure created an ease that lifted me up as I descended. The lightness of not having to exert allowed me to float in a silence void of thickness.

The harmonic balancer released the crankshaft and allowed it to spin freely with no argument. The freedom could be felt throughout the vehicle. Like landing on a cloud, the van hummed a sound that for the slightest instant convinced me of peace.

"Did the engine die?" Stopher asked.

"I think it's still running."

At the bottom the hill I observed the stop sign. I paused before pressing on the accelerator afraid to find that the engine, in fact, did die. I pressed and it purred us along thru the left hand turn and down to the park. Once we got parked in our usual spot across the street I turned off the engine and looked at Stoph.

"So, that was weird."

Like two people who aren't sure whether they want to address the ghost they have just seen, we sat quiet for a moment looking about aimlessly.

"I better take a look."

I popped the hood and saw a hunk of organized metal dangling, yet wedged, between the engine block and part of the frame. I scooted underneath and while lying on my back managed to get the hunk free and out from under the van. Holding it in my hand it meant absolutely nothing to me. This meaningless hunk would cost me money that I probably didn't have yet I understood nothing about it.

Chris and I decided that we shouldn't drive the van minus the hunk of metal, aside from the fact that the van had never once operated so smoothly in the whole time that I owned it, as it did those last two blocks; hunks of metal don't just fall from automobiles and make them run better.

"I'll walk to Albertsons and try to get Art on the phone. It's a Sunday night so he should be home," I suggested to Chris.

Art was now moved into the basement we had so desecrated with our debauchery after he had done likewise to his marriage. My folks deserved so much better. The half mile walk gave me ample time to consider just how fucked I could be, would be and was. It also went a long way at exhibiting how out of shape I was. Huff, huff—puff, puff.

He was around and eased my mind on a couple points pending if another current unknown point proved to be true. Basically, if the crankshaft remained straight and spun true, we were looking at four to six hundred dollars; if the shaft was bent we were going to be buried by the need of two to three thousand dollars. I had inspected it before walking to the phone. To my uneducated eye it seemed straight.

Since I had the triple A card Art advised me to go ahead and have it towed. That night we slept by the park and in the morning I called for a truck. We had it towed to the place where we had the timing chain done the previous Christmas. There we were told that the crankshaft was indeed straight. Whew! BUT, there was a metal pin stuck through it that, in part, used to hold the harmonic balancer in place. When the harmonic went the pin cracked and was now inconveniently stuck inside the crankshaft.

"But you can get it out, right?"

"It's in there pretty good."

"I can't believe you won't be able to get it out." I tried to measure my tone carefully.

"Ultimately, yes. The problem is what kind of damage is done to the shaft while doing so."

The portly fellow sat behind his desk uninspired by my desperation. His oily face had pockmarks that concerned him more and those not since he left high school.

"So what you are telling me," I paced my words evenly in an attempt to not have them make my head explode, "that the difference between me paying for a new harmonic balancer, and having to have the fucking engine re-built, rests solely on a four inch, metal, pin thinner than a pencil?"

"Yeah." He shuffled some papers.

"From five hundred to three thousand just like that," I said out loud to the wall opposite his desk.

"It all depends how much time he spends trying to get it out. He could get it out alright and have it cost you up to eight hundred or more," he said matter of factly. "You'll have to leave it over night."

At Steve's I called the folks who, although very sympathetic, in no way had the kind of money I might need.

"I'll put two hundred in your account first thing in the morning," Dad said.

"If you could that would be great," I said with a hollow gut. "Dad?"

"Yes."

"Do I have your permission to call uncle Bob? I mean would you be offended?"

"No, I won't be offended."

A silence filled the line, not so much uncomfortable as necessary. He knew I had tried, I knew he cared; Dad saw little use for expectations beyond one's self or those that they love. There were a million things he would have me done differently along the way but I didn't do them. I was out here trying, and that, he respected.

"I'll know where I stand by three o'clock our time."

"Good luck, babe."

"Thanks, Dad; thanks for everything."

I hung up the phone and felt disappointed in me for him. He is not a saint, but often plays one in my heart.

Out in front of Steve's, I leaned against his Honda Accord while Chris stood just off the curb in the street staring at the sky.

"It's a pretty day," he said.

"So we got that going for us."

The sun sat in a clear blue sky sparsely spotted with fluffy white islands that drifted in isolation. My heart felt like a lead weight in my chest.

"Want to call uncle Bob?"

"I won't call," he said sharply, without anger. "What time is it?"

"Almost two."

"We call at three?"

"Yeah."

Our whole existence, as we had come to know it over the last year, was in doubt. We had only just now come to find our groove, feel a part of the street, seeing the possibilities. I knew a moment like this would come along eventually; I thought I'd have more time. All the money we had wasted harassed me, every bottle, nickel of weed, and extravagant meal. I stood there remembering the night during our first month in Santa Monica when I had to have steak dinner off a fire grill, and we ended up driving forty minutes into Manhattan Beach to eat at a Sizzlers. The money spent on the food was bad enough. Two weeks later we saw that there was a Sizzlers in the neighborhood. Moments like that haunted me along with gallons upon gallons of booze that sucked the will out of my money. Why am I so fucking needy! I cried in my head. Will I ever grow up!

"I can't go back." I broke the silence if only to stop from hearing myself think.

"I'm not going back."

"What?"

"Worse case scenario, I'll grab the Ovation, the laptop, and my bag of clothes."

"And what?" My voice shook with a low brewing anger.

"And nothing. I'm not going back." Chris' eyes were hard, his voice dug into his words.

"Right."

"Believe what you want."

"What about the Strat, the Martin, the PA, all the writing, our whole life?" My voice took turns between scolding and pleading.

"If you can bring it home with you, great; if not, we'll cut it loose."

"So you're a bad boy now."

Stopher shrugged.

"God you're full of shit."

"I'm not going back to Chicago, and I'm not getting a job." His voice maintained its certainty as he took a few steps down the street before facing me again. "I can't."

In those two words I saw the break in his eyes that betrayed his voice.

"It's not in me any more," Stopher said through a weakening pose. "I can't be a man—I haven't been a man for so fucking long now and everyone still acts surprised. I won't go back there and be a burden because that is what I would do, it's all I've ever done; I'll pay the price here, if it becomes too much, I'll drown a bottle of pills with a bottle of booze and take a walk into the ocean."

My initial anger came from him making me look weak and whiney. How dare he say that he could live here without anything but a guitar; the nerve of implying that he could do without what I am petrified of losing. I danced in my head, believing him on alternate steps, dismissing him disdainfully on the others.

"You think you could do it?" I asked with my own answer in hand.

"I don't know."

In those words I could see that he was already tired of the thought. I wanted to beat him down into admitting that this was all talk, that he was every bit as dependent on the things that I was. Part of me needed to hear him bleed the fear that I bled, succumb to the tears of a tune called, "WHY ME, WHY ME?" All of me wanted to slap his face and shout, "Stop making me look bad!"

The sun moved very little, and the fluffy, white islands bumped overhead. The days warmth did not burn nor embrace, the ocean blew kisses inland.

"I'll call uncle Bob if I have to."

"He has kids of his own, and even more grandchildren," Stoph warned.

"I'll just ask," I whined.

I wanted to tell him that I knew he was a fraud, and maybe I did, maybe I had already. I don't remember ever saying it out right. Looking back on it I have an admiration for Stopher about that moment. Who cares if he never would have lived up to the pose? In that place, at that time, he tried; with words, he built himself into a stance, on to a platform that insisted he live up to something. Stoph prepared himself for the worst by saying, "What can I do for myself, by myself." I ransacked my brain for ways I could keep my precious little boat afloat with shouts out to those who had already done for so many; people, who by all rights, should have been left alone to sort through their remaining years. Mom and Dad, had too little money; Grandma was in her nineties but I'm sure had more money than Mom and Dad; uncle Bob was a strong possibility to have the means; and then there was Jack Kubitz, Dad's business partner. Outside of them Sukey was the only person I knew who had money, but I didn't know her well enough. I actually considered Steve for a half a second. I swung my arms wildly while Chris spread them out gracefully to the open sky of our fate.

"You'd really tough it out here?" I asked with an insertion of doubt that had incredulity for itself.

"I know I don't know nothing, Tommy," Stopher cracked a smile while referencing the scene from the Coen brother's classic, MILLER'S CROSSING. (Coolest film of all time.)

"Up to now you've been convincing."

"Dave, you know I'm weak and a coward."

"Yeah, but ya talk real good.

"Yeah I do."

"I'll beg for the money before I give up, but I don't think I could give up on all our stuff and take to the curb."

"If the worst happens, we'll go back to Chicago, you'll get a job, buy another van and then will come back," Chris said pragmatically, then flashed an overtly charmed smile.

"What if I can't?"

"You always could; you're the strong one."

"Do you really believe that?"

"At the moment, yes. Still, just in case, do we have any money for a bottle of pills and some booze?"

At three o'clock I made the call.

"My name is David Smith; '90 Ford van—white."

"Yeah, just a minute."

I heard papers shuffle, a door open and shut, voices murmur. In the lifetime that he left me waiting on the line, every muscle in me knotted, my brain as well, I whispered with the receiver raised away from my mouth, "Give me this; please just give me this."

"Mr. Smith."

"Yes."

"Yeah, we got the pin out and it'll be ready tomorrow around noon."

"How much?" I crushed my eyes with their lids and clenched my fists.

"It should be about $600, but that is not exact."

"Great, thanks so very much."

We had Steve give us a ride to pick up a few things from the van to get us through the night. Neither Stoph nor I even considered for a split-second asking to be put up by anyone. I know Sukey would have said yes but that felt beside the point. I had, only moments before, been on the cusp of begging for three thousand dollars to keep my dream alive, from just about anyone. Through all the turmoil of not knowing what would befall us, surrounded by my weakest tendencies and most pathetic reactions to adversity, I felt a need to cleanse myself. Stopher and I came within a breath of having our fate cursed by a thin metal pin; of having to choose between the curb or going home, or even worse: Getting a job! We had enough money for a motel but that feel didn't like an option either. Void of words we arrived at a "walk the walk" kind of agreement.

So Steve took us there then to the park. Stopher and I walked from the lot over the basketball courts into the picnic area and claimed a table in the park's southeast corner. By this time the sun's light headed seaward while still holding court. I had my sleeping bag, Stoph a blanket, we each had a pillow wrapped up inside them; the blue guitar was slung over my shoulder; and for that, "at home" touch, we packed up the five-inch screen TV along with an inverter and a battery to watch Monday night football in the park.

"You sure you want to do this?" Steve had asked as we departed from his car.

"I need to do this," I declared with more pride than was warranted.

The tall chain-link fence squared off the edge of the park by a drainage ditch on the east and a dirt alleyway on the south. The public golf course across the alley stretched out more eastward than southward but it sufficed to make up the view in both directions and westerly as well. Joining us in that corner on another bench were homeless Mike and "his lady". Mike had been homeless in California going on ten years. He was in his mid to late forties and about my height with a round head on thick, curved shoulders. We had seen him at the showers but really met him at the park. Like us he and the women were regulars. Other homeless would come and go there, on foot or in vehicles, but few made it home the way we did.

There was the large mulatto man in a red van that gave Stoph and I the creeps. I know—who are we to be creeped out by anyone? He had this lumbering innocent quality that reeked of serial killer on the verge of birth. It was just a feeling you get, knowing that it is nothing more. He always wore the same black tee shirt and light blue denims with a floppy white fishing hat. The locks on his driver's, sliding-side and back doors were apparently not enough because he had padlocks added to each of them. I knew the key locks worked because he made a ritual of turning the key in them, checking their security and then slapping the welded flap over the hook to further prevent entry. The passenger door however needed no such surplus of defense. He probably never used it so simply welded it shut from the inside. I gained a few isolated peeks inside when he sat with the side door open on warm days, always polishing something small. My glances found an orderly world of cabinets with thin drawers, commonly seen in an electrician's workshop, a stool, and a neatly made bed in the back. He gave the impression of a handy man of sorts, yet his van perpetually suffered from what sounded like a rod knock.

Whenever he sat in a stall in the bathroom he had an old transistor radio from the seventies in his hand with a news report blaring, spoken by an announcer from the same long gone era. Also, the man had an odd habit of having to reach from his squat over the bowl—there were no stall doors—across the aisle to the sink to rinse his hands between wipes. He cut chunks off an apple with a pocketknife while moving his bowels. Fruit is great for such movements; I don't trust a man who eats on the toilet. His eyes were hidden behind darkly tinted glasses and whistled constantly—I have a thing about whistling too; I hate it.

Of course the man in the red van was strictly a morning to early afternoon occupant. When he drove off I didn't see him many other places. On occasion I'd see him at the Albertsons, but very rarely. He lived his own mystery; I lived mine. Only mine didn't feel like a mystery to others in my mind. To me I was an open van for the world to gaze at in disgust, envy or apathy. I had at times wondered if the man in the red van ever questioned himself over us but came to the conclusion that he did not. Through the dark glasses I imagined eyes that did not consider the world at large. He lumbered, he whistled, and polished small things that I could not see in his bear-like paws. No, he did not consider me at all.

Mike wore dark glasses but his eyes came out through his bright smile. Unlike a lot of homeless that meandered from place to place, line to line, bottle to bottle, Mike's every stride held a purpose onto itself. His gray beard was that of someone's favorite uncle, his attire that of an adventurer; sturdy, drab green, army pants, flannel and dark blue sweat shirts, army-green, knit cap and a backpack that contained necessities to endure the rain and cold. His "lady" was a dark black woman who wore the same heavy black skirt, that seemed like it had been taken off a wardrobe rack from the set of an old western picture, everyday, with more skirts just like it piled on her body underneath. Her tops fit the same mold and again contained layers. Her matted hair completed the cliché' of a black women in a 1940s Hollywood movie. Oh, she was crazy, and to throw out another cliché', she seemed very bright in a clouded, buried way.

They argued quite often, or I should say, she berated him for insisting on helping her. Mike used the phrase, "my lady" but I had a hard time imagining much intimacy between them, or her with anyone. Without speaking a word she had an abrasive air that permeated from her very fiber. She exuded dignity as well. Her tall full muscular frame could easily be detected through the ridiculous amount of clothes that she tried to hide in. Mike brought her food, coffee, magazines, and she took them gruffly. He, at times, would exhibit the need for a more extensive communication from her even though she had made it clear that she lived outside such notions; bring what you want, I'll accept what pleases.

Their arguments, from a distance, were her marching about ranting animatedly, and Mike listening, waiting for the moment he'd be allowed to interject a question or comment. From that view one might assume him a saint attempting to ease the insane. But as their routine played itself out over and over, and on occasion I had been closer to hear more of the content, I could see that at the crux of things Mike attempting to gain some form of that intimacy I could not imagine in her. It made me think of all the times I had to try to get my ex-wife Donna to understand or care about things pertaining to my needs. My Dad kept telling me that just because what you're asking for is reasonable, there comes a point when you have to acknowledge that it may not be possible. Either that or knock your head against the same wall until your blood covers it with your reasonable desires and intentions.

I saw them converse leisurely and laugh as well, and that has its own intimacy. So they lived and fought over the facts of their lives on the benches in front of the baseball fields while Stoph and I did the same across the street in our van.

When the sun finally vacated the park completely Stoph and I had settled on to our bench with the TV's glowing images of Monday Night football as we glowed from cheap vodka. The Steelers and the Giants went at it while we looked on casually. It didn't matter all that much to us who was playing but I guess we were pulling for the Steelers. As kids I rooted for the Cowboys and Chris the Steelers but we loved them all—Bradshaw and Staubach, Swan and Pearson, or Lenny Dawson and Otis Taylor in Kansas City. The game and those who played it now meant less and less, but we still felt the faded connection enough to keep tabs throughout the season, and on that night felt even closer. We had come so close to losing so much that it warmed us to be roughing it out in the cool September air with some old friends glowing from a five-inch box.

Mike and his lady sat on a bench ten feet away from us. Mike had come over to socialize a little and hear our van story. He proved helpful in telling us where we should bed down for the night.

"A cop may drive through the parking lot, but no one will look back here. The thing you have to worry about are the sprinklers. They come on around five am in this part of the park. That's why we sleep on the other side of the fence that runs along the ditch."

"It doesn't get wet there?"

"No."

"Well, thanks for the safety tip."

He didn't drink but took a few hits off the joint we had flared and then returned to his bench to lay on top under the glow of the starry sky. His lady never spoke to us and in fact avoided us along with every human being other than Mike. I had seen her smile at children though, in that longing kind of way that wants to reach out and touch them; make them feel safe; gain their beauty shed on them your belief in it. She seemed the child herself when alone on the benches. She had a Game boy that she played incessantly and was prone to giggling fits brought on by the games in her head. The woman had the body of a long ago frontier wrapped around the mind and spirit of a child in the sand. I generally like to be left, and leave people, alone. I'd have liked getting know her and her story.

As the game progressed Stoph and I started to notice that she reacted joyously with every Steeler advancement toward the goal line, and always a beat or two ahead of the images on the screen. Not so surprisingly was that she had an earpiece hooked up to a radio. (The radio broadcast had a shorter delay.) That she was an avid Steeler fan surprised me quite a bit. I don't know why. Maybe it was that she seemed so bent on ostracizing all of society and its entanglements from her life; maybe I couldn't get over the fact that she looked to belong on a farm in the middle of a prairie; maybe I couldn't imagine her outside her own head long enough to follow someone else's game let alone taking a rooting interest. The fact was she got down right giddy with excitement over their every success.

Stoph turned the TV to face her direction and we moved to the benches other side to inviter her to look on. At first she didn't notice, when one of us voiced the invite, all the joy in her face went blank. She moved away abruptly and only allowed herself enjoyment of the game once we understood that she was to be left alone.

That night was also the first time I saw organized football in Santa Monica's parks. Not soccer, but good ole American football. The field was full of three or for different teams running drills and conducting scrimmages. I had been there a year and that was the first time I saw kids sporting full gear, pads, helmets and all. In the park of my youth back in Chicago, you couldn't walk through Portage Park on an a late summer or early autumn evening and not find the place lousy with kids ranging from eleven to fifteen, heading out to the field from all directions preparing to be yelled at for the next two hours.

I quit playing organized football when I was twelve because of the ridiculously zealot coaches and their Napoleananic dreams, but it felt good to see that a version of it still existed so far from home. There was comfort in seeing that my childhood, for better or worse, had a life in the present world.

The game ended, the bottles emptied, Chris and I sang a song or two, softly, a tad slurred and not all that well. We did it more out of romantic imagery than from a physical desire. By ten o'clock the park started to feel deserted, as the lights dimmed dark spread throughout. A basketball bounced and a few set of feet shuffled around it to the accompaniment of grunts and expletives. Soon that faded into steps off the court and into cars that drove to homes.

I didn't think of myself as homeless for a second. I was of the one nightstand taking a tourist's approach. Tomorrow my van would once again house and roll me to my bidding. A muscle of toughness did flex within me though. I felt how cool it was to be me as a silly pride swelled 'neath my chest, and I sat on the picnic table, feet on the bench, nursing the last swallow of vodka, and waiting for the camera crane to pull out and the director to say, "Cut!" The fear had passed, fate smiled and I got tough. If things had gone really wrong I would have cried pathetically, begged for a savior, and failing having one answer me, gone home a failure. Instead, I was asked only do endure one night sleeping in the elements and the elements were not that bad being made even friendlier by the cheapest of rotgut.

Stoph and I followed Mike and his lady out to Marine Avenue and around the day care center into the dirt path that ran along side it. They settled in their spot and Stoph and I went down a little further. I wrapped the TV in a towel and put it with the inverter and battery into a small duffel bag placed under my pillow. Inside my sleeping bag I found more than enough warmth and I smiled.

"Hey, Stoph, look: I'm homeless."

"You sure are Vuma. You sure are."

"Do you think you could have stayed out here if the van went down?" I whispered.

"I don't know. I don't know nothing."

"I'm feeling awfully lucky for a guy sleeping near a ditch."

"You are lucky; and cursed."

"D'oh."

"D'oh, indeed."

The next morning we woke up just before six am. Mike and his lady were already sitting on the benches by the field at the front of the park. The sun was bright and the sky clear—my hangover objected to both. We had only been awake a short time when Mike made an announcement.

"A plane just crashed into one of the towers."

He had the earpiece and radio that just last night made his lady so very happy with news of a solid Steeler performance. His voice held some shock, but no terror, it informed on his distance from the event.

"One of the twin towers in New York just got hit by a plane," he said again.

I remember not caring very much at the time. I could see the fascination grow steadily in his face, Stopher too. The frontier woman-child had ambled over to the three-level, silver bleachers off the diamond's first base side to lie down. Stoph grabbed the duffel bag out of my hands and began setting up the TV. The hugeness of the event climbed slowly into the moment where we we're standing and eventually on top of it. As it did I was taken aback by the fact that I still did not care very much. I looked over Stopher's shoulder along with Mike to see the pale-faced network mouthpieces trying to get a grip. The biggest news story of their lives just fell from the sky and they had no script. Luckily for them the images did all the talking. In those first minutes no one said terrorism but no one believed it an accident either. Before much sense could be made of it the second tower got hit. Soon reports of the other planes came in and the whole nation was gripped with fear. Who? Why? How? After an hour of replays, reaction, empty speculation and the falling of the first tower I spread my plastic tarp out on the grass near a small tree, hugged my sleeping bag and went to sleep.

All of this had nothing to do with me. My moment of truth had come and gone on 9/10; 9/11 belonged to the rest of the country. There were no cameras or national concern hovering about me when I stood in front of Steve's car fretting over a phone call I had to make to a stranger who might or might not remove a metal pin from my crankshaft safely. I stood there and Chris stood there. That was my whole world—my van and my brother—9/11 did nothing to change that.

Obviously as the days went by I got angry, felt the fear and experienced sadness over the loss of life; goose bumps ran up and down my arm when I heard the stories of people doing heroic things. A hellacious, horrible thing happened, the kind that every generation lives through at least once if not more. Where were you when Kennedy got shot? Who did you kiss the day the second Great War ended? What kind of snack food did you serve for the moon landing? America got its hat handed to it and I was waking up in a park.

As the noon hour approached I prepared myself for the two-mile walk to the mechanic's. Being that we were on the opposite side of the country from the tragedy, traffic, and the life that made it so, went on as usual; no one called in sick and the banks all opened. That said you could feel a difference in the air walking down the street. Most of it came from within. Your mind knew what had happened and part of it wondered if who ever did what was done had clocked out for the day. The mind also knew that every other mind would be filled with same shock, questions and apprehensions. Not a single car had music on the radio (every station became all news); the grocery lines all had the same conversation; in any office or other place of work, the break room TV sang the same opera and the day's work got little attention. The service industry was probably the least affected, burgers were flipped, lawns got cut, houses cleaned, and yes, vans fixed.

With each step I took toward the mechanic the largeness of something, that in the end, had nothing to do with me echoed. Of course all things are organically related, but I'll let the former statement stand. I in particular had made a point during the last year of withdrawing my membership from society. I lived in my van and offered the craft of my playing, the content of songs, to those that walked, shopped and worked on a given street. That was the whole of my commitment to them. As big as 9/11 was, as deep as its effect ran through the core of our perception of life in the grand ole U.S of A, bombs were dropped and worlds were rocked all through history right up to the last word I just wrote, and quite often by us. I knew before I left Chicago how done I was being a party to any government, institution or organized ideology, but in the days that followed 9/11 I saw it with a new clarity.

Somebody held so firmly and dearly to the belief that they were right, that they had been so wronged, that they gave their life to take thousands of others in the name of said belief. One general response from us: BOMB THE HELL OUT OF THOSE BLOOD THIRSTY MUSLIM SAVAGES!!!!!!

The only difference between 9/11 and what so many third world, Middle Eastern countries have endured is that this time it happened to us, on our turf. The impregnable got knocked-up but good. Don't get me wrong, I'm not justifying anything that had been done to us, I am simply not allowing us to justify our past and future actions. (Oh, we'd have actions in our future.)

I wrote a song addressed to those that saw fit to kill innocent office workers in the name of disdain for American capitalism, ironically titled, YOU'RE SO VERY RIGHT. I don't remember a single line or a note of melody. It was like the song that I wrote about being chased by that gang-banger after witnessing, and thereby spoiling, the attempted mugging way back in our first November—I liked the music; the lyrics were actually pretty good; but I guess they were both too specific. Even that isn't the truth as much as the thing that made me write it was too specific. If in each case I had somebody to give the song to, for them to sing, it may have served us both well. For me they became songs that I needed to write to help me walk away from the events themselves.

That night in the comfort and safety of the great white van, that faithful Ford, our sanctuary on wheels, Chris and I watched the footage over and over again. It was hypnotic.

The next day we had to decide whether to play or not; our first thought said, People will be offended at our lack of solemnity; the second offered that folks would welcome the immediate return to normalcy while appreciating music's soothing nature. The latter notion pointed out that we were broke.

The usual Wednesday farmer's market set up shop on Arizona between fourth and second, so we took that as a sign that our coming out would not offend. The Raven showed up at her usual late time, hustling into the restaurant without noticing us. Once stationed on her perch she smiled haggardly, which seemed the appropriate, wordless greeting of the day between all associates who are seeing each other for the first time since the attack.

"Let's keep it mellow," Stopher whispered before the first song.

"Right, nice and friendly like."

He did, EVERYBODY'S TALKIN', OPERATOR, and his very own, apt for the day, spiritual, GENTLE MOON while I did SPRINKLER'S CHILD, STAR BY STAR, (Mom's lyric written for Josefa's wedding) and anything else that spoke of children, family and love. At the end of the set the Raven dropped this note in our bucket:

Chris & Dave,
A pleasure to see you boys! Thank you so much—the day after
all that crazy bombing—we need some happy voices. You
boys really are great. You shine.

You could feel hollowness on the street that day. The crowd was smaller than usual and the people that did venture out carried with them a respectful, somber tone. Laughter along with any boisterous behavior didn't feel natural so no one partook. People did smile but wearily, and that weariness made the smiles feel all the more genuine. "Good to see you," seem to be the greeting of the day; good to know that somewhere, anywhere, people could see other people under relatively normal circumstances, extend hands, share a meal or just a few simple words before going wherever they were off to. Self-awareness permeated through each footstep, "I am here, I am walking unmolested."

Fear lingered behind all of the gratitude as well. That first day after 9/11, anything felt possible, vulnerability colored and informed on the slightest glance or the deepest stare. America had been educated on how touchable it was; this lesson we did not wear well or with ease.

We had a decent tip-day, nothing spectacular, but at least twenty or a bit more. When the money got dropped it was done so purposefully. No one walked by hurriedly or with an absent mind as they do on most days. On a usual day there are always at least a few that express a marked appreciation for our being there, adding something to the streets on a given day. On the day after 9/11 not a single person tipped us without at least going out of their way to catch and hold our eyes with theirs. The looks and words offered all said the same things: "Thank you for making this day seem at least a little normal," or "This is a day that needs beautiful music," and simply, "Thanks."

I had already come to realize before that day how much some people got from street musicians everyday. To see someone stand out in the middle of a workday and say this is my task, this is what I offer the world. They, most of them, know that no one who plays on a weekday in the street is getting anywhere near rich. The average stiff has weighed the odds of risking one's time on pursuing any endeavor that doesn't involve some form of punch-clock, and laid their arms at the feet of conformity. Some find better compromises than others, some even find a life more fulfilling than their childhood fancies, but most know intimately the resignation that earning a decent living in this country demands. So they see a couple of guys who went the other way and on top of that, they have talent. A dollar or a few is their way of telling us, "Good luck, don't give up," and "The world needs dreamers with a solid backbone."

On 9/12 each person that tipped us liked knowing that we were still dreaming with an unyielding bone planted firmly in our backs.

A couple days later as we were packing up after a set she wrote:
And they move on...
taking with them the silky smoothness that can be turned to
raw-edged grit that is:
R&R CROSSING
Paw mark

Oh, we were getting to her.

The promenade had yet to regain its usual life force. The crowds were still smaller, but slowly more jovial; still restrained but less so. On that Friday while Stoph and I were playing we saw Terry Bradshaw walking down the street dressed in sweat pants and shirt. A striking woman accompanied him and they both moved aimlessly about. They passed on our left, and out of the corner of my eye, just as they were on the other side of us, I saw Terry pause to look back at us.

On the following Sunday the NFL shut down out of respect for the tragedy. So Terry had no studio to sit in front of a camera in and act goofy with Howie and James. Just like on the previous Friday, except this time he and the lady were accompanied by another big guy in sweats, Terry, wearing the exact same sweats as on Friday walked, by us playing, on the same side, with same leisurely amble. I had remembered that we were playing something bluesy when he paused to look back towards us on Friday, so since we had just finished a song, I called out to Stoph, "ONE-STEP."

"Well my baby told me, 'Ya got to take it one step at a time," Stopher roared.

Sure enough, mid-way past the first dinosaur, Terry stopped dead in his tracks. Being on second guitar I could move around and nonchalantly check to see what they were doing. He stood there for the first verse, during the bridge inched our way. By my lead break they were just off to the side. At the end of the song Terry came up to us with that big country boy smile of his.

""You guys are great, just great," he said, throwing four dollars in our bucket.

"You're pretty great yourself," Stoph muttered through his school boy giddiness.

"Yeah, you were a great one," I added. (Actually I don't remember what I said, but it was something idiotic like that.

Terry stood there, not looking quite as tall as I thought he would of, shaking his head waving that hillbilly smile. "I saw you out here the other day and you guys are the best."

Stopher and I nodded our childhood-crush ridden, bashful smiles and mumbled incoherently. As I said before, we watched Terry Bradshaw play on television in our formidable years, years when you believed in football heroes, years when you wanted to be them, years when legends seemed realer than they would ever seem again. Tom Cruise could have given me a blowjob, so what? Terry FUCKING Bradshaw said we were great, and the best.

The next Sunday the NFL opened for business because tragedy could only cut into so much profit. We couldn't let the terrorists win and blah, blah blah.

A lot of stirring things got said on TV, and just as much left me swimming in banality. But it was on the third street Promenade that I was most moved. The Saturday after that fatal Tuesday, a stage was set up on the furthest north end of the Promenade. On it were gathered religious leaders from all the biggies: Jewish rabbi, Catholic priest, Muslims, Hindus and even a chick thrown in for good measure. They all spoke well enough and preached a similar message of tolerance, understanding and peace. One of them, a black Baptist preacher, was the master of ceremonies. He spoke first and, in between each speaker, gave the introductions.

"I will not say much, as there are a number of scholarly, spiritual leaders here to share with you their words; their prayers. I however have one sentiment that I feel holds the gravity of the day, and I will say it now, and I will say it after each speaker. As you hear the words, as you come to know them, as we work our way through this day on to others, I ask that you say them with me. The words are simply these, 'Let peace begin with me.' Before we move on please join me in saying these words once more. 'Let peace begin with me.'"

Chris and I stood at the back of the Saturday crowd during the day's noon hour and looked on with mild curiosity. All performers were asked to come join the rally or at least not play until it had ended. I saw no other performers in the crowd but was fairly certain that none ignored the request to keep the promenade silent during the event. I had graduated from hopeful agnostic to certain atheist just recently, but had pretty much never gone in for any organized religion. All speakers hit the right notes and spread a fine message, but it was from the black Baptist that I found myself being stirred. After each speaker he stepped up to the microphone with a contained force and repeated the mantra.

"Let peace begin with me."

The next one got introduced and they would get lofty, even a bit pious then pull it back for an all in all fine sermon. The big black Baptist stepped up again.

"Let peace begin with me."

The next speaker took their turn and with each return to the microphone the big Baptist gathered up his momentum where he had left off.

"Let peace begin with me."

It got to be as if all the words in between were these the meaningless meanderings of a dribbling brook bouncing off the rocks, a droning hum that served no other purpose than to lull the listener's ears to the waterfall of the big Baptist's payoff. Only when he spoke that one simple request; when those five words curled up on his and our lips; when all the exterior commotion and superfluous rattling subsided in the name of that one clear, concise concept of individual choice; only then did wisdom find inspiration, did I feel lifted beyond the previous day's circumstance.

"Let peace begin with me."

Stopher and I both were surprised to find ourselves energized by attending the service.

"That guy had IT," Stopher surmised.

"He did have something going besides the words themselves, didn't he?"

"You felt his blood heating up with each refrain."

"That big Baptist nigger was alright."

Stopher laughed at the absurdity of the comment.

"You go too far, Dave; you could have said, 'Silly negro,' but no."

"If it ain't vicious, it ain't funny."

So that was how 9/11 looked from the streets, a park, out of and back in, a van down by the ocean.

A few weeks later, on Mom's birthday (five days before mine) I began another story for the Raven:

The night wore on her patience as the road on her wheels. She slouched back in her seat, pulled her cap down over her brow and caught her eyes in the rearview mirror.

"One more year," she muttered under breath.

The rain painted the night in an appropriate mood.

"Okay," she defended against her reflection, "I'm going."

With its engine in gear, the cab went in search of fares.

He stood for the rain to fall on and the wind to whip. Guitar in hand he seemed uncertain of his next move. Fuck "seemed"; he hadn't a clue in years. For every song sung, every note played, he carried the imprint of a dead end brick wall on his forehead.

At the moment the cab came around the corner he raised his hand slapping at the rain and shouted, "Well, fuck you too."

She pulled over mistaking his disdain for the want of a ride.

He looked through the window with a puzzled pause.

"Ya need a ride or what?" she asked impatiently.

"Define, 'what,'" he responded.

"'What,' is what I say before I put my boot tip up someone's ass for wasting my precious time," she explained academically.

"As tempting as that sounds, I'll take the ride," he decided, and got in back.

Once he settled in, she asked the million-dollar question. "Where to?"

"That is the million-dollar question."

(Didn't I just say that?)

"Hey, I don't have any money for ya, so you'll have to give it up for free," she persisted.

"Can't we just drive around?" he asked.

"Look: this ain't no social club. This is a business situation," she informed him. "Your money for my gasoline. Do you remember the aforementioned boot tip?"

"How could I possibly forget?" he stated dryly.

"Show me some money." She paused. "Now!"

He rummaged through his pockets with the thought of the wet, the memory of the cold and the sudden desire to avoid both. Fumbling with a few crumpled bills, he produced a fifty.

"Let's start with this," he declared.

She contemplated kicking him out, then opted for the fifty and drove off.

That was all the time I had for that installment. At the writing of it I was aware of who played whom in the story, as I am sure she would be too. Romance lived in my words a faint hope that I had yet to believe believable. Still the story paralleled us accurately enough. She drifted in place and I drifted along. She worked a meaningless job toward some elusive success at a financially better life, while I let the rain of monetary failure fall around me where it deemed, in order to find meaning in what I held dear.

A couple of days later she wrote this:

I cannot say it enough—you sound so VERY good! You know I just adore you boys. And Dave, you know what your voice does for me— Don't blush, but I feel I have a crush every time you croon!

A fan. Paw mark.

Hello; a crush? Yeah, but signed a fan. I began to wonder if maybe I had reason to get my hopes up. Of course all I had to do was find the moneyless wallet in my back pocket, see the three hundred pound, drunken slob staring out at me from any store front window, and my ridiculous floating, feathered hopes saw the hard ground rising up fast to introduce them to my lead booted reality.

Ever since the day Steele told us that a few folks thought we were from Kentucky, Stoph would occasionally refer to us as Hillbilly Heroin. Sundays quickly became Hillbilly Heroin day. On those days the set reflected our most rural side with songs like, SUNDAY SCHOOL, (Chris') or THIS LAND IS YOUR LAND, by Woody Guthrie; songs that in general were folkie with a touch of drug induced guitar, R&R style. On the day before my birthday, the Raven made this request, via a post card:

Hillbilly Heroin for Halloween,

I know it's weeks away but I'm feeling kinda vulgar.

(It's not me, it's all that ocean fresh breeze.)

On the front of the post card was a carved pumpkin. In its wicked eyes, she wrote an *R* in each one and the nose got a, &, while the mouth read, = *They rock.*

The next day, October 6, was my thirty-seventh birthday. On the way out to the promenade we stopped off to pick up a half-gallon of vodka. Going through the intersection of Lincoln and Santa Monica an approaching car turned into me head on. He didn't seem to be making a left-handed turn; it was more like he decided that he wanted to be in England, so jumped lanes. In one split-second the car was directly in front of me and moving on as if I wasn't even there; this guy sat behind his wheel staring out blankly from his windshield harmlessly. I swerved into the lane he had just vacated in the middle of the intersection only to have to swerve back from whence I came to avoid a very surprised, and very scared woman in a tiny blue hatchback that for a moment saw nothing but the end of her days. The where-with-all to look back to see what became of the instigator of all the trouble was not upon me so I held to the wheel, swallowed hard and hoped for a safer rest of the day.

"Happy birthday to me, I guess."

"In the fucking morgue," Stoph breathed out heavily.

The Raven was at her post and cheered us on with even an added gusto. Early in the week she asked me what I had planned for my B-day, and I answered rock-n-roll.

"After that?"

"Well after the night set with the drums, Stoph and me will probably tip a few with Earnest."

"That's not good enough; leave it to me, I'll come up with a little something."

I tried not to write anything into it beyond friendship, while Stoph leered enough for the both of us.

During the noon birthday set the Raven gave me a post card whose front was selling pork. The advertisement read:

I SCREAM

YOU SCREAM

WE ALL SCREAM

FOR PORK LOIN

The Raven drew screaming lines all around the last, SCREAM, and added to the bottom:

And DAVE SMITH on his B-Day

On the back where her usual messages go, she wrote:

DAVE,

HE ROCK
Love ya, Love ya, Love ya,
On yer Birthday and any other moment, millisecond.
Otherwise-
They Rock, "HE" Rock

After the set we went into our usual waiting mode and the Raven had for me an assignment.

"You got a story to finish," she said handing me a few cards and a pen.

"But it's MY birthday; shouldn't you write me one?"

"Uh uh, it don't work that way. Besides you haven't finished the last one you started." She smiled wide and hard. "We still getting together tonight?"

"No, I got another gorgeous, honey-gold temptress to entertain me, and she tells stories."

"Yeah but she don't love your songs like I do, does she?"

"No." The game I had begun faded with the truth she spoke and I could feel the pain she saw in my eyes when I answered. "No, no one loves them like you."

She headed back to her perch. "I got a shift at Monsoons tonight, I get off elevenish."

I watched her go and felt embarrassed, but only a little. Over the last year we had been an equal gift to each other, it deserved to be felt and seen in our eyes, placed on our words, bubble in our veins.

From her perch she shouted, "Get to work on my story, birthday boy!"

I wrote:

They drove, the rain fell and time passed.

"Nice cap," he said, breaking the silence.

She nodded apathetically.

"I mean, it's no fedora," he continued, "but it does have a certain quality that some may confuse with style."

She found him in the rearview mirror and looked him over.

"Well at least it's not bent in all the wrong places," she countered.

(I have a line in the title track of our first CD, FINAL CALL, about my gray fedora being bent in all the wrong places.)

"You noticed that," he said with a smile as he removed his hat and held it in front of his eyes. "You ARE perceptive. Yes, indeed my gray fedora is bent in all the wrong places; poetically speaking as well as literally."

"Why don't you fix it, or get a new one?" she asked.

"Because, then it would not be mine. I've earned every crevice and they mean something to me."

"Such a fuss."

"Indeed."

Silence again prevailed.

The cab moved through the city with no intention of getting anywhere.

"What does the dent in the front to the left signify to you?"

"To never get married again," he answered immediately.

"Smart dent," she said.

"Indeed."

"Are you any good on that thing?" she inquired in reference to his guitar.

"I'm a fucking genius," he stated matter of factly.

"Well this I gotta hear," she laughed. "Play me a little something."

"I really shouldn't," he said.

"And why is that?"

"Because there is a seriously good chance that you'll fall madly in love with me if I do," he said solemnly, "and though you are quite stunning, I just don't have the energy for it."

"Oh, you do go on," she said turning her head to see if maybe he was joking. He was not. "Nobody is that good sweetheart, trust me."

"Hey, you're already calling me sweetheart and I haven't played a note," he pointed out.

"My cab; my rules," she said. "And I say, play or get out."

"Okay," he said with resignation, "I warned you, so don't blame me."

"I won't."

He pulled out his guitar and filled the cab, the night and her soul with a gentle sound that made angels weep.

I watched her read the story from the side of the dinosaur platform. Her duties only allowed it to be done in pieces. I could tell what made her laugh and when a line touched her so that she had to read it again. On those of the latter her nose crinkled and eyes sparkled; her shoulders gave a subtle roll and her hair brushed the cheek on one side of her face. On those she had to re-read she laughed the second time as if she found humor at being moved. When she managed to read the whole thing through a couple of times her eyes sought me out and almost scolded me, but playfully so. "What are you trying to pull here?" they said. The Raven had this smile that wrapped you up in warmth all the while bleeding you dry; all at once narrow and sharp while achieving an open valley of softness. Her smile and eyes worked in unison during moments like that, they both spread out around you before slicing directly through your center.

I raised my arms to her penetrating stare and bumped my shoulders, "What," I mouthed.

She folded her arms over breasts and tapped her black boot tip on the ground, causing hips to join the rhythm.

"You wanna piece of me," I mouthed again, wondering if her lip reading skills gathered my meaning.

A customer intervened and the Raven returned to work.

A little later she rushed from her perch to shove a couple more pumpkin cards into my hand before dashing wordlessly back to work.

Hey Mister would you be so kind as to put pen to PAPER for a Red-riding hood(lum)...? OR ELSE.

I laughed at her at play with words and sought out her eyes but found them busy at work shuffling bodies into tables. My first thought was to continue the story but I didn't have the energy for that specific beast, to finish it off just right. I re-read her plea-and-or-threat and got an idea.

Years lay dust on stories told. So much that the words survived by time don't necessarily equate with the events they supposedly represent.

For example:

The wolf died at the hands of a red-hooded gown-flowing vixen. Oh sure, these days it is believed that the wolf fell victim to his own appetite for destruction. Not true. The poor wolf's only crime was looking too long and listening not close enough to the hot breathed promises made by the Queen of a kingdom, which existed only in the moment of her touch, then vanished with her smile. Because smiles do turn to sneers and a sneer from her slices and dices the will of the strongest men. What was a poor wolf to do but offer the moment its humble services? All in all, fairness aside where it normally resides, the wolf died happy.

I knew something was up with us that night and I didn't have a clue; I was all over the map. I think I wrote those words to let her know that I knew I'd be lucky to receive whatever she'd offer, and that if she had an idea about the coming night that she didn't want to live beyond it, I was game.

I still had to wait around an hour and a half to play the six o'clock set when the Raven finished her shift at George's. She ran up heaving her big, black, canvas bag that passed more for a survival kit than a purse.

"Great set today, boys," she said smiling at both Stopher and I. "Have a good one tonight."

She started off, then stopped to make a quick motion to me to come near.

"You'll wait for me outside Monsoons?"

"Eleven?"

"Maybe eleven thirty."

"I'll be there."

I watched her rush off; an elegant kid in a long red strapless gown and long black boots, heaving a bag more suited for a soldier going off to war than a fleet-footed Raven headed to another restaurant to stand around and look pretty.

Earnest showed up about twenty minutes before we had to play and we set up our stage. That night we rocked, had tuning problems, endured missed cues, rocked, survived a train wreck and then rocked some more. The money left us each with close to twenty, so not a bad night at all.

"What's the plan for the rest of the evening, gentle men?" Earnest asked as we packed up the gear.

"Dave here, has a birthday date," Stopher informed.

"Riding the Rave on his birth day, eh?"

"E, I wish I could brag on your being right, but I'm trying not to get my hopes up," I confessed.

"She digs you; I can tell."

"She loves the music."

"Trust the Big E; I can tell."

"Well, I won't know anything until after eleven."

"So let's get this stuff in the van and have a few birthday toasts," Stopher declared. "You got a few hours to kill."

"Yeah, but I better pace myself, just in case."

"Just in case; I love you guys."

Whenever Earnest had nothing else to say, or wasn't sure what to say, he'd say that: "I love you guys." I know it was a genuine sentiment that he felt and what better feeling to fill any void than that.

We had a few drinks by the van and smoked a joint. Stoph offered me a couple doobies for the road but I just took one. I decided to let them get settled into their own party at Albertsons and hang out by myself taking in the promenade scene. I had my plastic liter of cheap vodka; a beat-up old gray fedora slanted across my head; and an abused, if not quite equally so, black double-breasted suit jacket over my black tee shirt. With all that I cruised up and down the three, carnival invested streets a spectator of sights and personal hopes.

The Bowler boys held court in the center square between the two dinosaurs that had endured so much of myself and others—how grateful they must have been to be wires and leaves. As much as Chris and I had attempted to be diverse from one set to another, the day in and day out grind of the first year, and the years to come, would find more than repetition repeated to inspire insanity. The Bowler boys weren't here as much between moving their act up and down the street and getting gigs on cruise liners, but within a two hour stint they regurgitated the same bits that are themselves as old and tired as the prehistoric beats depicted by wire and leaves, over and over again. Still, in the warm

October night, under the influence of digested substances, or simply allowing oneself to be fed by what was given, I smiled at the jokes and enjoyed the enjoyment of others. A gust of wind rustled up through the dinosaurs' hindquarters, over its spine and out of the eyes and mouth, tickling its leaves. The dinosaur cracked a smile too.

I moved on down the street to see the silver robot, who made comic geniuses out of the Bowler boys, making some schoolgirls giggle. He offered one a lollypop before, with slight of hand, snatching it from their grip. A small boy on his dad's shoulders sat off to the side on the curb with wide, joyous eyes that snatched at the lolly from his distance. With every attempt the schoolgirl made, the boy lurched causing his father to tilt. He laughed cautiously because he was too involved in the escapade to be overtly frivolous about the matter. When the girl had finally been given the sweet treat the boy applauded riotously.

I would not fully relinquish my bitter disdain for the silver robot, I would always disapprove of the way he crowded other performers, but I did see his worth for the first time. He did not serve my purpose but he served someone's.

The whole street bubbled with folks in search of a night that made the rest of the week palpable. I saw the necessity of my job at work through others. I was glad not to be performing, fighting for their attention, their dollar, I was happy that my shift had ended. I had my friendly buzz and I had a date to fly with a Raven.

Monsoons was a restaurant/club on the promenade's north end by Wilshire. The Raven had only been working there a month. Unlike George's, she did not stand outside soliciting, but instead received those who came of their own accord. It had a couple of bars, a dinning room, and a musical lounge upstairs; keeping track of the seating at George's was two plus two compared to the numbers that filled her head while maintaining the flow at Monsoons. She'd last another month there before getting fired.

I sat along the cement platform that framed the small dinosaur spewing water from his mouth into a pool. From there I could glance through Monsoons' front door to see the Raven flashing her flirting smile at the next customer. I sipped my vodka.

"This is so just a friend thing," I said under my breath, but out loud so that I would better be able to listen. "She likes your music, the way you sing. You are a fat slob with no money and no money in your future. The van is your home, your brother is your roommate. This is nothing; this will never be anything." I sipped the vodka assured that I had been convinced.

I looked through Monsoons' door and thought that she had smiled at me. But a figure then stepped into my view from the other side of the doorway and I realized that her smile was his. He had a pale green, silk suit draped around his tall fit frame. The man's haircut cost more than I had made in the last two weeks. I could see him lingering around the reception area as his friends left to be seated. After a few verbal exchanges and chuckles with the Raven, he took her hand softly into his and bid her a good night.

I repeated my previous warning.

At eleven she looked busy so I walked down the promenade again to its most southern end at Broadway and slowly made my way back. When I got there the Raven was standing outside talking to a short well-dressed man in his late thirties. The smile she gave him looked all too familiar sending a cold chill down my back; not your smile, I thought—it just felt that way. Her smile made everyone feel that way.

"Dave, hi," she greeted me. "This is my friend David, a musician and a great writer; we're going out to celebrate his birthday tonight."

"Congratulations," he offered.

"Thanks, but I didn't do much; just avoided killing myself for another year." That's it, I told myself, cynical and surly, cynical and surly.

"This is David too" The Raven kept things moving. "He's a photographer; he has a showing next week."

"An artists who makes money; now that is impressive." Cynical and surly, cynical and surly. (I actually was impressed.)

"Oh no, I do commercial photography, this is just on the side," he said apologetically, yet with an underlying smugness.

I nodded politely.

"Well, we should get going."

"Great to see you again. Enjoy your birthday."

Photo boy went to kiss her lips but the Raven gave him a cheek.

The Raven took my arm and we headed toward Broadway.

"Thank God you came along."

"You seemed to be enjoying yourself." Aloof joined cynical and surly.

"I went out with him once and then just bumped into him tonight waiting for you."

"Oh, is that the guy who-"

"No, he was Persian."

"Oh, right; exotic foreigners. Right."

"He kissed with his tongue on the first date, and I was like, 'I don't do that.'"

"You don't, well fuck this then," I said breaking from her arms, heading in the other direction.

"Dave," she said laughing as she tugged me back in line. "I don't do that with him."

"And me?"

"Let's get some Champagne first, do this birthday right."

First? The plot thickens. From that point I left aloof alone to go fuck surly and cynical in any order they wanted. While trying to keep my highest hopes at bay, I decided to let confidence take a swing.

We stood on the emptying street of a Saturday night on the promenade's south end after she had secured her liquid inspiration from the Broadway restaurant/specialty wine store. Voices echoed up and down the street from those whose night was fading as the dinosaurs spit water perpetually. I held her bag; she the Champagne, her eyes questioned mine. For a moment I managed to rob her of the moment's control. Her bare shoulders, basked in the neon, flexed until her smile relaxed them.

"You have to kiss me now," I told her.

"Not here."

"My birthday is almost over."

"Only technically."

"I need you to kiss me on my birthday."

She checked her watch, which was set ahead to remind her that she was always late. She did the math.

"Two more minutes."

"You have to do it now."

"Have to?"

"It's a federal thing; not just local."

I saw it. I saw the concession. Not in her eyes, not in the face, but in the romantic mist that surrounded her, in the moment that had come to exist at the insistence of all others that had passed before. She had to kiss me and she knew it. She wanted to kiss me and I knew it. I set the bag down, stepped in closer placing my palms around her forearms as her chin lifted and tilted to accept me; softer than romantic mist itself we kissed. Her lips fell upward into mine, my arms enfold her, one around the lower back, the other taking the shoulders. Our mouths opened ever so slightly to allow the tongues to slide together momentarily in a warm grasp; nothing so gentle had ever happened to anyone anywhere; not frenzied, just mouths embracing each other's warmth, pulling and pushing exteriorly to create a rhythm designed to invite passion while keeping it at bay. The interior was no more than a side bar compared to the outer rims of the lip's meshing, holding, giving, taking.

It was not a long kiss, but it made its point.

"Happy."

"Yeah."

"Let's get you a guitar."

We stopped briefly by the van and I picked up ole blue.

"You got an old blanket you don't care about?"

"I got a sleeping bag that I don't get along with all the time."

"Bring it."

"You gonna say, hi?"

"Is Earnest there?"

"Probably."

"Nah."

She never did like Earnest.

"How's it going?" Stoph asked.

"Life is funny."

"Ha ha-funny?"
I gasped thoughtfully.
"Funny-strange? Stopher offered.
"Just funny."
"Yes it is."
"Go get her, Dave," Earnest slurred.
"You boys have been busy."
"It seemed like the thing to do," Stoph answered.
"It always does don't it."

Walking back to the car I was happy to know that Chris had Earnest. Even though spending your birthday with a beautiful woman was every man's wish, I would have felt guilty leaving him alone. I still felt a tad guilty. And I would have gone whether he had Earnest or not.

She drove up the PCH toward Sunset BLVD. and turned left off that on to some small winding road that lifted us up into the canyons among the glamorous homes perched like majestic hawks on a ridge. Their wide, tall windows seemed to serve as the bird of prey's eyes, looking upon me disapprovingly as I had clearly traveled into where I did not belong. On so very many levels they were right.

"I come here a lot with dogs."
"They're into architecture?"
"You'll see."

The car's headlights threw themselves about at every twist, exposing things in snapshots. All very telling. At the top we came upon a turn around that was marked by a thick single bar/gate. She turned around and headed back down the hill.

"Well, thanks for the tour; it's always nice to know how I'll never live."
"Shut yer trap."

Almost immediately she pulled over.
"Saddle up cowboy."
"Can't we just talk first?"

We loaded up the guitar, sleeping bag and another bag for her Champagne along with a few other things that she hid from me, then headed back up the road on foot. Beyond the single bar/gate was a wide dirt road that led into the wilderness. Along the left of the road was greenery that held back the mountains rising ever upward and to the right greenery in the form of knee-high shrubs that led to where the mountain shot dangerously close to straight down; where gravity waited to show off. The city of Los Angeles sat off in the distance sparkling as if that made it innocent.

"Funny how being way up here in the middle of nature makes the city below look like nature too. At night anyway," I observed.

"I never look that way when I'm up here." The Raven walked on.

The dirt road slanted up and taxed my breath while the Raven seemed to move easily. Within a hundred yards she stopped to let me catch up.

"We go this way," she pointed to a thin trail that shot steeply up through the brush and winded out of sight. "Or we could walk further up the road and come around in on the other side; that ways longer, this one is tougher."

I had the blue guitar in a gig bag that strapped itself to my back so I opted for the short, tough journey.

"Can you carry all that?"

"I got it." My male pride couldn't help but feel challenged even though she was in solid shape, went hiking and running on a regular basis, and I had been living on a strict regiment designed for an early death.

The Raven ascended the trail easily while I struggled a bit, but to my credit not all that badly. (I was a jock once ya know.)

The trail came out to a relatively flat, rocky area. In fact, it seemed that we now stood upon a single boulder whose true vastness no one would ever come to know. Not far off stood a small crooked tree whose trunk bent and twisted while its limbs sprouted to form an old man's palm turned upward spreading his fingers, begging for a magic elixir to make him young again. We stepped off the boulder on to the grass and spread the sleeping bag out under the tree. From there you could still see the city sparkle in one direction, and see where the dirt road trailed off into the dark in another. Stepping away from the tree facing westward the ocean waited to be seen. The clear night conspired with a healthy moon to show all.

"Sing me a song, bitch," the Raven chirped.
"What'll ya have?"
"STAR BY STAR."

I sang my mother's words with hopes that they would get me some action. Oedipus-shcmedipus. I stood over her because my ill shape found no comfort sitting with the guitar, even when my body had seen better days I was never one to sit cross-legged. She sat slugging Champagne from the bottle propped up by the other arm and her legs curled around those vivacious hips. Only the Raven, dressed for a grand ball, sitting on a beat up old sleeping bag on a mountain in the middle of the night, drinking expensive Champagne like it was a bottle of Boons farm wine, could maintain elegance in the face of white trash or vice versa.

I sang to her at first but, as is my way, the song won out and I went where it took me. By the end my eyes left the mountaintop to climb my soul, which jumped over the moon, in search of the search, and the girl got set aside for the thing she loved about me in the first place. With the last note just beginning to fade from the guitar and my voice with it, she cut them both short with her body and mouth respectively. Unlike the night's first kiss, this one went from zero to sixty in an all out frenzy. At first I left the guitar between us being that it brought us together to begin with. Soon I slid it out of the way to feel the whole of her against me. Just when I thought things would progress she pulled away.

"Play me a song, bitch."
I pretended that she had never left, groping the air in front of me.
"Should I leave you two alone?"
I slid my hand down to where her ass had been.
"Hey, that looks like fun."

She stepped back into where I imagined her being and we resumed. Eventually we made it back to the sleeping bag and the guitar was set aside in favor of us playing each other.

I'll cut the suspense and tell you right now that I did not get laid. We did a lot of heavy kissing and groping. At one point she got on all fours and purred like a kitten encouraging me to inspect her. I slid my hand up her dress, leisurely making my way up her thighs until I finally graced her wetness. All the while I kept waiting to wake up, have her slap me or at least have her be offended. When I actually reached there I realized that I was drunk and not at my most coordinated. I feared my best work not being at my disposal, so merely lingered to tease and then withdrew. She returned to a sitting position and I instantly knew that I had made the right call. She would have stopped me any second any way.

"So, you don't wear panties."

"Nope."

"Just on special occasions, or never?"

"Almost never."

"Good to know."

"Even more fun to find out."

"Indeed."

I sang a few more songs and went to have a drink.

"Here drink this," she said handing me some of her Champagne. "I'd rather you taste like this than cheap vodka."

"Fair enough."

We paused to smile at each other.

"Did you like your story today?"

"I did. What is with you and that hat; it's so eighties."

"I told you before, I've always loved fedoras. And I wear them because of the thirties, not the eighties; Cagney and Bogart see."

"At least you don't wear vests."

"I love vests, brought one with me but lost it on the trip out."

"Luckily for you."

"Yeah, it was."

"You have such great hair," she said running her fingers through it. "If you'd stop combing it so much. What shampoo do you use?"

"Don't; use soap."

"Soap? And no conditioner?"

"Nope."

"David," she scolded, "you can't keep doing that to your hair. And take that pony tail down." She reached up and removed the scruffy from the back of my head.

"Yes, dear."

She smiled and kissed me softly, then I her.

"You know this is just for tonight?"

"I didn't; guess a part of me figured."

"I like you, and your voice totally does it for me but I'm getting near forty and I can't be fooling around, I wanna get married and have a house."

"Well thanks for tonight." I looked around at the surroundings. "I couldn't have imagined a better way to turn thirty-seven."

"I appreciate you; your talent, the way you write; the kind of person you are. You and your brother; you're like family."

"Family? You really know how to hurt a guy; say I'm like a brother and I'll smack ya."

With that she slapped me.

"If anyone does the smacking around here, it'll be me."

"Yes, dear!"

"You liked that, huh."

"Actually, I did. A lot."

"You're a sick fuck; I like that."

"I remember when I got this hat." I changed the subject, lying on my back. "My ex-wife got every one to chip in on it for my twenty-fifth birthday. It was the first fedora I ever had that didn't come from the Salvation Army; we've played a lot of rock-n-roll together. I remember a tripping my brains out with Stopher sitting by a lake in Wisconsin and laughing our asses off. The hat fell off and I thought I'd lost it. We sat there all night laughing and talking. I let the hat go because when I thought about trying to reach off the pier, a headline flashed in my head: DRUNKEN MAN DROWNS IN LAKE LOOKING FOR HAT."

"Good thinkin'"

"More than just a hat rack."

"Yeah, shoes too."

I did a double take before getting the joke.

"Clever girl."

"So how'd you get the hat back?"

"When the sun peeked through, and I sobered up a little, I saw that it got caught on a splinter from one of the poles and was able to reach down and pick it up. It was soaked through; didn't wear it as much after that; I had gotten another hat to get married in, a black one."

"How appropriate."

"But when the marriage started to fall apart I lost my taste for that one and have been wearing the grey one ever since."

"But you have such beautiful hair."

"Well, I tend to wear hats in cycles and I have been wearing this for a while. I could be due for a break?"

"You should; I'm the one who has to look at you for two hours a day."

"It's the least I could do.

"The very least."

"But my Mom gave me this great railroad crossing pin that I have on it."

"She'll understand."

"She is awfully understanding."

"And you're just awful."

"Yes, dear."

It got cool and she tired. I wrapped her up in my suit jacket, which she asked me to not wear any more either, and in my arms, she drifted off to sleep. When I was certain she wouldn't wake I slipped away and looked out off the bluff into the ocean. It had all been so perfect—except for not getting laid—a beautiful woman who loved my songs and made me laugh, out in the wilderness under the moon; it was the best birthday I ever had. I stood there soaking it in, not wanting to forget a single detail; the way she smelled; the form of her mouth against mine; the shushing sway of the tree; and how the night hovered respectfully, not too dark not too bright.

The details did fade but the essence has not. It was the best night of sex I never had.

As the sun crept up on us I had managed some sleep but not much. We rose stiffly in our bones but comfortably with each other. I kept waiting to see regret in her face or detect it in her voice but it never surfaced.

"Have some gum." She did not ask.

We made our way back to the car in a silence void of awkwardness. On the drive down the PCH I watched the water smiling.

"You got nothing and you're smiling."

"Cool ain't it?"

"Yeah, darlin', it is."

Coming down 11th toward Marine she said it again.

"So last night is over and we're just going back to before, okay?'

"I understand."

"Just friends?"

"Friends." I smiled warmly with ease. She couldn't possibly grasp how fortunate I felt.

"Okay; just one more."

She abruptly pulled the car over to the curb on Marine after the turn off of 11th and pulled me close to kiss me hard. The passion filled her and she me.

"David! Why are you so cute."

"Practice, years of practice."

She kissed me again, this time with less intensity, more longing.

"I suppose you'll tell your brother everything."

"Yeah." I laughed harder and longer than even I thought was warranted.

"But no one else, especially on the promenade; I don't like people knowing my business."

"Sure."

"I mean it. I am a very private person."

"Sweets, I am way too grateful to be unaccommodating. Trust me."

She dropped me off at the van and Chris sat in the driver's seat hurting from the previous night's drinking. He got out and walked around so I could climb behind the wheel. He looked me over curiously, but tired.

"Well?"

"Happy fucking birthday to me."

"Did you?'

"No, but it was amazing."

"Good." His happiness for me came through wearily so. "Are we playing today?"

"No, we are getting drunk!"

His face widened, "Now *tha*t, is good news."

CHAPTER THIRTEEN

The high of having a romantic evening with the Raven floated me along a few days. By the time I felt withdrawal, and that she was in fact serious about never kissing me again, she showed up at Albertsons. I had just only had a couple of drinks and had a big pot of food lying in wait for when I could get no drunker; Stoph and I had our system down. With cheap vodka raised to my lips she appeared at my window.

"Startin' without me, eh?"

Her hair waved and curled down around her shoulders framing those narrow eyes as they peered out at my stunned expression.

"Did we have an appointment?"

"Get your dumb ass out here and give me a hug."

I stepped from the van and her into my arms but not before engulfing the vision of her long black margarita skirt that got to her hips ahead me. The top she wore with the skirt was usually dark and always an afterthought for me.

"I'm taking you for a ride."

We drove to her favorite liquor store on fourth near Pacific but that was closed so she settled for the one off Main. I followed her toward the door dragging my feet.

"Why don't you try walking instead of scuffling every where you go?"

"I'm pacing myself, sergeant."

She stood at the front door until I realized that she was waiting for me to open it. In that moment I held back, not because I was uncouth, I saw a power struggle afoot. This beautiful, dark bird held pretty much every card and I feared that I might be a patsy in the making. She obviously had just come from being wined and dined by some well to do sap, and was now slumming with art-boy. Of course that's all good and fine, I thought, but I could feel her well under my skin and decided that a physical example of aloofness would do me a practical service. I knew that she liked and respected me, but having been her friend over the last year, I also knew that she collected men, making boys of them all. We had crossed the threshold of platonic intrigue, even if we never kissed again I held out hope for more, and she understood that as yet another card in her deck. On top of that Donna had been a feminist who would just as soon hold a door for me as I her. I appreciated that about my ex-wife. Woman so often want it both ways, so I harbored some resentment on that issue. All this raced through my mind as I ambled for the door.

"Something wrong with your arm?"

Her eyes rolled, "Oh, a tough guy."

She opened the door, walked through making sure that it shut in my face.

I could feel the ice beneath my feet. Between her humor, knockout figure and love of words, falling painfully in love with her was perpetually a breath away. I had to protect myself. On the surface the fact that she was so very much out of my league along with her being a tremendous flake, a bit of a spoiled brat and also, thrown in for good measure, one who never failed to remind me that I was poor fat and poor, you would think all that enough to keep my sight clear. But then you never kissed her.

That night, like so many to come, was spent sitting in her car talking about how frustrated we were being who we were; making out with mouth and hands; telling stories old and new; re-canting our aforementioned frustrations in favor of reveling in our respective glory; and then back to making out. It was as if I had gone back to my high school years in some regards. Except this time I wasn't nervous. Being middle-aged you might think that making out was no longer sufficient. Again you have never kissed the Raven—or me for that matter.

"I just wish I could get my shit together. Being a house-sitter I see what they spend their money on and I know that they actually paid someone to design the whole look and theme, and I'm like, 'How do people get so rich with such awful taste?'"

"Either mommy and daddy, or because they have such awful taste."

"I had a great job designing the windows of high class Art-boutique once, and not just the windows but the gallery as well. A week or two into working there I realized that my keeping the job was based on sales. The pressure got to me and I quit. It was only a few years ago but I think I could handle it so much better now. Working at the restaurant and getting dog clients has really helped me with my verbal skills."

"Why not try it again?"

"Cause I'm full of shit."

"In my twenties, I managed the band: got the gigs, sent out the mailing lists and put some nice press-kits together. The sad part is that we hadn't got the music right yet and now that Chris and I have…I just don't have the stomach for the business side anymore."

"Now you're all stomach," she said patting my belly.

"Gee you're nice."

"I'm such a bitch. I don't know why."

So she went from riches to rags and fed me her leftovers. Well, sometimes. Mostly she'd put them in my lap and then after drinking her Champagne needed to eat something and ended up picking at whatever she gave me until it was gone.

"Oooh, my tummy's burning."

There goes what's left of the rack of lamb.

"You're too poor to appreciate something like this anyway," she consoled.

At the end of each night we'd park in Albertsons down the same row from the van and she'd lay her head on my shoulders taking up my hand in hers. I loved the way she squeezed my hand with a pulsing firmness. From one moment to the next the hands sat loosely intermingled before surging into a desperate grasp. It reminded me of the chill I'd get from contemplating death; shooting like a string-thin, raging river up and down my spine, then gone. I think in her mind she became overwhelmed by some loneliness or fear to the point of seeking comfort in the grip of my flesh. It could have been that she was falling for me too, but I tended not to indulge that theory for very long. I simply settled on gratitude for being the hand she wanted in hers, whatever the reasons. We'd sit quietly for an hour, sometimes more. Often she slept while my mind wandered and wondered. Even in her sleep her hand periodically tightened around mine. Intermittently her head rose as if I had called to her. I only had to kiss her forehead and she faded back down. For all my sexual tension and her flirtatious agendas it was in those clinches I remembered that she was a woman who never knew her father, and I a father who's daughter lived far away. A lot of elements went into creating what we were becoming, that played a part as much as any of them.

The promenade remained the focus of my life. It had to. The Raven would come and go, and I purposefully reminded myself that her most sincere intention was to one day never return. Besides, I didn't come all this way, leave all I had left, to fall in love. I had hoped for some sort of musical glory but had now settled into being an anomynous legend. The world may go by on a daily basis indifferent to my intentions but my intentions would be played out all the same. The dollars fell, not at a high rate, but they fell all the same, now and again some would have to stop to offer their love beyond monetary expression.

An old gentleman in his seventies planted himself firmly in front of us during one song smiling with his eyes closed. The song went on and on, he stayed on, listening intently, bowing and tilting rhythmically; his eyes, though covered by their lids, sank and heightened in their socket along with the songs arranged dynamics; the man lived the song as we did.

When we finished he slowly arrived from where we had sent him.

"I studied music." He spoke carefully. "I say this because I want you to know who you are talking to. I have conducted orchestras all over the country and I know music, I know what it is to be a musician; I know what takes to be one."

He paused to see that we accepted his words.

"Your arrangements, your execution; the interplay between your instruments and voices—you understand music at an extremely high level. I come out here a lot; I am old and don't have anywhere else to be. I see you boys and how much it means to you when you play."

He paused again, this time to catch his breath.

"I know you get all sorts of people saying all sorts of things; some good, some bad. Music was my life and I love hearing it in your hands."

"Thank you," we both said, hoping that something in our voices came through to express not only gratitude, but also the depth and belief we placed in his knowledge.

He put up his hand. "I thought you should know."

The old man walked away and we never saw him again. I say this now knowing that I could be romanticizing, but I remember seeing him around a lot before that day. It was as if he had picked that day to speak up because he knew there would not be another.

Around that same time (I think late September before my night with the Raven up in the canyons) Drifter resurfaced. I say resurfaced because the previous June a guy who referred to himself as Drifter approached me by our usual spot. I was waiting between sets on a Saturday with Angel. It could have been a Thursday, but I do know that Angel was there. He talked about being a guitar tech on some big time tours like Van Halen or something. He said that he loved Stopher and mine's act.

"When I'm not teching for the big boys I help put together some smaller shows. I gather the talent, offer 'em up to the money boys and then sign on as road manager. Would you and your partner be interested in something like that?"

Drifter looked like just that: dusty, road worn and pushed along by a cop in every county.

"That is what we hope for everyday that we come out here," I replied as honestly as possible. While I tried not to get excited I've seen enough movies to not be dismissive.

"Well I'll be back this way next September or October with something to offer you all."

"Unless that big record deal finally comes through, we'll be here."

...IN A VAN DOWN BY THE OCEAN

Sure enough Chris and I were finishing up our second set by the fruit-smoothie stand north Arizona and I saw a familiar face sitting on the curb smiling.

"You all remember me?"

Stopher hadn't been there so he did not.

"Actually I do," I said slowly, but not getting the name.

"Drifter," he said.

"Right, guitar tech/road manager extraordinaire."

"You boys looking for work?"

"Always."

"I got something for ya then."

"We have drummer who knows a few sets of our material?" I offered.

"Nah, it was you two that I seen and it's you all I'm hiring."

"You're the boss.

Drifter laid it out that we would meet a bus in Santa Barbara, do fourteen dates in roughly three weeks at rock/bluegrass festivals down the coast then up to Oregon, and we'd get $500 a night. All the details combined with him telling me way back in June that he'd be standing here in September with an offer had me convinced that he was for real.

"You got a fax number? If not we can go to a Kinko's, or some place like that."

"Steve?" I said to Chris.

"Or Sukey."

"Where are you headed now?"

"Well that sort of brings me to my next question." His voice dropped. "How do ya'll feel about acid?"

"We are very much for it."

"I got a whole liquid vile of some of the best stuff you are ever likely to come across. If you boys could help me run some errands and then take me over to 14Below, there's some friends of mine who do a Dead Tribute, I'd take real good care of ya."

"Let's go over to my friends first and see about that fax number then we'll take you wherever the hell you want."

A three-week tour that could open up all sorts of doors for us and free acid in one fell swoop; praise the lord!

Sukey gave us her fax and said that she'd keep an eye out for the contracts.

"They should be here within a couple of days."

"Not a problem.

We drove Drifter to a few places on Venice beach where he appeared to do some business pertaining to the liquid journey in his vile. At the last stop he came back to the van.

"I run into some prime bud here boys but I can't spend what I got. Seeings how I'm covering the trip," he shook the vile at us, "I was thinkin' you all could spring for the weed."

We gave him a twenty, he got the bud and we headed for the club.

As it turned out the acid was no good, or just plain water, he smoked most of the overly priced bud and we never heard from him again, by fax or otherwise. It seemed an awfully elaborate scam to get us to buy weed we got to smoke some of and give him a lift. At the club the whole band knew him, seemed excited to see him. We got in for free and the band was all right. I didn't even question that the fax would come, even Stoph felt confident, or it least hopeful. Steve seemed a little skeptical but not overtly. A few days came and nothing, then a week and then another. By then I had given up for the most part. It wasn't until the day we were supposed to be in Santa Barbara that I washed away the rest of my faint belief. He even gave us an exact date, November 8th

"If only we knew where the bus was going to be."

"There isn't a bus, Dave; there never was one. He was just some loser trying to feel big."

"I'll never believe anyone again."

"There ya go."

Dad offered this: "This offer was not for real—the next one will be."

I needed someone to say that, the fact that it was Dad helped even more. It was him saying, I believe in your talent; I believe in you.

Life went on, the promenade is where it went. I took solace in the fact that I didn't say anything about it to the Raven during the first week I waited on the fax. By the time I told her about it I talked much more reserved on the whole matter so when it didn't happen I looked less foolish in front of her.

It was right around then that Angel sent me a Dear John letter. I had been trying to think of a way to tell her about the Raven so when I read it I couldn't have been more relieved. Even when I was still in Chicago I wanted her to feel free to pursue anyone and anything, and had told her so. She wrote me that the long distance thing had become too much, that she had met someone she wanted to know better. She was sweet but a tad dramatic about it considering all I had said previously on the matter. Still she felt an obligation to me and I can understand that. I called her saying we were fine and that I would remain a good friend. I told her about the Raven, whom she had met, and she seemed impressed.

"Watch out for those hotties," she warned with a laugh.

"Oh I know it's just a passing fancy for her, but it's nice to be fancied at all."

So the promenade gave me a place to exhibit my wares, a chance to attract a rare bird, and a venue for delusional wannabes to color me their mark. It was also a street where they filmed a lot of commercials and various other projects ranging from school kids to professionals.

Steele, ever the street-musician's liaison, advised us early on, "They have permits to shoot, but they don't supercede your right to play, so cut yourself a profitable deal."

The first time a film crew asked us to move on I asked for a twenty and they jumped at it. Then my price went up to a hundred and they balked. I quickly settled at fifty. In the case of the college kids or rag-tag independent I requested only a tip; five or ten bucks. But in those cases they never asked me to move on, only to stop for ten minutes or so. Quite often they wanted to film us. A lot of performers had a strict rule about being filmed; I couldn't have cared less. "Gimme a buck, I'll be in your movie." I lost count of all the documentaries I might be in, or all the interviews we'd given to school papers, or independent publications. Like I've said, we'd achieved a bit of a celebrity status.

Some TV shows and movies have been shot on the promenade but they either shot inside or came out after midnight; no shake downs there for the little guy.

On October 20 I finished the cabbie story for the Raven:

By the time the last word came to terms with the notes final sound she had given the cab to the side of the road. Behind her eyes, tears boiled until they could no longer be contained; emotion won out.

"I'm sorry," he mumbled," I didn't mean to reveal you."

She laughed to the accompaniment of a salty waterfall. "You're not as bright as you sometimes sound," she commented through it all.

"I hear that a lot," he agreed.

"I'm not sad, I don't feel joy, and yet I'm crying." She paused. "I don't cry, I never have. Now I have all this unidentifiable emotion. I mean, I'm lousy with the stuff."

More tears fell over her words and she let them have the moment because they were going to take it anyway. Occasionally she laughed at herself if for no other reason than to show herself aware of the spectacle she had become.

He attempted to put the cause of her display in its case but she motioned to him to play more. He did. She cried in unison, sniffed to the beat and laughed on cue. After a time that knew little of hours or minutes and had no interest in seconds, all fell to a calm silence; she had nothing left.

"How do you feel?" he asked.

"Like a child that has been scared to the core; lost without knowing from where or whom; who is found by no one other than herself," she answered from an exhausted haze.

"And that feels?"

"Infuckingcredibly good! Refreshed and worn; ready to start again but...unsure if I had ever started before, and in the end, I don't care."

"But you're not hopelessly in love with me?"

"No, but I am grateful."

"For what?"

"You know."

"I think I do. I also think it's time that I go."

"I think you're right." She smiled.

He opened the door to find the rain gone and a warm breeze welcome him back to the evening air. His feet aimlessly took him down the road while his mind floated about himself and where he had been. Miles trampled beneath him as the sun crept upon the night, leaving the sky hinting at the coming day. It was then he stopped and found a tree in the middle of an open field all to itself as if to give the horizon the finger. He went to it, sat, removed his hat and scratched his head. Without warning his eye burned, his heart swelled, his knees shook, lips trembled and tears poured from him without pain and in no relation to thought. The tears had done the deciding, and it was they who would decide when to stop.

She pulled up in front of her house and sprang from the cab happily, then stopped. Peeking her head back inside through the front window, she looked at herself in the rearview mirror.

"One more year," she said cheerfully.

I look back at stories like this and wonder if I was making things up or making insightful guesses at the future, or romantic musings on the present. I won't tell you now how I was right or wrong because those terms are useless in translating these stories' worth. I will say that as I read them off the bent, crackly withered post cards and write them into the computer before me that I feel like a ghost walking through a house, unsure if I had ever lived there, but very certain that *it* is haunting me.

During the first week of November, instead of getting ready for our mini-tour with Drifter, I helped the Raven move into a rented room in a house. It was on Rose in Venice at the end of the block from the beach. The owner lived in the carriage house out back and rented out the main house's three bedrooms. She was to share the house with a gay guy named Will who seemed nice but a sloppy drunk, and a French woman who she immediately came to despise.

"I hate that Frenchie," Quoth the Raven.

She rented a twenty-five foot box truck when a large cargo van would have sufficed.

"More is more. Besides, the Macho Princess moves her stuff in trucks, not vans."

I drove; it felt good for me to show her how easily I could handle it. She knew from my stories that I had a class B, but I enjoyed showing off the skills of my past life. On top of that, as much as I never wanted to do it for a living, I too liked the macho visual of being seen behind the wheel of a truck.

Having spent the last year or so living in her phasar, she had all her excess property in storage at a friend's house, most of it clothing. Lots and lots of clothes. She did have a TV, filing cabinet, desk, lamps and couple of chairs as well. When we had the truck loaded, and she loaded with the better part of a bottle of white wine, she leapt from the curb into my arms, shouting, "PDA!"

I caught her and her mouth. Nothing had ever felt so right in my arms. (Yes, my daughter, my mother, yadayadyadyada; not the same thing at all.)

Her body slid down as we kissed until her feet touched the ground. The world went away taking all my fears and dreams with it. Yes she was beautiful, and Goddammit, she was hot. Something else though had to exist for me to feel the peace holding and kissing her gave me. Maybe I just wanted to believe that I had to have something more and she could have been any sexy nymph. But the fact remained that there was more to her in my eyes. We spent a year talking and laughing; I was not the one to be holding her by her own definitions. So at least on her end, something deeper was at hand. That alone could be enough for a man to love a woman, being valued for your inner worth, and that worth edging her on to set aside all that was not and probably never would be. She had always talked of superficial things and would continue to do so as time went on, but these were the arms of a poor, fat guy she jumped into—wildly talented, extremely funny and smart, with the prowess of a sexual dynamo to be sure, but fat and poor all the same. I will always give her credit for that.

"Thanks for helping."

"You are very welcome.

She stayed in my arms. "Squeeze me."

The Raven loved to be held hard.

"Higher."

I moved my arms up around her back just under the shoulders.

"More."

I flexed but still held back afraid of hurting her.

"More."

I gave more.

She grunted. "Yeah."

It got to the point where I could have been a man dangling from a beam at the top of an unfinished skyscraper with no help insight. No longer was any of my strength in reserve, her small, sturdy frame disappeared into me while holding her own. Then, crack-crack-crack.

"Did you hear that?"

I stood back, my hands sliding down to her waist. "I'm sorry, are you okay?"

"Yes, it felt great. Do it again."

She gave a tiny jump into me and squeezed as I smiled hard, giddy with giddiness. There wasn't any other crack but they were merely a fringe benefit of what we were after anyway. Her cheek slid up and back against mine until she settled her lips over mine.

"WE have fun, huh, baby?"

"Yeah, we do."

She stepped back and reached her hand down between my legs to firmly grab my cock.

"You're having a little too much fun."

I blushed.

"You're cute, baby."

I have moved furniture for a lot of friends and family in my life having good times along the way. This was better.

Like the promenade, the showers had come to feel as much mine as anyone else's, and like the promenade it had more than its share of annoying people. The Mouth beat them all. As his title might imply, the man talked and talked loud with absolute certainty on any subject. I don't remember seeing him until that second November but I could just have been blessed by the luck of timing. That luck ran out.

"On the road, once I'm back on the road sleeping in fine hotels with the fine women I'll be gathering from the clubs after my gigs, I won't give this place a second thought. The road cannot come soon enough;

I may never get off it this time. No more dragging my ass in these stalls with all your dirty asses; waiting while some dumb motherfucker cleans his underwear, or pots and pans or what have you. Look right there; brother they got mirrors and sinks out here, you don't need to be brushing your goddamm teeth and shaving your homeless face in the showers; people are waiting on you, son."

While I whole-heartedly agreed with him on the shower edict having vast amounts of room for improvement, listening to him speaking on any issue drained me. He had a piercing, tinny, nasal tone, yet contained a full body volume. For two weeks after I first saw him he ranted, from the moment he stepped through the door, all through waiting his turn, continuing on while he showered, up to and not at all ceasing upon being finished and dressed, about how the following Tuesday, then Thursday, on to Monday, back to Tuesday, how he was a memory waiting to happen in this Godforsaken town. The contempt that he held for all that passed through there, the town and the showers both, lifted at his wings. The man soared on disdain, fueled to the point where if one only listened to his words they would swear that he not once walked among those he belittled, that his home was not a red mid-seventies Volkswagen van, that he was there to shed his filth just like the rest of us.

Of course, like so many others who attended the showers, he lingered long after his obvious task was complete. Pacing back and forth, the Mouth spouted on about the newest conspiracy theory flying down the misinformation highway. Someone usually got suckered into a debate with him, and the Mouth charged back zealously self-assured.

"Do you watch the news? Do you even know how to read? This country is run by oil companies, they don't need a reason to do a single fucking thing."

"Yeah, but you just said-"

"I know what I'm talking about, I know what I've read; I bet you saw CNN last night, watching through the a storefront window not hearing a goddamm thing, and now you think you know something. That is the problem with you homeless rabble, you have no information, you stand there with your hands open and head empty waiting to swallow whatever they're giving."

The Mouth was not a big or an imposing figure; he stood a little short of my five ten frame; average build; not a pushover but no menacing threat. His light complexion did not betray his African-American heritage, his constant indignant rage colored him as black as coal, though he clearly saw himself as an intellectual. In fact he did come off as well read, and on occasion said things that made sense, but he was all over the map. What the CIA had been guilty of one day could be laid at the feet of Al Sharpton the next; the Mouth had no allegiances. What he had was the desire to speak and to be taken as an authority unquestioned. Much like the world leaders he berated on a daily basis.

The Mouth never went on the road and soon ceased mentioning it. My first guess at what he would have done on the road was being a stand-up comic. The fact that he came off as utterly humorless soon over took the opposing speculation that all his political pontifications might somehow be related to a Dennis Miller type of shtick. In the coming months he talked of working the clubs and private parties, and it became clear that he claimed to be a DJ.

"Don't be talking to me about some Raggedy Ann pussy you salvaged from the dump. I'm talking about some fine grade A tail that you couldn't afford to dream about."

I could not tell you one hundred percent that everything said, from partying with strippers to running a website that would earn him enough money retire at fifty, was all bullshit, I don't even want to. I like indulging varying versions where bits of truth get magnified into the glory he portrayed. I think he did know enough about computers to build some kind of website, porn probably. What kind of money he made was as clear as him showing up at the showers everyday. Maybe he did DJ at a strip joint or two in his day; he didn't get so much as a waitress's area code.

When it came to the showers I believed the Mexicans and that was it. First of all they never made any outlandish claims and rarely spoke English. Most of them arrived before the doors opened and headed out quickly to wait on the street corners by the lumber or masonry yards offering themselves up for cheap labor. Quite a few of them actually had jobs, some had homes, but they were so over crowded that it was easier to get in a morning shower at the park.

There was one guy who I couldn't stand because he sang. It was even worse when he sang while listening to something on his headphones; when he sang without them he was a little softer and didn't remember the words as well. I have never heard a cat being strangled, least of all in Spanish, but I imagine now that I might recognize it if I did.

Then there was Brenda and Susie. They took longer showers than women on their wedding days. Some of the guys guilty of taking too long were genuine nut jobs. They stood under the water shaking and mumbling as if trying to appease the voices in their head or drown them out. Other crazies were simply obsessive-compulsive washing their hands thirty times after each body part got theirs. In those cases I was certainly annoyed but took it a little better.

There was one guy who I thought was schizophrenic that stood under the water with his eyes closed as if listening to angels. He never had soap but he didn't smell bad either. For the first ten minutes he stood perfectly still, then he slowly stretched his arms and legs. Pretty soon he was well under way doing a full yoga workout in there. For months I had not seen him speak to anyone, figured him lost in his head. One day while waiting for food, I observed him speaking with someone. I didn't hear all of what was said but he was articulate, void of static. As I moved closer it became obvious that he was not at all crazy—just an asshole who did his yoga in the showers.

Susie had long, stringy, thinning, blonde hair and lived in dark blue late eighties Volkswagen. He showed up around eight always parking in the furthest corner from the showers. The man definitely saw himself apart from the rest. Brenda lived in a white Chevy, mid-eighties, and was tall, thin, but not boney. He had short brown hair, not quite full- not quite scraggily mustache and beard, and gave the impression of a blue collar working man who was good with his hands. Even the book wormish spectacles he wore did not detract from that. They both sauntered from their vehicles each morning with a sense of their own royalty. Susie hadn't worked in years, either living off a family fund, or a settlement of some kind but I'm guessing not social security like so many others. Brenda had the grease of work on him one day and white powder of drywall on him the next. Neither seemed to be druggies or alcoholics.

In the shower they stood in their respective stalls talking sports and cars along with some current events unless Brenda didn't show that morning. In that case Susie would volley back and forth with the Mouth. The Mouth, by then fully clothed, shouted from the drier side of the half-wall, while Susie sudsed and lathered taking whatever opposing view was at hand. On the days they found common ground the subject got immediately changed.

I bit my tongue most of the time but less as the years wore on. One day Brenda was berating someone for complaining at his taking so long.

"You got a problem?" he shouted from his stall next to mine.

The little Mexican who had spoken up backed down but Brenda had more steam to blow.

"I'm standing right here minding my own business. You should do the same!"

He went on for another five minutes, no closer to being done while I was finishing my shower up.

"You got a problem!" he shouted for the millionth time.

"Yes!" I answered. "We all have many problems. And yes, you number among them!"

"Whatta you gonna do about it?" He faced me.

"I can't make you be decent. I'm not going to do anything. You insisted on asking over and over again if there was a problem, now you have your answer. We all have a problem, okay." I stood squarely in front of him not wanting a fight but unafraid of anything he might do.

"That's what I thought you'd do, nothing."

He went back to his stall victoriously taking his sweet ass time as he always would. But at least he shut up about it.

Poor Martin, the elderly Irish saint who brought food to the park two mornings a week, he too had his ear opened and gutted by the Mouth's tenacious appetite for attention. The man came to feed bellies and left with an earful of one man's diatribe on the governments assault on the poor, or the Third World's plans of global domination. What you have to understand is that agreeing with the Mouth's general stance on a given day doesn't make listening to him any easier. Agreeing with him made the Mouth uneasy at first, caught him a little off guard, but he'd muddle through by changing the subject or going on as if you had yet to fully comprehend what you thought you understood. When he was argued with or his data doubted, a litany of source documents and references were implemented at will; when he found someone siding with him he went through the same process but with a perpetual double-take look attached to his face talking even louder, his nasal passage sounding even more narrow.

The short Pakistani man remained silent at all times. Years later I did catch him talking to himself but mostly in mumbles, definitely in English, but mumbled English. He wore the same blue and white-checkered jacket and white soft-domed baseball cap every day, though neither was particularly clean they never appeared to get any dirtier than the first day I saw him. The man meticulously brushed his teeth and shaved with same ceremony. In the showers he took his time and cleaned his underwear as if squatting by a river in a time only written about. After 9/11 I kept waiting for someone to attack him out of some misplaced patriotism, but no one ever did—not even verbally. Mark one for humanity.

Like a lot of people in the showers he came prepared with an ample supply of newspaper. Most used it to keep their newly cleaned feet off the mold-infested floor while they dried themselves. I did it as well in the beginning but after a couple of months saw it as kind of silly and pointless. (I did start wearing flip-flops during the second year; Chris still uses newspaper.) Mr. Pakistan not only laid it out under his feet before disrobing but also on the bench to protect his bags from people's asses. He stood patiently holding his things until the proper amount of space became available to aptly spread his things out in the manner he deemed civil. He annoyed me to no one end, but then pretty much everyone did.

There was one time early on that I do remember him talking. It was to the black G.I. Joe who came in every morning to shave his head. I am certain that he showered once in a while but I can't envision it now, he always had a hearty stench to him; his clothes were in perfect order, even looked ironed, but he smelled terrible. Joe was one of those men who carried the American flag in his eyes. I don't know that he actually served in the armed forces but I feel certain that he at least tried. To me, insanity would be a prerequisite, but my guess is that the boys in green draw the line at schizophrenia. "Uncle Sam is the only voice we want you hearing around here, boy!" His shoes and belt buckles shined as did his deeply rich brown head.

One day as Joe set down his things on the bench in symmetrically formed stacks, Mr. Pakistan observed him with a keen interest. Finally he spoke.

"You and I are like same."

Joe did not look up.

The older man in his fifties approached the young one not yet thirty.

"You like me."

"I like me." Joe held back his eyes.

Mr. Pakistan seemed a tad entranced. He approached no further nor did he retreat. He remained, staring almost fondly with a hint of curiosity. I remember thinking, and this was before 9/11, that Middle Eastern men, homeless or not, had their own best interest in hand when they sought out anonymity. Up to this point, other than cleaning his underwear in the shower, he had achieved that nicely. Striking up conversations with young, clearly mentally challenged, men dressed in military garb, was going the wrong way.

"Stop looking at me." Joe did not remove his stoic stare from the neatly arranged items stacked beneath him. He had long since finished but continued to eye them as if a better form could be attained.

"You do not understand," the elder man smiled hopefully and reached out a hand.

Joe slapped at it and stepped into him. "You and I have nothing in common. I am nothing like you; you are not like me. Leave me alone."

"Yes we are very much the same, not like these," he said indicating the rest of those present with his hand. "You and I are not like them."

"I done told you, I done told you," Joe's eyes fired up than receded instantly to their usual cold distance. He returned to his things, collected his cream and razor, then went to stand in line for the mirror.

Mr. Pakistan went to follow when Surfer Burn-Boy intervened.

"I think you best let him be."

Mr. Pakistan looked deeply into him in attempt to convince Burn-boy how little he grasped of the situation. He stood silently communicating, then returned to his own daily tasks and never spoke to anyone again.

The two men were both victims to voices, anal retentive and homeless, but I don't think Mr. Pakistan was on about anything so surfaced or obvious. He saw something, felt something and came close to getting his butt kicked over it. For the next week or two I wanted to ask him about it, then never thought about it again until now. Today he is just another guy whom annoys me as he stands in front of the mirror with one hand at the back of his waist as he brushes profusely while his shirtless, small, round, hairy belly protrudes out over his belt. On that day I got curious about him because he seemed so very certain of the importance that he and the young G.I. confess their connection.

Surfer Burn-Boy was one of those guys that belonged to a place. For him that place was the showers. I saw on my first day there he was well aware that he was where he belonged. He wore a seashell necklace and banana-yellow shorts that screamed surfer, but he had a soft Texan accent. His body had pink scarring all up and down his body that I assumed were from burns. I got couple of those and although mine were thicker and rougher I deemed them close enough to come from similar events, so Stoph and I dubbed him Surfer Burn-Boy. (I learned in time that he had some sort of rare skin condition but by then the title Stoph and I dubbed him with had been ingrained.) He had a healthy attitude spurred on by a sunny disposition. He seemed the kind of fellow that couldn't be where he didn't want to be so he'd find a way to want to be where he was. Each morning he managed to be able to afford a few tallboy beers. He talked about having work to be at that always involved something being cleaned up. A lot of guys talked about a lot of things, the Mouth being the loudest and best at it, but Burn-Boy's talk was permanently grounded; I had no trouble believing what he said. Of course none of it was said to me because I wanted nothing to do with any of them; get cleaned-get out.

Walking into the showers was like walking into any corner bar, full of talk and bullshit. Men need to talk and pretend someone's listening and that is easier when there's a bunch of bodies mulling about the room. Even the homeless need a social club.

Chris and I became permanent fixtures at the sunsets that second year where Hollister Ave. met the ocean. Since we rarely played nights we were there pretty much every Sunday through Thursday. After the time fell back the sun fell around five-and would bottom out around four-thirtish before the days started getting longer again. Watching the sun set into the ocean was something I only saw in movies growing up in the Midwest. It held magic as far as I was concerned—walking off the blacktop of the lot, over the bike path's cement and on to the sand down to the shore—the colors that the sky offered ranged from pinks and burnt oranges to misty grays and white lined blues that all meshed into night by the sun's final withdraw. Along the way purple hues got discussed, but not every night. Stopher and I stood listening to the music of the rising waves that crashed at our feet dwindled into shadows of their former selves. Sometimes we talked, others we said nothing, instead standing separately together except for the times one of us would drift off along the shore. The sky appropriately commented day in and out on the remarkableness of our journey. From the sand one looked up into it feeling life; knowing death; beauty wrapped itself around the mundane; eyes where shouted at while the ocean said, shhh.

One night, not long after my fantasy night up in the mountains with the Raven, I along with Stopher and Earnest leaned on the fence that divided the temporary lot from the long-term parking. I was full on my recent glory and the sky supplied his, and we all had glory in the form of a plastic water bottle that held water not. Well, the sky didn't, but the three men beneath it did. (I had buzzes on top of buzzes.)

"You boys going to be making your nightly pilgrimage down to the shore?" Ernest inquired.

"You know that we will," I said.

"It is still so new to us," Stopher added.

"I love you guys. You're the only ones that I can really talk to about literature and music. Everyone else I know are tweakers and gear heads. You two…you guys walk down to the shore for the sunset."

"We're still caught up in novelty of it all."

"I beg to differ," Earnest shot back at Stopher at once. "You are artists through and through; don't ever change."

"I don't think that's possible anymore."

Earnest looked at me, then Stopher and shook his head. "I love you guys."

With that Earnest put his palms firmly down on the waist high fence—to his taller frame—and jumped it clean. I, feeling aglow with my current stature in life as a man of art that attracts fascinatingly, beautiful women, forgot in that moment that I had become a fat middle-age man that, while reaching many heights by way of the soul, his body could not soar along side in any literal sense. I had enough sense at my disposal to know that I could not, even when I was in better shape, hop the fence in the gazelle like fashion of Earnest. The fence rose above my waist just over my belly-button, so I pushed palms down as I jumped with feet, purposely falling forward, reaching with my right hand down the fence's other side, and with a tug, pulled the rest of me over in a swooshing flip that ended in a dull thud. I did land on my feet and actually succeeded in what I had set out to do. Although somewhere between my swooshing and thudding I felt a tear in my left heel.

I was able to hobble to the shore where Earnest joined us, as he usually did not. We didn't stay long as there was smoking to do in the van. In social situations such as this Stoph sat in the driver's seat, our guest rode shotgun, and I crawled in the back up to my bed. I put my right knee up, gripped the inside of the doors with my hands and pushed off the ground with the left foot. Now I had done this on several occasions void of self-mutilation. Apparently whatever damage had been done to my heel flipping over the fence lied in wait for my next stupefying gesture. I pushed off and this time not only did I feel a tear, I heard it. It hurt a little at the time but the next day after the liquor no longer traversed my blood, I realized the full extent of the injury. For the next two months I had a severe limp that begrudgingly got better over the next six.

The next time I saw the Raven I could hear what she thought. "Add crippled to broke, fat and drunk."

I had another physical reoccurring ailment to contend with. My voice. Throughout my twenties and into my thirties my voice would periodically shut down. Living in winter places my whole life I chalked it up to colds and the like. In my late twenties I started getting allergic reactions from the spring and fall changes that resulted in sinus headaches and some throat problems. Of course a life of drinking cheap booze and smoking pot didn't help. I would later come to find that switching to vodka from bourbon made it much worse. On top of all that I was now singing four hours a day five days a week for the last year. Two of those hours was singing back up for Stoph but it all added up. So there were sets where I couldn't sing certain challenging songs, like the bridge in TINY DANCER, Floyd's TIME and the Sam Cook (Sam didn't actually write that one—forget who did—but Sam really did own that sucker) song that I did. I also took huge chunks of sets off leaving the majority of the lead vocal work to Stopher. That didn't happen much the first year but during the next two it would get worse. The few times when we did three two hour sets in a day to get work in with Earnest proved disastrous to my throat taking a couple of weeks to fully recover from.

The Raven came by more and more but always singing the same song.

"You're not my boyfriend; couch potatoes need not apply."

"I don't even own a couch."

"David, I'm an active person, I like to go running and hiking."

"Bring it on, well the hiking anyway; my knees are probably retired from the running."

"All I am say-"

"Look, lady, don't let the pile of flesh fool ya, I'm a jock and I'll keep up. Trust me."

"I want to go places that I can't afford; sailing, I wanna learn how to scuba dive, go back to Europe. Ya got nothing, Dave. You got less than nothing."

"Nope. You are right about that, I got nothing and lots of it. That is unless you count the shit loads of talent in my fingers and at the tip of my tongue. Oh, and all that wit, humor and smoldering sex appeal."

"You are cute, baby."

"You do what you want, sweets; you know where to find me."

If I had a dollar for every time she insisted that we have that conversation I'd have enough money to buy all the things she wanted. It took me a while to figure out that she kept us going over that same ground to keep her from forgetting to remind herself not to fall for me.

"Don't fall in love with me," she warned.

"I am sincerely trying, kid."

Still she came by the van unfulfilled by the night's previous companion and off we'd drive in search of a dark street, alley back way or empty lot to park. The kisses became more inflamed while the hands traveled more intently, but our clothes stayed on—ajar and tattered, but on. One night I made the mistake of confessing that having my nipples caressed drove me wild. Like Bluebeard's mistress she had to see what that entailed. I did my best to contain the passion that arose within me but she pushed too far, too often, for too long. Actually it only took a couple of minutes for me to lunge from my seat, over the gear-shit and wrap her up within me under deep throaty kisses and flexed fingers on hands that sought the truth of her matter: How could you, why would you light a keg of dynamite unless you want to see it explode? Of course I stuck to the practice of keeping her clothes on but her shirt came up and my mouth found her firm honey brown breasts.

I spent as much passion as I could while remembering that she had yet to offer me anymore than I had been getting, so after the initial frenzy had been served I retreated.

"Sorry."

"It's okay."

"Well, now you what it does."

"I was a little scared there for a moment."

"I would never do anything that you didn't want me to. Please believe that."

"I do, it's just that you were so…"

"Yeah I was."

"That kiss was like mouths fucking."

"Really? That is so sweet of you to say."

Soon she would cut straight to the chase and drop a card in my bucket during our noon set telling me that she wanted to see me that night. She held to her freedom to go with anyone she pleased but indulged it less and less. Part of that was my getting deeper into her blood and part of it was because she needed help organizing her new place. A project that would require attention over the next few years. The notes in my bucket came to include cries for help, whether working on her apartment, getting her car in or out of the mechanic's shop, or helping her keep appointments with dogs. My favorite notes were like this one:

Save it 4 later…Dave,
I mean it! I think I may have to BUY yer
Last set out from under you so I
Don't get leftovers 2nite.

Sometimes I'd have to take a ten or twenty from her because she knew that if I sang a second set on the promenade that I'd have no voice left to sing for her and if I didn't sing a second set on the street I wouldn't have any money for mine and Stoph's dinner or the van's tank. At first I felt bad about it but came to realize that she preferred the business aspect of it; keep things nice and professional like; a man paid for his time is a man held at an emotional distance; no love affair lifting off here, folks, just money exchanged for services rendered.

On those nights we'd find an isolated spot on the darkened beach or the park if not too cold. Coco played excited witness on quite a few excursions, wrapping her leash around our already entangled bodies and ole blue to boot, trying to win back some of the attention. The house she lived in was often empty from seven to midnight or, at worst, Will, would be around but mostly stayed up on the second floor. The main floor had an entertainment room at the front with a door closing it off from the rest of the house. It used to be a part of the front porch but now was walled up into an extra room. The room was a small rectangle with a couch at one end and shelf holding a stereo and TV on the opposing one.

The Raven set up candles on pieces of marble she took from her room, some on the floor a few on the windowsills. Two of the marble pieces were a foot and a half squared while the others were jagged fragments just big enough absorb the melting wax; the large pieces, white swirling in gray; the smaller ones a somber red with what could have been a swirling form of green.

Indoors I usually brought the Martin while outdoor serenades were left to ole blue. The Raven liked ole blue more, it's color went better with my eyes and the strap that went with it had a sort of red and black Native American thing going that pleased her as well. In time no matter where we were at I brought along ole blue. The house had cats so Coco rarely, if ever, joined us there.

I have had the women in my life like hearing me play but the novelty wore off, as did my other charms. Donna genuinely seemed to love my music but that did not last. Once when we were trying to sort out what was wrong with our marriage she said:

"You don't to play for me any more."

"You got that backwards; you stopped listening a long time ago."

And that was the truth.

The Raven heard me sing two hours a day for over a year now and was getting greedy for more. Sure, it wasn't every day but it was more than anyone had ever put up with before. Of course some of it was based on an emotional connection to both Stoph and I, then eventually a growing physical one between she and I. Everything that grew between us started out from her love of words and music, our words and music filling that need better than anyone else that came along. She had other favorites like Mel and James, Los Pinguias and a few others, but she'd be the first to admit that we were the ones she missed the most when our schedules did not align.

No one else got these notes:

You guys are great! RE: Please play for me later?
You made a shitty day a good day.

Yes it was more than the songs we played, it was the jokes we made on stage, it was how she liked to joke along, it was who we were, it was who she was, it was us getting her and her getting us.

Chris and I broke into our musical exchange called The Game where we break out of familiar patterns and ignore keys trying to create an unusual dialogue between the two guitars. When it worked it was Coltrane or Monk good, when it didn't it was still brave and interesting. The Raven hated The Game and often frowned when we went into it.

When we finished one that pleased Stopher and myself she shouted from her perch:

"I dissonant like that."

Apt wordplay; what's not to love about that? (I was in a band called Apt Wordplay—Bob Dylan)

Just as she went from going out to dinner with money bags then slumming it with me afterwards, to dropping me notes of planned events between us, the very next week I wouldn't see her off the promenade at all. That pattern played out again and again over the years: a few weeks inseparable, ten days apart. We'd share pained glances on the promenade during the days apart, then a joke or two through two hours of music. Ultimately I'd get this note:

Boys,
Too many distractions from R&R. And that's all have to say about that!
(Miss you) Can we hang out Mon. or Tues.?

From the bottom line she drew a cartoon voice bubble and planted a big lipstick kiss in the middle of it.

It had only been a month or so since our night up the canyon, I couldn't have been more like a yo yo on a string. As much as I thought myself just another guy she kept in the wings, one that pertained to a specific fancy she indulged with me when it needed indulging, I couldn't help but sense a real bond building between us, that I was special, maybe even more important than any of the others.

The night she took me to see MOULIN ROUGE encouraged the latter. First of all she had seen it before and found intensely romantic, dramatically sensual.

"It's ridiculously romantic just like us," she said to me as we walked from the car.

As we got near the theater, which was on the promenade, she pushed a twenty in my hands and dashed off saying, "I'll meet you inside."

She didn't want to be seen going into the movies with me. That momentarily had me stumbling into the above former category of just being another guy. I said something about it inside. "Don't want to be seen socializing with the help?"

"I don't like people knowing my business. Especially people where I work."

I didn't quite buy it but let it dangle.

I did love the movie, which I did not expect too. I generally find that movies like THE ENGLISH PATIENT portray love on too surfaced a level. They say, "These two people are soul mates," and I have to just go along. I assumed MOULIN ROUGE would be like that and on some level it was, but with all the music and costumes of a surreal world it allowed me to more easily swallow the pill. Having the Raven at my side with her hand in mine, head on my shoulder, helped me to open myself up to the experience. We even made out a little during the movie which I hadn't done much of in my life.

After the movie we walked out on to Arizona Avenue towards Second Street and she forgot to worry about being seen. She leaned into me leisurely as we ambled around the next corner talking about the movie. She steered me into the courtyard of a brownstone where we walked up to the doorway and kissed. Our noses were cold, tickling each other's cheeks and we let them. My nose was a bit runny and it ran on to her cheek.

"Sorry." I stepped back and turned away to wipe my nose. It had been running a lot lately so I had some napkins with me. "Another benefit from living in a van, I guess."

"It snots so bad."
"Okay, I think I'm ready for more."
"Snot now, maybe later."
"You already did that bit."
"I'm a pretty girl; I'm allowed some repetition."
"Yes, dear."
"One of my Alternates is always telling me how quick I am but he isn't very funny himself."
"What's he do."
"Stockbroker. He's my New York friend; smart guy who makes a ton of money but-"
"Smart and quick is different."
"Yeah. See I spend time with these dolts and my wit gets dull from not being tested."
"Enter fat guys in a van."
"Exactly."
"So are any of your Alternates funny?"
"One or two, but not like you and your brother. Sometimes I like to watch you two talk about anything. It's like watching TV."
"So how many boys or Alternates to you have at your mercy? Currently."
"Oh, four or five. Five."
"And am I one of the five."
"Na, you're a Staple."
"How many of those do you have?"
"You can only have one Staple. The next step after that is boyfriend, and then all the Alternates get cut loose."
"A Staple, huh?"
"Don't be gettin' any ideas. Staples that live in vans with no future never make it to boyfriend. Sooner or later I'll find an Alternate to make Staple, then you'll get demoted down to being one of my boys."
"No." My voice dropped any hint of humor. "I won't ever be one of your boys, Alternate, and I'm not your Staple: I'm me." I paused, then gently put my hands on her shoulders. "Don't ever refer to me as one of your boys, to anyone: one of your boys, friends, or your mother. If

you talk about me at all have enough respect to not group me in with the others. Even if that's what you think of me."

"Oh, darlin', I don't think that about you; we're friends, best friends; family."

"I don't want to be your brother."

"How about kissing cousins?"

"Well, it is a start."

The next week we set about painting her room. Something we should have done before moving in all of her stuff; the walls had problems breathing. We started by moving everything to the center of the room and throwing a plastic tarp over it. I should say that I started by doing those things while she searched out the right motivational music and popped open a bottle of wine. We barely had room enough to maneuver but we managed. That was the night she turned me on to Jimmy Smith, the great jazz Hammond organ player. I had faintly heard of him, no doubt caught some of his music listening to the jazz my Dad would have going on the radio in the kitchen growing up, or in the van since I had arrived. The Raven had a best of CD, we listened to it over and over the next few nights as we sanded and painted the walls and trim, and then tried to make the room look less like an inadequate storage facility. She also played some old time, blues guys singing dirty, old time, lyrics on to a scratchy piece of vinyl that retained purposefully every scratch in its transfer to CD. Songs with lyrics like:

I'm the cock of the walk, baby
So walk them chicken feet on over here.

"That's nasty, huh, baby?" the Raven called from where she kneeled painting.

I loved her playful side, the way she held the line of adult themes over and throughout a child's glee. Working with her was a lot like play-acting: In one scene we were the friends on the verge of a kiss while moving furniture out of a house into a truck; in the next we were the comfortable couple (although she went out of her way to say we were not) painting up the new apartment to begin our lives; and of course all along the way I had this fatherly warmth that took pride in her every clever remark, that wanted to heal whatever disappointment she suffered.

The work could also be absolutely frustrating. The Raven had not exaggerated her ADHD (Attention Deficiency Hyper Disorder—the Hyper not being at all a superfluous addition.) When we were getting ready to paint by moving boxes around she would open one and start looking through it.

"I have such cool shit."

"Can I set this out in the other room?"

No response.

"Ray?"

"Oooh, I forgot I even had this."

"RAY!"

"What?"

She'd wake up from her revelry trance unaware that she had gone away. Or she returned pissed that I had the gall to intervene.

Before we could paint she had to have the right music to set the tone. Soon she'd have her past life call to her through the songs that played soundtrack to a moment that she had forgotten about.

"I have a deliciously short memory," she often explained.

But that was a double-edged sword she seldom remembered the downside of. According to her it meant that she could enjoy repeated readings of an article she liked, or viewings of movies. It also aided her in moving on from boy to boy because it is hard to be attached to something you don't remember much of. She also had a habit of not finishing any book she loved reading because then, in her mind it wasn't over.

"Yeah, because you're not reading it."

"But it is there, forever waiting."

"Because you'll never read it."

"I like knowing it's there."

That is not so much related to her ADHD but it feels like a cousin to me. I do understand what she means about not finishing something that you don't want to end. A little.

"But everything does end, and your not reading it is just another version of it ending."

"But I didn't read the ending, how can it have ended?"

"You having not read the ending doesn't keep the experience from ending if you're not reading it."

"I'm corn-fused."

"It's a matter of choice, I guess."

"I choose bliss."

When you showed herself to her the Raven had a good habit of not running or building a wall of denial. She knew that she was ridiculous, she saw how far she wasn't getting and never doubted herself a spoiled, pain in the ass. She just knew that she was worth it. Yeah she was.

The most frustration I suffered during my marriage was having Donna be caught in the act of being a bitch, or unreasonable, or lying, or anything and she would either completely change the subject by bringing up an old argument or look blankly into my eyes and confess utter bewilderment as to what I was talking about. The Raven had no delusions of being the smartest or the most altruistic person in the room. In fact she regaled in her vampness.

On occasion I'd say, "It's not something to brag about."

Her answer came in the form of narrowing her almond eyes into a penetrating, entrancing glare while enticingly rolling her tongue across her upper lip.

"Point taken."

Another growing bit between us that started with her tugging at our beards, or giving Stoph and I running body slams, was her slapping me around.

In our early unromantic days on the promenade she greeted us by tugging at our beards affectionately, but not without inflicting pain. At the park when we were standing around the benches or outside the van, then later down by the sunset, she would sneak up on us with a running body slam to our side or back. Usually one of us saw her, thereby leaving the other with their back to her approach. Lifting a finger to her lips that also indicated playful eyes, the one who observed her was pretty much helpless to speak up. She got so much joy out of it and that gave joy to Stopher and I both. Being physical in her tomboy way was how she expressed her love to us. Plus she liked being one of the boys; in her mind this was how boys played.

As our romance bloomed, although she continued to categorically deny that it had, she took to slapping me. Hard. I instantly understood it. I absolutely loved it. There was actually a quick conversation in my mind about it:

"She thinks she can push you around."
"She just likes to be physical."
"She wants to belittle you."
"She simply likes the dramatics of it."
"SHE IS TRYING TO SEE HOW FAR SHE CAN PUSH YOU!"
"She only wants to make things more exciting."
"She wants to dominate you into a subservient role."
"Really? That sounds kind of sexy."
"You want to be dominated by a woman?"
"That woman? Fuck yeah!"

All of the thoughts flew through me the first time she did it. The fact that she kissed me firm and hard right after it, then slapped me again and kissed me even longer and harder still, made the conversation somewhat moot at the moment.

But I did think about it at a greater length laying in my bed one night. I decided that every single statement could be true, the positive and negative. At the heart of it all what struck me most was how much *I* liked it, what *I* got out of it. Secondly I believed that it was not an issue of respect. She didn't slap because she had no respect for me or in any attempt to rob me of my dignity—a petty theft at best. The actual truth laid quite contrarily: The desire to slap me and the comfort level that allowed her to do so freely spoke to our kindred spirits more than one's superiority over another. Yet I do admit that her insatiable appetite for control fed her motives in how she treated men, or her boys. The Raven's inner world chaotically unfolded from one incomplete thought to the next, while the outside one tugged her by the tick of a clock she couldn't read fast enough to keep up. With men she relished the one arena where she could make the rules, set the clock, then change it when the time failed to suit her.

Did I mention that I liked it?

I had been married, raised a child, had assorted heartaches and disappointments; loved and lost; failed myself and others; and somehow grew up into a man. I kept telling myself that it was too soon to be falling in love. Sure, I had known her for over a year but we had only been romantic for less than two months. On top of that she was a judgmental, spoiled brat. I allowed myself the infatuation with all its chest swelling and mind racing fantasies, but convinced love to lay low, calling caressingly from an intimate distance.

CHAPTER FOURTEEN

Chris had gotten food stamps a few months back, and a couple of hundred bucks in financial aid from the state of California to boot. We blew the money void of frugality, chalk full of haste. The money was a one-time gift while the stamps were promised for three months at one hundred and thirty a pop. By the end of November they would run out and then I would apply to get another three months. So I went down to the Rio Rancho office on Pico a little east of Sepulveda and waited with the rest of the leeches. I say that and it sounds callous, I know. For myself, I looked at it like a government grant, to further my work. My Aunt Dorothy and her troupe back in Providence lived off the things. Of course they worked with inner-city kids and taught classes for the betterment of the community, but in our way so did Stoph and I. We didn't teach classes but we gave something of worth to the community. The others in the chairs of the Rio Rancho offices, sitting in the rows, standing in various lines, had their own stories. I know some were doing their best to get by while others did all they could to get away with as much as they could. The older I get the less interest I have in sorting through who is deserving or not of whatever is it at hand. Is the bucket empty? No? Well let's all get in line in an orderly fashion and see if there is enough to go around. When the rich no longer have big homes, several cars and more servants than family members we'll revise the discussion.

I sat half listening to the names droning from the overhead speakers trusting my brain to tell my ears when mine the speakers spewed. I first wrote a letter to dear old friend from my grammar and high school days. Linda and I played opposite leads in a production of MY FAIR LADY.

In high school we remained casual friends but at a Halloween party I discovered that she had a crush on me. The attraction wasn't there for me but I thought her great: a smart, funny broad of the highest order. We ended up fooling around; one thing led to another and we went to the senior prom together. I had already quit high school by then but she really wanted to share the night with me. Yes, that was when we both lost our virginity. She knew that even if there had been a mutual attraction our lives were going in different directions. She would go off to college out of state while I was already hell bent on a life of rock-n-roll. Her collegiate career led her on a traditionally defined path that served her well professionally and we all know what became of me.

Linda did me the greatest favor by making that prom night happen. It was a relief to get the sexual conquest burden off of me but neither of us knew what we were doing. The real fun came earlier at the dance where we stole the show on the floor and shined as the fabulous performing duo we were. Giving her my virginity was as right a thing as I have ever done in my life. It was as clumsy as it was beautiful, as illuminating as it had remained a mystery.

The years went by and she stayed in touch. I attended her wedding with Donna, Linda she saved me a few dances. Again the floor belonged to us.

She always wrote me on my birthday and I would get her form Christmas letter as well. It always took a month or so, but I wrote back every time. No, I never bothered to learn her birth date because I am an asshole. She had been the one to pursue me as kids so it seemed appropriate (in a self-centered way) that this came to be the way we stayed in touch.

That was the year she told me about her marriage falling apart and how she feared for the well being of her two kids; she feared them scarred for life. I told her that scarring the ones we love is what people do best and most often. I offered up experiences to make her feel less alone in her guilt, and my love to make her feel less alone. I sat there waiting in the pool of financial miseries of humanity with our collective hands out and thought how hard it all is for everyone, in everything.

I told her about the Raven, how I felt myself slipping into that dangerous territory where the heart and flesh pool their efforts to convince me that practical worlds can be overcome; that romance on a foundation of true love between friends who have the hots for each other can set aside reservations rising one above contradictory motives or aspirations. The words, "I'm in love with her," did not find the page but as I read back the words that did, I suspected that they might as well have.

In conversations with Stopher I avoided the words too, but I was becoming more and more aware that the truth of the matter spoke for itself, that I was on the verge of being in some deep shit. The Raven had been clear from the outset: We were having fun and nothing more. Her favorite phrase was, "I appreciate you." (Like a good wine, I thought.) She was at play and I was the game, she danced on a tune I played from my station as the dirt nourishing the tulips. Still, beyond that, something was going on. I had done my share of unrequited pining in my life as a youth but had grown into the kind of man whose ego had to be served in order for interest to be held. As much as she tried to paint the picture of a casual embrace I knew in my blood that something was happening to her, under her skin, within her blood.

I also knew that those thoughts were not ones to be indulged. I had to assume the worst, I had to get myself, on some level, to believe that I would never be more than another one of her boys. I didn't want her saying it or even thinking it, and I really couldn't buy it myself, but needed a counter weight to how hard I was falling.

After my letter to Linda I wrote this:

Feel for flight
eyes closed head back
Dig in—let go

Love is not in the knowing
Cause ya don't
Ya think
Ya believe
Ya hope

Feel for flight
Arms spread faith in tact
Help yourself—float don't ask

Crashing awaits your future
It is what it is
what was
what does
Because?

You wanted to fly
You wanted to love

"Let's make chicken soup," the Raven declared.

I sat riding in her car watching the night fly by her window along with early evening traffic.

"Okay."

Daylight had no voice by the five o'clock hour so the night gave us time for such undertakings as soup would require.

The house on Rose was empty for all intents and purposes. Will could be heard rummaging about upstairs but seeing him would be momentary at best. We unloaded the bags on the spacious counter that centered the roomy kitchen. (I love a good kitchen.) Once she had found the pot and cutting board I went to work.

"I like cooking, but I love being cooked for," the Raven said mischievously. (The woman could make mischievousness out of a solemn prayer.) "There is something about soup that says, 'Welcome home, soldier'."

I cut the carrots and smiled.

"I was dating this guy once, and I was sick, and he brought me over a can of soup. 'That's not soup,' I said, 'that's an insult.' He didn't last long."

"I should say not."

"You're making fun of me, huh, baby?"

"Yes, dear."

She took me by the shoulder and turned me toward her to give me a slap and a kiss. She lingered for a moment in my one arm while taking note of the knife dangling at my side. Her hand slid down that arm on to the hand then over the blade. Her mouth moved slowly toward mine as she lifted the knife, still in my hand, placed it between our chests, and in the name of all that is sultry, kissed me again, and I her. Our motion rolled like silent waves as we pressed deeper and deeper into each other, feeling the metal cool on the other's skin through our clothes. My free hand took in the terrain of her back and caressed the curve of her sumptuous ass. Falling in love or not, this was fun.

She pulled back and her eyes shone what I had sensed in her blood. In that moment I had no questions of my worth to her. If I was a toy, then I played with her as much as she did me.

The Raven gave my cheek a half slap that betrayed the intensity in her face; almost an anger. In that instant it seemed she became aware that her footing was not what it should be and that her assumed upper hand had turned over. Suddenly her teeth lunged at my jaw and dug in, enjoying the bone. I dropped the knife and surrounded her with my arms in attempt own her; I couldn't get close enough to her. She gnawed at both sides of my face while my hands traversed in a quest to understand every rise and fall that her body offered; up the middle back to blade's of her shoulders; down to feel the bones of her hips thrusting against me; from the downward slope of her ass, as formed by her tight, gray skirt, to dig into her hamstrings flexing and pulsing as she rose on to the tips of her toes to better consume my face; then around to the thighs where I slid one hand to their inners, while not plunging to where I so wanted to plunge all that I was; the other hand returned to her most wondrous ass to aid the exploration of aforementioned thighs. Again I could not get close enough.

She soon took my hands and placed them on her ribs and without being told I knew that she wanted me to clutch them free of her breath. Her hands wrapped themselves around my waist to give her leverage in converging our loins to better feel what the other offered, to get a hint of a taste.

As suddenly as it erupted she pulled away looking immediately, and of course purposefully, as if nothing had transpired.

"Cook my soup, bitch," she said with an indifference that held an underlying menace.

"Yes, dear."

About ten minutes later I heard Jackson Browne's, LATE FOR THE SKY being played by Will upstairs. The Raven took note of my surprised pleasure placing a hand gingerly on my shoulder as I continued to work, and smiled. She liked to see me happy. It gave her something that words might be able to explain, but would defeat the moment in doing so.

Finally she said, "We have fun, huh, baby?"

I looked up to fully appreciate her stare. "Yeah." I paused. "We really fucking do."

The day before Thanksgiving Stoph and I went with Ernest to a church on sixth and California for a free turkey dinner. The line was long but efficient and those involved wore a relatively sunny disposition. There were a few drunks but were well behaved. I was getting a kick out of being there, to be among them, I didn't know why. Maybe it was because I had been living this way for over a year now and had earned some sort of right to be there? It could have had something to do with festiveness that surrounds people on both ends of giving and receiving during the holidays. I missed my family, as I did the Christmas before, but I felt at home being away from home this year. On top of that there is something about a stuffed turkey with mashed potatoes and gravy that signifies a special day. I have cooked those meals, know the work that goes into them, and couldn't help but feel loved by a bunch of strangers slaving away in an unseen kitchen.

All the volunteers, from those who helped with the seating to those who brought food to the tables, were genuinely jovial and heartfelt in their goodwill. On other days I could see me feeling shame at being in need of such kindness. That day would come again. On this day I saw and accepted my role of being one that others could take pride in lending a merciful hand.

Usually in big crowds like this I get suffocated by annoying conversations that invariably are populated by liars looking to carve out grand identities for themselves, or in search of a symphony of sympathy. Instead I smiled at their imagination and truly in my heart wished them all well. The asshole in me took a day off and allowed myself to accept them on whatever merit they offered. I even went beyond listening and joined in on a conversation or two. The credit was not simply due to my own magnanimity but also lied in the spirit of those around me. We were all having a good spiritual hair-day.

YEAH US!

The next day Stoph and I took our mutual hangovers and sprinkled them with a hair of the dog before heading out to the promenade. Pretty much all of the stores were closed and only one or two restaurants opened up, but all of the movie theaters would encourage enough foot-traffic to make our playing a set worth while. George's Bistro, where the Raven perched, remained closed but Bravo, next door, served breakfast and lunch. So we set up down by the benches as close to the two movie theaters as the fire laws allowed.

The Raven had planned to spend part of the day with her mother then go out with her Persian, New York stockbroker and his friends.

"You're not my boyfriend," she reminded me.

"Yes, dear."

I was actually kind of glad because it sent a clear message that she could maintain a solid footing where we were concerned. It put me in my place and I needed that to be done for my heart's own protection.

The street had a hollow sound to it when we first started playing. We were the only performers, none of the carts were rolled out and even the homeless had other places to be; charitable feedbags aplenty ruled the day. Our guitars and voices accompanied the solitary air without diminishing its loneliness somehow; like a pin dropping in a silent hall but not. After a while the music and the emptiness of the space usually so cluttered merged and created its own atmosphere. We started an hour early and played through the noon hour because no one was there to tell us to move on. The people who came out to catch a movie were mostly the ones that didn't have to cook or host an event at their homes. They had a few free hours so took the kids to a movie. Along with them were those hiding from holiday depression or just hiding. There weren't a lot of folks that indulged the music but the ones that did, did so generously. By one o'clock we had a couple of sawbucks (ten dollar bills) a few fins (five dollar bills) and a handful of singles (dollar bills).

Chris sang a few Christmas songs and that added to the day for a few passersby, we were glad to do it. We would have played up until two at least except for the Raven showing up just before one.

"You boys wanna join me and my mom for dinner?"

"What about your date?"

"I can do that later; Thanksgiving dinner is for family."

Stopher's initial reaction to any social invitation, let alone a last second one, is always negative. I'm the same way but I had a bit more vested in this proposition than he. I may have been introduced to Carol, the Raven's mom, once before but I don't remember it and if I did I'm certain that it was only in passing. Not being a "boyfriend," I guess I should have had no cause for alarm, but the Raven's protest aside, all intentions of purpose served up the same apprehensions one would assign a boyfriend's status.

"She just wants you," Stopher said when the Raven left us alone to discuss.

"She said family and I think she meant it, and that includes us both."

"Family."

"I know. Look if you don't want to go I won't either. I don't even really want to in the first place."

"You should go, it'll be a good move."

"I'm not leaving you alone on Thanksgiving, Chris."

He rolled his eyes. "I got vodka, weed at least twenty bucks and football; I'll be fine."

"Still."

He paused and I could see the decision adjusting in his face.

"We'll go."

"Really? Are you sure?"

"It'll be fun; I've always got the van to hide in."

God bless that white whale of a Ford.

We followed the Raven up then down the 405 into the valley. Carol came to the door a tad out of sorts and apologetically so. She felt a little under the weather and not quite up to the tasks of the kitchen. While I was sorry to hear about the former the latter gave me a hopeful smile.

"Carol, I love to cook, in fact I would consider it a favor to be able to be in the kitchen on Thanksgiving."

At first she seemed uneasy about my putting together a big feast: Did I know what I was doing; basting a bird and carving was one thing but what about the gravy; was I privy to the fine art of getting the potatoes properly whipped while retaining their heartiness; would I use mayonnaise or sour cream in them? And so on.

Early on she kept coming in from her bedroom to check up on me, and saying: "Let me know when the potatoes are peeled and I'll take it from there."

" Make sure not to cut them too small or too big before boiling, then leave it to me."

"Make sure to heat up the milk for me to mash them."

Finally:

"Just make sure you use the mayonnaise instead of sour cream."

Most of the day she laid down in the other room and called out the warnings of her imminent arrival to do things in the proper fashion, but when all was said and done the meal got made by me in the manner I had always done with a single exception—I usually used only milk and butter, sometimes adding sour cream in the potatoes. She did come out and crush some garlic into them, which was a nice touch I must confess. When things were close to being served she took over the kitchen to make a few pies from a ready-made crust, "I like to make the crust from scratch but I had too much to do today."

By the time the pies came out of the oven to cool the Raven and I had the table set and the food covered in tin foil in serving bowls and on platters ready for consumption. Carol, while not overly complimentary seemed pleased enough with my efforts and did not criticize anything with the exception of taking her plate back to the kitchen to re-heat in the microwave.

"I just like my food fully heated."

Stoph observed to me, free from her ear range in front of the microwave, "It was fully heated when you put it all on the table while she was late getting the pies out of the oven."

He meant no malice but simply wanted to make sure that I did not take on the failure she implied.

Throughout the day the Raven went back and forth between spending time with her mom in the bedroom and keeping me company in the kitchen, and peeling a few potatoes. Cooking on a holiday with such a traditional feast on the menu made me feel close to my Mom and that was company enough. As I said earlier, Mom had threatened for years to never cook again, and succeeded in small intervals, but whether she hated it or not, in my mind cooking big meals for the family was equated with a love so deep that words failed where food said all.

Whenever the Raven joined me in the kitchen we both played house, not ostentatiously, but it was there for us both and did not need pointing out. I'd be standing over the sink cleaning as I went to keep from being buried by pots, pans and dishes at the end of the night, as was my way, and she'd slip beside me with an arm around my waist and her head on my shoulder. I kissed her forehead and she my cheek while her hand fell over mine under soapy water.

"Thanks."

"It is my distinct pleasure."

She'd lift her head off my shoulder to look me in the eye, "You're so dramatic."

"I think dramatic is overstating, but I am being something."

"Oh, you're something." She slapped my ass parentally. "You're a pain in the ass."

I glanced down her backside. "Now that would be a pleasure beyond distinction."

"Baby?"

"Yes, dear."

"Are you being nasty?"

"I'm afraid so."

"Well don't stop on my account."

"On account?"

"On account I like it."

I turned to face her, sliding my hand down around the ass in question and our mouths melted into one another and the cameras rolled.

Stopher, who had written a lyric the day before, spent a good part of the afternoon with the Ovation sitting on the front stoop working out the music. It started with the line:

Royal weddings and dirt-poor love

He didn't know where he was going with it but he liked the line. Then came:

Through the ocean fog I see the desert dust

Now that came because when he was writing it a fog rolled off the ocean and made him think of the desert.

Hitchhiking angels and holy bums

That refers to us and all travelers:

Royal weddings and dirt-poor love

The song goes on to describe journeys in a transcending way while throwing in specifics from our life. Lines like:

Living in a mansion, living in van

Look both ways when you across this country, woman child or man

And the transcendent ones:

Living for a moment, waiting on the lord

Laying on a bed of feathers, sleeping on the floor

In the last verse he came across what I think was in him that got the song written in the first place:

I half raised this girl, (Aubrey) *now she's half woman and half child*

Today is her birthday and I'm off two thousand miles

Ya see I got this funny job, where I got no place to live

I wrote her this letter; it was all I had to give

(Into the chorus' last refrain)

Royal weddings and dirt-poor love

Through the ocean fog, I see the desert dust

Hitchhiking angels, and holy bums

Royal weddings and dirt-poor love

Stoph is writing his own book and I, for the most part, have decided to enter only my lyrics into this account of our journey, but the above excerpts from that song were too much a part of that day's story not include them. First of all, Aubrey's birthday did occur just two days before and subconsciously got him to write that song, the song therefore becomes a document of the life I am trying to speak of; secondly it illustrates what it is he and I do, and what drives us to do it; thirdly, you'll have to wait to see.

Earlier in the day the Raven asked if we wanted to invite Eric or Steve. I knew that Steve had plans but called Eric, got his machine and left a message of where we could be reached. He did have plans for an early afternoon dinner invitation that, apparently, left him with a bad taste in his mouth, emotionally as well as the food being awful, so when he got home and heard the message he called to see if it was too late. Since we had gotten such a late start he ventured out to join us. We started eating without him but he got there soon after.

"It was put together by some of my hiking friends so I was surprised to see the room filled with smokers; on top of that the girl who invited me came with a boyfriend, which I can't begin to understand how our singles got that crossed; I got home totally depressed and heard your message and felt like crying at the thought of having missed the chance spend a family holiday with people I love; well these two fellows, although I'm sure you and your mom are lovely people. Anyway, thank you so much for the invite."

"Actually I thought I dialed Steve's."

"Serendipity doodah."

"I'm just glad you made it."

"Would you like your plate heated," Carol offered.

"This is more than fine."

"Let me heat it up." She removed the plate of food from the table.

Before he could object I said, "Let her. Please."

The conversation flowed and the food got passed around, and re-heated, and soon full bellies quieted the room.

"There's pie," Carol announced.

"I have not nor ever shall argue with pie," Eric declared.

"Too bad; you might actually win that one," the Raven observed.
"It all adds up," I smirked.
"I was told there would be no math," Stopher joined in.
"Huh?" Eric said before following the flow.
"I get it," the Raven chortled, "Pie, add, math."
"She is a quick one. Quicker than me anyway."
"Well, Eric," I said, "one does not necessarily imply the other."
"True enough."

Eric and Stopher retired to the couch while Carol cut the pie, and I started working on the clean up. The Raven floated among the three groups chastising the boys for not having their guitars out, picking at the whipped cream, and pulling me off to the side to steal a kiss.

I felt so loved, so desired, so mischievous: her mom in one room, Eric and Chris in the other with, she and I in the hall between. She was always busy pretending that we were nothing more than friends, fretting over what I told my friends about us (I told her flatly that Stoph would hear of pretty much everything) and afraid that our mutual associations on the promenade would speculate behind our backs; to have her unable to keep her hands and lips off of me, with Eric in one room and her mom in the other, was quite the boost to my ego. I partly considered this to be just another one of her games, me an interchangeable part, or at the very least just a holiday whim to taunt her mother with. Of course when she approached me with whipped cream on her left breast cooing, "I've stained my frock, whatever shall I do?" I licked and sucked it clean like any good sport would. At one point, as the night grew long, I tried to shake myself from the dream.

"Shouldn't we get to wrapping things up; you have late date."

"I already called and cancelled; I didn't want to be any where else—with anybody else."

I thought to make a joke that belittled me and saw in her eye the same knee-jerk reaction, but we both drew a thoughtful breath instead.

"Oh, baby, what am I gonna do with you."

"Cherish me, baby, just cherish me," I said all Elvised up.

She cackled in my arms, "What's that from?"

"PEGGY SUE GORT MARRIED."

"I thought I recognized that; you're such a dope."

"What? I loved that movie."

"I don't know, there's just something dopey about Nicholas Cage—not specifically from that film, just in general."

"That moment always killed me."

She smiled sweetly. "You're such a dope." Then she kissed me hard.

With most of the cleaning done and desert consumed we sat around the living room and the three men passed around the guitar while the women folk tended the fire. The weather required no such flames but the Raven insisted upon it. Even after something went wrong with the flue and smoke wafted back out into the room.

"Honey, put that dang fire out before we all get smoke inhalation," Carol scolded.

I enjoyed seeing her mom put her foot down. My guess is that it never came down enough while she was growing up.

With the fire quieted and the patio door opened to allow the smoke somewhere to go other than our lungs, the men showed off their talents. I was tired and my voice was in the midst of one of its fragile periods so I only sang a couple. Besides there was more cleaning in the kitchen awaiting my attention. Eric got playful and played some Kinks, which got him doing his Mick Jaggar imitating a chicken posing as a rock star.

After one such exhibition I heard the Raven shout, "Do another squirmy one, more squirm, more squirm."

I came out of the kitchen and smiled along but I have to admit, seeing her give that kind of attention to Eric made me a little jealous. "Hey," I thought, "I'm the dancing monkey around hear." The funny thing is that whenever I got to funk-out on the promenade the Raven would try and tone me down. The fact that she wanted Eric to make more of a spectacle of himself instead of me only pointed out the lack of emotional investment in him. I still felt a little jealous. I stood in the back of the room smiling and sincerely enjoying the performance, while in a corner of my head I pouted insolently, "Love me! Over here; love me."

After that Stopher played ROYAL WEDDINGS for everyone. With all its travelogue qualities and spiritual content it fit the day perfectly.

We were, all of us, on a journey to ourselves and grateful for the company present, and others far away. The Raven beamed with every knew phrase uttered, reveling in the fact that she was hearing such a creation fresh from its shell; knowing that not a single soul outside the room had been blessed by it; and somehow feeling a part of it coming into being because the music was written under her wing; she being the one who brought us all together on this day. I saw all that in her from the first verse on and to this day question none of my assumptions. Her love of a squirming Eric, the ability to instantly grasp the historic beauty of Stopher's song, were just two more reasons for me to fall in love with her. She sank into my arms on the couch during the song drifting from her mother's and I could feel that she wanted to be close to me to further mark the moment's importance.

Carol too was instantly drawn to the song. In fact, as much as I had immediately liked the song, I think they both understood it on a level that I would have to come to eventually. It could have been that they were so unaccustomed to being present at such births that their reaction could have been as intense regardless of the song but I assure you it wasn't. It was the right song for the right people at the right moment in time. Such a collection of events exists to show us something about ourselves and the people we are with. Watching them love that song verified something for the Raven in me and showed me a side of Carol that I would not often see.

At the end of the night as we were leaving I gave Carol an uncertain hug. I knew that I was not what she envisioned for her daughter but she did gather up the respect I had earned that day and showed it to me in her eyes.

Then she said as I pulled back from our not completely awkward hug, "Take care of my little girl."

I stood stunned momentarily, then quickly recovered and tried to invoke the manner of one who had just been told to drive carefully, which could have been all that she meant for me to infer. I do think she saw something that night in the way the Raven and I fit together. Obviously her daughter had previously talked a lot about the rag-tag fellows in a van down by the ocean, but seeing us in the glow of a family atmosphere struck the depth of our possibilities in her mind, and perhaps in her heart.

I drove the Raven's car home while Stopher followed in the van. She was sleepy and I think wanted my company a little longer.

"I love to drive when I'm not driving." Her head nestled against my shoulder. "The hum of the wheels on an open road, the purr of an engine climbing a hill."

Her eyes closed and her breath heaved. All on my shoulder, all in faith of what it carried. I knew she would be asleep soon if she were not already so I decided to keep myself company by humming. I started soft and wordless but soon found my way into one of my favorite show tunes.

"*I have often walked down this street before but the pavement always stayed beneath my feet before. All at once am I several stories high, knowing I'm on the street where you live.*"

In the eighth grade I played Henry Higgins in a production of MY FAIR LADY. The above lyric was sung by a supporting character, Freddy, but ON THE STREET WHERE YOU LIVE always had a special place in my heart because of its gorgeous melody and full-blown romanticism. Even as a kid I was a theatrical little son of a bitch. I was the only twelve year old in the history of twelve year olds to come home from school all moody and listen to Jackson Browne's LATE FOR THE SKY. Most kids my age were still listening to KISS. My musical precociousness was due to being the youngest of six kids, all of whom were the product of two intellectuals, although the hambone dramatics of my psyche cannot be traced up the family tree.

I remember being heart broken by a girl that year in eighth grade, (who coincidentally turned out to be my sister in-law, Alice years later) and I'd walk home from school going out of my way to pass the street she lived on so I could sing ON THE STREET WHERE YOU LIVE. I'd be strolling along all cinematic like belting this song out and quieting down beneath a whisper when someone approached from the other direction. A month after Alice broke my heart I started dating her sister Donna (who would, years later, be my wife) and a month or so after that she broke my heart, (a performance she would repeat years later) so once again I found myself on that same street singing that same song.

When Donna and I were married and taking a long drive I would break into that same song along with my other favorite show tunes until she hushed me for changing keys once too often. Aubrey and I used to love to sing, I COULD HAVE DANCED ALL NIGHT, on long drives when we tired of our novelty, road songs. She never mentioned me changing keys.

That Thanksgiving night as the Raven snoozed, I crooned softly to myself trying not to disturb her while maintaining a single key. Changing lanes—not keys. When I felt her stir I hushed.

"Sing," she sighed as if talking to her dream. "More singing." Pause. "Don't stop."

I smiled and sang every show tune I knew out of the valley and into Santa Monica.

"I'm not your girlfriend," she said adamantly.
"This we know."
"I can do what I want; I can do who I want."
"I don't need to be at the goddamm Christmas party."
"But I want you there. I want you to play. I want to show you off." She tapped her foot to give her irritation another voice. "Esquire is connected, you know? There might be someone who could help you at the party."
"And I'd love to play, I'd love to get connected."
"But you won't go unless I promise."
"You don't want a life with a fat, miserable failure who lives in a van and I don't blame you. You come for me whenever you need a fix and then run around looking for Mr. Rich, I mean Right—wait, no I mean Rich. I accept all of that. I don't like it, but I see my lot in life and understand its limitations. But if you want me at that party I'm not going to be put in a position where I could walk into a room to find you under the mistletoe. Is that so hard too understand?"
"I want people to hear you?"

"And I appreciate that; Sweets, things have gone too far. I can't be sure that I'm in love, but I'm definitely in deep; I have to protect myself a little here. You seeing other people, is one thing, but me seeing you with them? I have no interest in that, it would hurt too much."

"Alright, but you're not my date."

"Just as long as no one else is either."

"I have other friends coming."

I dropped my head feeling her trying to slip through some verbal loophole. "I really want to be clear about this, Sweets, I don't want any misunderstandings: If I'm there and I catch you necking or even flirting with some schmuck, I'll feel like a fool. I don't have to be there, you'd be free to do whatever you please. Just don't make a fool of me, I'm begging you."

So it was agreed that I would attend the Christmas party thrown by her landlord, Esquire, at 55 Rose Avenue. Making her promise an evening of fidelity left me ill at ease. I kept thinking if you need this from her you are setting yourself up to be a chump. Fuck the party; don't go; or go with no expectations. I couldn't not go because I wanted to be there in case she was right about making connections and because I wanted to be at a Christmas party with her. Fools do foolish things and end up looking…you guessed it: Foolish.

Things started swimmingly enough in the beginning. The Raven moved about quite a bit but made me feel wanted, gave me my due time-wise. I got to meet Monica, who was a successful dog walker in a way that eluded the Raven; or that she eluded in her own distinct, and always fashionable, way. I liked Monica; she laughed in all the right places. She was also one of the Raven's rare friends of the female persuasion. Alexis was another but more of an acquaintance really; she laughed indiscriminately. Her tiny waif frame whispered like a leaf whenever she giggled. Despite having a sort of educated air and having had something published recently, she ultimately came off on the dim side.

I ended up spending a good part of the evening's first half with them at either arm. Monica only knew the Raven while Alexis did move around with some familiarity but appeared to be strategically holding herself back in our midst. It was then I detected her sniffing for money. Up until that point she had paced herself in the background with the blue-collar artist and the enterprising, recently divorced, young woman. She didn't say much but simply and subtly drifted off further into the crowd where shiny things glittered and ice made you feel all warm inside.

But by then the Raven had rejoined us, and Alexis was mostly dead weight anyway, little that there was.

"It's time for some music," She slurred. "Anyone wants to hear some actual good music join us in the entertainment room." She indicated the small room at the front of the house just around the Christmas tree.

That was my cue so I went to where I had my guitar waiting and got it out. I was followed pretty much only by men all in their late twenties to early thirties. I recognized one of them from another of the Raven's picking parties. Monica and the Raven were the only females in the room.

I sang well enough but I was nowhere near my best. My throat had been worse but I only had a half hour in me at the most. I kept it simple singing songs that weren't too demanding like SEARCHING, UMBRELLA and SPRINKLER'S CHILD. All in all they had a good enough time, as did I. I'd stop playing to let a conversation unfold, after a bit someone would ask for another song. And the someone wasn't always the Raven. (Only about two-thirds.)

Out of the blue the Raven, who sat on the floor with her back against the closed door of the little room, took to periodically leaning forward just enough to open the door and stick her head out to shout, "The real party's in here with us; not out there with you fucking losers."

Her shouts went unchallenged from the other room so there remained an uncertainty, by me and I think Monica, as to whether she had been heard in the other room at all. When this thought occurred to the Raven she waited and listened. The second the music of one song from the other room's stereo ended she pounced on the silent gap.

"If you want to hear some real fucking music, it's all in here."

Most in our room ignored the outbursts and concentrated on their own exchanges.

"What are you doing?" Monica asked

"Just tellin' them," she turned her head but left the door closed and yelled, "FUCKERS, where the party's at."

"Why are you so angry with them?"

"I think our little Raven has had her feathers ruffled once too often," I offered to Monica. "Huh, Princess," I shot at the Raven. Getting caught up in her theater drama had turned my tongue a tad acidic.

"That's Macho, to the likes of you." She turned and opened the door. "And the same to all you mother fuckers out there!" Her drunken sneer returned from the door than vanished. "Play another song, baby."

"Okay."

Opening the door, "Now this is music, only you mother fuckers wouldn't even know it."

"Thank you, dear."

"Nobody puts Vuma in the corner." Pause. "Huh, baby."

"Huh, baby."

"Now play me a song, bitch."

"Raven!" Monica scolded.

"Ahh, he loves it."

"What can I say, she's got a way of makin' a guy wanna get roughed up."

I didn't notice her leave but I did take note when she had been gone for a while. I had my guitar packed up and was thinking of heading back to the van. The obnoxious drunk thing she had going that night was beginning to wear thin, if it was going to get worse I just as soon not be there. Monica had been gone by then so, momentarily, I debated a slip-into-the-night kind of exit over a track-her-down-to-where-she-went-off-too-mistake. As I first started down the hall to her room to get my coat I guess a part of me already knew. Her door was locked and I heard two voices on the other side. My head leaned against the door searching for a breath that would lead me to a graceful departure. I knocked.

The Raven's voice mumbled inaudible from her side of the door. It then rose some in indignance while remaining inquisitive. "Who's there?"

"I would like my coat."

There was more mumbling coupled with some rummaging. "Why are you leaving?"

"Can I just have my coat?"

"Want don't you go back up front and I'll bring it to you?"

"Ray, can you just drop the game, give me my coat and let me get the fuck out of here?"

"Can't you wait up front?"

"Look, I know you're not alone. I asked for one goddamm thing from you and you couldn't do it. So give me my coat and then you'll be free to do whatever you want with whomever you want."

The door opened, the Raven stepped out, and some short guy slipped out behind her to head outside.

"Why don't you stay? You're the 'whomever' I want to be with."

"Really? Well I've been here while you were in there with him."

I stormed passed her found my coat and went to leave. She put her arms around my neck.

"I wasn't doing anything with him; we were just talking."

"What-fucking-ever, Ray." I pulled her arms off of me to walk away, but stopped for another word. "I didn't have to be here; I begged you not to make me the fool; I told you this was the one thing I would not stand for."

"Nothing happened!"

I stopped again. "BULLSHIT!"

The Raven caught up with me on the sidewalk along the tall white picket fence.

"Baby! Wait. I don't want you to go, can't you just wait a fucking minute?"

"I'm not one of your fucking boys. Even if we were 'just friends,' which by the way we are so fucking not, there is a way you treat people who you supposedly care about; there are lines you don't cross and you just pissed all over it."

"I'm sorry. Nothing happened."

"If nothing happened, why are you sorry?"

"Because you're hurt and angry; because you think something happened and I don't blame you for thinking it. I know it looks bad, but I swear to you nothing happened. I was drunk and I needed some quiet. Dev was just looking out for me in case I got sick."

"Good ole Dev; what a precious sweetheart."

Somewhere in there the Raven threw herself at me in a fit of passion. At first I held her back in some sort of feeble attempt at dignity, then decided that that was a boat whom had sailed and had its belly ripped to shreds by a curvaceous reef. So I kissed her and I kissed her angrily. We tore into each other grabbing and pushing and tugging and digging, as if some underlying truth could be found in the fabric of our clothes; as if maybe our skins were trying to tell us something. So they called out and we dug in, separating molecules from molecules but getting no further than surfaced heat. The more her mouth pleaded with me the more I believed their previous words. Maybe nothing happened, maybe she felt nauseous and Dev offered a watchful eye. (Everyone reading this is thinking, "Chump isn't a strong enough word.")

The kisses ceased as she laid her cheek into my chest.

"None of them mean anything, you're the one I care about."

"See, I know that." I forced her to look me in the eye. "I know that we have built something between us. I know that it scares the shit out of you. The last thing you want to do is fall in love some fat loser."

She smiled, "Baby, if you were a loser you wouldn't be so fat."

"Probably not the best time to see how clever and cute you can be."

"Sorry."

"I know what we are and I know what we have. I don't think you do."

"You know I love you," she started to say before quickly muffling the last three words against my chest.

"What did you say?"

"I'm not going to ride off into the sunset with you, David."

"But you did say what I thought you said."

"It doesn't matter what I said or how I feel. This," her hands bounced back and forth between us, "is not going to happen."

"I'm not letting this stumble into another one of your tired rants. I knew before you tried not to say it anyway; nice to hear it though, muted as it was. Listen, lady, we're both drunk—well you're sloppy and I'm a couple past a friendly buzz—what you did was selfish and stupid but I still love you anyway."

I'm not sure if this was the first time I had said it, but if I had it was in the same off-the-cuff-not-really-saying-it manner. Still it was known between us that I had been falling hard for a few weeks at least. My reasons for holding back at all were purely defensive.

So we went to and fro living the evening over and over again as drunks and romantics tend to do. She never admitted to kissing Dev, although for a moment she did concede her drunken state and that something could have transpired without her remembering. In the sober light of the next day, even if you tracked her down and asked the question on her deathbed, she stood fast that nothing happened in that room.

On the front porch I heard the occasional giggle as the dwindling remains of the party gathered there to eavesdrop on the spectacle of intoxicated lovers quarreling over hours in a sandglass. At the time I felt stupid, and at the time I saw the humor from their end. I also enjoyed the hysterics, and battled back and forth between indulging them and attempting to extricate myself. The thing about the Raven and I was that we both lived in a perpetual cinematic state in our head. That's partly why we were drawn to each other and that's why we we're so entertaining to those on the porch. Well that and our being folly personified.

We had to be out up against that fence for at least close to two hours. When she wasn't crying or yelling I was scolding, we both laughed, and did some serious necking. She had revealed previously a good deal of her emotional baggage to me, but that night held it up to the light of a living dimension. I knew about her unstable childhood and a father who wanted nothing to do with her but I physically saw the scars in her eyes that night; I also so the pretty, manipulative girl trotting out her psychosis' to dress up her bad behavior in a sympathetic gown. And like everything else she wore it well.

Finally I announced that I had to piss. I walked up through a parade of thinly veiled chuckles at my expense, through the empty living room, down the hall and into the kitchen. Just as I was about to step through the door to the bathroom she rushed up onto my back and, though I carried her, it was her momentum that carried us into the next room. Her feet slammed the door and she crawled up over my shoulders and head, fell into my arms placing her on the floor and kissed me. Before I could say anything she was behind me again shoving me up against the sink, holding one of my arms behind my back by the wrist.

"This is the confessional; I want you to know something about me." She paused as if turning a knob in her throat to accentuate the following words. "I'm going to want to fuck you in the ass." It was a whisper that held a knife.

My tongue stumbled out of the gate to form not so much words as a collection of clumsy sounds. Firstly, I wasn't sure I heard correctly. Maybe she said that I would do it to her, or something completely different. I was afraid to repeat it for fear of offending.

"Did you hear what I said to you, bitch."

"I think so, but why don't you say it again to make sure."

The Raven was a playful sort and didn't always mean everything she said to the fullest extent of her words. She did sound serious—but she was still drunk—although she had sobered up quite a bit—besides, all the emotional roller coasting riding we had just been through could have warped a spring in her brain—she did sound serious.

"At some point, if you want to stay involved with me, you are going to have to let me fuck you in the ass." She punctuated the last part by twisting and shoving my arm higher and deeper into my back.

"That certainly is a conversational twist in the evening."

"I'm serious; I've done it before."

She had told my about a small, but physically impressive, Persian doctor that she had been involved with who turned her on to the whole slapping guys around thing. He used to goad her into hitting him. I did like when she slapped me once I understood it as a warped form of affection.

"Will this be a mutual exchange?"

"Maybe."

I freed myself, turned and took hold of her as she held back her mouth from mine. I paused with the thought of whether I could be accountable for any answer. I decided that no court would convict.

"I want you to fuck me in the ass." I knew that I didn't have to mean it.

I think I did.

When I left we understood each other without having to admit to anything, and as for evening ending revelations? that got set on the back burner. Dev and his friend gave me a ride back to the van. I refused at first but she insisted I not walk on my bad heel. Dev turned out to be a nice enough fella, charming even.

I didn't see her for a few days after that and when I did she was sheepish. Her memory needed a boost but most of it came back to her minus absolute clarity on the minor details.

"I said what?"

"Oh, something about them being mother fuckers and how the real party was with us; stuff like that."

She covered her mouth with a hand. "No one said anything to me at the house."

"Maybe they didn't hear, or maybe our little soap opera on the front walk made up for it?"

Any discussion of anal sex went unapproached.

The next time I saw her I was drunk. I had asked her earlier that day after my set if we might get together later; she said that she had a date. She must have cut it short because she showed up at the van by ten. On other nights I sometimes drank slower in case she might drop in on me but the scene at her Christmas party left a bitter taste in my mouth. Unfortunately it didn't diminish how I felt about her. Between the bitterness and my unrelenting fondness, little room remained for being casual. I was falling in love or had already fallen and she continued to bounce around like a super ball that always landed in my lap—in my chest.

Of course when she showed up I felt blessed to see her. She wore a long red gown but not the one she took me up into the canyon in on my birthday. This one was made of felt with long sleeves covering her shoulders and neck. A lot of the evening's details remain blurry to me but the soft red cloth circling her neck and wrists, holding up her breasts and cascading off her hips is with me always.

She gathered me up from the van and I stumbled along gleefully, free from any and all defensive reserve. My heart would not break tonight, I wouldn't have noticed if it had; pain belonged to the realm of daylight along with the stiff joints of dehydration.

In her room on 55 Rose I stood among the clutter not bothering to seek out a place to stand let alone sit. Her loft bed, which I had no interest in mounting anyway, boasted a couple of suitcases, a large cardboard box and various clothes strewn about. The floor looked like a department store's aisle after being visited by a tornado. The only chair in the room, and I only guessed it to still exist because I had moved her in, could have been in the far corner between the closet and window, for the pile of assorted clothes and shoes carried the faint shape of one beneath the mound of leather and fabric; imagine a snowman melting over warmer days with its hat and mittens gone and only a rotted piece of orange mush to remind you of a once pointed nose; the mud invades the white and the shape shifts but if you look at it objectively you are able to reconstruct what once stood. Chairs, desks and dressers all had similar fates await them in a room designed by Raven. Or should I say a life lived by a design of mayhem that is the Raven? Of course there was not enough cognitive thought in her world to claim design. There was only the way she would like to be and the way she was, which implicates us all.

The Raven had gone off to attend something or other and I took a swig from my bottle. A few minutes went by and I realized that it might be a while before her return. I was drunk and tired, not merely sleepy but tired of being a decoration in someone's life. I thought I knew myself to be important, and so what if she had to fight off her affection for me, the fact remained that she did fight, and from my vantage appeared to be winning, because I felt lost. I couldn't convince her to embrace poverty, or make big money on her own; I was as hopelessly me as she was hopelessly her. So I got on my knees and began to clear a space on the floor for my body and in fact a floor I did find amidst the rubble. I drifted off unconcerned of any possible reaction she might have.

I awoke to her rummaging about trying to create a space for herself on the floor with me.

"Drink this." She held out a bottle of Champagne.

"I have this." I held up my water bottle of rotgut.

"That's rotgut. I want to taste this when I kiss you."

I took the Champagne.

We kissed awkwardly searching for spots clear enough to rest our respective limbs. I noted a difference in her demeanor from other nights. The Raven always had something up her sleeve or at least went out of her way to make you think she did, or was just a natural state of her affairs. On that night not only did she have a sleeve full, but I began suspect that she was going to reveal said fullness.

She lay back on the floor away from me and cooed, "Do you want to see my kitten?"

"Can I look with my tongue?"

Her gown rose up to her thigh, "That's not looking, that is licking."

I kissed her inner thigh and then the other. "What's that?"

"That's kissing."

I kissed them both again exposing her flesh more to my tongue while biting a little with my teeth. I moved higher.

"Oh, my goodness, what big teeth you have."

I crawled up under gown and made a most miraculous meal of her "kitten," as she coyly dubbed it, and took careful note of what she said as I had begun in earnest. "We're not fucking," her heaving breath gasped, as my tongue got lost within her kitten.

"O'tay 'Panky," came my wet and muffled response from between her legs.

Up in the canyon on my birthday I wasn't sure if she had tried to offer what I received that night on her floor, but I think I played it right on both counts. If I may be crude and uncouth for a moment, let me say that I have never indulged in such a pussy as I did that night. It had none of the human salty after taste, which I had acquired a liking for, and all of the silky, foamy goodness that one would associate with the nectar of gods. Her inner flesh curled in wondrous directions that my tongue read like a map. As lovely as I found it to be that night I knew it had to be even more so because I was drunk and my senses were at half-mast. (Yes my cock was on full throttle but that is beside the point.) At times I wasn't sure if I had the right rhythm going but before I knew, she was cumming and cumming hard.

"My, GOD! Where did you learn to eat pussy like that?" She pulled my face up to her and kissed me, then licked around my mouth to taste her on me.

"You came?"

"Couldn't you tell; you're such a beast." She kissed and licked around my mouth. "I could've cum sooner but I got greedy and didn't want it to stop."

Now I know it sounds like bragging but in the end I think it had more to do with how deeply we were connected emotionally, and that sexually we simply had similar sensibilities. If you like the same books as someone there is a chance you'll like the same movies too. And of course, I am one sensual, sexy motherfucker.

We kissed and talked a little more but I had already fallen asleep on her floor once that evening so she thought that she should get me home. I didn't make any moves to get reciprocation because I was too drunk to care and just glad to have gotten into her panties. (Not that she wore any.)

The next week the folks came into town and it was great, as always, to see them. Free meals and even better than that, great conversation. Our life in a van and on the streets had been defined and I loved holding it up for the folks to see. They wished peace of mind and good health for Stopher and I and we were achieving none of that, but we were as close as we were likely to ever get. Dad marveled at our simplicity and Mom relished in our sunsets.

I made pizza at Sukey's and Eric, Steve and some of Steve's other friends came to indulge. Ernest came along as well but the Raven had to work. She could have dropped by afterwards but she wanted to keep her distance. The folks had met her on the promenade but she felt uneasy about getting any closer.

"I'm too close to you and your brother as it is. If I like your folks as much as I think I will…I'm in deep enough, thank you."

The pizza flowed, music got passed around, and the folks couldn't have been more pleased. Ernest refused to join in on the conga because, as he stated, "I'm a drummer." He did talk a little poetry with Dad and tried not to speak too ill of Robert Frost while insisting on mispronouncing Rimbaud.

"He is an interesting fellow," Dad had observed. "He seemed to know that Rimbaud was a homosexual yet stood fast unaware."

Mom smiled brightly all night. "You really have found a place for yourselves: The music, the joking; you are all so clever and take such pleasure in each other."

Before they left town the Raven came around and decided to have the folks over to 55 Rose. I was nervous and excited to have these separate people that I loved in an intimate setting. I knew that their first observation of her would be that she is beautiful but flakey; her substance washed away under a brilliant smile that tried a little too hard; her soul simultaneously afraid of not being seen and being found out.

The day that we were to go there, Mom made an announcement.

"Your Dad and I want to fly you home for the holidays. Aubrey will be there and you can surprise her."

Chris was up for it instantly and gratefully while I put on a similar face that betrayed my true feelings. Yes I would like to see home again, full of all the people that have helped form me; and of course I wanted to take Aubrey into my arms in hopes that the distance could melt between us until the previous life we had built surrounded us, belittling our time apart. On top of that were the kids of my brothers and sisters whom I had just gotten to know before disappearing; Eileen and her sweet Keely had not even heard the song I wrote for her after she came with Aubrey to visit.

Obviously my being in the middle of the mess that was the Raven and I tugged at my heart-sleeve telling me that I wanted to stay and play. In the time I'd be in Chicago whatever spell I had cast could be broken—hell by the time I got to the airport. Something deeper spoke to me on the subject as well. Not only was I addicted to playing four hours a day-five days a week, but everything else in California was mine, from the van in which I slept to the sun that I watched go down into a salty horizon; mine and whatever I made of it. On the streets of Santa Monica I was that guy who played the promenade, in Chicago I was the youngest of the Smith clan, which I was proud to be and still…also I wanted to come home a conquering hero, not be flown in by Mommy and Daddy. No, at the heart of it all I was in the middle of something; the Raven yes, but so much more than that; I was in the middle of a declaration and it felt wrong to take a vacation.

"If we're going to go to all the trouble of flying you in we might as well have you for a good while," Mom said cheerfully. "How does three weeks sound?"

I know she thought she was doing Chris and I a favor and she was, absolutely she was. Yet I stood there with an empty smile realizing that not she or Dad could see my struggle. Chris spoke to quiet my silence.

"I can't wait; it'll be a much needed break."

Somewhere inside me I was on the verge of telling them no, I wanted to stay and play through the Christmas season that I missed out on last year with all the van troubles and Angel's visit. Mom's enthusiasm slowed my lips but the thought of seeing Aubrey ended any words I might think to say. If nothing else I owed it to her to be there.

"And we won't tell Aubrey or Grandma," Mom concluded joyfully. "What a surprise it will be. You could both walk into her front room with your guitars, singing."

"And I can meet Aubrey at the airport." I heard myself say happily.

Yeah, I would, I thought, and it will be wonderful.

That night I stood at the front door of 55 Rose with the folks minus Stopher. (He opted for the tranquility of solitude in the blessed van.) Frenchie came to the door saying that the Raven had called to say she'd be late but please come in and have a seat. Mom had bought a bottle of wine, which I was of little help in picking out.

"I know she likes white," I offered.

To the Raven's credit she was not at all as late as she was apt to be and showed up not far behind.

(Author's note: One year has passed since I began reliving this journey)

She entered briskly and cheerfully holding a 12-pack of Coronas with a hint of pretension, which was understandable.

"I bought beer," she declared triumphantly.

"I have wine," Mom countered, with a more subtle enthusiasm.

"Oooh, let's drink yours," the Raven smiled.

"I'll have a beer," Dad said in his grounded fashion.

"I'll-"

"You'll have beer and like it," the Raven cut me off.

"Yes, dear."

I wanted beer and she knew it.

We all settled on the curved couch in the corner of the living room opposite the Christmas tree. The Raven and I sat together on one side, the folks the other. Awkwardness would be an over statement but so would have casual comfort. The Raven wore her knee-hi shiny, black boots under a shin low, form fitting, grey skirt that went perfectly with the elegant yet ski-lodge-type, long sleeve, top that swirled around waist, breast and shoulders in an array of maroonish reds and varying whites, gripping her upper body most flatteringly. Her long, dark hair, teased to perfection, jiggled in unison with each giggle and bounced off every bit of laughter. Being beautiful to her was breathing—tonight she was stunning.

"I just came back from an interview for a TV show called the BACHELOR; some new reality show—it ran a little late."

"How exciting," Mom said. "Did it go well?"

"It was fun. I don't really expect anything to come from it. I was standing in front of the restaurant when these women were walking up and down the promenade scouting for participants. It was in the neighborhood so after work I stopped by. It was fun."

"A reality show?" I said, only partly keeping my disdain at bay.

Dad sat silent.

"Oh, I don't think I'd do it; still, a free vacation."

"Why not?" Mom agreed.

"Because they're awful tripe and demeaning? I'm just thinking off the top of my head here."

"Anyway," the Raven brushed my comment aside, "I made the interviewer laugh and I got the feeling that I wasn't the usual fare he came across."

"You mean vacuous?" I offered.

"Oh, don't be a snob," said Mom. "It could be a wonderful experience."

Dad sat silent.

Now mom, given all the facts of what the show eventually became, and even at the moment she sat there on the couch, certainly had a sense of what I was talking about but preferred to remain a good and encouraging guest. That and a free vacation is a free vacation.

Dad sat silent and smiled politely.

The topic of conversation drifted into music and her life as a dog walker. Mom always got a kick out of the different lives people lived so the evening bore some pleasant fruit. Dad too enjoyed hearing about the nuts and bolts of how people made their way and I liked watching them learn about her. They didn't stay for very long but they had officially met the woman for whom I had fallen. On the subject of music, the Raven beamed her pride on to Chris and I.

"Your sons not only make my job at the restaurant easier, but their music...their words and music are extremely important to me. Oh, and I am a fan of your lyrics as well, Barbara." Mom nodded her thanks. "I appreciate them on a level like no one else." She looked at me and smiled. "They know that." Looking back to the folks. "So I adopted them and they adopted me."

"They both speak very affectionately about you," Mom said.

Dad smiled at me, "All the time."

"We're the best of friends." Quoth the Raven.

"Right, friends." I said to her then looked at them.

We all smiled knowingly of the swamp afoot.

Before they left mom took a couple pictures of the Raven and I in front of the Christmas tree. One of those pictures is taped on the ceiling of the van over my bed. I used to look at it a lot more than I do now. At times I've wanted to take it down and tear it into a million pieces but know that I'd regret it soon after if not that very second.

The folks drove their rental car back to the motel and I stayed behind to tell the Raven of my eminent departure.

"You get to see your kid, that's great."

"But I'll be gone for almost a month."

"Hey, we had our little fling and this will give us a chance to pull things back to where they should be."

"Do you even care that I'm leaving?"

"Of course I'll miss you." She paused to place a hand on my cheek. "You know this couldn't go any where, it's gone too far already; it never happened."

"Just a dream, huh, baby?"

"A nightmare more like it." She started to laugh but saw that I wasn't. "Oh, darlin' you know I appreciate you and your brother."

"My brother isn't here and he hasn't been here for a lot of things. Stop always trying to group us together so you can imagine a bigger distance between us than there is."

"You go home and enjoy your family and I'll get back to being more vamp-like."

"Oh, you're vamp-like enough as it is."

"It's going to get more so. You need to believe and accept that."

She took me to a Japanese soup place on Olympic called Ramen Yai. The Raven loved going there for the enormous bowls of delicious soup and to hear the waitress shout out their orders. I ate only the little she insisted I try, it was awfully good but I couldn't get past how she took my going with butterfly wings. Did I miss something? Was I that alone in what transpired emotionally between us? Could she be that flakey and or aloof? She slurped and smiled and talked as if it were just another day. I was leaving in a few days and she didn't care.

I saw her after that before I left; she gave me a keepsake. Down on the boardwalk under the pier they have these machines where you put 51 cents in and out comes a penny flattened into a thin elongated oval shape. One side is blank and smooth while the other has a picturesque view of the pier, although mostly you can only make out a fairest wheel. It read: The Promenade in Santa Monica—alonge the bottom curve beneath the Braille-like embedded scenery. I immediately decided to keep it in my pocket at all times as a good luck charm. I am romantic, cinematic and at times overtly sentimental. Oh, and a chump

Speaking of chumps, romantic and otherwise, I wrote this for her between sets on the promenade just before I left for Chicago:
But for her breath—warm and welcoming
But for her smile—soft and curvaceous, deep with out end
But for these and so much more I am reaching forever in search of receiving

I have been so blessed yet I crave more glances thrown my way, one more smile to blind the sun from the day, one more kiss scented by her breath
It is a wish made by a man whose wealth at her hands dwarfs any concept of what is actually deserved
By greed I am defined
By desire driven

But for her breath
But for her smile
But for her eyes
Only a fool would place anything above

I am no fool
I wrote this the same day:
Careening through a dream
Colliding with a moment
Teasing every desire
Tip-toeing around every atonement

Moseying about my journey
Motoring to a conclusion
Sauntering for the sake of a saunter

Savoring my many distractions

I'm leaving and arriving with every step
Both ways and none at all
Alone in the world
Together in a tomb
Dichotomy dangles
Deliciously in bloom

She promptly placed lipstick marks on either side of the card of the former one and showed it to me before I left for the day. Of the latter she said, "A bit of the Cat in the Hat; cute though; any time you can combine dichotomy and delicious is okay by me."

I smiled.

"You do have a silver tongue," she confessed. "And you ain't bad with words either."

On the plane I wrote her two letters: one pathetically romantic and gushy, the other funny and wise. In my time away I would write several letters and send a tape of some songs I recorded that were her favorites of mine. She wrote no letters but ended up calling me almost everyday. Our conversations were mostly casual with a little mush, from both ends, thrown in for good measure, but I didn't consider it much comfort. Her life went on without me like a light, summer breeze. After the second week the significance of her calling me all the time remained lost.

"She is calling you everyday," Mom finally pointed out. "I'd say that qualifies as, 'being hooked', in more than one person's book."

I love home. I love Chicago. In all my travels away there was always a part of me that couldn't wait to get back. I had built a life with my wife and daughter in Nashville, but whenever we came to Chicago for a visit I relished in every second. Sure there were things that I wanted to get at in Nashville. Yet, in the house where I grew up, I felt whole. Whatever waited anywhere else was in addition; outside my core; something that existed in hopes of carrying me back home. Chicago, when I left for California was still where I was ultimately headed. On that first return from California I found that changed.

The Raven played a role in that but that part stood on the frail, wobbly stilts of romance. As far-gone as I might have been at the time, my rational mind still spoke to me. It reminded me that despite all I felt, or thought I felt, for the Raven, she was just a soft, beautiful drug coursing through my veins: yes she was more than a body to me and we had shared genuine feelings and deep-rooted connections, but she had not yet become a match for the roots buried beneath the years of my life in Chicago. The effect she had on me there was immediate and surfaced—powerful and daunting, but immediate and surfaced. No, there was something else afoot. Something she was a part of but also existed without her.

In Santa Monica I played for my keep, known to all who knew me as the artist I sought myself out to be; I slept in a van paid for in full by me; four hours a day five days a week I stood behind a guitar and said, "This is who I am." As much as I was jonesing for a Raven fix, I sweated out the lack of time performing even more. Uncomparatively more. The Raven, as deep and true as I had begun to believe our love could become, walked upon my earth as man in the face of existence. Music and words rose with the creation of the first sun. It was they who brought me to her in the first place. At home I was the failure back from the road with nothing to show for it, who needed every meal given because he had no money. Out there I was the same failure but a failure in process. Each day presented the chance to show my wares, make enough to eat and even strike gold. At the end of the day my head laid on a pillow in a van I provided for myself.

Understand that none of my family saw me as a failure, those are my words and for me they only hold up in the most specific light. The people at 5103 hold me and my efforts in the highest of esteem. Whether they always agree with my methods or condone my discretions are separate issues. They love me and I love them, I give them my pride and they me theirs, period.

Of course the main reason, and probably the only, I came back to Chicago in the first place was to see Aubrey. I told Stopher after the folks first brought the whole trip up that if wasn't for Aubrey I would have stayed behind.

Stopher said: "I believe you; I'm going no matter what."

Chris and I got to the airport a good hour before she was supposed to land. We took the train to O'Hare; Dad was to meet us with the car outside at the terminal. Once we located her gate Stopher begged off.

"You two should have this moment alone; I'll look out for Dad and meet you by the baggage claim."

"You raised her too; are you sure?"

"I know my place."

I stood off to the side when the passengers filed off the plane and through the gate. I found a large enough pole to conceal me while giving a clear view. She came off seeking out a familiar face while half expecting to head down to the baggage claim by herself; no longer the child that had be looked after every instant in a big crowd. Moving slowly she scanned gaining speed with each step until her feet found the tiled floor and saw the sign pointing the way toward the proper escalator.

"My, god," I thought, "she has grown."

I stepped out from behind the pole and followed taking note of the purplish, reddish streaks in her hair, and the tightness of her jeans wrapped around a burgeoning figure. Her back to me I still couldn't get over the shock of how much make-up she wore. I let a hundred feet go by as I closed in. The smile on my face grew hard and a little embarrassed. Of course she would be glad to see me, she'd be fucking ecstatic. The time and distance could never be a match for what we had built and still...

"Hey, Breeze-child," I said, a whisper above a whisper.

Her whole body went stiff and she turned to face me knowing whom she would see.

"Daddy!"

She was in my arms.

I had always been a giver of firm hugs but the Raven had me trained in the art of back-cracking, spine-tingling hugs so Aubrey gasped.

"I can't breath."

I pulled back.

"You're so tall, you look great."

"No one calls me Breeze-child but you, so I knew the second I heard."

I kissed her forehead and hugged her again, this time in a more humane fashion. Down at the baggage claim she ran to Stopher and water filled my eyes to see them. I loved how much she loved him.

The trip was filled with reunions, eyes standing back to take in old, familiar but long unseen faces. For Grandma we put on our guitars outside her door and walked in strumming THE HOUSE OF THE RISING SUN, a song she loved to hear me sing, she howled with surprised excitement. It was great to be home, it was all that anyone could want, to be in a place where love lived in the walls; Chris and I told stories and heard them in return; we played football with the nieces and nephews in hopes that we might discover who they had become; Aubrey and I went to our favorite neighborhood restaurant alone; Joel called us to come play guitar and drink beer in his smoke filled room; Mom and Dad beamed in the evenings as we sat around the front room singing songs; Dad's eyes seemed perpetually wet, his smile likewise open for never ending business.

Although Joel was the resident nutcase and diseased-mind, it was Art that haunted me. Joel had found his way through hell and within it remained himself somehow—sweet and profound. Art seemed lost in anger even when being pleasant. It was good to see him but I'm not sure what he saw of me. Of course that had always been a problem between us. He lived in the basement where Chris and I had dwelled but he kept it locked when he was away, sometimes even when he was at home. As far as Santa Monica took me from home, as much as I wanted to be back there during my visit to Chicago, I was never as far from home as he constantly seemed to be.

Aubrey only stayed for a week and we saw enough of each other while allowing the space to spend time with the family members in our respective age brackets. It didn't snow a lot but one night we bundled up and walked to the Portage Park School playground and rolled around in the dark winter night watching the snow gently drift down through the street lights to fall all around us. I spun her on the tire, watched her try the slide without much success because of her snowsuit and sat on a swing next to her and talked; we were still us. I could tell she had more on her mind than she spoke but then, not everything needs to be said and others are wanted for one's self.

When she went back to Nashville I had over two weeks left in Chicago. Without Aubrey there I got more and more restless.

I talked to the Raven a lot, sometimes that helped and sometimes it worse. She called on New Years Eve and that meant a lot to me. By the time we boarded the plane to Los Angeles even Chris was eager to get back. The van, which had sat idle in Sukey's driveway for almost a month, started up like a true champ. It was a Sunday but too late for us to get a spot on the promenade. Chris needed a couple days to adjust anyway. I decided to take my bike out from the side of Sukey's house and ride along the shore on the path. Of course I ended up on the promenade and stopped by to say hello to the Raven. She was warm but distant as was her way with me on the promenade the more we became involved.

"I don't want people here knowing my business," rang her mantra.

She kept her distance but we still played for her and with each song she melted a little more. She still wanted me to write for her while I waited to play and there too I made attempts at chipping away at her resolve, though not with obvious romantic advances. And not all of what I wrote had designs on her but in fact the opposite. Some were more in the lines of concession speeches of sort. In the end I simply did what I did best: I talked about me:

I'm not or have ever been closed to myself—the world is another story. That is to say, what flows from my being does so for it's own survival. So I babble when bubbling beneath my thoughts trying to breath air; I collect calmness when words float free from connection to a concerted concept.

But what I am is where I am; who am at a given moment, for better or worse.

I've been contemplating a life with no more love than I have already been given. Certainly I've had more than my share.

Still it wounds me

I ache in a space that can't imagine being healed

Unfortunately I fear the possibility practical; mathematics have spoken. There is only so much love and I have made my choices.
Clarity has its price
I spread my fingers with open hands at the end of arms that attempt to ask no questions. But that is a lie, for they desperately want answers. Of course love is neither an answer nor a question.
It is simply what I want

Earnest was glad to see us and told us that he moved southward down the shore for the sunsets.

"All those tweakers were getting on my nerves."

So the Ocean Park entrance became our new haunt. I liked it better there; it felt more spacious; there were no bike rental shops our burger joints, just restrooms, the sand and the water. Down on the shore there were a few large boulders to sit on that made it more comfortable and cinematic.

CHAPTER FIFTEEN

The folks came for a visit the first week of February. It was a short stay, we had only recently returned from Chicago, but it never ceases to serve my soul to see them. The Raven joined us briefly for a walk down to the shore by the pier. She had to get back to work so she and I walked ahead. I still had the bum heel and was using a cane I got from my ninety-two year old grandma during my visit home. The Raven sprinted out in front of me at the end laughing at my feebleness as I trailed. She stood apart from me and smiled mischievously. We paused in silence. Slowly we moved closer together and embraced—cautiously soft. She allowed my lips to approach her but removed them as we touched.

"We're not going back."

"How's about forward."

"Ya are not neither."

The next day on the promenade I wrote this:

I wish I were an answer—a solution so serene that all would seek me out. What a light I would cast across this vast wasteland of queries; a beacon for all the lost; a final destination for all who travel.

Alas, I am but a shadow of my own doubt

Eh, answers are overrated

I think that last one was as much about the lack of tips, love and recognition I got from the promenade and music world in general, as any plea to her, if not more.

The night the folks caught a train back to Chicago, Chris and I decided to hang out and see them off. In the hour or so we had to kill we each did some walking off on our own around the historic station.

It was a grand place that belonged in a climatic scene of some kind of 1950s, cinematic intrigue. Every room had high ceilings and all the woodwork, from the benches to the expansive doorways, shined with an age that told wonderful stories. Chris and I had been walking separately down two opposing corridors when coming out of a turn I saw Chris talking to a stranger. The stranger, apparently, had some grade A magic mushrooms that he had to unload before catching his train in ten minutes.

"Kind of a sleazy thing to do while you're seeing your parents off," I said, when we had held a private counsel on the matter.

"I can live with that," said Stohper.

"I saw an ATM in the other hall?"

"Sounds like fate to me."

We paused.

"Shroomies, Vuma."

"Shroomies, Stopher."

"Who knows when we'll stumble on them again?"

So we went for it all the while forgetting the number one rule about purchasing anything from a stranger, let alone drugs; never buy anything from anyone at bus and train stations or airports. Our collective eagerness had led us astray and when the folks got on their train, and we were in the van pulling out on to the road, I was almost certain that I saw the stranger who had supposedly boarded a train north forty minutes ago, huddled with another stranger, no doubt telling him about having to board a train in ten minutes. On the ramp to the highway, I told Chris.

"Never buy drugs at a train station; I know that," he said.

"Whatta ya think?"

"In for a penny in for a pound; we have weed, we'll get a bottle and hope for the best."

Part of our initial willingness, other than our childish want for it to be true, was that Steve was out of town for a few days and he always left a key for us so we could bring our batteries back and forth and use his Gizmo. So we had access to his VCR and nineteen-inch, colored television. If luck had laid with us we would be in a secured room watching our favorite concert footage tapes or one of Steve's videos and tripping our brains out within the next two hours. As it turned out the mushrooms would have been better use in a red sauce over pasta. We did, however, go to Steve's, get drunk, smoke some weed by the pool, and watch live footage of Stevie Ray Vaughn, Billy Joel and Jackson Browne.

I was in a stupor faintly hovering over being passed out by nine o'clock when I recognized the voice on Steve's machine as my old friend Bill Schlegal, who had coincidently been the man who gave us the videos we were currently watching and always treasured. Chris too heard that it was Bill and picked up the phone. I sat through blurry eyes in an even blurrier head and watched as Stopher's face turn to shock, his eyes water. He kept up his composure long enough to take in what Bill had said and finish the conversation.

He hung up the phone and said: "Bob Johnson is dead; he killed himself."

I think I understood and believed him at once. I saw his face bloom into an intense red as Stopher began to shake from his shoulders up. Tears streamed down as his hands could not keep them from coming. Like Sam Spade getting slipped a Mickey, I faded to black. An hour or so later I re-surfaced to Stopher sitting there, listening to FUNKIN'OBNOXCIOUS, a cut from our first CD that I had credited Bob Johnson with a co-write on.

"Did you tell me that Bob Johnson is dead?"

"Yeah," Stopher said with a laugh that sounded angry.

"You talked to Bill?"

"And I called Scott."

"Fucking Bob."

"Fucking Bob." Stopher raised his drink and smiled his displeasure.

I had known Bob since before the fifth grade but had not become friends with him until then. Like me he loved music and baseball and discovered pot at an early age. To sum up: life beat him up and smacked him around like every one else, and like so many I have known he didn't take it very well. One could easily say that he was manic depressive or bi-polar. He had all the traits and on top of that he had a natural brilliance that made everything else all the more frustrating. No one hit a curveball quite like him; he was a natural on the drums; understood music in general on an organic level; and had an excellent mind for academic science. That he never found a solid enough footing in any of his talents, and that the world refused to see him as special enough to encourage him or throw him a single bone, bitterness and a hereditary chemical-imbalance dissolved his resolve into a series of delusional rants that alienated him from all his friends and family.

He came to my wedding, we had stayed in touch over my travels to Nashville, but I saw him slipping away even from that distance. Bob, The Boomer as I liked to call him, was always crazy and at odds with the world; he never managed to rise above the fray of his own self-disappointments coupled with a demanding world whizzing by on all sides pushing him deeper into himself. In the years I spent living in my parents basement, between Nashville and California, it got to the point where I could no longer be in a room with him. If it were just Bob lying about being begged by the Northeastern University baseball coach to join the team—despite his being thirty, overweight and still having only the credits of a sophomore, I would have indulged him—I did indulge him. He got paranoid, accusing me of betrayal; he was simply lost in his own anger, swinging at anyone trying to stop him from drowning.

Although just a few weeks before I left for California he called me, full of humility.

"I'm sorry about everything; do you think you could be my friend again," he said, calmly.

"I've never stopped, man; you were the one angry with me."

"I know."

He would come by a few times, still telling stories of imminent success.

"I started a training program to be carpenter. The foreman said that, with my skills, I should blow through orientation in less than half the time. I'll be making fifty Gs by the end of the year."

On the night of our going away party Boomer was there and seemed sad. I could see him no longer clinging to the carpentry business as a life raft as he drifted between beers. We stood away from the others by my front steps. I was getting ready to leave and spend the remainder of the night with Angel at a motel.

"I bet you do great out there. You and Chris have the talent and discipline to make it happen."

I saw him trying to meet me; I felt his love wanting to be known.

"I don't know about the carpentry anymore. The guy running the thing is two-faced; says one thing and does another."

"Still answering phones at that pizza place?"

"Yeah, come by anytime and I'll get you one free."

"Thanks."

We drank our beers and I searched for what it was that I wanted him to know.

"Bob, I'm not going with the thought of any great success. I just want to be happier—not even happy—just happier. That's what I want for you; find something to make you a little happier, whatever that is."

He smiled and I saw those crystal clear, blue eyes of his sparkle off the streetlight. For that moment I saw only the kid I had grown up with, void of the disappointment, minus the anger of having been a failure. Boomer was a sweet kid, a good man who would never be able to stay afloat. And I loved him.

I never cried for Bob. My journey consumed me; I didn't have the energy to spare. Chris insisted on writing a song for our fallen comrade, I ended up writing some of the words with him. We played it for a couple of years but it faded from our set. It was a song worthy of Boomer's memory (Oh, it jammed), but it faded anyway. One line has stayed with me and it is this: *Blue eyes on a fast bike.*

Bob Johnson, after drinking most of the night before, woke early one morning and shoveled the walk in front and along the side of his house. The house he had lived in all his life, the house his mother still lived in and had repeatedly asked him to leave from. Afterwards he took a six-pack of beer into the garage, closed the door behind him, got in the car, started the engine and closed his beautiful, blue eyes. They found a bible next to him; maybe he sought god, maybe just forgiveness. I do know that he wanted off the ride; he wanted peace. He wanted to be a little happier. I hope he found at least that.

I talked of Bob's death with Stopher just the other day.

"He was losing his home and had no friends to take him in; if only he knew how pleasant it could be being homeless out here," he said.

With Bob's death I began to understand suicide. Yet when considering Stopher's recent remark I wonder if Bob had another card worth playing? Even so, I do understand.

The week after the folks left, the Raven took me out to see a boat she was thinking of buying.

"I could live at sea."

"Do you sail?"

"I could live at harbor."

"Like living in a van."

"It's a boat; completely different."

The guy who met us at the harbor to show her the boat, was Mark, a tall lanky yet filled out man about my age with a rugged outdoorsy air but a somewhat tender demeanor. He was an independent contractor who worked just enough to pay for his many mountain climbing and scuba diving expeditions. I would find him later to be competition for the Raven's affection. He was not the first, just the first I got to know. That night we sat in the boat's main cabin playing guitar and drinking beer. Mark was a good picker and a fine singer. We jammed while the Raven sipped scotch from her flask and called out requests. My voice had been burnt from singing four hours that day so I mostly jammed along. At the end of the night Mark gave the Raven an endearing hug, which at the time I didn't think much of...I wondered about it a little.

The next night the Raven and I went back alone and ended up in the boat's bow bunk where I, in a more sober state, reminded her of my other talents.

"Baby! What do you do to me?"

"That voodoo that I do, so well."

On the ride home she scolded: "I can't always be driving you home."

I knew exactly what prompted it.

"Lady, drop me off anywhere you like."

"What about your foot?"

"I have a cane."
"I'm not starting up with you again."
"You're doing an excellent imitation then."

So it began again, the late night drive bys, the longing stares from her perch every time we played for her on the promenade, and the final, definitive, absolute declarations of our demise.

For all my drama with the Raven, life for Stopher and I still revolved around music and writing. Stopher was in the middle of yet another screenplay; I had begun my second novel. One of my favorite moments in a given day again found it's fullest bloom beneath her arrival. Obviously she shared in our music on the promenade, but also on days we didn't play and took turns with the laptop at the library on Santa Monica and Sixth (the old building), during my second shift stint I'd often look up from my work to see her standing there, dressed in whatever elegant, exotic attire she chose for that day at work. She usually got off around three and I tended to knock off from three to four so it worked out nicely. It was that moment I cherished—not just then but now—playing (actually being) the diligent writer, hacking away at the world armed with words for hours then having this incredible vision wrapped in a colorful sarong, sporting a black tank top and donning a wide-brimmed straw hat stand above me; a call to come play.

"Look, my belly is so brown."
"Indeed. Hmmm, indeed."

On the promenade between sets she did her best not to know me, when she wasn't engaging me to write for her or brandishing her fist humorously like a school ground bully in a cute cartoon. Depending what went on between us the previous week or the night before I'd write of my yearning and frustration in some form or another, not always necessarily pertaining to her.

Here are a couple of examples:

Shapes saunter in a collection contained in a changing ocean
Colors collide, sizes vary—none failing to please

The eyes surmise what arms can not hold
where words falter before being formed

The night is final
It neither speaks nor listens
An endless stream of what may or may not be possible in infinity takes from the day

Each night holds its own
And this one is cold

More shapes, all desirable, all worth what you'd give
but not necessarily what they'd take

Random thoughts rally against any arrival of a specific conclusion
Doubts dance with apprehension to the tune of a cynic's insistence
Self-pity serves the moment well:
"Poor, poor, dear," it caresses the sourful soul

Indignancey has no place here yet perfumes the atmosphere for fools to smell of when avoiding their exclusively painful truths

The sun lies in wait
but will luminate little
more than what already is
Simply brighter

Shapes saunter, eyes follow
Shapes saunter, eyes follow
And another:
A world lives in a moment in her arms
I go there when it is offered
Clenched for comfort
all outside the embrace tumbles through meaningless mumbles
Soft in her roughness
giving she receives
A moment in her arms

is a moment for the filling of me
To the eyes it seems I, the larger of the two
am holding her
To my heart it is I in her
though she is within me
A world lives in a moment in her arms

I pray the moment comes again

The Raven preferred that the vagueness of the former be given to her on the promenade, lest it fall into the hands of others who were otherwise blind to our affections. Although we were now entering a time when we became the gossiping speculation of all the regulars, from Franz the balloon man to Vince the actor/political activist, and Bible John to a few of the homeless, she insisted our secret lay with us and us alone.

So I tried to be more topical when I could. Like with this one that I wrote after I observed a small boy watching the mime:

The little boy's eyes were butterfly wings filled with wonder. Patiently he watched the white face explain all by saying nothing.

Love life—the message came.

The boy already did.

But will he remember this unnecessary message as the years tumble around him, weighing in doubt on his shoulders, surrounding his every move and challenging his every belief?

Some messages are meant for saving until you need them to save you.

The man moved

The boy laughed

The man frowned playfully

The boy's eyes turned to circular question marks

Moments amass to form our lives only if we think to preserve them. If we let the moment go it will. Of course it is bound to go no matter what we do. But if we treasure and wish them well, they will come back when we call.

In my mind I call to the boy. I know he can't hear. I call anyway. Maybe to myself. But in my mind it is to the boy.

The little boy happily walks away with those who have brought him out of the collective consciousness and into the separate.

I wrote this one in response to all the sad, needy, lonely, annoying, bullshitters that vied for my attention in hopes that if I heard their stories that they would miraculously turn to fact:

His words were incessant. They rolled on and on, one after another. Maybe he was lonely? Maybe every person he ever knew swallowed the barrel of a gun to escape his never-ending prattle.

Had I a gun, I would have joined them with glee.

Oh for the love of silence; the lack of a voice drumming in my ear.

"Did I mention the time some producer wanted to make me rich and famous," the man continued to drone. *"Yeah, well I was gonna do it but my heart wasn't in it."*

Right, I thought, his heart. It couldn't possibly be that he was delusional!

If only I could form the words, "SHUT UP! Won't you, for the love of all that is sacred, please stop talking? Is it not within the realm of your depleted sense of reality to see that I have been beyond polite, that I have indulged you more than could be reasonably expected of any fucking saint?!"

He seems like a nice enough man, so I allow that I am simply an asshole; an unruly fellow unfit for a civilized world. If this be the case, I grant permission to lock me up. BUT PLEASE, let there be peace and quiet. And if that cannot be arranged, then may I inquire into the possibility of having my ears RIPPED from my head, BURNT to a crisp and its ashes buried at the bottom of the deepest ocean.

PLEASE!!!!!

The Raven laughed hard when she read that one.

One day the old man, Billy, who no one could agree on whether he was Asian, Mexican, Alaskan our even human, was banging away at his drum set and singing, HOTEL CALIFORNIA to the same beat he sang WANTAN AMERA. I could never get over the expensive equipment he had. Here was the man whom the rotation rules of promenade were invented for, just to keep him from taking stores and restaurants hostage until they paid him to leave. Of course the rule did not come into effect until he had made enough money to buy all this wonderful stuff and make CDs. That's right: plural. I could never decide whether he was mentally slow or a genius. Danny, the singer songwriter from Manchester, England, said that he talked to Billy on a bus once.

"I kid you not, mate, he was acting all excited about how good his new CD was coming along."

Delusional wins again.

So I wrote a bit similar to the last one, about Billy as he played one time in front of her restaurant but the Raven wanted none of it. His constant banging drained her of all humor on the matter.

In the world of physical, lust, love or however you want to classify it, the Raven sought blood. Not necessarily literally but in spirit and effort. The fact that my cheeks remained unscarred the next day had nothing to do with her being gentle, and did not stop the bone of my jaw from remembering her teeth vividly. Eyes may water but all in the name of good-not-so-clean, twisted fun. The day after one such exchange of flesh for romance, the Raven wrote me this note:

Hey You,

You give good ear! (Referring to the day's music)

I bite your other cheek off! You made me; I had no choice. As Malcovich said in DANGEROUS LIASONS, "It is simply beyond my control."

To which I responded:

She chewed my cheek casually as you please.

I said: "I think I might need that back."

"Can't have it," she muttered between bites and swallows.

So cheekless, and better for it she assured me, I attempted to put on a brave face. I had no idea how integral a cheek could be in such an endeavor.

When she finished, a coo followed by a belch announced her pleasure.

"Good?" I inquired.

"Alright," she mused, "but I've had better."

"So you do this often." I concluded. "Eat people's faces."

"It's a hobby," she answered flatly.

"Ya see I would think there'd be a law against this sort of thing."
"Shows how wrong ya can be," she smiled.
Suddenly she set a soft hand on my remaining cheek and whispered with a lilting sincerity that covered me in calm comfort.
"Nothing will ever be alright again," her words warned.
"Were they ever?"
"Of course not."
I nodded appreciatively.
She bowed benevolently. And then was gone.
If I had my cheek back I probably wouldn't take the kind of care, give it the attention it needed; love it is at it should be loved.
So I am of one cheek and one mind. I am the idiot that let some fancy dame eat his cheek.

Yes, we were on again the ride she designed from moment to moment. She steadfastly remained determined to keep her options open while I relinquished pride and dignity in favor of having nothing to feel bad about. As Valentines Day approached I felt the queasy stench of jealousy in my gut, assuming she we would go out to dinner with the one who offered the most expensive, elegant evening. In anticipation of that I wrote a poem as a gift to give her after my set that day. The pseudo-holiday fell on a day that I knew she'd be working and us playing. What I had written burned a hole in my heart for days, wanting her to read it instantly, believing and scoffing simultaneously in, and at the worth of, these collected and cleverly arranged words. To do battle with my anxiety I wrote this philosophical distraction to myself and gave it to her:

I tilt to the breeze
It lifts as it laces through my hair;
eyes closed—soul opened
I'm sure I've felt one before, but for the tense of this purpose
I propose to let the memories merge 'till there is only one;
a lifetime of breezes converge
Fear joins anxiety in their obsolescence
Jealousy with anger follow suit
Appreciation enjoys the peace of an idle mind

Certain that all moments chase the breeze
I let it go to allow room for the afterglow
Where the breeze sweeps, the glow settles
into arms that choose to embrace
And as is with all
The glow, which came after falls
into itself and fades as a song
Ahh, 'till the next breeze has come and gone

That was one of those of which she said after, "It was a bit much to take in all at once. I'll have to read it later."

Sometimes, when we got together later in the night, she would have me read them to her and I'd take questions. Ultimately everything I ever wrote for her ended up in a box. "Ten years from now when I've forgotten the whole sorted affair. I'll have them to tell me what happened." So she said. "My memory is deliciously short." So she explained.

"Mine is painfully long." Was my response.

"That is why you are a great writer."

Only she could compliment me so while slicing into my pain exquisite.

On Valentine's Day she wore an old fashion satin, sock-hop kind of dress. It was red without sleeves and bore her shoulders unfettered by cloth as well. It had a bow just below her cleavage and rose up just above the knee, which was uncommon for the Raven who usually favored the long flowing look. She wore similarly dated black and white shoes to complete the time travel. Cute doesn't begin to capture her being.

"It's fun," she explained her themed attire.

"A throw back to a more innocent time," I offered.

"I don't know about innocent," Stopher said referring to her cleavage, "but it sure as hell looks like fun."

"So are you gonna give me that Valentine poem today?"

"Not that you are deserving, but yeah. Do you want it now, or should I give it to you after the set?"

"Why don't you read to me when we hang out after work."

"What, no money bag suitor tonight?"

"I'm taking my mom out to dinner, but that's later."

I had never been so happy to hear about any one taking their mother out to dinner in my life.

We only played one set that day because she got off work at three and I wanted to be there when she did. She set aside her usual rule about socializing on the promenade because she wanted me to buy her a tee shirt off one of the carts. I felt guilty and pathetic at how easily I went along, because my money was Stopher's money, and any extra should have been sent to Aubrey.

"Fuck it," Stoph, "so you spend twenty bucks on her."

What a partner.

From three until five we hung around the cart as she hen-pecked over every single detail in the process of getting the words "GIMME PAWW" written on the black shirt in glittered studs. By the time we finished, the sun left the promenade all but dark. We went to leave for her car, as we did I placed my hand around her waist. She said nothing but I felt her back twinge. Once by the car she spoke.

"I really hate when guys have to claim their property by handling me."

"And this because I dared to touch you in public?"

"I'm not your girlfriend."

"We were having such a nice time, Sweets; we laughed and talked; we were just being, you know? I've seen guys do what you're talking about and that's not me. There's this thing called affection, maybe you've heard of it? I was expressing affection, not ownership; sorry to offend."

"I'm sorry. You're not like that, you're right. Just no PDA, especially on the promenade."

"PDA?"

"Public display of affection."

"Unless it's you giving it to me?"

"Exactly."

"You decide when and where?"

"And how much."

"You are a piece of work."

"Is that polite for bitch?"
"Clever girl."
"Oh, baby."
With that she ran and jumped up into my arms to kiss me.
"Now that's some fine, PDA," I said.
"Huh, baby?"
"Huh, baby?"
With that she dropped me off by the van at Albertsons.
"Do you want me to read you your gift?"
"No, read it when I pick you up in a couple of hours."
She was good to her word and came back three and a half hours later.
She drove down 11th because she hated Lincoln, but turned east on Ashland instead of going up to Marine and heading west.
"Where are we going?"
"I hate going to my place. There's no real privacy and always that Frenchie. I used to park the Phasar here all the time because it's a dark and quiet street."
We pulled up behind the Phasar that was parked along the curb by a row of tall bushes that hid the house from us and us from the house. Once inside the Raven slipped into my arms and kissed me like a true Valentine.
"Sing me a song, bitch."
"Request?"
"Pink Floyd, no wait that's a belter, huh?"
(I do a killer version of TIME.)
"I know, CRYING ON THE SHOULDER OF THE ROAD. And remember, nice and twangy like."
I sang the song I wrote in Nashville oh so many years ago, then sang, NO DOCTORS PLEASE, a song I wrote with Mom, and a couple of others. In the meantime she crawled under a big billowy sleeping bag, changed out of her cute little dress, into her robe and sipped Champagne. Of course when I say sipped, I mean gulped it from the bottle.
"Now read it, baby!"
I read:

To the Klassiest of Kittens:
I want to thank you for giving me back my romantic heart. I had stopped believing in its rhythm; a deaf ear led by blinded eyes.
Blinded by disappointments, failed expectations
Deafened by a lack of faith
in my own beauty's ability to be seen or heard
Then I heard you smile
It shattered my every pretense; engulfed my defenses

A symphony could not orchestrate the music of your smile
To listen to your smile is to be silenced by your eyes; too profound for words

And yet those eyes and that smile are but tools of a soul in flight
A soul that sings so a smile can be heard, a soul that glows with such grace that it cannot be contained within its own eyes.

So it is not the smile; it is you
It is not the eyes; it is you

Are all my words merely a plea to a kiss? If that be so they are still no less true.

And what of a kiss? Is it no more than mouths at play? Teasing tongues, lacing lips, offering only a moment's pleasure? So let it be so. Moments have been given to lesser endeavors

Yes I have found my romantic heart
It pulses in my palm; gentle not frail, tender not soft, full of wonder not lost
It beats for the sharing not taking
Feed your soul of my heart and it is I who am nourished
I will do the same for mine with yours and it will be we who flourish
And if it be not love I speak of
then it be not love I need

"Read it again baby, read it again!"
I did.

And again and again until she pulled me over her and in, my mouth all consuming, my breath all knowing. I consumed her flesh, taking her ankles in firm of hand never having her hands know me beyond the surface. I gave for the sake of taking what that offered, asking and receiving nothing more. Her ecstasy remained, for that night, a one-way street and that was fine by me. *"I have often walked down this street before. But the pavement always stayed beneath my feet before..."*

It could have been her having me pay my dues or that my body, fat and grotesque as it was, had no worthy claim to reach any sufficient height of ecstasy at her expense. At that moment I took no offense, even imagining the rules holding steadfast. The Raven was playground enough for me. On top of which her every groan combined with her body writhing on my touch to fill the banks of a memory I would soon run to swimming from shore to shore. The macho Princess was my queen I served faithfully at face value all the while faintly hoping that other walls may fall.

"You're like a Greek God," she exclaimed pulling from between her legs by the hair after a job well done.

As superficial as it sounds, I loved being the guy that could make this hot, sweet, beautiful, creature hotter and sweeter. (Her beauty was beyond my improvement.)

The next day on the promenade she wrote:
Whew..!
That set was similar to my last brush with...EDIT...EDIT.
Over before I knew what hit me! BAD BAD BAD Raven! Surprised?
What? Huh? Well I've got to say I'm in a bit of a stupor at the moment
And boy howdy it feels good. It's a little like this...(here's the vision)
Grey matter on a squeaky kiddie pool-float, sunny day, not a care in the world.
Got that? Yea, it's good 2 be my grey matter when nuthin' else does.
I wrote:

*There were moments when I thought my breath wouldn't return
I didn't care
From my chest through her fingers my breaths belong to her now
Pleasure gripped my throat and I gasped
Air fast became meaningless as it seemed to serve only as a distraction from her touch
To quote her: "It's good to be grey matter when nothing else does."
Indeed at that moment not only did nothing else matter, nothing else was
Sitting under a sunny sky soon to be fading
I measure each breath gratefully
Life floats about and I smile:
Good to be a part; nice to have survived the passion
I would, without a single moment's hesitation, offer up my breath to such passion should it pass my way again. Sacrifices have to be made if adventures are to be had*

Oh we two did have fun.
Soon after I wrote my first song for her called, THE RAVEN. The music leapt from an upbeat, jazzy intro to a thoughtful, standard-like musical prose.

*I stumble over myself
Feet tangle with the years
Putting my life to the light
I know who I am; I have no fear of mirrors
Then the Raven wrinkles her nose
over a curvaceous smile under spacious eyes
And all my answers question me, "Are you sure?"*

*The song I sang for me
Now too sings for the Raven
The music sails under her wing
For as long as she is listening
It will be*

For the Raven and me

My voice reveals me putting words to sound
If the soul exists it is speaking now
Fingers find the music
Lifting the voice, sending it soaring
And setting it gently down
The Raven's head tilts slightly
Her eyes find me—suddenly I'm more
At that moment even her daggers seem kind
Peace on a hurricaned shore

The song I sang for me
Now too sings for the Raven
The music sails under her wing
Words float around us
As our eyes bring us closer
Me on my perch she on her's
The song was mine but now it's ours
For as long as she is listening
It will be
For the Raven and me

That song was what we had been before our first kiss and why it came to be. It was the first of many to come, and while one of the later songs to come was to be my favorite, none would ever be more apt, or accurately depicted the beginning of something that, in my wildest dreams, did I ever allow myself to think possible.

One day amidst all this romance the Raven bustled over from her perch—big, black, canvas bag over shoulder—to thank us for the previous set. Stopher and I smiled at the elegant spectacle.

"Good set, boys."

"We broke a few windows," Stop conceded.

"Hey, Dave," her voice suddenly went soft and hidden. "Wanna have some lunch with me by the car; I'm in the bank lot, meet me there in about five minutes."

Stoph and I exchanged a puzzled glance.

"Too many busy-body eyes out here."

I dropped my head while Chris' eyes turned hard.

"Heaven for fend," he said.

"David, you know how I am about my privacy; are you going to come or not?"

I looked at Chris and he turned away in disgust before walking off.

"Okay," I softly emitted, keeping my eyes to myself.

"I got Greek," she offered, then stopped before leaving. "It's nobody's business out here who I lunch with."

"Whatever," I answered the ground after she had already had her back to me.

"You're not going to meet her?" Chris scolded me.

"I'll give it her this once."

"Fuck her!"

"She just likes her privacy."

Bullshit!"

He was right.

"Fuck her," he hissed.

"Don't ever ask me that again," I announced as I arrived at her car.

"David, yo-"

"Call it privacy all you want; you're ashamed to be seen with me, or you don't want to scare off any prospective suitors, or both. Either way, fuck you, I won't do it again."

"There are plenty others who'd be happy to-"

"Fine," I turned to leave, "go find one of 'em."

"David!" She ran to cut me off and wrap me up in her arms. "Baby, you know I only want to hang with you."

It was just another never ending circle we'd run in, one of many that led back to us. I knew that there were other performers, and customers from the restaurant, that had designs on her, even a few whom she may have had a design on, or at least a notion of one. I knew her hang-up on privacy to be true, and I knew my other suspicions to have merit. She was free to do as she saw fit while it lay upon me to draw my own lines of defense.

"From now on I walk off with you or you eat with someone else."

"Okay, baby," she placated.

In the future she would arrange the same type of meeting by saying that she had to call a client, or run an errand, so that it appeared an organic happenstance. She also walked off with me in tow enough times to satisfy my ego.

Back in October '01 I began doing a little yoga and a couple of basic exercises. By February '02 I had added three sets of ten push-ups and fifteen sit-ups. Nothing compared to what I, in better days, had been capable of but a welcomed start. I sometimes did two or three sets of each at night when I felt able. In the day I laid out a plastic tarp by the short bleachers that looked out on the baseball fields of Marine Park. Over the next couple of years Mike's pioneer lady would suffer through as witness to my workouts from her vantage point of sought out shade as I slipped the feet of my bent legs under the bleachers to give me leverage for that endeavor. (Mike was always off gathering in the mornings.) I felt bad on the days that shade fell mostly where I huffed and puffed, but there was only one spot by the bleachers that had the needed level ground. Some mornings I'd wait as long as I could for the sun to shift the shade to a preferable distance or for her to wander off of her own accord so as not to crowd her. (We were neighbors and I tried to be a considerate one.) At night, in Albertsons parking lot, or down by the ocean, the front tire of my faithful, beloved van held my feet.

One night the Raven came by Albertsons with her mother Carol in the midst of one of my sessions and the elder woman remarked: "Is he doing that for you?"

"It's for himself but because of me," the Raven answered proudly.

On my return from visiting Chicago I began long, daily walks along the shore as soon as my heel allowed. At first I went from where we had parked to the Santa Monica pier and back. Soon that seemed too easy so I started walking in the other direction towards the Venice pier, figured that to be close to two miles each way. I usually started by four-thirtyish and ended about an hour and a half later. That time was reduced over time to an hour and that time to even less. I remember walking and watching the sun fall over the water, forcing the sky to change its opinion of color in regards to the clouds. I'd pass runners and joggers going each way and scoffed at their intent focus on body over soul. I used to jog and enjoyed it but with my weight and beat up joints I surmised my running days better left to a younger man I would never again be. Of course my ego wouldn't allow me to leave it a logical course of age and physical limitations; they were fools missing the smell of roses growing in the sky and I was the wise old man taking it all in.

Out on those walks I began to slip the chains that had grown all over inside me. Between the morning yoga and the early evening walks a thaw occurred in my very marrow. Bitter days on the promenade got left there among the footprints to be washed away into the vast salty soul cleanser. The Raven continued to haunt me but by the end it invariably concerned me less than when I started. I was becoming a me I had always known yet saw so very rarely.

"You're like Art," Chris had once observed. "Once you sink your teeth into something you have the ability to get obsessed. I see your eyes narrow and know that something is going to get done."

Those narrow eyes were upon me and they, ironically, opened up a world long gone from me.

I also took to taping up photos on the ceiling of the van over my bed. It happened in late November 2001 while Stoph and I were lying around the van listening to jazz in the rain. We had been getting all these pictures of our nieces and nephews; Aubrey and Madison; and some taken from the folk's previous visits. I laid in my bed looking over the stack of them through lovingly buzzed eyes and thought, "It would be healthy for me to see these more often." I immediately began to tape them up void of scheme or forethought. Just one after another side by side, end to end.

Eileen sat at a booth in an IHOP skeptically viewing her son Jake's exaggerated face of authority, as his index finger raised itself to punctuate a circular mouth; an outside shot of 5103 with a Christmas wreath on the front door. (I took a few shots around the house during my Christmas visit and this one, with some others, got added as time went by); I also gathered up the back yard—so different than the one from my youth, with it's twin apple trees, decorative fountain, purely aesthetic garden, bearing none the edible profits of the past; Linda stood adorned with a psychedelic tank top, son at her side, a mountain woman and child (she of eighth grade Eliza Doolittle); Aubrey sat in the snow during her first visit to Chicago without me, bundled in a snow suit I bought the winter before I left and a hand me down coat from future-stepfather-Larry over it , having just made a snow angel. Her expression like her greeting hand, carried a casual resignation that didn't so much surrender as set aside any need to fight—who she had been or become; a close up of Aubrey had her face framed off center to the right. Her smile, genuine and easy, revealed the braces she had gotten a year after I had gone—she colored the braces in with blue ink before sending the picture to me. Her thumb print mistakenly smudged up the left hand's upper corner opposing her forehead; Chris, mom and I in a Venice sunset by the shore—Stopher's eyes were wide and his mouth tight, Mom easy as her smile and proud of her boys, I still wearing the beat up old fedora leaned in and felt loved; Grandma sitting at her dinning room table looking relaxed—a way I don't think of her as often as I should; Art at the tender age of fifteen, sitting in a rocking chair that Eileen had gotten for Christmas when we were all too young to see it as nothing but a waste of a Christmas wish. He wore the red, black and white checkered, flannel shirts we all had growing up—the only kind of clothes that could stand up to us. There is not a trace of anger in him, he seems confident and unquestioning about who he is, who he should be, they are the same—that is to say, they were then; the chair Joel sits in is a lazy-boy type in my grandma's front room. He wears a blue bandana and his usual distracted smile. As he sits there, no doubt thinking about asking for something, I am out in California wanting a dream or two of his to be fulfilled by Chris and I; Mom and Dad sit in the booth of a restaurant and physically they are apart. Mom's eyes take in the lens while Dad's stand up to it, unthreatening, void of submission. They are so different but on the same page, I'll never imagine one without the other; Aubrey, sleep still in her eyes leans over Madison's half-brother Tristan. He of the perpetually sweet and goofy smile seems glad to have her around. The boy was supposed to have been dead by now time and time again, he'll always be in need, never do a single thing for himself, but he seems to be able to love Aubrey as much as Aubrey, Madison and Alice (his mother) love him; Aubrey and Madison attempt to do my famed potato dance. Madison's face scrunches up as she tries to appear rounder in body, as does Aubrey, although she seems to achieve the necessary pivot-wobble that makes a potato dance; Portage Park School before the outside portico vanished into the new building built on to it. I played in and around it all through grammar school, chased down foul tips off of it during our summer swift-pitch games in the school yard, and got married to Donna in between its pillars; the old garage still stands up on my van's ceiling. Little did I know when I took the picture during my Christmas visit that it would be torn asunder and built a new the following summer; Madison wrestles a large dog to her will; Art's Sean and Tim hold guitars along side Eileen's Jake while Keeley majestically indicates them from the background as a queen does her court. The guitars were gifts from Joel, who would give lessons as well. Lessons, to my enjoyed surprise, Jake and Tim would take to almost seriously; Erin, Art's little girl, holds gingerly the violin Joel gave her. The fact that she is standing out in the alley behind 5103 holds a poetry for me that explains how a pure love can't help but be found when it is so consistently and obviously there. Erin's mother wanted her to hate not only her ex-husband but also his family. For a time evidence could be held toward that favor. I ran that alley, my brother's ran that alley—it was ours and those whom we befriended and had befriended us, now it was also Erin's; Madison and Aubrey sat bundled up in mittens and scarves surrounded by cubes of stacked snow arranged to the effect of a fort. It stood on the front lawn of the little house Donna and I had rented in Wisconsin. It was the first time I lived anywhere but the neighborhood I grew up in. I remember what a baby I was in adjusting to that. I had built a lot of forts in various spots on Pensacola between mine and Jerry Samack's yard down at the other end of the block with the Disviscour house in between, but the one up in Wisconsin was the most important; me, Dad and Chris huddled around a bench on the Venice pier—like Mom, Dad's pride was evident. Chris could be seen holding a plastic water bottle that held cheap booze—his jovial demeanor spilled forth as did mine; Josefa and her husband Ross sit on a beach with their three boys Guthrie, William and Rory. I barely knew Guthrie, William a little less and Rory not at all. To them I am the legend of their mother's words; Art holds Sean as a baby. Sean almost didn't survive being born and because of that struggle, in some ways with some things, always would; William and Rory sit in front of their Christmas tree in a house in Michigan that Chris and I helped our sister's growing family move into. Other than that weekend and one other I have never been there and now they live in Indianapolis.

There were more of the same group and others of the extended family like the Jungels and childhood friends, including my brother in-law Scott who simply became a brother. Those were put up in the cab where Stopher could see them. Pictures like the one with Bob Johnson looking lovingly drunkenly at Chris with his arm about his shoulder, taken at my bachelor party. I had left photos for Chris to tape up by his bed but they never got taped so they ended up in the cab or a box. Other than the handful of ten to twenty that went up that first afternoon under a November rain, the photos went up one to a few at a time over the ensuing years.

The point was to see where I had been and how those younger ones were changing—my daughter, my Madison, and the kids of the brothers and sisters whom share my scars and victories. It helped me to keep my conscious self in touch with my sub-conscious and all it's ghosts—friendly or otherwise. My heart and soul had them safely in tow but I had come to need them more, probably because I felt me slipping away from them.

I don't remember in what order they went up as some came to me at different times, though after a few months of posting them, I began to get more discretionary. Obviously the most represented face was

Aubrey's. The picture of the Raven and I in front of her Christmas tree was the only one of her but it was centered for optimal viewing.

In the following summer heat the photos, all taped together as one, peeled and drooped at the edges, swooning to the wind from the windows as we drove. I dutifully kept at it with tape, trying to keep the many times, places and faces as one. By the next summer I would concede that the photos needed separating into smaller groups if they were to hold their places. That project took much careful tape removal and scissor snipping. I would then be faced with the fact that parts of the plywood that was my ceiling simply would not be stuck to over a time. So some photos were removed to the cab's ceiling while others got lost or boxed. All those mentioned above remain in view and are viewed with appreciative love.

Another change in our van life arrived that February (2002 for those playing at home); it came in the way of cooking. That is to say, where we cooked. We had just finished shopping when the rain started to threaten. Hurrying to the park we watched the sky with worried eyes. The subject had been batted around before between us; there were safety concerns and a lack of actual knowledge to satisfy them. Parked at Marine the rain fell and I looked at Chris.

"Let's cook in the van," I said with confidence.

"I don't know."

I pulled back the curtain to reveal the rest of the van. "I won't even have to get out to set it up."

I climbed over the driver's seat on to my bed and crawled toward the back. I was able to, from Chris' bed, get at the pot, utensils, cutting-board, stove and propane tank. It took three trips but I set up the tank on the guitar cases and the stove on the water cooler between the two front seats.

"We'll roll down the windows and clear any paper away from the flame," I explained.

"What if the gas leaks?"

"There are only two places it can leak from, we'll be able to keep an eye on both; propane you'll smell instantly."

So it was then we began cooking in our beloved van. No more long walks to the other side of the park, worrying whether someone would call the authorities on us. The chopping of vegetables and cutting of meat was a bit tight, but I leaned one end of the cutting board on the stove and the other up against the steering wheel, which worked out fine enough. Now I just stand outside the driver's door with the cutting board on the seat.

On the promenade I made an enemy of Ned Timms and his wife—he of the flying fingers and she of the hot blood. They had been vying for the two o' clock time slot along with Arthur, the one-man band. Arthur had left a speaker to mark his territory and went back to his car for the rest of his gear. Within minutes of his departure the Timms showed up with all of their gear in tow. I had the noon slot wrapped up so it had no ill effect on me, but I was asked for an opinion on the matter. I thought of myself as friendly with both parties and had no wish to choose sides. When Arthur had returned his pained expression looked to me for justice.

"Arthur was here first but not with all of his equipment; I'm not sure of the rules on that," I said, maintaining neutrality.

"You asshole, you take his side," Mrs. Timms shouted. "You have no talent just like him, neither one of you should be allowed to play out here.

So much for neutrality.

"Look, lady, I didn't even make a claim on the rules, I simply pointed out the facts."

"You hate us, you are always trying to fuck us over!"

"I stopped your bucket from getting robbed once."

"You are a petty, jealous, no talent asshole!"

I looked over her shoulder to see Ned filing his nails.

"I don't know where any of this is coming from, but you're out of your tiny little mind, lady."

"You are calling me crazy! You insult me!"

"You called me a no talent asshole."

"You are an asshole. We will make you pay!"

"Fuck you, lady," I laughed.

Her face lost all expression for a moment, then filled up on indignant shock. She turned toward her husband for chivalry. The funny thing about these two is that on stage, Ned treats his wife like a second-class citizen. Whenever the timing of a number shifts, it is she who shifted it; if he misplays a note, it was she who drove him to it; Ned is the talent and the reason that they make so much money. Off stage that dynamic holds to form, at least on the promenade (she waits with the equipment to hold the spot most of the time while he disappears), although I'd assume it is the main fabric of their relationship. It is only in moments like this that I have seen the power tip her way. I was not the first performer that Layla spewed upon with her misplaced righteous rage, her royal tantrum antics. Here she draws the line that Ned must cross if he wishes to have sex, ever again.

As he approaches me I can see that his heart is not in it, and not because he doesn't share her outrage—he more than anyone believes himself to be god's gift to the promenade if not music itself. These confrontations are beneath his stature, add to which, he is a small man compared to me. Not just in size either, he knew my reputation as one who goes out of his way not to fuck with anyone's time.

"You can't talk that way to my wife," he said firmly, with resolve.

"She's the one out of line and you know it, Ned."

"People come here to see me, not one man bands and not…"

"Losers like me?"

"I always thought you knew your place."

"Well that is damm benevolent of ya, Ned."

He tilted his head just so, as if to say, "We both know, just apologize and get it over with."

I tilt my head to mirror him and paused.

"Go fuck yourself, Ned. You are the worst kind of snob, your wife is a nut job, and I have more soul in my little pinky than you have in your whole, useless body."

His beady little eyes narrowed making them ever so much more beady. Ned turned on his heels, gathered up his gear and headed down the promenade in search of another spot to play. Layla shouted all the way past me her tidings of asshole, no-talent, throwing in bum for good measure.

Stopher walked up at that point.

"Everything okay?"

"Just another Saturday on the Nod."

I explained the scene and he laughed, "I always thought she was a looney."

"A great fuck though, I bet."

"Of course, I assumed the great fuck was implied."

I still drank but did so less because of the Raven's more frequent visits. She started requesting that I leave my bottle behind when she swept me off.

"I don't want to taste that nasty stuff when I kiss you."

Fair enough.

I ate less as well. I didn't want to worry about having to shit, or passing gas when I was with her.

The kisses were coming my way more easily. She stopped worrying about what Chris thought or any of the strangers that happened by the van whether we were parked by Marine or down by the sunset. Oh, she still dragged me out of the front seat and to the back of the van.

"Stand up and kiss me like a man."

Then I'd lean against the van as we kissed until she noticed and pulled me back off it to slap me.

"You're always leaning against something, or scuffing your feet on the ground as you walk."

"My boots are loose."

"Your screws are loose."

"Let's get tight with a screw."

"We are never fucking."

At first those claims made me feel like I had been out of line. As things went along I thought of it as her just, while sincerely meaning it, being playful. Physically things had escalated. During one of her house sitting gigs—the music producer's place where Chris and I had attended that first picking party she threw the year before—I stayed with her for a few days. It started with her throwing a picking party. There we're a couple of new performers from the promenade, a player I had never met before. Stoph and I brought along Eric. The Raven liked Eric; loved to watch him get squirmy. Eric resented the, "Dance for me monkey," mentality of the Raven, but still enjoyed being squirmy for her that night.

While she played host to all she continued to hide me in corners for glimpses of her affection. Unfortunately for me there were too many people creating very little opportunity. She did however request songs from me out of turn and always gave whatever song I sang her full attention.

"I don't know who she thinks she's fooling," Eric said the next time we spoke, "she obviously has a major thing for you."

I thought so too but loved hearing others re-enforce the theory.

I slept on the couch that night and spent the next day alone with her. We sat out on the balcony under a brilliant, clear sky. The sun had a friendly beat and she obliged with a tank top and shorts. After a few songs and a couple of glasses of wine, the top came off.

"We're not fucking," she informed softly as her shorts fell to the ground. "I'm just getting some sun."

I remember telling myself to snap memory shots for old age (Click.) I didn't even mind not fucking. The theater of it all combined with the fact that she was good company, who liked my mine, put my libido at ease. Sitting in a chair across from me with her feet on my lap, or laying down on the balcony floor with a towel, it was all very natural.

"Lay down with me."

I laid beside her and we embraced with a kiss and things progressed until she jumped to her feet.

"Ooh, wait."

She disappeared into the house only to return quicker from anywhere than she had ever done before. She set down a jar of peanut butter and a plastic squeeze bottle of honey.

"Mamma's serving lunch."

She dressed herself in honey, first down around her breast and on to the belly. By the time I made it to her kitten she had insisted that my eyes be closed. So it surprised my tongue to find her usual foamy silken terrain turned chewy and dry, and salty.

I lifted my head to show her the mess my mouth had become.

"Hmmm, peanut butter pussy."

"That's nasty baby."

"Huh, baby?"

I buried my face in her again furiously trying to get past the novelty food to attain the main course. When I did...

"Huh, baaabyy!" she heaved and sighed.

Orgasms were beside the point at this juncture; we were just playing. There was too much muck about for our senses to rise. Soon she had me sitting in the chair naked. I had a moment of being embarrassed to be seen in the light of day, but I was fat, she knew I was fat, and I knew that she knew. I never had honey sucked off my cock before. I never had any thing sucked off my cock before. (Probably whipped cream once or twice.) It was nice. Not really the thing of serious sex but a fun little romp to tell stories about at bachelor parties and such. Just being able to look down at the vision between my legs and thinking that I should be waking up any second now. (I sing a Smokey Robinson song with the line,...*a taste of honey is worse than none at all.* After this day we always shared a look on the promenade whenever that line I sang—well, most of the time for the next year or so.) I didn't wake up but it didn't last long either. The Raven liked cinematic moments as much if not more than I did, and even pornos have cinematic value, but moments get played then have to make room for the next moment. She retired to the shower. I assumed that seeing me naked was enough to make anyone feel dirty.

To my surprise she said, "Don't get dressed, wait for me in the bed downstairs."

On her clean return we went at each other in earnest minus the paraphernalia. I gave her my usual treatment and she reciprocated: I said, SHE RECIPORCATRED. Fat guy and all. Things were now getting very interesting.

She was into it enough but I still felt a lack of attraction. Or maybe she didn't love to suck cock the way I love to eat pussy. Still, if I had a male body to match her female goddessness, she might have been different. That is not to say that it, or she, wasn't wonderful, or that she fled the room vomiting afterwards. No, it was civil to say the very least. The fact that she did it again the next time we fooled around and then not again for quite a long while after certainly indicated something. She still got me off, just not with her mouth. It hurt a little but my perspective was healthy enough to understand and be grateful for what I got.

There would still be a week where she stayed away or that when we did get together it was just heated make-out sessions. We were both such good kissers that it was probably better than a lot of other people's sex life, all by itself. She said so herself.

In the month of March she moved into her own place. It was a little beach house that had been compartmentalized into three units. There were two other likewise structures on the lot divided by a driveway with one across from hers and the third at the driveway's end. At least it offered more privacy than her last place. Of the three units in her house only one other was occupied most of the time. The house across the driveway from her was always empty and the one at the back of the lot was only a dual dwelling unit that remained half occupied by a single family made up of an older Mexican couple and their middle-aged daughter with a toddler of her own.

Before we could move her in the Raven wanted to paint the walls and floor in the main room. Other than the bathroom and kitchen there was only the one room. She also had her "friend" Mark, the independent contractor/mountain climber/scuba diver/boat owner/whatever do some work on the plumbing in her bathroom. That is he sent his under paid Mexican crew to work on it for her. At the time I decided not to think much of it. We had a deal that if she ever got as heated with someone as she was with me, she'd have to tell me. Actually all that was said was that if she fucked someone I would have to know for health reasons. But in time, I'd specify the former and find that she had stayed within those parameters anyway. Of course, those were fairly vague parameters and all answers she gave rested on my believing her words. I have, for the most part, accepted them at, if not, face value, then a close facsimile thereof. Mostly I just wanted to know if anyone had at her kitten and were they as good as me. Mark never made the grade, or got a chance to get graded. How close he came I have decided not to indulge.

The night we painted the floor is one of my favorite sexual memories. I didn't get laid but she introduced a disturbing game. Her hair was up in pigtails and she had on grubby shorts and an old tee shirt. Add to that a spot of brown paint on her cheek and nose. If ever she looked the part of a little girl it was that night. With all the woodwork and the floor half painted we began kissing as we kneeled on the floor. She happened to have just put a big, round, grape lollypop in her mouth. We started to share it as we kissed.

"Mommy says this is my lolly," she spouted with a pout, and turned her back to me.

"Good girls are supposed to share." I played along.

"I wanna be bad." She laid back on to the floor.

Okay, I thought. This could get a tad twisted. In the beginning I was every bit of gamed, but as it progressed I remembered that I had a daughter. The Raven liked to dominate and I liked to be dominated, to a point; she held all the cards in our relationship, I played along. But as she slithered the lolly enticingly about her kitten lips whilst I shadowed it with my tongue, she talked about how mommy wouldn't like this, I considered the concept of trust. When you create these kinds of sexual scenarios the lines of propriety blur one's discretion. That is kind of the idea. The problem was that we were not even fucking yet, and according to her never would. Finally I decided to let her continue calling the shots, play whatever role she set out for me to the best of my ability, improvising strictly within the confines of her design; tricky but intriguing. Hell, only months before I verbally consented to be anally probed, I guess incestuous make believe could be considered fair game in that realm. So I went with the hungry daddy and ate my little girl into her delight. The lolly survived the event little more than half way consumed. My orgasm went unattended that night but when I left she made a gift to me of the remaining lolly. I promptly teased it all the way home to the van, searching for the flesh that once engulfed it, and finished it off in bed along with my pent up passion.

From faux incest to beating off with a lolly in your mouth ain't your average night, it's better.

During one stretch of her running off to be wined and dined in the face of resisting the charm of my artistic poverty I took the opportunity to get good and smashed. The Raven had seen me drunk, very drunk, and drunkified beyond redemption, but she had not seen me smashed to smithereens. Stoph and I sat in our blessed Great White Buffalo down by the ocean washing the sun from the sky with good ole Kentucky bourbon. Sometimes cheap, charcoal-filter, gut rotting, esophagus cancer-causing vodka just isn't good enough. Well it was good enough for Chris that night but not me.

I drank it fast, I drank it hard; I drank it as if life itself grew from its brown liquidy goodness. In part I drank as a fuck you to the Raven and her need for fine things that insists on lots of money, and in part, I drank in pleasure to be reacquainted with an old, dear friend whom loved me for all I was, only asking that I spend a mere eight to ten dollars. I had tempered my drinking for too long, eyeing the street for her arrival, peeking perpetually in my side mirror for her appearance. "Today, to live is to drink."

Woo-FUCKING-hoo!

Of course she showed up. Of course just minutes before I was slurring my disdain while belittling any fondness or genuine emotion for her I might possess. Then her black Neon filled my side mirror and it must have been there before I noticed for when I did, she miraculously already stood at my door's side. My dull eyes said to my numb brain, "Hey, her car (way over there)—hey, her (right here.)"

I bounced off my seat on to my feet in mid-stumble like a giddy kid lured to a candy store by Stranger Danger. She must have really missed me because she either didn't fully comprehend the extent of my state or didn't care. Her smile held an apology that she would never speak. It flashed the instant her face appeared at my window and was gone in the next. I can see it so clear sitting here typing. I can also see me not seeing it then, just as clearly. All I knew then was that she couldn't stay away; that she had yet to find someone she would rather smile at, apologetically or otherwise.

She led me to our place at the back of the van, most assuredly gathering up my unstable thudding at her heels, she kissed me anyway. After which she shoved some gum in my mouth. On every other day, even if I was sober and just brushed my teeth, she would have made me chew the gum before allowing me to kiss her. That is an exaggeration of course but a rule of thumb with her no less. On that day she wanted me to feel loved or at least desired. An acceptance of me glowed about her. It didn't last long as my debilitated tools of speech and general lack of coherence exhibited themselves.

"I couldn't stop thinking about you, David," she scolded.

"I cursed you a time or two myself." That is what floated through my brain. What came out was more like, "Icurred—I youatimetwo mthelf." I pointed a crooked finger as if to guide the gibberish into making sense. Next I fell to raising a brow off my eye and tilting my head to indicate more clearly how clever and charming the words sounded inside, before lips and tongue got hold of them.

"You are absolutely smashed out of your mind."

"Well, that is a matter of relative interpretation, semantically speaking." Again, "Wellthht isammaer of rrhblgks nsvgnw." I never quite finished pretending to get that one out.

"Come over to my car; you need some food in you."

She reallycares alloyttabuitt me. Yeah, I started messing up the words before they left my head, too.

She couldn't find anything but a piece of beef jerky and I couldn't even chew that. If ever she needed more ammunition against any thought of a life with me I was doing my utmost to provide it. I must have put a few sentences together because I know she laughed and kissed me a couple more times.

Stopher got out of the passenger seat and walked around to the other side.

"I gotta get parked for the night," he said before getting behind the wheel. He was good and drunk but nowhere in my league. Anyone who wants to be disgusted or offended by how many times we drove drunk has the right; I offer no defense. (I've already entered into the record that I'd feel as safe or safer with a drunk Stopher or Vuma—not the way I was on that day—behind the wheel than most sober people on the road. That being said, we were wrong every time we did it. That being said, we'll probably do it again.)

Stopher said the next day that he waited a long time for me to return to the van; I remember him starting the engine and hitting the horn a few times. Eventually he drove off leaving the Raven to contend with a sloshy sloshed Vuma. Whatever fun or enjoyment she had garnished from our little visit vanished with my van's dissolving exhaust.

"What's he doing?"

I lifted an arm and try to point as if to explain the word leaving.

I don't remember much after that but as she told me about it a couple of days later certain images appeared in my memory. I remembered her trying to get me to eat a hamburger and me not being able to keep it afloat in my hand; it seemed hell bent on diving for the floor beside her passenger door. For some reason she thought that a hot dog might be easier to hold so she bought a couple or four. Her plan was to show up at the van with two for Chris to insure that he would not eat mine.

"You need to eat something." I remember her saying that a lot.

"I need to lay down in my bed." I remember not being able to say so ceased trying.

It would be almost a month before I found the hot dogs that she assumed Chris had taken from me. They were dried, petrified sticks of breaded meat between the driver's seat back and so much stored uselessness.

She didn't see me that bad often but even once would be enough to conjure up a respectable amount of apprehension in any level headed girl. Level, she was not, and still she gathered up pause. Not enough though, at least not in any lasting doses.

She continued to run and seek something worthy of keeping her away from me with little success.

"Ain't none of you good enough. Maybe I just need to keep juggling a few at a time to be satisfied; to get what it is that I need."

"Maybe you need to be a bit more understanding and less demanding."

"And live in a van with you?"

"Or live in a house with someone not as interesting, or live however you can afford to live on your own."

I had similar conversations, oddly enough, with Eric. He tried so hard to meet someone to partner up with for the rest of his life, inevitably failing to realize their expectations or them his. As hard as it is in this life to find somebody to strike that impossible balance between sheathing ones sensibility into another while mutually expanding each other's horizon, it grows exponentially impossible with every item of criteria we insist piling on, until all we can see is what they don't possess. With Eric one such criterion was smoking. He would never involve himself with someone who smoked, regardless of any other qualities.

"What if your soul mate happens to smokes?"

"Then she is obviously not my soul mate."

We, he and I, have danced around to that tune countless times without movement from either side. It struck me as downright hilarious that Eric and the Raven would have something so vital in common. He was an educated male, far from dawdling in the shallow pools of materialism, she was not; she sought stability through dependency, he did not. Yet their different versions of surfaced indulgences left them adrift on the same raft. Well maybe different rafts but in the same murky waters to be sure.

I was sitting in Steve's studio mulling over the similarities of these two very different people in my life, both of whom I had become very, for very different reasons, fond of. The phone rang and I heard the Raven's voice on Steve's machine. Being that he was in the shower and that it was for me, I picked up the phone.

"Are you going to play tonight?"

"Tuesday is my day off."

"I'll tip ya, but good."

"Suddenly, a drunken, poverty stricken, loser, has become quite the man of importance."

"Oh, darlin', you know I appreciate you. I appreciate you more than anyone else."

"I just sometimes wonder if you give that the important consideration or status it deserves."

This led the conversation back round to the familiar territory of how no one is enough, that every man falls short of her many requirements.

"I'm seeking pros but getting' nothin' but cons."

"So what am I?"

She paused with a sigh in search of a concise thought.

"Baby, you're a pro in cons' clothing."

"Yoink."

"What's that?"

"That's the sound of me stealing that line; it's a good one."

"You like that? That was a good one, huh, baby?"

"Huh, baby?"

"I said, HUH, baby!"

I turned my voice down, low and gritty. "Huh, baby?"

"BABY!" she squealed. "That's some gravelly, velvety goodness, ya got going there."

"I know."

"Stop it, baby!"

"Are you sure?"

"Where are you?"

"You called me, I'm at Steve's."

"I'm coming over."

For her and Eric, I wrote this song:

Pick your poisons or live alone
Light a candle for each expectation
Feel safe in the satisfaction
You never settled for less than a perfect home

I know it's hard, don't make it harder
You need what ya need but something
Will always be missing
For you and me and every self-made martyr

Rings of smoke decorate your disdain
I know there are parts of yourself that

You'll never be able to spare for change
But list get long when list we're making
And being buried by words is your first mistake

To know one's self is needed, that's understood
But hard-fast rules defeat the purpose
Of hearts in search of being nourished
Until ya feel it, you don't know what's good

So pick your poisons or live alone
Light a candle for each great expectation
Settle in the satisfaction
Let the candle's fire consume your perfect home

Chasing pros but catching cons
Forever weeding the good from the bad
But don't forget that there are pros in cons' clothing
It takes time and a leap of faith
To know what ya have

So pick your poisons or die alone
Light a candle for each great expectation
Feel safe in the satisfaction
You never settled for less than a perfect home
Let the candle's fire consume your perfect home
Playing solitaire with your wish-bone
Pick your poisons or die alone

Soon after I wrote this song for the Raven; (The opening lines were lifted from conversations about Zen philosophy with Dad. Actually one line came from talking with Art, who of course was quoting what Dad had relayed to him.)

Stop thinking and solve all your problems

Drink from any cup, half or full
Just know that it's already empty
The end is in the beginning, the moments your only chance to rule

You're always running late busy trying to run free
You can't seem to accept yourself
Tell me now, who else where you gonna to be
There's always someone else to be
To be

So much to want, you can't help but feel the weight
Hard to believe that you're all you need
Or that your disappointments are appointments you made
Lick your wounds dry or let 'em bleed

You say something needs changing
It seems that something always does
But hand in hand with all your planning
It is what it is just because; it is what it is just because
Just because

Answers aren't always asked for
Maybe, baby, I should just shut up
I really don't have any anyway
Except for maybe that crack about a broken cup

You're always running late…
You say, "Something needs changing"…

    Of course both of these songs were me trying to convince the Raven that she was denying some deep philosophical truth concerning us: Not only should she love me on my terms, she would grow spiritually by doing so; in the end her loving me would be me doing her a favor. Pretty clever, huh? No, she wasn't buying it either. In fact she never quite liked the JUST BECAUSE song because she thought I was being critical of her. Chris wrote a similarly themed song inspired by her called, OFF-SEASON SUNSET. The Raven cared way too much about what other people thought of her and Stopher compared that with how the sunsets are more beautiful during the non-tourists time of year. The sun falls into the water from late fall to early spring. The rest of the year it falls into the mountains up towards the north horizon. The punch line is that both songs speak as much to ourselves as they do her. I don't preoccupy myself with what others think to her degree, but I let the world shove me around in my own way. And neither Chris nor myself are graduating from any Zen institute any time soon. I feel the weight of what I don't have; my desires cut into my peace of mind. So she didn't like either song that much in the beginning but they did grow on her because they were good songs and, in the end, the Raven was not one to hide from herself completely; what she didn't like in the songs originally she came to own.

CHAPTER SIXTEEN

In late February Eric announced his intentions to walk the Appalachian Trail, beginning at the end of March. Since his falling apart after failing to strike it big with his first CD, Eric had drifted away from his artistic roots. He did do some community theater in Philly and took some acting classes in L. A. but stopped writing pretty much altogether only playing other people's music. He would soon become a disciple of Laurence Juber, an amazing finger style instrumentalist. What he did do was spend as much time in nature as he could. He went for hikes into Topanga Canyon and sometimes drove out of town for weekend camping trips. All this led him to the conclusion that he walk the entire Appalachian Trail.

Whenever we got together for one of our marathon conversations over at the Soup Plantation Eric still talked about his desire to write. He wanted to write a book called TWENTIES, about, well, his twenties. When he brought up walking the trail that ran from down in Georgia up into Maine, all I could say was, "Wow, you really don't want to write."

"Maybe I'll write about the walk?" Eric pondered aloud.

"Nahh," said he, Stoph and I.

So there was a big get together in Sukey's house a couple of weeks before he was to leave. I made pizza, we all sang, and Steve, Chris and I each wrote a top ten list to send Eric on his way. It had become a tradition that for each of our birthdays, Ty included, we wrote top ten lists. Eric's walking the trail was a big enough event for us to honor it thusly. At one point Steve pulled out a kazoo. It was that kind of party.

The Raven came and brought her mom, Carol along, as she had become more comfortable with my crowd, allowing that they, in fact, knew that there was something between us. The Raven was particularly tickled by the use of the kazoo. She and I had been joking about them the other day because Arthur, the one-man band, used one in his act. (She was not a fan of Arthur's.) Something about it being the first resort of an unimaginative mind in a music store. She had liked Steve but still found an off-putting quality about him; an air of stuffiness playing at being loose; a harshness toward others dressed in humor; and, "…that head too big for his skinny body". But the kazoo somehow had the reverse effect one would think, making him more endearing to her.

The party had hit its zenith, having already begun to slowly settle toward goodbyes, when Steve informed me of an urgent message on his machine. It was Donna telling me that Aubrey had written a suicide note. She was understandably in tears when she left the message and I called her back immediately. Donna answered.

"She wants to talk to you but she's a little afraid; be easy on her," Donna warned.

"Of course."

I had always been the hard-ass, disciplinarian in raising Aubrey, but I didn't think I needed to be told to take it easy on a thirteen-year-old girl who had just written a suicide note. Donna tended exaggerate Aubrey's feelings in a given moment, but I did allow that the kid might think me disappointed in her for, I don't know, giving up on the ultimate game.

The inside of my head felt suspended in water, yet hovering above somehow. I believed her to be in pain but couldn't quite accept that she was truly contemplating it. Not that she didn't have her reason— we've all got reasons. Living with her mom all this time without me around…Donna is a good person, but can tend to leave one feeling foggy about where they stand, and reality in general gets fresh coats of paint at a moment's notice. It made perfect sense that Aubrey would feel isolated and deserted, even if I had stayed in Chicago. Still, as I held the phone in my hand and voices spoke, it all had an eerie staged quality, dream like.

Before bringing Aubrey to the phone, Donna read me the note. Nothing in it surprised me, she had been moved around too much growing up and as she was getting older, friends got harder to make, the one constant in her life, me, went away, and she had always struggled in school. But even in the note I detected a sense of acting out for acting out's sake. I don't mean that Aubrey attempted to con us, or rub our faces in all the things there indeed were for us to feel guilty about; she wanted to see the words written down; somewhere, somehow the thought occurred to her that killing herself could be something to consider. So she did.

"I don't think it is something I could ever really do, but I did started wondering about it, and that scared me." Her voice, at first shaky, settled with each word. "We haven't talked as much lately-"

"I'm so-"

"It's not your fault. You've been calling; the timing's just been bad. Daddy?"

"Yeah, Kid."

"I really miss you." She fell apart all over again. "I'm trying, I really am trying to be strong. I don't wanna be the reason your dreams don't come true."

"Let's set my dreams aside and talk about what you need, what you want. You've indulged me more than anyone could deserve to be. You have been great and put up with a lot of bullshit because of who your parents are. If you screamed at me or hated me I'd offer no argument."

"I love you, daddy, I'm not angry at you, or mom. I don't even know what it is that I want to say, or want period. I just felt alone; we did everything together, dad. I just don't have that with anyone here."

"Your mom does the best that she can."

"I know, but it's not the same."

"Even if I was there, you're getting into that time of life when you need to begin separating from your parents anyway."

"And I'm starting to make some good friends too, in fact there are a few I really want to meet you; I talk about you all the time."

Right around here I thought that killing myself was the least that I could do. I had put her through so much and ultimately failed her where she needed me most. So what if she chose to live with her mother, so what if they insisted on going back to Nashville, I knew she would need me, I should have sucked it up and followed. I was a big piece of shit.

"Dad, could you think about coming here to stay for just a few months?"

"Of course I'll think about it, I already am but-" What? What could I honestly say here other than that I am too pathetic of an excuse of a man to have the financial wherewithal to be able to get there, and too self-involved to convince myself that I should get a job for raising the money. "There are a lot of logistics involved. If I said yes today, and I'm not, it would take at least a month or more to get up the money and that's assuming that the van would survive the trip. Once I'm there I'd have to get a job to live and get up money to come back. Because, Aubrey, I'd be coming back to California. Right or wrong, I've started something here; I nee—I *want* to see where it leads."

"Alice has a house you can stay at rent free, and you don't have to stay here that long, I just need to have you around for a little while."

"If I come I'll have to work no matter what, and I'll have to make money to come back so I might as well be there building up my savings, stay for a few months, maybe longer."

"Mom says you can stay at Alice's house for the whole summer! We're all living out here in Lavernge, the house is in Nashville so you won't have to deal with mom barely at all."

We talked some more about less urgent things and left the rest open. Before I hung up I had talked to Donna, Alice and Madison, who all were in need of a distant, calming voice. Each of us in our own way took Aubrey's pain personally, Aubrey too; we all thought that if we were better people the drama could have been avoided.

"I feel better knowing that you know what's going on," Madison said.

The last thing I said to them all was that nothing had been decided, no miracle cures were forth coming. To Aubrey I said this:

"Promise me that you won't hurt yourself or anyone else until I see you again. And remember, Breeze, if everything that you hoped for falls apart, and you're convinced that no more options exist, instead of killing yourself you get on a bus and come to me, or go to Chicago and the Folks; you are very loved by some good people. Don't ever forget that."

"I won't, dad; thanks."

"I'll call in couple of days when I've sorted some things out and have a plan."

"I love you, daddy."

"I love you, Aubrey, and I'm proud of you for speaking up. Get some sleep."

I let the party in on what had happened and what might be happening. In my mind I was not automatically going back to Nashville. I felt the Raven's eyes on me as I spoke. She watched me tenderly but with a reserve. One of her hands was always touching me, offering support. If I glanced her way she smiled softly, graciously. I remember thinking how well she smiled actually; how it held zero forcedness; appeared organically appropriate; how it wanted to be there for me when and in whatever specific way I needed it to be. I thought, I am wounded and she loves me.

As the night's conversation returned to Eric and his journey, the Raven and I slinked away into a dark corner of the yard. She kissed with an intentional firmness.

"When will you leave?"

"I don't know if I'm going."

"Oh, you're going, it's the only way I'll ever be rid of you."

She spoke with a twinkled eye but I knew truth lied within. She wanted out of us and couldn't do it herself. Also, she wanted me to be the kind of father that would drive across the country when his daughter called, the kind of father that she never had. As much as she wanted me to go so I'd be gone, I'd have been a disappointment to her opinion of me if had I stayed.

"I was never even here," I said mocking her gently.

"Exactly."

It hurt and fed my ego to know that her feelings ran deep enough to want me against her better judgment. The hurt being that she judged me unworthy despite her wanting me.

The Raven tried to get a head start on my leaving by staying away on her own. It took me three or four days to agree with myself that I should indeed go. I sat in Sukey's den on a love seat holding a phone in my hand waiting to hear Dad's reaction. The phone offered nothing, regardless of all I had just spoken into it. Dad was not of the mind to tell people what they were supposed to do. Besides, I knew what he wanted me to do.

"I should go."

"I think you should."

For him that was sticking his nose way in. Any thoughts I had meandering about my soul of weaseling out of the trip melted from my grasp. Dad would not have been hard on me, he doesn't believe in expectations so how disappointed could he get? All his Zen wisdom aside, he had a value system like everyone else, so somewhere inside him something would rub the wrong way if I didn't follow through in a way befitting the son of one Robert Smith. Whether I paint him accurately on this or not that is how I felt.

"I have some money, but not enough to cross the country. Well, that's not true, I have enough to cross if absolutely nothing goes wrong."

"You should have some cushion," he agreed.

"I plan on working when I get there and with me not having to pay rent, I should be able to pay you back for once."

"You've paid us back before."

"Not often."

"No, not often. David, you know that if I can help I will; first comes your Mom and mine's boat, if there's anything left…"

"Two or three hundred?"

"Which."

"Three; I won't get a job the first day I'm there."

"We can handle that."

"We won't be leaving until the end of the month, probably the first week of April actually."

"It'll be in your account by the end of the week."

My throat joked, sending heat to the back of my eyes. Damm! I don't want to cry here, I told myself. Be a man for fuck sake. I should have gotten off the phone right then and there.

"I'm sorry for putting you through all this." The heat pushed it's liquid to fill the sockets around my eyes.

"You're not putting me through anything. Look, you are trying to do something that I think is good for you. I wanted the life I have; you're not me."

"I'm just tired of having to ask you for things."

"Well, the good news is that I don't have much, so…I'm retiring any year now, you know. The well will dry up and you'll be on your own, babe."

I laughed as the tears built up. Again I thought, get off now.

"I just want you to be proud of me and what I've done with my life."

"Oh, Sweets, I am, I definitely am. Your mother and I tell everyone about our boys out on the road, and how one day we hope to follow."

My red face shook as I tightened the lids down over my eyes. The tears came anyway. I couldn't speak, Dad knew better, so we sat on our respective ends and listened to me cry. I don't know how long it took, but I did regain some semblance of composure and tried to wrap things up.

"I'm such an idiot."

"We're all idiots; bozos on the bus, kid."

"Right. Thanks for everything, Dad. Tell Mom too."

"I will, and you're welcome." He paused. "Life is hard, and you didn't make it any easier with the path you chose. You are trying to do the best you can; your mother and I see that. We love you."

"I know. I love you too."

I don't remember Dad ever trying to seek out my approval. With Aubrey I tried to be half the man my father was to me. Funny thing is that I spent a good deal of time doing things with Aubrey that Dad rarely did with me. But he had six kids and never planned on being anywhere else other than the home in which they were being raised. From the day I knew enough to form an opinion, I had no doubt about having the best parents in the world: smart, compassionate, strong and enlightened. So growing up I sought for them both to think well of me and then, did the same with Aubrey. I think she has some of that for me, but with all the time apart I assumed that the hero worship aspect of it has diminished greatly. Maybe not. You'll have to read a book by her.

So the Raven stayed away for a week after all this happened. During these periods, so many over the years, I'd get notes like this on the promenade:

I MSS YOU!! Your velvety voice is kicking my ass. I MISS YOU!!
I MISS YOU!! Went to the Home Depot to look at some things I MISS YOU!!
I MISS YOU!! to help store all my shit more manageably. I MISS YOU!!
I MISS YOU!! It wasn't the same with out ya. I MISS YOU!! !!!!!!!!!! !!

Or:

The following message is brought to you by sappy romantics, dramatists, lovers of good music all over THE promenade patio, Kleenex and the number 8...I feel I may be needing one. (Kleenex, not the number 8) MISS YOU

MISS YOUMISS YOUP.S. (2 hrs. later) Blatant destruction of all things subtle and artsy courtesy of DAVID SMITH and schleps who come before him. MISS YOU

She came into work one day and walked up to my spot on the promenade full of smiles. She had been staying away but was glad to see me, excited at the prospect of hearing Stoph and I playing. I on the other hand, had nothing but angst-ridden disdain for each smile; the wider expressed and deeper immersed in goodwill that they were, the more offended I felt.

"I expect no less than a world that's in the process of being rocked."

"Go fuck yourself," I said, harshly beneath my breath, as venomously as possible.

"What's your problem?" she asked, still partly smiling.

I saw that she hadn't yet fully decided if I had truly been angry or was playing at it. I also detected her doing her utmost not to let anyone notice the disharmony of our moment.

"You want to run around and stay away from me? Fine. Just don't come up to me out here like things are hunky-dory. Pretension is not one of my strong suits. Got it?"

She retreated to her perch trying hard not to look the part of a dog beaten with its own tail.

"That's not cool at all," Chris hissed in my ear. "Grow up."

"Fuck you."

"Yeah, fuck me"

We went about our set that day and played our asses off, like everything in the world depended upon it. Everything did. I had to show her how important it was that I did what I did. I had to show me. I tried not to vent all my fury at her but ended up giving her a solid dose. I doubt anyone other than the three of us picked up on it, but to Stoph, her, and me, it was palpable. I felt me trying to pull back but I also felt her loving it as much as she hated it.

In the middle of the set she dropped this note in my bucket:

Let's just say, I don't appreciate this drama! Do not do this again!!

(She crossed those words out then turned the card on its side and wrote:

I'd like to interrupt this fight by noting that I am enjoying having, that I'm sharing this fight with no one other than you...so FUCK YOU!! I'm getting all hapless romantic about having a fight with a hapless romantic.

(This part she circled with squiggly lines—then wrote under it:

All I'm saying is that I've missed you and was looking forward to seeing you and don't know what this is all about. But look forward to to to...

P.S. Ya ever consider a kazoo.

I left the promenade that day with a smile for her and a vented soul for myself. I didn't see her that night nor did I think that I would. There was a part of me that continued to hope. The next time I saw her at work she stayed away and kept her morning cheer to a minimum. While waiting to play I wrote this:

Kazoos collide carefully consulting their own destruction with the grace of a conductor waving wildly, madly, purposefully of course.
Or maybe you've never considered a kazoo.
Big mistake!!!
Nations have fallen, history made, and futures horribly altered over such ill-conceived errors.
Lipstick traces on a postcard unveil an off key melody's envy
And pray tell, what in the fuck-sake could that possibly mean?
Let us assume nothing while pretending something resembling worth
Suddenly I realize that her smile must be, at all costs, stopped.
Why? A valid question
But fuck you anyway. Call it a kazoo casualty
How? Important question
Again I point the good senator of California to the precedent set by code A-478k, which clearly states, and I quote, "Fuck you."
So we don't know why and can't figure out how and by now are not even able to remember what it is we are supposed to do.
Serendipity saved by the bell.
Or was that a kazoo?

Chris and I made good money early and were looking forward to the evening set. I was in a great mood; I didn't have her, but I had me; I had what being me was all about; on that day it flourished—financially even. In between I wrote this for the Raven:

I was thinking, "Be clever while creating images of grace and beauty." A good plan, because that is what I do best.
But something is in my way and I'm almost certain it is me
Or maybe it is her
Something I want to tell her.
For it is in such matters that grace clumsily clouds the vision and beauty falls short of the simple truth of the matter
It is amusing how suddenly serious I feel. I could just say that I love her. But she already knows that.

You would think that I had a bad day, how my mood weighs heavily, pushing heart into soul, forcing them to converse about the possibility that they are one and the same.

Fact is, I'm having a great day and the heart and soul agree when they say, "Tell her again."

Okay

"Raven, I'm in love with you."

So there's that.

During my last couple of weeks we spent every day together. My target date for departure was April 5. I made overtures at using these last days together for having the best sex our bodies could conjure.

"We are never going to fuck."

"We do pretty much everything else."

"Besides fucking."

"What is so precious about fucking, is it some misplaced allegiance to your Catholic school days?"

"I did go to Catholic school; I do believe in God, and yes, I still have the uniform."

"Baby!!"

"Huh, baby," she teased.

"HUH, baby," I groaned.

"Huh, baby," her hot breath, whispered just beneath my lower lip while whisking over the back of my tongue.

"We should be fucking! You know it would be great, fat as I am, you know you won't regret it."

"Baby, you are a master pussy eater and probably the best kisser I've ever known."

"Oh, well then by all means, we should most definitely never fuck."

"Darlin', I can't get rid of you as it is. If you do me like I think you will, I'll be stuck forever."

"You have the most interesting way of stroking a man's ego."

"It's a gift."

"Then why do I fill cursed?"

"Because it's *my* gift."

One night after fooling around she started complaining about everything from the way I scuff my boots against the ground to my every major decision regarding how to live life. In the midst of all that she slipped in that her "friend", the stockbroker from New York would be visiting soon. I don't know where in all of that I made for the door, but I did so loudly.

"I have neighbors, if you don't mind," she scolded from her bed on the floor. (We hadn't set up the loft bed yet.) "Some of us have to live among the civilized, and pay rent, and get along with the rest of the world."

"IS that what you call what you do? Getting along?" I stepped back from the door. "You get along by having others carry your load, and the reason you need so many, is that your load is so un-fucking-reasonably large."

"A roof is not unreasonable."

"We're not talking about a roof and you know it. In fact we shouldn't be talking about any of that and just leave it at this: This is what and who I am; it doesn't get any better or worse."

"Oh, I'm betting it gets worse."

"Fuck you, Raven. I walk easily and my boots are a little big so they scrape along the ground; and there is only so much I'm willing to do for money, the list getting shorter by the minute; I'm willing to live with nothing and I'm willing to live without you, I never expected to have you in the first place; you want money and don't care where it comes from, by all means, marry a stockbroker. "

"It's an honest living and he's a good man."

"I'm sure he loves his mother dearly, oh and I bet he likes dogs. Gee, your standards for decency are so tough. As for an honest living, do you have any idea what stockbrokers do? They move numbers around without considering for a single instant that the numbers are people. Companies get bought and sold, stocks shift from one account to another, and all the while some schmuck pushing a broom in a warehouse loses his job, or a factory gets shut down. So, the stockbroker and his clients make more money than they need and another family man joins the unemployment line."

"You don't know any more about the stock market than I do, except for what you see in movies or read in a book."

"I've read and seen enough to stand by what I said. All I'm saying is that at some point, *how* you make money has to be as important as how *much* you make. It's a vicious, dog-eat-dog world out there and I ain't biting."

"You're too good, too silver tongued for me, David; you have an answer for everything."

"You'd rather I stuttered?"

She came to my arms and they took her in. I held her naked body as my hands traversed. All the arguing turned seriously silly in my mind. I knew that she baited me; I knew that she wanted us to be mad to make things easier for her to walk away from. I stood back from her leaving my hands around her waist.

"I love you, Raven."

"Oh, darlin', you're just lonely and bored."

That sparked my anger all over again. I pulled my hands off of her.

"Hey, just cause we play around like high school kids and you hold sex over me like a twinkling yo-yo, don't forget that I've been married, I raised a couple of kids and that I am a fucking man! Maybe not much of one, by some standards, but a man all the fucking same!"

She dropped her eyes looking for an escape.

"Maybe you don't love me-

"I appre-"

"Spare me your appreci-"

"Hey, people throw the word love around all the time and it adds up to nothing; to really appreciate someone, the way I do you, in some ways, means as much or more than love. I don't appreciate just anyone."

"I know, at the very least you appreciate me and I'm grateful. I'm grateful for every single tiny shred of interest you've given me. But goddamit, Ray, look at us. You have all the reason in the world to stay away from me and you can't. There is not one iota of the things you talk about your future holding that I possess, and yet I'm here. You put me here. You drive down to a van in the corner of a deserted parking

lot time and time again to drag me here. If it ain't love it's a hell of a lot more than appreciation."

"Oh, baby."

"Okay, I'm a pleasant distraction, a shiny wind up toy that sings your heart's desire, so you like to have me around. Fine. We'll leave you out of it then, it'll just be me. Yes I was lonely and yeah, I get bored, but this is something else. I love you; I'm in love with you, Ray. You can't write that off anymore, it is as real as I'm standing here."

We kissed long but soft. Tender flesh consoled weary souls. In my arms she settled in for the sake of a moment's peace, we let the room go silent. When she looked up into my eyes I could still see her fighting. It wasn't the kind of fight that asked to be challenged. To the contrary it begged that I surrender. I dropped my arms, turned to the door, opened it and stepped through. On the other side I leaned toward her as she hid her voluptuous body from the view of anyone who might choose to lurk up an unassuming driveway at two in the morning. She stepped back from the door as she opened it wider, offering me a return.

"I love you," I said, then leaning in further, "madly…" I stepped away from the door spreading my arms out like bird searching for a friendly wind, "gladly."

I left.

Before leaving for Nashville I did my best to finish up the never-ending task of straightening out the Raven's apartment. The more I organized, the more shit she pulled out of storage for me to make fit in her shrinking apartment. I got her loft bed put together which created some floor space for me to stash stuff and finally the influx of incoming blood reached a temporary coagulation. That night she asked me to stay the whole night. I had fallen asleep there before but my snoring usually woke her up, plus I had a schedule with Chris to adhere. We had reached a summit in our organizing her apartment and in our relationship. This did not imply, however much I did try to infer it in to being so, that the act of intercourse was at hand.

Wild passion did ensue, as always it was incredible. We bumped and grinded void of penetration, her teeth did gnash at my jaw, she did offer her wrist to my mouth for likewise consumption. We filled the sandbox that was her bed with our sweat and enthusiasm that eventually landed us in a spent heap. I held her afterwards, nothing fit so naturally in my arms before or since. I never slept well with others beside me until a couple of years into my time with Donna, but even then, we sought out our sleep separately. With the Raven's limbs tangled up in mine, her warm, sweet breath dancing off my cheek, curling up under my nose, I at first made an attempt to break free out of habit. She, having already found the first stage of slumber, tugged at my every move to slip to the empty side of the bed or simply grunted gingerly, like a child fighting off sleep at a party.

My main problem with sleeping in close proximity with others was the timing between our breaths. I'd try to stay in tune with theirs to keep from being a bother to them and end up not being able to breath unconsciously, and therefore not fall asleep. Breathing became a task that required all my attention. So at first I invested energy in failing to free myself from our heap. As I briefly laid in momentary surrender, the Raven squeezed my hand in hers. She was fast asleep; I had done nothing to cause it concern, yet she reached out from her dream-state to give me affection. I felt my eyes heating up, water bubbling from them as I raised my head to better look down on her while not disturbing. It happened again. She tightened her grip around my hand. It was then I saw it; it was at that moment all doubt faded. In the light of the morning, when words and movement crowded and clouded the day in the name of useless agendas, doubt would certainly again have its say; but there in the dark while she slept; there where she could not control or edit thought and motion; there where we lay in a connected mess on opposite sides of consciousness, she told me, she said it: "I love you." Her mouth immobile, her thoughts a placid pond, her body a subtle tool, she took my hand with hers and told me.

Say what you want, think it away with logic, explain all the speculation I would have to employ; I don't care. I kissed her forehead, then her lips; both softer than sleep itself.

"Hmm," she said.

"You're welcome," I whispered.

This was the first time she told me that she loved me. I know, she let it slip when drunk out in front of the house at 55 Rose, but we were fighting, the night heightened in dramatics, she was sloppy drunk and took it back the instant she blurted it out. No, there in the dark she owned up to all we had been building and accepted the thing that we became.

I fell deeply asleep in her arms.

Of course within a an hour or so we untangled to stake out our own portions of the bed so the sleep could go deeper still, but falling asleep in her arms remains a watershed moment for me.

I did rise before the sun and walk to the van because the day has its needs and they couldn't be served from her bed. I couldn't get back to sleep so I lay there until Chris awoke to begin our day.

On the promenade during our set the Raven dropped a card in the bucket. She formed the shape of a heart by writing the letter z, one after another and drew an arrow through it. After the last z she put *Ray*, upside down. In the middle of the heart she wrote:

A
Picture
Sez
A 1000
Of' 'em

Before we left I wanted to record a few songs for the Raven and let her make a list. She chose: PICK YOUR POISONS, HARD-EDGE BLUES (Mom's lyric), BLACKBIRD (Paul McCartney), ROYAL WEDDINGS (Stopher's), PAINTED EYES (Mom and me again) and EMPTY EYES (another of mine). She had others but we would be lucky to get to those previously mentioned.

I asked Steve, as a going away present, to give me an hour of recording time for free. He thought a moment and said, "Okay." It was not an easy going, "Sure, no problem, what the hell" but more of a, "Yeah, I guess so, well alright, an hour ya say, I can do that maybe."

Steve had done more for Chris and I than anyone outside our family. If not for him, I don' know how Stoph and I would have survived the first two years. We were still charging our batteries at his place and using his gizmo, although we were beginning to experiment with our own PA with the batteries out on the promenade. The reasons being that we wanted to be less of a bother to him, also it was better suited to do battle with Earnest's drums. On top of that we used his phone a lot, we were always coming and going for the batteries so he had to leave a key for us under his mat. During the first year we asked to use his place to watch videos while he was out and he was great about all of it. Toward the end of our first year in town he had to draw a line because we started coming around too much and sometimes he'd come home late at night from a gig to find us watching tapes. A lot of the time I was passed out in the van, so it was just Chris—a drunk Chris. Once he pointed it out we backed off. So yeah, Steve had done more than anyone could ask.

On the other hand we were there for him as well. If he needed some muscle to hang speakers in a theater he was doing sound at, we were it; when he was making his silent movie with his girlfriend we helped out; if he needed to use the Strat for recording; or move furniture, whatever. He had been a good friend and we did our best to return the favor.

All this being said, we still had a sore spot over the recording we thought he had offered to us before we left Chicago—one of the main reasons we left Chicago. Over the phone it was more like, "We'll make records, don't worry about the money, I trust you." When we did make the one CD our credit was not as abounding. Stopher took this more to heart than I. There was an irrational side in him, and he knew it to be so, that wanted Steve to open up his studio to us once every year or so to document our work. Yes we would do our best to get him some money, but money should be beside the point. Stoph had no real righteous rage; it lived inside him as a mostly benign, fairly insignificant tumor.

That was the history with which we entered into this latest favor. The Raven came to watch the proceedings and that ended up adding to some of the ill will. From the beginning Steve had a less than cordial attitude, though still mildly pleasant. When I had asked for the favor I thought that I had said an hour or two; I should have definitely asked for two.

When you pay for recording time it is customary that the clock begin when the engineer enters the room to set up the mics and board. I was not thinking in terms of a formal clock. I should have. In reflection I would have just had Steve record me singing a few songs on the Martin and then let Stopher sing a few. That way the set up would have been much less and we would have had time to record all the songs we wanted void of incident. The thinking was that this was for the Raven, and she would have wanted us to record as the act she had come to know. Getting a solid mix between the two guitars and vocals took up more time. It had been my intention not do any second takes, not be at all precious; I just wanted to do this for her. So when we got through the first four songs I was shocked to hear Steve say, "That's an hour."

I had hoped to get through at least ten.

"Really?"

"Set up, mixing; that takes up time."

I stumbled for the words that might ease us out of such a restricted business environment. The look in Steve's eye told me no such luck.

"I know I said an hour and I should have kept the set up simple with one vocal and a guitar, but I had hoped to get in a few more."

"You asked for a free hour and that's what I agreed to."

He was right; I had no moral inroad to demand anything.

"How about just two more? No second guitar or vocal—just one take on each and we're outta here."

He begrudgingly conceded with a father's disdained disappointment. Chris ripped the Strat from his shoulder and stormed out in a huff. I took Steve's superior tone and implied bitch-slap, thanking him graciously and apologetically. The Raven looked up at me with a sort of stunned expression. She never claimed to be of great insight or quick on the up take and caught my eye to see if she accurately surmised the moment. With Steve occupied by a button or two, I nodded my head with a raised brow over a rolling eye.

I thanked Steve for his time when I finished and apologized for the lack of communication on my part as he burned a couple of copies for the Raven and me. Outside by the van Chris was short.

"Let's get the fuck out of here."

"Was it me, or was Steve kind of a jerk in there?" the Raven asked.

"It wasn't you," I said.

"He's a fucking precious prick," Stoph hissed. "Let's get the fuck put of here."

We all went to the park to hang out, soon the Raven and I drifted off on our own, ending up at her place. Chris knew as well as I that Steve owed us nothing, that in fact, if a debt lied in wait of payment it laid with us. Still he couldn't let go of the superior, parental attitude with which Steve did his best to make me feel small.

"We're fucking leaving town," he shouted. "We could not come back. It's not like we're asking for a big party. No, we dared to 'Take advantage' of his precious little board."

"He's done a lot for us," I reminded.

"I know that; and we've done for him. We took off a Saturday to stand around watch him shoot his cute little silent film; we did it gladly. Of course we don't have a price tag on our time. Hey, when it comes to his stuff, his phone, he's as generous as it gets."

"He's used to being paid for his time."

"He's come to expect it like royalty. When we worked on his film we were involved because we just wanted to play in the sand with him; we threw out ideas; offered some enthusiasm. Not for money."

"No one is offering us money for our time."

"That is so beside the fucking point!"

"I know, you're right."

"I mean get some perspective; we're not taking advantage of him— it's us! He should want work with us! He should be grateful."

"We weren't even making a CD for money."

"It was for me," the Raven finally joined in.

"Every man knows that you don't make a guy look bad in front of his girl," I said.

The Raven didn't object to the term, 'his girl,' for the sake of the discussion.

"He fucking emasculated you!"

"That was pretty weak," the Raven agreed.

When she and I left Stoph was still fuming. I should mention, like with most recording sessions, that Stopher was drinking. He would have been every bit as offended sober but it should be on the record anyway.

So Chris ended up going over to Steve's to apologize. As mad as he was, as much as he felt justified in it, to some extent, he was his father's son and knew that no one owed him anything. Steve had been a good friend, if in this one instant he came up short of Stopher's standards then the least Stopher could do was accept the bad with the good. Here, ironically, is where Stopher made a mess of things. Steve obtusely picked up on none of our resentment. I had tried to mask mine but Chris, to the Raven and I, couldn't have been more transparent with his. He didn't want to leave town with an ill taste in his or Steve's mouth so went over to own up to his childish whims.

"Steve, I'm a big baby and I'm sorry for getting mad," he said walking in the door.

"About what?"

"You know for storming off because you were being such a clock master. It's your studio and I don't have any right to expect favors you don't want to give; you've done so much already."

"Okay." Steve played along, still a bit in the dark.

Standing next to Steve was one of his writing partners, Jacob. He smiled.

"We asked for an hour so that's what you signed up for; if I wanted you give me love, I should have just asked for it."

Jacob, who had not been there when it happened, seemed to understand more than Steve, what had transpired. Jacob laughed sweetly.

Steve only nodded.

"Anyway, I'm sorry," Stoph offered again. "I'll let you two get back to work."

When Chris told me about it later I thought, well that was nice of him and good that it all got put to rest.

The next day, when we came for the batteries, Steve asked us to sit down for a talk. The tone in his voice sounded disturbed, like the time he asked us to sit down and then proceeded to tell us that we were taking his space for granted. Which we had, and had since stopped.

"I'm upset and hurt by your being angry with me. You asked me for a FREE hour, which I am not generally comfortable doing, and I said yes. I feel like I have been a good friend to you, and of substantial help in your earning a living, so when Chris told me about being angry, I was to say the least, miffed."

"But he said he was sorry," I countered, "and that he was out of line."

"Well, I certainly appreciate that, but the fact that he could be angry with me in the first place, I find disturbing, frankly."

"Well let me say that you are right," Chris interjected, "I have no right to be upset with you."

I could see Stoph's pride vanishing behind gritted teeth, sliding down the back of his throat. Stoph knew at the moment something that I would not catch on to for another month or so.

"To be fair, Steve," I said, "we all have the right to be angry when someone's out of line. I mean you were a bit of a jerk."

Stopher winced from his chair by the door. "Be pretentious, Dave, be pretentious," he telepathically said.

I did not hear.

"Oh, I'm a jerk for giving you a free hour of studio time."

"No, more in the way you treated me in front of Raven."

"It's a guy code thing," Stopher offered gently. "You don't make a friend look bad in front of his girlfriend."

"Even when that so called friend is taking advantage of me."

"Taking WHAT?" I should have let it be.

From that point things escalated fairly quickly. I should have known, as did Stopher, that Steve would never own any of his behavior—he never did before. He's like most folk, they all admit to being a flawed human being but can never seem to cop to a specific charge. The beauty of being a fat slob with a severe drinking problem is that everyone can see it, you can see that they see it, so you are pretty much cornered into a sense of humility.

The frustrating thing with Steve was, every time it seemed that I, or Chris, articulated a point that you could see made sense in his eyes, he jumped the subject.

"You have helped us but we've helped you too. And in the midst of me doing something for you it still befalls upon me to treat you with respect."

"And I did not?"

"No, ask Stopher, ask Raven; the three can't all be wrong."

"I didn't know you two were serious."

"And that justifies a lack respect, how?"

"I'm tired of you two coming to the parties here drunk; you're already trashed before you walk in the door."

"I do that but Dave never does."

"What about that one Christmas when Angel was here?"

"I was cooking all day and extremely upset about spending the first Christmas out here away from my daughter; is this really the time you want to choose to throw that up in my face?"

"You know it's one thing for me to put up with it, but now you're subjecting Marie to it, and she is a woman that I love."

"I didn't realize that we did her any harm."

"Of course you didn't."

"Is this really what you brought us here to talk about?"

"I didn't want to bring this up, but business has been really bad, my equipment needs to be seriously updated and I'm going to have to go into some major debt to get it done."

"Have we done anything to stop you from making money?"

"I just have a lot of pressure."

His eyes filled with water, not enough to spill out, just enough to bring things to a halt. Things became so muddled from the conversation's origin that I felt the need to offer peace on the most sincere basis I could mange.

"Steve, I owe you more than any single person in the world besides my folks. Chris and I have survived because of you, we continue to survive because of you. If in anyway we appear to be unaware or ungrateful of those facts, please hear me now, we are not." A few tears built up in my own eyes. "You have in the past asked us not to come around drunk and we responded. You have allowed us to do so when we recorded because you see that as a different arena, so we still do. You now say that our drinking at parties is a problem, okay; we won't drink or we won't come. As for your financial state, well, we are the last guys to be of help there." I laughed.

Steve chuckled.

"We love you, and like to think that we have been of help to you."

"You have."

"And we'd be more than happy to be of help again."

"I appreciate that."

This is where I should have let things settle, although what would come to pass, according to Stopher, was inevitable regardless.

"But just because you do wonderful things doesn't mean we won't call you on the times that you're acting like a superior shit."

He laughed hard. In the end he didn't mean it.

"Well I am glad we talked," Steve said.

"I am too," I agreed.

Stopher nodded.

Outside in the van Stopher said, "We'll have to find somewhere to charge the batteries when we get back."

"What are you talking about? Every thing is fine."

"Trust me."

"I felt like we reached a real understanding; you heard him—he seemed good with us."

"Trust me."

I should have.

A few things that at the time held the promise of a possibility at being an opportunity reared their taunting heads in the days before our departure. The first being in the form of an overture made by Q'orianka's mother, Sasha. Q'orianka was the twelve year old girl with the grown up singing voice that I, on so many occasions, got to witness rake in the bucks while Chris and I had to search them out with a magnify glass and tweezers. Her mom liked our act, appreciating our gutsy, organic rendition of rock-blues. "You sweat every ounce into each moment," she had said. Sasha came upon the vision of us backing Q'orianka for a set here and there on the promenade and then maybe taking it to the clubs. Also she thought that we could work with her on writing some songs.

"I have an original blues song that would be good for her voice," I offered.

"But no sweet, sunshiny, baby doll lyrics," she warned in her softened but apparent German accent.

"I don't do 'baby doll'."

"Good."

I told her of our impending travel plans and though she was disappointed Sasha's interest did not wane. In September, or whenever we returned we would pick up the conversation. It tickled her to no end, picturing her little dew drop of a rainbow being backed by two burly, surly, grizzled, aged rejects from the 70s. And she loved our lyrics. One time she stood in front of us as we played, I sang a phrase that so pleased her she said, "Shit, if you're gonna lay down lines like that," and she tipped us a fin.

Stopher's response to the proposition, after she left, was true to form.

"Ain't never gonna happen."

On our return from Nashville we sought out Sasha, at first her interest, though not as animated, held up, but it never did lead to anything. I hated the thought of collaborating on someone else's agenda but knew the kid had talent and a real shot. Money aside, I did get a kick out of a scenario that had Stoph and I mentoring some future pop star. It sounded like a cute Hollywood movie anyway.

"What did you expect," Chris said when nothing came of it, "it's us."

On our last Saturday on the promenade a woman approached us after dropping a five-dollar tip. She worked in the office at the TROUBADOR, the historic club where the likes of Jackson Browne and the Eagles had built their rep. She asked if we'd like to play there; she said that the manager would love us; she said that we should call; she gave us a number; she said we should call this very Monday.

"We're leaving town Tuesday night and won't be back for at least a few months, probably not until September," I said with numbness that reeled.

"Oh, that's a shame."

"We've been playing out here for almost two years hoping someone like you might happen along," Stopher said, as if talking to a recently absent wind.

Sensing our heartfelt disappointment she offered to buy a CD and give it to the manager along with her praise telling him of our "when" and "wheres".

"Call him when you know the month you'll be back."

"We most definitely will; thanks so much," I said.

After she left I looked to a stunned Stopher. "Why, of all the days, why does she show up now?"

"Because it's us."

I did call the Troubadour a month before our return only to fine that the management changed and so did the booker. No, we never played the Troubadour.

The next day during our second set, by the fruit stand, while we were doing the very new song that I had written for the Raven, JUST BECAUSE, a couple of men stopped to listen. One was slight of build, casually dressed, the other with the build and motif of a biker. They listened intently and drew near as the song progressed. During Stoph's ending lead break the casually dressed one walked off only to return with a third man in a suit, but no tie.

"Hi," the casually dressed one said, after we finished. "That was an amazing song, is it on one of these CDs?"

"No," I explained, "I just wrote it last month."

"If I tipped you ten dollars, would you play it again? I'd like my associate to hear all of it," he said referring to the man in the suit.

I played the song again and they seemed every bit as interested as the first time, even had deeper responses to some of the lines.

"We are making a film," he handed me a card, "and your song, the lyrics and arrangement both, are just a perfect it."

"It almost sounds as if you wrote it after reading the script," the biker said.

"There is no recording of it?" the suit asked.

"No."

"Could you make one?"

"The problem is that I'm leaving for Nashville this week for at least a few months."

"Could you record it there and send us a copy?" the biker asked.

"We'll make a point of it," Stopher chimed in.

"Here's my card and address," the casual one said, "call me when you're settled and then again when you have something to send."

"How much are these?" The biker knelt down to where our CDs sat displayed along the neck of the case.

"Ten."

He picked up FINAL CALL.

"That has some great stuff on it; excellent production," Stoph encouraged.

"There might be some things there we could use," the suit mused.

So they bought the CD, wished us well and said that they hoped to hear from me. Yes, we were giddy, of course our hopes soared, obviously the ensuing months were decorated with bubbling conversations of how this could be it, and no, nothing ever came of it.

This ain't a mystery novel, folks.

It simply turned out to be another one of those moments that tells our story in a nutshell. We did find a way to record it in Nashville, in which Donna was extremely helpful, and we kept in contact with them diligently. Unlike so many that came our way, I think they were for real. But like so many movie deals, theirs fell apart. I talked with the casual one on the phone several times from Nashville and he sounded excited all over again when he heard the demo we sent. A few conversations down the line I could hear the absolute deflation in his voice. It had nothing to do with the song; it was the sound of a man whose blood, sweat and tears were about to get washed down the drain.

"A lot is up in the air right now." It sounded more like they had all crashed down around him.

Previously he said things like, "Check in with me next week," or, "I'll know more at the beginning of the month," and, "The ball is set to roll any day now."

The last conversation ended with, "I'll call you when I have any news." By the time we got back to California his number had been disconnected.

The fact that these three, so-called, opportunities came just before our departure made no real difference in the results; only made them more dramatic. Well, maybe if we were there to strike when the iron was hot on the Troubadour thing, but I doubt it. I remember when we had first started playing out on the promenade. We had been there only a few months. This guy named Yarbrough was a regular performer at the House of Blues in L.A. playing for the lunch crowd a few times a week.

"You boys don't belong out her," Yarbrough said. "Here, call this number and ask for Lisa. You tell her I said that you was hot."

He sounded like that was that; but we were us.

It became our mantra when things appeared to be on the verge of our getting any steady gig or making real money:

"Remember, it's us."

On my last night in California I laid napping up in the Raven's loft bed while Stoph supposedly did the same back in the van. She had to work but wanted me to be there when she got home. I had hoped for a goodbye fuck, but alas, no. In fact she spent part of her evening looking to give Danny, the Manchester folkie a ride. He was without a place to stay and she offered him a bed in the Phaser (camper). In return he was to paint her bathroom. Of course this led to twinges of jealousy on my part. I kept waiting for her to tire of my music and me, in favor of the next artist of the month.

"He's just a kid." She would say. "Besides, all his songs are fluff; some are alright; he is easy on the eyes."

"Thanks, you almost had me relaxing."

"Oh, baby, I'm too old to be running around with twenty somethings. But I am leaving you; I'm already gone."

"You were never here."

"Exactly."

Danny was just one in a line of possible replacements for me as her resident artistic plaything. Still, as much as she warned me, and as much as she wanted me to know my place as a transient wind, she always gave my due.

"You and your brother are the best writers out there and no one's voice does to me what yours does. Besides, I'm fondle of ya."

Eventually she came to lay in my arms and we kissed softly but slept mostly. At one A.M. the alarm she set for me told me to get up.

""I'll drive you," she said.

"Go back to sleep."

She held me tight and then she held me tighter.

"Don't leave me, baby."

I laughed painfully hard. The woman who could only tell me that she loved me with her hand while she slept; the one who desperately wanted me gone; was the same to need me in a way that I have never felt needed by anyone.

Don't ever tell me that life ain't the funniest thing going.

I walked down Rose Avenue as I had done on so many nights. Passing huddled figures with who knows what in their heart—malice to goodwill no doubt—made me nervous. Venice and Santa Monica, for all the glamorous history their names conjured, in the end, were small towns and the streets where left to those that lived on them within late night and early morning. I still, at that point, had not yet gotten comfortable passing strangers on the narrow pavement in the dark quiet. With each step closer to our encounter another muscle in me would flex-up to the ready; black, white, or Hispanic; short, tall, slight or muscular; only expensive clothes put me at ease. I rarely ever came upon a body dressed any, or much, better than me.

On my neighborhood streets back in Chicago and even some in the surrounding area's tough 'hoods, I had come to feel a sense of ownership. Not so much thinking myself impervious to attack, but rather if it were to happen I would be where I was from, and that soothed me somehow. I guess the logic is that if you are going to get gotten on your own turf then you are going to get gotten; an inner belief such as that was a wall of defense in itself that those who approached you could sense. Maybe it's bullshit, but it was a comfort I had back home that I did not yet have in California. (I do now though and have for quite a while.).

Either way I passed a figure on Rose, a couple more on Lincoln, all void of incident.

Stopher sat up front just starting to nod off a bit with cheap vodka on his breath.

"I figured you'll take the first shift, but I'm fine. I made sandwiches."
I stood outside his passenger window.
"I guess we're going to Nashville," I muttered.
"It'll be good."
"It fucking sucks."
"Yeah, it does; but it'll be good."
"I know."

I walked around to the driver's seat and started the engine without getting in. Standing in front of my blessed great, white buffalo Ford, and whale of a van, I put a hand to the hood. Stopher joined me.

"She's gonna take us across one more time," he said.
"Two more."
"Two more," he amended. "And then some."
"I know that it's foolish and counter to wisdom to love an object…"
Stoph laid his hand on the hood. "I love'er too."
The Raven's Neon pulled into the lot and came to a halt at our backs.
"Well, you gonna drive it or fuck it."
"Both?" Stopher mused.
She got out to give Stopher a goodbye hug.
"I'll miss ya, babe," Stopher said.
"Take care of yourself, Stopher."
Stoph sat in the van.
"Have a good trip and don't come back," she smiled.

I kissed her, squeezed until I heard her back cracked and kissed her again.

"Oh, David, what am I gonna do with out you? Who's gonna take care of me?"

"You'll find someone. More like a few someones; I do an awful lot," I said, lasciviously at the last part.
"And you do them so awfully well."
"Yeah, I do."
"We're being nasty, huh, baby?"
"Huh, baby?"
"HUH, BABY!!"
I kissed her forehead and whispered, "Huh, baby?"
I got in the van and drove to Nashville.

We chose to go without the sun's consent in order to spare the van's engine any desert scorn. When the sun pierces through the high blue sky to beat the desert floor, the bickering deafens. We would be well through Arizona before any genuine heat could question our or the van's resolve. There were stops for gas, food and bathrooms but nothing else. One of us could always sleep while the other drove. Late Thursday morning we pulled off highway 24 at the Harding Place exit. Aubrey and the rest lived a couple more exits east of town but would still be in school or at work. So our first visit was to an old friend named moo goo gia pan.

The goo is good.

At three o'clock we pulled our road-weary buffalo into the driveway that the directions had led us to. Donna's proneness to move every year or so had stayed true to form, Aubrey got to know yet another neighborhood and another town. At least she had Madison to keep her company. The four bedroom, ranch style house, sat on a lot big enough to build two more houses at least. Knowing Donna, Alice and their collective offspring, they would need every inch.

Aubrey busted out of the back door toward the van and I scooped her up as best as I could. I love words. I love to tie'em up like neat little bows on a packaged image, deliver them full of insight and aglow with wonder. But all I can tell you here is that I love my daughter and she loves me. God, it was good to see her.

Time lost can't be retrieved, repackaged and squeezed into the present. We can only live in the framework of where we are; Aubrey and I would not spend 24/7 catching up. She had school and friends up in Lavernge while I would be staying in a house half an hour away in Nashville where I would have to find a job. The whole point was to have me around, to be in a position where I could be turned to. I came out during the week early on before I started working, and also on the weekends even after, or she came down to the city with me. I was divorced dad all over again. She would call me when there were problems at home with her mom, Alice or Madison, and I refereed as best and as impartial as I could.

She didn't want to come to the city every weekend because she did have a life with her friends, a thirteen year-old girl only had so much interest in hanging around with a thirty-seven year old man, and vice a versa. The fact that we were father and child or that we loved, liked, respected and enjoyed each other would not alter the previous equation. Donna was disappointed and tried to fight the math.

"You are here to spend time with her," she complained.

"And I am, but I can't force her beyond what's natural. I'll come up and baby sit if you want to go out on some of the weekends she doesn't come here but other than that, it is what it is."

The van had been acting up for months previous to our journey and the trip itself was the knockout punch. Alice was able to lend me her mini van to get around to find a job and fix the van. The folks came through with another few hundred to help get it fixed quicker.

"The less you have to depend on them the better," mom said.

I went downtown to sell plasma at the "donor" bank there as I had done to supplement my income in the years that I had lived in Nashville before. Ty had turned me on to the racket. It gave me forty bucks a week. Within two weeks I had a job driving a cement truck for ten bucks an hour but continued selling plasma when I could. It rained a lot in Nashville so my hours were not consistent. I drove for a family owned business with thirteen trucks: Lawson Re-mix. Jim was a charming, friendly guy who took me at my word for the most part. I had never poured cement before and his trucks were all front dumps, which required more skill and finesse than the rear ones. I'm sure he received a good reference from my last employer, Nashville Lumber, but it wouldn't have been as easy with some big corporate operation.

I was trained by a real sweetheart of a guy they called Cornbread. Cornbread came off as genuinely kind while somehow maintaining an edge about him. It wasn't that he didn't see what dickheads people could be, he simply saw who he'd rather be; how'd he envisioned his business getting done; and followed thru accordingly. He also wrote country songs. I never heard any because he saw himself as a work in progress and immediately got the impression that I was a finished product. In the week I rode with him we talked music mostly, and a little life. I gave him a CD by the third day and that justified and solidified his initial assessment of me in his mind. The next Monday he came to work after listening to it thinking even more of whom I supposed myself to be.

"I only listened to about half," he said excitedly, "because I liked to listen careful and a few times over before I move on. I'll yell you what you and your brother are though, you are the real thing."

Being the head driver on the lot he took the route of cheerleader. He praised everyone but had a way of making each driver feel singled out. And the truth was that they were a good crew.

"Ed," Cornbread said to one driver, with a smile that wondered, "how do you do it? How do you rock? How do you rock so very hard?"

He said the same phrase to all the drivers but assigning each a special inflection. Nothing drastic, but there all the same. For me he gave it a confidential tone with a dose of conspiracy.

"Hey there, Dave." He'd move in close and look around the small dispatch room where no secret could be whispered low enough to stay one. "I just got to know; why do you rock so hard? I mean how? And Why?"

"It's not just in the rocking," I played along, "but in the rolling as well, Cornbread."

"That is too funny, Dave," he exclaimed. "You here what he's doing over here, Boss man?" he'd say to Jim. "That is TOO funny."

That was another of his favorite phrases, "Too funny." Whether he was telling a story about yesterday's run or repeating something told to him by another, he ended it with, "That was too funny," and sometimes he'd throw in, "I was cryin', absolutely cryin'."

After about a month I started saying, "Or is it just funny enough." Cornbread seemed to like that. He liked people to play along and I think he appreciated it on the level of being challenged. When I had done it enough for my taste I stopped but he kept it going for me: "That is TOO, TOO funny," he'd be saying loud and joyfully to whoever was in the room, then to me out of the side of his mouth with a bit of lead in his boots, "Or is that just funny enough, Dave, just funny enough."

I liked Cornbread in a way that I don't take to folks very much. He was Iowa grown, tall, and thin haired with a subtle curl here and there but all painfully yellow. We kept talking about getting together outside of work but never did. Real good guy though.

I have to admit, as much as I hated working for a living, it felt good to be a truck driver again. It is a part of me that belongs to Grandpa on my Dad's side. I got my middle name from Walter and he drove a gasoline truck for a good twenty years or so. The man could build or fix anything he put his mind to; it's where Art got all his gifts. He didn't think much of Dad's literary or educational pursuits, "This world is gonna eat you alive, Bobby," he had been known to tell his son.

I watched Art be the kind of boy and man that Walter encouraged his son to be and felt all of their blood in me. I loved the smell of fresh cut wood and words; I longed to build a house or make a chair just as I crafted songs or wrote a book; but I was all intimidation and no talent when it came to the former. When I first stumbled into being a truck driver I sensed that void being filled. At the end of a day filling in driveways or foundations I drove my beloved, loyal beast to atop the rock mountain at the back of the yard, swirling around the rugged gravel path, waving a soft-spoken greeting and farewell to a fellow trucker coming down, knowing that we both met the day cool of head and steady of hand. I climbed my rig, hose in tow and washed out the day, after letting the barrel do the same. I loved being an artist more than anything, I was an artist more than anything, but this was in my blood too, not as much, but it was there. If I had to face a lifetime driving a truck I would most certainly be miserable, yet the years I gave to it soothe and complete my soul. That part of my soul had been served years before and it was nice to make its acquaintance again.

The Raven called me more days than not and then there were would be a week where she faded, leaving me feeling cold and forgotten. She took some scuba lessons through Mark, her mountain-boat man, and got certified. I was happy for her and worried that it solved her interest in this Artists-boy.

Eric dropped in for a visit, taking time off the trail and taking a bus west to see Chris and I. We went for goo, And THE GOO WAS GOOD. I forget how far he made it up the trail, but he did himself proud. He was back in California well before Stoph and I.

Ty too came to town from Austin, Texas to play the famed Bluebird, so we got to have a few drinks with him and sing a song or two.

I set up our PA in the back of the house to keep my chops up, though Stoph joined me less and less. I even went to a songwriter's night or two for want of an audience.

But most of my time was spent working and hanging with Aubrey. Madison didn't come as much because of the smell in the house, the smell being Stopher and myself. It used to be where she lived for a time. On Saturday nights they both preferred to go to the roller rink out in their neck of the woods, so to give their mothers a night off I'd drive up there to play chauffer. Mostly I'd drive them there and someone else would pick them up. I remember the first time I took them in my van; Aubrey asked to be dropped off around the corner.

"I don't want to be seen getting out of this thing."

"This THING took me across the country to see you, and this THING keeps me from the cold and rain. This is not a THING, this is my van and you should be damm proud of it! And if not that, don't ever speak ill of it to me again."

I pulled up to the front door.

"I love you, kid," I said to her as she stood outside the front door. "But you gotta show some respect. And I'm sorry."

"For what," she smiled.

"This."

I blew the van's horn hard long and hard so everyone would turn to see her standing next to it talking to me.

Aubrey dropped her head and laughed. "Okay, dad, ya made your point."

With all our stuff inside the house the van was left relatively empty except for a few odds and ends, and the photos on the ceiling.

"That's my dad's girlfriend," Aubrey pointed out to her friends when I gave them a ride. (Oh, she got over her van embarrassment.) "Hey, dad, roll us around."

When I had another van or first got this one, I'd ride around empty parking lots at night with her, Madison and sometimes a few neighborhood kids, making herky jerky turns that threw them every which way. Hearing her ask for it now that she was a teenager, with a new set of friends, warmed my heart. I knocked'em 'round but good.

One sunny Saturday in an abandon parking lot I gave the wheel of my beloved Ford Buffalo to Aubrey. We circled gingerly. She had been behind the wheel of her mother's car before but that could not prepare her for the monumentousness that was my great white whale.

"It feels like a big ship," she said nervously.

"You're running with the big boys now," I congratulated her.

It only lasted about ten minutes but I did get a kick out of seeing her mange the wheel, look out over the hood; sitting in my seat tickling at my perspective.

Back during the years I spent working in Chicago between my first stint in Nashville and going to California I drove a little four-speed Golf hatchback that belonged to dad. I used to let Aubrey shift the gears for me while I managed the clutch. She stumbled at first when trying to down shift but all and all had a knack for it. I would never get to be the one to teach her to actually drive, like I had taught her so many other things, but it was nice to have had those two fragments with her.

In going to the plasma I got weighed twice a week and saw evidence of progress. When I first arrived in Nashville I weighed 280ish, which meant that I had lost twenty pounds since that night on my birthday up in the canyon, at least. As the weeks made months I went down into the seventies, sixties and fifties by the time I left. I woke up every morning for work at five; I did some yoga; three sets of twenty pushups; and three sets of twenty-five sit-ups. For dinner I stopped after one huge bowl instead of my usual two, and I took long walks whenever I could. On the weekends I went with the kids, or by myself to the hiking trail by Radnor Lake. It wasn't a real mountain but a hell of a hike. A couple of times I tried running near the house but decided my knees weren't up to it.

I wrote two songs while there, both for the Raven:

I tell her that I love her
She says, baby you're just lonely and bored
I ask if I could simply hold her
She laughs, greedy boys always want more
I can't say that she's wrong; she can't convince me I ain't right
But she'll hang for as long as my voice pulls at her blood and puts clouds in her eyes; pulls at her blood and clouds her sight
I love her—Madly, gladly

We're so good at playing
It's hard work to do anything else
She keeps the world waiting
While we stack another day on the shelf
Meander down any aisle, time's a tool without power
Yeah I get lost in her smile
And all the while hours make the moment ours
All the while hours make the moment ours
I love her—Madly, gladly

I like to talk about forever
She swats at the buzzing bee
I wish on "ifs" and grand endeavors
She calls me a drama queen
Grab my collar, slap my face; color me a happy man
Shove me all about the place
Call it another case of pleasure mocking me where I stand

Call it another case of pleasure mocking me where I stand
I love her—Madly, gladly, Madly, gladly

Other than stealing from our life, like the way she called me a drama queen that is always buzzing or the way we love to have her slap me, the Raven contributed one line. She had written a poem for me in my absence and read it to me over the phone. There was a line in there about my gravelly, velvet voice pulling at her blood that I liked, but I only use it in paraphrase form. She still wanted a writing credit when she heard it. She did not get one. The first time she heard it was over the phone.

Whether in Nashville, Chicago or Santa Monica the phone played as big a part in our romance surviving as her watching me on the promenade. The phone also added the specific plus of her only being able to hear my voice void of the life attached to it; no unsightly, cluttered poverty on wheels to have to look at; no "van-aroma" (her terminology) to ingest through her nose; just my voice with its silver tongue conjuring all those cleverly designed words to the tune of a gravely velvet goodness swirling sultrily in her ear. Sometimes I'd use a guitar but mostly it was about the voice. (Once she did ask me to set the phone and just riff a bit on the Strat, plugged in of course, but that fix didn't translate as well.)

I sang her favorites mostly, slipping MADLY GLADLY in only twice.

The other song, I started writing not as a song but just as a way to work through a melancholy mood that had me down. It was within one of those weeks where she hadn't called much:

I was looking for something to feel good about. So I put on some Jackson Browne. His sorrow informs me of my heart. They converse to the tune of laughter; common truths tend to make that sound—mmm, that sound
You're not my everything and that's enough for me
It doesn't really matter what you don't in me see
I know the truth of your beauty; it's what I'm going on about in the first place

So you're not my everything, and that's enough for me

My mother finally told me that I was not adopted. It's a joke she's been playing with for years. Still I know that she's my sweetest one. It's not something she completely owns, but what I know about love starts there—it's all there

I'm not your everything and that's enough for me
It doesn't even matter if we don't find what can't be seen
You know the truth of my beauty; it's what got you coming round in the first place
No I'm not your everything, and that's enough for me

I have a child and other than myself she's my main concern. But as wings insist on flying simply because the wind begs, she asks for more than any of my offers. I answer with who I am and no better, so she knows where my fires burn—ooh, they burn
Now all I've lost is measured up against what you found
Through it all please, pay close attention to the sound
Of your heart beating and your soul listening to the truth of my being...
Yeah, your heart beating and your soul listening to the truth of my being...
Around

No we're not our everything and that's enough for me
It doesn't even matter what you don't in me see
We're not our everything and that's enough for me
It'll never ever matter if we don't find what can't be seen
Cause I know the truth of our beauty; it's what we're on about in the first place
No, we're not our everything, and that's enough for me.

Oh, I'm a drama queen. But it's like I've told her a million times, some things are dramatic. That one had too many bellowing parts to sing over the phone.

We were in Nashville less than a month when the letter from Steve came. I alone suffered the shock for Stopher knew. Oh, he knew. I could almost hear the anger shake in Steve's voice right on the page. Not the shake of a dangerous fury but that of wounded indignation. Although addressed to and affecting us both the words themselves pointed directly at Stopher.

"Chris you say I never apologize; I say all you do is apologize." Because he does so much wrong we inferred. He felt humiliated and betrayed by our lack of gratitude, it was as if we never had the conversation in his studio where we went over every little thing, hashed out all the ill will and came to a mutual understanding.

"Did I dream the whole affair?" I asked of Chris.

"Yes and no."

"I'm calling him."

"What's the point; he won't hear."

"I'm not trying to get our battery privileges back, I wanna know what the fuck happened."

"You know what happened."

I did. I called anyway.

We had a nice chat actually and I came away feeling better about things. It help me set aside the soap opera of the day we recorded and the day I watched him scatter from one issue to another like a cockroaches from the light. He had put in his time, he had done more than anyone's share; we needed to wipe our own asses. Shit. (Of course that type of independence would not be achieved for another few years.)

Steve so appreciated the way I responded to the letter that he offered to ask Sukey about plugging into one of her outdoor outlets in an out of the way corner in her yard. That came to pass as our batteries' new home. We bought a big, blue plastic tarp to wrap them up to both protect them from the rain and make the row of batteries less unsightly. And of course on our return we would strictly use our PA, although I think he offered us to continual use of his gizmo. I thanked him but knew it better to make a clean break.

Our relationship underwent a makeover after that because harsh things were said. Mostly by me. I called him out on his aloofness, his inability go beyond intellectual conjecture and wise-ass one liners—not that day on the phone from Nashville but back in the heat our previous exchange. The funny thing is that it was Chris who got the ball rolling and him again that took more of the offense at Steve's emotional frugality; but it was my verbal assault on the day in question that laid into Steve most pointedly; when all was said and done Steve chose to hold the grudge against Chris and he him. Once the battle began in earnest Stoph all but dropped his arms and I lashed out. As the initial dust settled, Stopher stood philosophically removed and I groped for solidity of common ground. Yet, in the years that ensued I let go of the battle that occasionally stirred in Chris and that Steve pretends never happened.

All that said, we love Steve and he loves us. Letting and being let down by the people you love is par for the course; it's what we do.

The plan of me living rent-free until September so I could be with Aubrey and rebuild my savings got cut short.

"Alice is renting out the house the first of July." Donna told me over the phone.

"I thought I was invited to stay as long as I needed."

"Yeah, but Aubrey is doing so much better and Alice needs the money."

"I told you that coming here would break me; the van crashed and burned on the trip; I had to borrow money from the folks. I made it clear that I would need the summer to get back on my feet if I was going to leave California."

"She has a mortgage, Dave."

"I didn't make the offer, I accepted it."

They really wanted me to leave by mid or early June but July was their idea of a compromise. I called Mom and explained that I had the five hundred I borrowed but now that my trip was being cut short, if

I paid them back it would leave my savings depleted. I tried not to so sound like a baby about it, but I am what I am.

"David, screw the money and get away from those women now," said Mom. "You know I like Donna very much, but it is not healthy for you to be around them."

Bless that woman.

Despite Mom saying to forget the compromise and leave the first week of June I opted to wait for the last week so I could make a little more money and take the kids on a camping trip up into Kentucky near Six Flags.

We drove and sang all the same old songs. At the campsite the kids had the same old squabbles but we ultimately had the same old fun. After a full day at Six Flags I decided to save money on a campsite and drove the four hours back to Tennessee. We re-lived a bit of our old glory; it was a nice way to end things.

There had been talk of taking Aubrey with us to California, seeing the Grand Canyon on the way, putting her on a plane home after a couple of days on the other end. I worried over the money. Luckily she didn't fancy a cross-country drive so we both got what we wanted. Though I still felt guilty about it because if I had forced the issue and insisted upon it, it would have been an important and beautiful time in our lives. Instead, Aubrey drove with us to Chicago to see the family, staying on with the folks for another week after Chris and I headed west.

As always it was great to spend time in Chicago with the most wonderful folk I know, even though the Raven and the promenade tugged at my sleeve all the while. I got a ticket for an expired city sticker on my van while it was parked at the end of the street on Pensacola. I kept my Illinois plates and drivers license at first because Chicago was my home and then because it was easier and cheaper. The city sticker didn't need to be kept up because the van was never there; still haven't paid that ticket.

The old garage was torn down and built up a new. The same cracked and oiled cement floor sat inside while a whole new frame huddled around it announcing inevitable change. It made me sad to stand within the foreign walls but not as sad as if I still lived there.

I'm just a visitor now.

The goodbyes were more casual than in the pasts, well except for Aubrey.

"I told you before and I'm saying it again, come to me when you think there's nothing else."

"I don't want to live in California, even if you had a house. I don't know if I have ever felt as strongly about this before, but I'm a Nashville kid now."

"I can respect that. But if things get as bad or worse than when you wrote that note, I want you to prom-"

"I PROMISE, God, dad."

"You got options, Sweets. Don't hurt yourself or anyone else without giving me a chance to show you another life. In an apartment or in the van, we could make it work. I know it. I guess what I'm really saying is that next time you come to me."

"Seriously, dad, I hear you and I understand. I'm fine; believe me."

"I love you, Breeze-child; I'm proud of ya."

"I'm proud of you too, dad."

"Oh, I see, but you don't love me."

"Dad!"

I drove for twenty something hours straight and would have made it all the way to Santa Monica without passing the wheel if it weren't for the highway closing in Nebraska. We got detoured to some desolate, side roads along the rolling prairies in a line of cars with no seeable end for four hours. Inconvenience aside it taught me something surprising: That the beauty of Nebraska's rolling green pastures, vast and full of wonder, matched in my soul, the spectacle of any mountain range, ocean view or desert floor. People laugh or scrunch up their faces in disdained disbelief when I tell them this, but the land I saw? lush personified. In reflection I understand how important it was to see; how profound that moment now resonates when a person, place or thing shows you how wrong you can be about beauty.

Would you like to see your manuscript become a book?

If you are interested in becoming a PublishAmerica author, please submit your manuscript for possible publication to us at:

acquisitions@publishamerica.com

You may also mail in your manuscript to:

**PublishAmerica
PO Box 151
Frederick, MD 21705**

www.publishamerica.com

PublishAmerica